L.B Cuore

Italian Conversation-Grammar on Otto's System

L.B Cuore

Italian Conversation-Grammar on Otto's System

ISBN/EAN: 9783337239787

Printed in Europe, USA, Canada, Australia, Japan

Cover: Foto ©Andreas Hilbeck / pixelio.de

More available books at **www.hansebooks.com**

ITALIAN CONVERSATION-GRAMMAR

ON

OTTO'S SYSTEM.

BY

L. B. CUORE.

FOURTH EDITION.

THOROUGHLY REVISED.

NEW YORK
HENRY HOLT AND COMPANY
F. W. CHRISTERN
BOSTON: CARL SCHOENHOF

BROWN'S
PRINTING AND BOOKBINDING CO.,
205-213 East 12th St.,
NEW YORK.

PREFACE.

This Grammar, based on that of Robello and others, claims to be all that is necessary for the study of the elements of the Italian language.

Great pains have been taken to present the verbs in a clear, concise manner; and though, for the sake of easy comparison, they are placed at the end of the book, the student is requested to study a part of them with every lesson.

It is hoped that this little work will fill the place for which it is intended.

THE AUTHOR.

TABLE OF CONTENTS.

	PAGE
ITALIAN GRAMMAR	1

CHAPTER I.
Pronunciation. 1
Etymology 15

CHAPTER II.
The Article 16

CHAPTER III.
Union of the Articles and Prepositions 21

CHAPTER IV.
The Noun 26

CHAPTER V.
The Plural of Nouns and Adjectives 32

CHAPTER VI.
The Cases of Nouns 40

CHAPTER VII.
Pronouns 46

CHAPTER VIII.
Pronouns: Personal and Conjunctive 55

TABLE OF CONTENTS.

CHAPTER IX.
The Adjective 61

CHAPTER X.
Adjectives: their Comparatives 67

CHAPTER XI.
The Adjectives: Superlatives 72

CHAPTER XII.
Augmentatives and Diminutives 78

CHAPTER XIII.
The Numeral Adjectives 82

CHAPTER XIV.
Relative Pronouns 89

CHAPTER XV.
Possessive Adjective Pronouns 96

CHAPTER XVI.
Demonstrative Adjective Pronouns 104

CHAPTER XVII.
Indefinite Adjective Pronouns 109

CHAPTER XVIII.
Indefinite Adjective Pronouns (continued) 115

CHAPTER XIX.
The Prepositions, *Di*, *A*, *Da* 121

CHAPTER XX.
The Prepositions *Con, In, Per* 129

CHAPTER XXI.
The Prepositions (continued) 135

CHAPTER XXII.
The Verbs *Éssere* and *Avére* 141

CHAPTER XXIII.
The Verbs and their Syntax 146

CHAPTER XXIV.
The Verb: The Subjunctive Mood 153

CHAPTER XXV.
The Infinitive, Gerund, Present and Past Participles 159

CHAPTER XXVI.
The Verbs *Andáre, Dáre, Fáre,* and *Stáre* 166

CHAPTER XXVII.
Adverbs 171

CHAPTER XXVIII.
Conjunctions and Interjections 179

VERBS.
Auxiliary Verbs 186
Regular Verbs 188
Irregular Verbs 214
Defective Verbs 246

Proverbs 259
Idioms 263
Vocabulary 266
Index 275

ITALIAN GRAMMAR.

ITALIAN GRAMMAR teaches the principles of the Italian language. These relate, —

1. To its written characters;
2. To its pronunciation;
3. To the classification and derivation of its words;
4. To the construction of its sentences;
5. To its versification.

The first part is called ORTHOGRAPHY; the second, ORTHOEPY; the third, ETYMOLOGY; the fourth, SYNTAX; and the fifth, PROSODY.

CHAPTER I.

PRONUNCIATION.

The Italian alphabet consists of twenty-two letters: —

A, a; B, b; C, c; D, d; E, e; F, f; G, g; H, h; I, i; J, j; L, l; M, m; N, n; O, o; P, p; Q, q; R, r; S, s; T, t; U, u; V, v; Z, z.

The letters *k, w, x, and y,* sometimes occur, but only in words derived from foreign sources.

SOUNDS OF THE ITALIAN LETTERS.

In Italian, every vowel must be distinctly sounded. The five vowels, *a, e, i, o, u,* are thus pronounced: —

SOUNDS OF THE VOWELS.

A, as . . . . in f*a*ther;
E, as . . . . a . . . . in m*a*de;
I, as . . . . ee . . . . in *ee*l;
O, as . . . . o . . . . in R*o*me;
U, as . . . . ou . . . . in s*ou*p.

REMARKS.

E has two different sounds, — open and close:

E open, as in MATE, NAME:	*E* close, as in GREY, PAIN:
Tèma, subject.	Téma, fear.
Vènti, winds.	Vénti, twenty.
Avèna, oats.	Méla, apple.

O has likewise two sounds, — open and close:

O open, as in CORD:	*O* close, as in BONE:
Bòtta, blow.	Bótte, cask.
Ròsa, rose.	Óra, hour.

To become thoroughly acquainted with the open and close sounds of *E* and *O*, three things are especially necessary: 1. *Practice;* 2. PRACTICE; 3. PRACTICE.

SOUNDS OF THE CONSONANTS.

The greater portion of the consonants in the Italian language are pronounced as in English. The following are the exceptions: —

C, which takes the sound of *ch* before *i* or *e*: otherwise it sounds like *k*.
H, which is used only to harden the sound of *c* and *g* before *e* and *i*, and to distinguish different parts of speech. It is never sounded.
J sounds like *ee*.
Q is never used without *u*, and is sounded like *q* in the English word *quire*.
R, which is sounded as if rolled on the point of the tongue.
Z, which is sounded like *ts* and *ds*.
L, M, N, and R are liquids, or semivowels.

PRONUNCIATION.

COMPOUND SOUNDS.

Ch sounds	. . .	like *k* in English.
Gh „	. . .	hard as in English.
Gn „	. . .	like *n* in the word ONION.
Gli „	. . .	like *ll* in the word WILLIAM.
Sci „	. . .	like SHE.
Sce „	. . .	like SHA.
Sch „	. . .	like SK.

Cc, followed by the vowels *e, i*, is pronounced like *tch* in the English word *match*.

Gg, followed by *e, i*, sounds like *dg* in the word *lodge*.

The exact sound of the letters can be obtained only by hearing good pronunciation, and by repeating after the teacher, as almost every language has some sounds which can only be learned by practising with an experienced teacher.

But, as an Italian teacher is not always to be found, we shall endeavor to give a few concise and practical rules, by which the student may make himself familiar with the language of Dánte, Alfiéri, Boccáccio, Ariósto, Tásso, Petrárca, Mafféi, Manzóni, and a host of other writers, whose works will never cease to form part of the *belles lettres* of every country.

Diphthongs, as we understand them in English, do not exist in Italian. Dr. Bachi, in his excellent Grammar, speaks of diphthongs and triphthongs, by which he means such a blending of the vowels that *each* is but faintly heard.

The apostrophe (') indicates that a vowel is omitted; as, *l'óro*, instead of *lo óro*, the gold; *dell' ánima*, instead of *délla ánima*, of the soul; &c.

The grave accent (`) is used on the last vowels of some words; as, *città* (formerly *cittade*): or as a termination which must be pronounced sharply; as, *avrà, amò, cessò*.

EXERCISE IN PRONUNCIATION.

A	Cása, música, dánza.
A	Felicità, darà, sarà.
E (close)	Béne, pedóne.
E (open)	Téma, péna, érba.
J	Princípj, provérbj, compéndj.
I	Inímico, cíbo, ripiéno.
O (close)	Córso, amóre, fónte.
O (open)	Póvero, tólto, pópolo.
U	Dúo, túo, súo.
CE	Cénto, céce, felíce.
CI	Pacífico, diéci, cíbo.
CH	Chiódo, chi, che.
GA, GO, GU	Gámba, págo, gústo.
GE, GI	Germáno, dígito, legióne.
GN	Campágna, magnético.
GLI (liquid)	Fíglio, fíglia, gli, méglio.
S (strong)	Sánto, stúdio, sénso.
S (soft)	Guísa, cása, cósa.
SCA, SCO, SCU	Scábro, scoláre, scuóla.
SCE, SCI	Scéna, scinto, fáscia.
Zz (z like *ts*)	Nózze, fazzolétto.
Zz (z like *ds*)	Azzúrro, mézzo.

REMARKS.

Double consonants must be *very* distinctly pronounced, thus: *immènso, im-mén-so; innocénte, in-no-cénte;* &c. Every syllable must contain a vowel, and cannot receive more than one consonant after it in the same syllable, but may be preceded by one, two, or three. All Italian words end with a vowel, except *il*, the; *con*, with; *non*, not; *per*, for; and a few others. The final vowel is, however, very often dropped for euphony.

READING EXERCISE IN PRONUNCIATION.

To impress the following exercise on the memory of the pupil, many English words are omitted. The pupil is required to fill them up: this can be done with the help of the dictionary.

PRONUNCIATION.

LA FANCIÚLLA DI BUON ÍNDOLE.
THE GIRL OF GOOD DISPOSITION.

La Marchésa Giúlia andáva in carrettélla a far vísita álla
The　　　　　　went　　little carriage to make　　　to the

sorélla che stáva in villa, e avéva con se solaménte una
sister who was country, and had with her only a

cameriéra e uno stalliére. Una ruóta della carrettélla si rúppe,
chambermaid and a footman.　wheel of the　　　　　broke,

e benchè per buóna sórte non rimanésse feríto nessúno,
although by good fortune　　remained wounded no one,

bisognò scéndere, e adattársi di andáre a piédi ad un
it was necessary to descend (adapt) prepare to go on foot

villággio lontáno di lì quási tre míglia. La Marchésa
　　　distant from there almost three miles.

mandò innánzi il servitóre per fáre avvisáre un carrozziére
sent before the servant for to make to give notice carriage-maker

che venísse ad accomodáre la carrettélla; il cocchiére rimase
which should come mend　　　　　　　coachman stayed

con i caválli, e la signóra prése a bráccio la cameriéra, e si
with the horses　lady took　arm

avviò.
set forward.

Éra sul mezzogiórno, e il sóle dáva lóro mólta nója;
It was mid-day　　sun gave to them much inconvenience;

dimodochè la signóra, non avvézza a camminare a piédi, présto
so that　　　　accustomed walk　on foot very soon

présto si straccò, e per riposársi ébbe ad uscír di stráda, ed
　was tired for to repose had　leave street

entráre in un práto dóve érano délle quérce. Là si mise a
enter　meadow where there were of the oaks. There she put herself

sedére all' ómbra sótto uno di quégli álberi, e guardò con
sit to the shade under one of those trees observed

piacére il bel prospétto che le éra dinánzi. A un trátto élla
pleasure fine prospect which her was before. all at once she

víde passár pel práto úna ragazzína con un fastéllo di légna
saw to pass through　little girl　faggot of wood

in cápo.
on head.

Ragazzína più béllа di quélla non éra mái passáta sott'
occhio álla Marchésa. Le súe cárni parévano látte e róse, i suói grand' ócchi celésti érano piéni di dolcézza, e sótto una pezzuóla di cotóne giállo, annodáta intórno al cápo, venívan fuóri le ciócche de' suói bióndi capélli, e dávan grázia vieppiù a quélla bélla fisonomía. La signóra non avéva fígli, e se ne addolorávа. A vedér dúnque quélla cára fanciullína, non potè a méno d'invidiáre la mádre súa; e dísse álla cameriéra di andáre a chiamár la bambína e condúrgliela. Quésta si avvicinò con un contégno modésto ma fránco, posò il súo fastéllo, féce un inchíno álla Marchésa, e le domandò se avéa qualcósa da comandárle. Niénte, rispóse la dáma; vóglio soltánto parláre un po' con te: méttiti a sedére quì sull' érba, e príma di tútto dímmi cóme tu ti chiámi? Rósa Lúci, al comándo súo. Il bábbo e la mámma li hai vivi? Il mío bábbo è mórto ch'è un pézzo; la mía mámma ha me sóla e si sta quì in un villággio vicíno. M' immágino che non siáte mólto felíci. Oh, perchè? Nói ci vogliámo béne, e siámo conténte. Ma mi páre che vói siéte mólto póvere! Nói ci guadagniámo il páne cón le nóstre fatíche

abbiámo délle galline che ci fanno le uóva; e la mía mámmı
we have some hens which make eggs
óggi è andáta al paése a vénderle, ed i quattríni si sérbano
to-day is gone to the country to sell them the money serves
per la pigióne di cása. E in che lavoráte voi per guadagnárvi
rent house. work you gain
da mangiáre? Nell' estáte noi andiámo a sarchiáre, e dópo la
to eat? In the summer we go to weed after
mietitúra andiámo a spigoláre. Ma se duráte tánta fatíca,
harvest glean. But if endure so much fatigue,
mangiáte mále e andáte mal vestíte, cóme potéte voi éssere
you eat badly go ill dressed, how can you be
conténte? Noi a tútte quéste cóse non ci pensiámo
We (of all these things not ourselves think
nemméno; quándo s' ha fáme si ringrázia Iddío di avére di
at all; when one has hunger one thanks God to have of
che satollársi, e ógni cósa par buóna. Se nói non abbiámo
what satisfy every thing seems good. If we not have
vestíti bélli, siámo púre copérte e decénti; sóno solaménte i
clothes fine we are yet covered are only
pígri che vánno sémpre strappáti e súdici; la mámma pénsa a
lazy who go always ragged dirty thinks
rassettáre le nóstre robiccióle, ed io già comíncio ad aiutárla.
to repair our clothes I already begin to help her.
Rosa, vuói venír méco a quel villággio? Volontiéri: tánto la
wilt come with me to that Willingly whilst
mía mámma fíno a stasséra non tórna; ma bisógna che
until this evening returns it is necessary
intánto io pórti a cása mía quésto fastéllo. E se lo comprássi
meanwhile carry house my if it should buy
.o? Allóra poi! ma cósta séi sóldi, veh! Éccoti sei sóldi
I? Then but costs six cents, hum! Behold
(rispóse la Marchésa alzándosi), pósa lì il túo fastéllo, e viéni
rising, put there come
con nói. Ma s' ella l' ha compráto, bisógna ch' io gliélo pórti
But if you have it bought, it is necessary that I it carry
(e voléva ripigliárlo), ma la Marchésa gliélo impedì, e prése
she wished to take it again prevented took
la vía del villággio, dóve arriváta, entrò in un albérgo (*hotel*)
way where entered
d' apparénza assái decénte.
appearance enough

Lo staffiére vénne a dírle che per accomodáre la sua
The footman came to tell her mend
carrózza gli bisognávano cínque óre. La Marchésa ordinò il
needed five hours. ordered
pránzo, l' ostéssa la condússe in úna stánza pulíta óve éssa entrò
dinner hostess conducted room clean where she entered
insiéme con le áltre dúe; diéde pói segretaménte dégli órdini
together other two; gave then secretly of the orders
álla cameriéra che uscì per eseguírli. In quésto frattémpo la
went out execute. meanwhile
Marchésa continuò a parláre con Rosína, e si trovò conténta
to speak found
sémpre più del candóre délle súe rispóste, e sopratútto délla súa
always more candor her answers above all
enerézza per la própria mádre.
tenderness own
La cameriéra tornò cárica de' vestíti che avéva compráti nel
returned laden clothes she had bought
villággio; spogliò, per órdine délla padróna, la piccína, e le
undressed, by order mistress little one
mise indósso úna camícia di cotóne, un sottaníno ricamáto, e
put upon her shirt cambric petticoat embroidered
úna vestína di séta colór vérde chiáro, con un ornaménto di
gown silk green light ornament
merlétti colór di rósa; pói le acconciò i capélli, cólle trécce le
lace then dressed hair braids
formò una spécie di coróna sul cápo, e vi póse una ghirlánda di
formed sort crown head put garland
fióri. Rósa dapprima facéva la ritrósa, e si vergognáva a
flowers. at first made shy was ashamed
vedérsi vestíre da signóra; ma pói, siccóme éra di naturále
to see to dress then, as she was by
mólto compiacénte, si sottomíse a tútto. Quándo fu assettáta
very complaisant submitted all. When she was fitted out
per béne, la Marchésa la condússe davánti állo spécchio, e le
fully her conducted before her mirror and to her
dísse che si guardásse. La piccína si guardò sott' ócchic
said that herself she should look at. little one regarded
néllo spécchio, sorríse ed arrosì.
smiled and blushed.

Che ne dici eh! disse la Marchésa; non ci arrésti
What to it sayest thou would have
gústo di stár sémpre vestíta in quésto módo? Sì; ma cóme si
taste to be always dressed manner? Yes how
può con quésti ábiti andár a tagliár l' érba e sarchiáre? Védi, se
can clothes to go cut grass to weed? See if
tu fóssi la mía figliuóla, com' io lo desidereréi, tu non faticherésti
thou wert daughter as I it should desire fatigue thyself
più in quésto módo; tu imparerésti a léggere, scrívere, e
more shouldst learn to read write
cantáre; e ti rimarrébbe ánche témpo per divertírti; io ti
to sing to thee would remain even time to amuse
meneréi a spásso in carrózza, e ti faréi giocáre in tánte
would lead would make to amuse so many
maniére. A me, la mía mámma ha détto sémpre che Dío sa
manners (ways). To me has said always that God knows
quel che fa. Dío ha volúto che élla fósse Marchésa, ed io
what he does. wished you should be
úna contadína, ma io pregherò Dío di dárle úna figliolína, ed
will pray to give you
élla è tánto buóna che il signóre la farà contéuta.
you are so lord you will make
La signóra Giúlia non si saziáva di accarezzáre Rosína:
satisfied to caress
facéva ammiráre álla cameriéra la gentilézza déi suói módi, le
she made admire gentleness
grázie délla persóna; e quésta, per far la córte álla padróna la
she to please the her
lodáva ánche più di lei, e la Rosína ascoltáva quéste lódi tútta
praise than she heard
confúsa. Vénnero ad avvisáre che il pránzo éra all' órdine:
They came inform dinner was ready
la Marchésa passò in úna píccola sála con Rósa per máno, e la
passed into a little parlor hand he
féce méttere a sédere a távola accánto a sè. La póvera
caused to put sit table at the side
fanciullína si vergognáva talménte, che quási piangéva ma
bashful so almost to weep
vedéndosi trattatta con tánta bontà, cominciò a rassicurársi un
seeing herself treated kindness began re-assure
póco.

La minéstra le párve si buóna, che ne mangiò assái
soup   to her seemed   of it she eat enough
e il lésso che vénne dópo, le párve una vivánda squisíta; e si
boiled meat   came after to her seemed   food   exquisite
saziò affátto; dimodochè, quándo vénnero in távola gli áltri
satiated   so that   when   came   the other
piátti per quánto la Signóra la pregásse, non potè più mangiáre.
dishes   begged   was able   to eat.
Il víno pói non vi fu módo di fárglielo bére; appéna l' ébbe
wine then   there was   to make to drink; hardly   had
ella assaggiáto si riscósse, e chiése che per carità le désero
she tasted   shuddered   asked   for charity her should give
dell' ácqua. Allorchè élla víde veníre le frútta e i dólci, mandò
             When   saw to come   fruit   sweets uttered
un grído di sorprésa. Un áltro pránzo! eh! Élla potéva
cry   surprise.   dinner   could
chiamáre tútti i ragázzi del villággio, v' éra da sfamárli tútti
call   children   there was to satisfy
Ebbéne Rósa, se tu vuói veníre a stár con me, tu saráí
Well   if thou wishest to come   to be   shalt be
trattáta tútti i giórni cóme óggi, e ánche méglio. Per me.
treated   days   as   to-day   even   better.
Signóra mía, faréi tútto per compiacérla; ma égli e
            I would do   to please you
impossíbile ch' io lásci la mia mámma, che non ha áltro che
                  should leave   has other than
me per ajutárla e vegliárla quand' è maláta. Io pagherò úna
      to help her to care for her when   sick.   will pay
dónna perchè la sérva. Si, ma quésta dónna non le vorrà
woman   for   her serve (that she may serve her).   would wish
béne cóme io gliéne vóglio e la servirà solaménte per
well as   to her wish   her would serve only
guadagnáre. La mía mámma ha préso cúra di me quánd' io
to gain.   taken   care
éra piccína; óra ch' io sóno gránde, non vóglio abbandonárla;
                                       I wish
quándo élla sarà vécchia, io lavorerò per dárle da mangiáre
           will be old   will work   to give her   to eat
cóme élla facéva per me quándo io non mi potéva guadagnáre il
as   did   was able to gain   the

páne. La Marchésa era intenerita dái sentiménti di quésta
bread.   affected by the

fanciúlla, e non ébbe più il coràggio d' insístere : le permíse di
                    had   permitted

ripréndere la sua vesticcióla, e tornár dálla mámma, che dovéva
to take again   dress   return   ought

cominciáre ad éssere in pensiéro per léi. Innánzi di lasciarla
to begin   to be   thought   for her. Before allowing her

partíre, l' abbracciò, ed empì le sue tásche di quéi pasticcíni
to depart, she embraced her   filled   pockets   cakes

e di quélle pastíne che éssa non avéva neppúre assaggiáte.
       that   pastry   had   not even   tasted.

La Rosína paréva un uccellétto scappáto dálle máni di un
         appeared like a   bird   escaped   hands

ragázzo che lo volésse ingabbiáre : avéva préso i súoi zóccoli
boy   who it wished   to cage: she had taken   wooden shoes

in máno, e così scálza corréva tánto lésta, che la cameriéra, a
  hand   so barefooted ran   so   quickly   to

cui la marchésa avéva comandáto di tenérle diétro, durò fatica
whom   keep   found it difficult

a non la pérder di vista. Éssa nonostánte arrivò al casoláre
  her to lose from sight.   notwithstanding arrived house

quási súbito dópo Rosa, la trovò nélle bráccie délla sua
      soon   after   her she found in the   arms

mámma, álla quále élla raccontáva che úna bélla signóra la
                        related

voléva condúrre con sè, promettèndole vestíti bélli e tre
wished to take her with her, promising her clothes fine three

pránzi ógni giórno. Io nondiméno son venúta via (aggiungéva
dinners every day.   nevertheless am   come   added

élla), perchè sebbéne io vóglia bene a quélla signóra, la* non è
              although   wish well

poi la mia mámma.
then

La cameriéra dísse a quélla contadína che álla súa padróna
                told

éra piaciúto tánto il buon cuóre délla Rosína, che voléva
    pleased   wished

---

* La for ella, she.

assicurárle úna pensióne di dugénto fránchi, e al suc ritórna
to secure to her   two hundred francs   return
álla città ne avrébbe segnáto il contrátto: le lasciò l' indirízzo,
       would have to sign   she left her   direction
e le raccomandò di venírla a vedére la doménica próssima, e
    advised   to come   to see   Sunday   next
menár con sè la Rosína. La dónna gliélo promíse.
to bring with her   it to her promised.

La Marchésa Giúlia, benchè non fósse avvézza a sentírsi
                    although   accustomed to hear herself
contradíre, siccóme d' áltra párte élla éra generósa e di cuór
contradicted, on   other hand
buóno riconóbbe che non avéa potestà di dispórre di Rósa cóntro
      recognized   power   dispose   against
il súo volére, nè di obbligárla a preferír lei álla própria mádre;
       will, nor   oblige her   to prefer her to   her own
perciò si determinò a fárle in áltro módo tútto quel béne ch'
therefore   determined   another manner all   the good
élla potéva. Accólse dúnque le contadíne con mólta affabilità,
she   could. She approached then

e dópo ch' élla ébbe parláto con la mádre, non si maravigliò più
   after   had   spoken   was astonished
délle qualità buóne délla figliuóla. Quélla dónna in fátti éra
                    daughter.   That   lady   fact was
tútta probità e delicatézza: conténta del súo státo, non invidiáva
 all   delicacy   state   envy
niénte i rícchi, i quáli dicéva éssa, son pur sottopósti, cóme tútti
ny one   rich   who   said   she are   exposed
gli áltri uómini, álle malattíe ed ai dispiacéri, e dovránno réndere
                    diseases and to misfortunes   ought   to render
un gran cónto délle lóro ricchézze, dóve non se ne sérvano in
        account   riches   where   serve (use) for
béne.
good.

La Marchésa féce álla Rosína il regálo che le avéva
               made   present for her she had
destináto, ed érano tre vaccherélle, le quáli élla féce consegnáre
           three young cows   which she made to consign
álla mádre perchè le conducésse con sé: ed aggiúnse, éssere
                  should conduct   added to be (it was)

súo desidério che la piccína non andásse più a lavoráre álla
her   desire   should go   work

campágna, ma badásse soltánto a véndere il látte e le nóva.
country   should care only   to sell   milk   eggs.

Siccóme pói, diss' ella, non déve Rosína stár mái disoccupáta,
But then, said   ought   to be ever unoccupied,

ndrà álla scuóla del vóstro villággio, il restánte délla giornáta
hall go   school   day

.o passerà da úna maéstra che le insegnerà a far la trína: álle
pass   teacher   her will teach   to make lace

spése che occorreránno per la súa istruzióne penserò io. Rósa
expense shall incur   I will think.

e la súa mádre volévano ringraziáre la Signóra, ma vínte dállo
                   wished   to thank

lácrime non potérono articoláre paróla.
tears   were able   word.

    Quésto benefízio non potéva éssere fátto a persóne più dégne:
                                was able   made   any one more worthy

l' educazióne sviluppò nélla fanciullína tútte le buóne qualità
                developed

che tralucévano in léi fin dall' infánzia. Un ánno dópo élla
    shone   her from   A year after

portò in regálo álla Marchésa úna trína lavoráta con sómma
carried   present   lace   made

finézza ed éra tánta da guarníre un vestíto. La Marchésa séppe
                enough   to trim   dress.   knew

che quélla famíglia, résa da léi agiáta, risparmiáva pei
                      rendered   saved

soccórrere i bisognósi, e spiáva tútte le occasióni per beneficáre.
succor   needy   spied (watched)

    Rosa éra entráta appéna ne' quíndici ánni, quándo la
            entered   scarcely   fifteenth   year

Marchésa cádde in una gravíssima malattía: súo maríto éra
             fell   in   very serious   sickness   husband .

in viággio: e non avéva áltro che la súa génte di servízio che
  absent   she had no others than   people   service who

l' assistésse. Lo séppe Rosína, e súbito, lasciándo úna súa vicína
her could assist.   knew   left   neighbor

a guárdia délla cása e délle vaccherélle, partì per la città
   guard   cows,   she set out

insiéme cólla mámma. Arriváte che fúrono, andárono álla
together   with   Arrived   they   were,   they went
cámera délla Marchésa. Éssa éra fuóri di sè, nè riconoscéva
chamber   She was out of her mind, neither recognized
alcúno; e da quéllo státo di delírio, cadéva poi in un profóndo
no one   fell
letárgo che paréva mórta. Tútta la génte di cása éra costernáta,
             appeared   dead.   people   confounded
la cameriéra, sommaménte affezionáta álla súa padróna, non
                    greatly   attached
sapéva far áltro che piángere, e non éra buóna a núlla. La
knew   to do   than   to weep   she was   for nothing.
buóna Lúci féce rizzáre accánto al létto délla signóra un
                made to be placed by the side   bed
letticciúolo: ed élla e Rosína vegliávano la signóra úna nótte
little bed   watched
per úna.

I médici s' intendévano con lóro per la cúra dell' ammaláta;
              depended   upon them   care   sick (lady)
e tútto éra adempíto con la mássima puntualità. In cápo a nóve
             fulfilled   greatest   At the end of nine
giórni la malattía pigliò buóna piéga: la Marchésa ritornò in sè e
days   took   turn   recovered
conóbbe quánto dovéva állo zélo e all' affétto délle sue amoróse
knew   owed   loving
assisténti. La póvera Rosína éra scoloríta dálle inquietézze e
                                           pale
dálle nottáte perdúte; ma i suói ócchi abbattúti ripigliárono
nights lost (sleepless nights)   languid   took again
la lóro vivacità appéna élla cominciò a speráre nélla guarigióne
                   as soon as   began   hope   cure
délla súa benefattríce. Ella con le súe premúre rése méno
                                                      cares   rendered
spiacévole álla signóra il témpo délla convalescénza; óra le
disagreeable   now
leggéva un bel líbro, ora le raccontáva quálche fátto interessánte
read   then   related   fact
accadúto nel suo villággio: voléva ánche pensáre a vegliárla,
happened   wished also   to take care of her

nè permettéva che áltri le facésse i bródi e preparásse le
                       others   should make broths

medicíne. In quésto témpo il marito della Marchésa tornò,
                                                               returned

ed éssa, ritornáta in perfétta salúte, gli mostrò quánto dovéva a
    returned   health   showed   she owed

Rosína ed álla mádre di lei, e gli dísse che oramái non le   dáva
                                         now   gave (had)

più il cuóre di separársi da lóro. Concertárono dúnque di
    heart   They agreed   then

méttere la Lúci alla direzióne délla cása, sicúri che non
 put   sure

potévano affidárla méglio: la fíglia pói non dovéva avér áltro
were able   should have

titolo che di compágna ed amíca délla Marchésa. Voi vi potéte
                                                                    can

figuráre, figliuóli miéi, quánto volontiéri accettárono ésse tále
          children   they accepted

proposizióne.

ETYMOLOGY.

PARTS OF SPEECH.

There are *nine* parts of speech in the Italian language
— 1. The ARTICLE; 2. The NOUN; 3. The ADJEC-
TIVE; 4. The PRONOUN; 5. The VERB; 6. The AD-
VERB; 7. The PREPOSITION; 8. The CONJUNCTION,
9. The INTERJECTION.

The first five are variable; the four last, invariable.

The change which the first four undergo by means of terminations is called declension: it refers to gender, number, and case.

There are two genders in Italian, — the masculine and the feminine.

There are also two numbers, — the singular and the plural: and five cases, expressing the different relations of words to each other; namely, the nominative, genitive, dative, accusative, and ablative.

The nominative case, or the subject, answers to the question *who?* or *what?* as, Who is reading? *The boy.*

The genitive or possessive case answers to the question *whose?* or *of which?* as, Whose book? *The boy's* book.

The dative answers to the question *to whom?* as, To whom shall I give it? *To the boy.*

The accusative or objective case marks the object of an action, and answers to the question *whom?* or *what?* as, Whom or what do you see? I see *the boy, the house.*

The ablative answers to the question *from* or *by whom?* as, From whom did you receive it? *From* my father?

CHAPTER II.

THE ARTICLE — L' ARTICOLO.

MNEMONIC EXERCISE.

LA *doménica sénto* LA *méssa*. On Sunday I attend (*the*) mass.*
IL *lunedì spéndo* IL *danáro*. On Monday I spend *the* money.
IL *martedì viéne* LA *sérva*. *The* servant comes on Tuesday.
IL *mercoledì stiro* LA *biancheria* On Wednesday I iron *the* linen.
IL *giovedì págo* IL *cameriére*. On Thursday I pay *the* domestic.
IL *venerdì riscuóto* L' *entráte*. On Friday I receive *the* rent.
IL *sábato aspétto* IL *sárto*. . I expect *the* tailor on (*the*) Saturday.†

The article is used much more frequently in Italian than in English.

There are two articles, — DEFINITE and INDEFINITE.‡ The Definite has several variations for the sake of euphony.

---

* In the translation of the Italian examples, words which cannot be expressed are inserted within marks of parenthesis.
† The pupil is requested to commit to memory the Italian words occurring in Rules or Examples, as their meaning will be seldom repeated. The conjugation of the verbs will be found at the end of the book.
‡ The indefinite article, *un, uno, una,* a or an, will be treated of in a subsequent chapter. (See chapter on Numeral Adjectives.)

THE ARTICLE. 17

DEFINITE ARTICLE.

SINGULAR, *il, lo,** masculine;   *la*, feminine.
PLURAL,   *i, gli (li),*† masculine; *le*, feminine.

REMARKS.

I. The article *il*, plural *i*, is most generally used; as, —

Il temperíno, i temperíni;   *il sigíllo, i sigílli.*
The penknife, the penknives; the seal, the seals.‡

II. The article *lo*, plural *gli*, is placed, — 1st, Before nouns beginning with *s* followed by another consonant; as, —

Lo spécchio, gli spécchi; lo spírito, gli spíriti.
The mirror, the mirrors; the spirit, the spirits.

2d, Before nouns commencing with a vowel, eliding the *o*, and replacing it by an apostrophe; as, —

L' ócchio, gli ócchi; l' amíco, gli amíci.
The eye, the eyes; the friend, the friends.

III. The word *déi*, gods, takes the article *gli*. We say, *Il Dío di Abrámo, gli déi del paganésimo;* the God of Abraham, the gods of the heathen.

IV. *Lo*, or *il*, is written before masculine nouns commencing with *z*; as, *Lo zío*, or *il zío*, the uncle; and after the preposition *per: Per lo cuóre*, or *per il cuóre*, for the heart. But, in speaking, *il* is generally used, except in the phrases *per lo più*, at most; *per lo méno*, at least.

V. *La* before a feminine noun takes *le* in the plural; as, —

La pénna, le pénne; la stánza, le stánze.
The pen, the pens; the room, the rooms.

---

* The Italians have taken the articles *il* and *lo* from the first and last syllable of the ablative Latin *illo*. In their use, euphony alone is consulted: *lo libro, lo pádre, il libro, il padre.*
† We find *li*, plural of *il*, in classical works, especially in poetry; but modern writers use *i* in preference.
‡ The article is given with every noun, so that the pupil may learn the gender of the noun

The *a* of *la* is elided before a vowel, and replaced by an apostrophe. It, however, takes *le* in the plural; as, —

L' isola, le isole; l' ánima, le ánime.
The island, the islands; the soul, the souls.

VI. The article *il* may lose the *i* if preceded by the words *che, tra, fra, e;* as, *Tra 'l sì e 'l no*, between yes and no. Such elision is mostly confined to poetry.

VII. The article *gli* loses the *i* before a noun commencing with *i*; as, *Gl' inférmi*, the infirm.

VIII. The article *le* loses the *e* before a noun beginning with *e*; as, *L' elemósine*, the alms; *l' érbe*, the herbs. The above rules are purely euphonic.

IX. As there are only two genders in Italian, English neuter nouns take the gender of the noun into which they are translated; and the article naturally takes the gender of the noun to which it belongs.

X. They say in Italian, *Vádo in chiésa, in strádu*, etc., I go to church, into the street, etc.; and do not use the article, because the church or street is not designated But, in *Vádo nélla chiésa di San Cárlo, vádo nélla stráda dóve státe di casa*, — I go into St. Charles' Church, I am going into the street where you dwell, — the article is used because the church and street are defined.

XI. So, likewise, they say, *Vádo in cása, in cámera, a létto, in cucína;* because it is understood that the person speaks of his own house, room, bed, kitchen; which nouns are defined by the circumstances.

XII. It is necessary to use the article in such sentences as the following, where the signification of the noun is limited: —

Vádo —   I am going —
nélla cása di mia mádre . . . into my mother's house.
nélla cámera di mio pádre . . into my father's chamber.
nel létto di suo fratéllo . . . in his brother's bed.
nélla cucína del vicino . . . in the neighbor's kitchen.

XIII. There are cases in which the article may be used or not; as, —

Audácia, fortúna, e virtù, gli déttero tróno e poténza; or, L' audácia, la fortúna, e la virtù, gli déttero il tróno e la poténza.

Boldness, fortune, and merit gave him the sceptre and the power.

In the first case, the nouns are considered independently, without any subsequent idea: in the second case, the article limits the signification of the noun by something relative to each noun understood; thus: —

L' audácia che spiegò in ógni imprésa, la fortúna che lo secondo, la virtù che lo distinse, gli déttero il tróno délla nazióne e la poténza sovrána.*

The boldness which he manifested in all his enterprises, the fortune which favored him, the merit which distinguished him, gave him the throne of the nation and the sovereign power.

XIV. The nouns Mr., Mrs., Miss, take the article, thus: *il Signóre, il Signór dottóre, la Signóra, la Signóra principéssa, la Signorína.* These words do not take an article when they are addressed to the person to whom we are speaking. The word *Signóre* loses the final *e* before a masculine noun.

XV. Proper nouns do not take the article; † as.

---

* When several nouns come together before or after the verb, and the article is used or omitted before the first of them, this article must be repeated or omitted before every other noun in the sentence.

† Names of kingdoms, provinces, mountains, and rivers, take the article or not, according to the extent of their signification; as, *L' Itália è bélla,* Italy is beautiful; *Stava in Italia,* he was in Italy.

Names of cities and villages, unless qualified by an adjective, are used without the article. The same rule applies to the names of a few islands: *Malta, Cipro, Creta,* etc.

The names of abstract substances, and those of gems, metals, etc., when used in a generic sense require the article before them; as, *L' óro e le pérle, e i fiór vermigli e biánchi,* the gold and the pearls, and the red and white flowers.

A noun preceded by an adjective takes the article before the adjective; as, *Il gran mále,* the great evil; *Il gran peccáto,* the great sin.

All words used as nouns require the article before them; as, *Il bello, il buono, the beautiful, the good; Son cérto del sì,* I am certain of the affirmative; *Ciascúno rispóse di no,* every one answered in the negative; *Il súo parláre mi piáce,* his conversation pleases me.

When a noun is used in an indeterminate sense, the article is omitted; as, *Non uómo, uómo già fúi,* now I am not a man, formerly I was a man.

Michelángelo, Raffaéllo. But it is generally placed before family names, particularly of illustrious or renowned persons, both male and female; as, *Il Buonarótti, il Sánzio, la Marátti* (the poetess).

XVI. Possessive adjectives generally take the article; as, *Il mío, il túo, il súo, la nóstra, la vóstra*, etc., my, thy, his, our, your, etc. Possessive pronouns always do.

XVII. Verbs in the infinitive mood, and adverbs, take the article when they are used substantively; as, —

Il balláre mi sécca; Non sò nè il quándo nè il cóme.
It tires me to dance; I know neither when nor how.

READING LESSON.

L' amóre e la mórte fánno eguáli i re ed i pastóri.
Love and death make equal kings and shepherds.

La glória è il sólo béne che póssa tentáre gli uómini.
Glory is only good which is able (can) to tempt men.

Il témpo, che forțífica l' amicízia, indebolísce l' amóre.
Time fortifies friendship, weakens

Le calúnnie sóno cóme le feríte che lásciano sémpre la márgine.
Calumnies are like wounds leave always scar.

La paúra govérna il móndo.
Fear governs world.

La prudénza è la guída e la padróna délla víta umána.
Prudence guide mistress life[2] human.[1]

EXERCISE UPON THE ARTICLES.

(The) fortune loves (the) youth.
fortúna (f.) ama gioventù (f.).

The scholar cultivates (the) memory.
scoláre (m.) coltíva memória (f.).

The servant (f.) puts out the light.
sérva smórza lúme (m.).

The evening I study the lesson.
séra (f.) stúdio lezióne (f.).

The shoemaker brings the shoes.
calzolaio (m.) pórta scárpe (f.).

UNION OF ARTICLES AND PREPOSITIONS.

WORDS.

Il páne,	the bread.	Io ho,	I have.
La cárne,	the meat.	Tu hái,	thou hast.
Il víno,	the wine.	Egli ha,	he has.
Le frútta,	the fruits.	Ella ha,	she has.
Le méle,	the apples.	Non ho,	I have not.
Il fratéllo,	the brother.	Ho io?	have I?
La péra,	the pear.	Hái tu?	hast thou?
La pésca,	the peach.	Ha égli?	has he?
Il fíco,	the fig.	Ha élla?	has she?
Il pádre,	the father.	Non ho io?	have I not?
Líbro, book.	Sì, yes.	Che, what.	Chi, who.

CONVERSATION.

Ho io la pénna?
Hái tu il temperíno?
Che há mio fratéllo?
Ha lo zio dél Signóre il líbro?
Che spéndi tu?
Chi ha compráto la cása?
Che cása ha égli compráto?
Che ha la Signóra?
Chi aspétto il Lunedì?
Che cámera hái?

Sì, tu hái la pénna.
No, non ho il temperíno.
Il fratéllo vóstro ha la cárta.
No, égli nón ha il líbro.
Spéndo il danáro.
Il Signór dottóre.
La cása di mio pádre.
Élla ha lo spécchio.
Aspétto il sárto.
Ho la cucína.

CHAPTER III.

UNION OF THE ARTICLES AND PREPOSITIONS.

MNEMONIC EXERCISE.

I giórni DELLA settimána . .	The days *of the* week.
Le stagióni DELL' ánno . . .	The seasons *of the* year.
Nélle stráde DELLA città . .	In the streets *of the* city.
Il lapis è SULLA távola . . .	The pencil is *upon the* table.
Siámo NEL cuór délla státe . .	We are *in* midsummer.
La pénna è NEL calamáio . .	The pen is *in the* inkstand.
Ballátè CON LE ragázze . . .	Dance *with the* girls.
Léggo cogli occhiáli . . .	I read *with (the)* spectacles.

UNION OF THE ARTICLES AND PREPOSITIONS.

§ I. If the article is used with one of the prepositions, *di*, of or for; *a*, to or at; *da*, from or by; *in*, in; *con*, with; *su*, upon, — the two monosyllables are joined for euphony.

REMARK. — In connecting the preposition with the article, *di* is changed into *de*, *in* into *ne*, *con* into *co*.

§ II. 1st, Contraction of the article *lo*, and its plural *gli*, with a noun : —

SINGULAR.

Lo	. *spérpero,*	the havoc.
Di lo . .	DELLO *spérpero,*	of the havoc.
A lo . .	ALLO *spérpero,*	to the havoc.
Da lo . .	DALLO *spérpero,*	by the havoc.
In lo . .	NELLO *spérpero,*	in the havoc.
Con lo . .	COLLO *spérpero,*	with the havoc.
Su lo . .	SULLO *spérpero,*	upon the havoc.

PLURAL.

Gli	. *spérperi,*	the havocs.
Di gli . .	DEGLI *spérperi,*	of the havocs.
A gli . .	AGLI *spérperi,*	to the havocs.
Da gli . .	DAGLI *spérperi,*	from or by the havocs.
In gli . .	NEGLI *spérperi,*	in the havocs.
Con gli . .	COGLI *spérperi,*	with the havocs.
Su gli . .	SUGLI *spérperi,*	upon the havocs.

This article, before a vowel, is written *dell'*, *all'*, *dall'* *dell' amico*, of the friend.

Lo	*L'* . *amico,*	the friend.
Di lo . .	DELL' *amico,*	of the friend.
A lo . .	ALL' *amico,*	to the friend.
Da lo . .	DALL' *amico,*	from the friend.
In lo . .	NELL' *amico,*	in the friend.
Con lo . .	COLL' *amico,*	with the friend.
Su lo . .	SULL' *amico,*	upon the friend.

Before nouns in the plural commencing with an *i*, we write *dégl'*, *cogl'*, *dagl'*, etc.; as, *Cogl' infelici*, with the unhappy.

§ III. 2d, Contraction of the article *il*, and its plural *i*

SINGULAR.

Il		*fazzolétto,*	the pocket-handkerchief.
Di il . . .	DEL	*fazzolétto,*	of the pocket-handkerchief.
A il . . .	AL	*fazzolétto,*	to the pocket-handkerchief.
Da il . . .	DAL	*fazzolétto,*	from or by the pocket-handk.
In il . . .	NEL	*fazzolétto,*	in the pocket-handkerchief.
Con il . .	COL	*fazzolétto,*	with the pocket-handkerchief.
Su il . . .	SUL	*fazzolétto,*	upon the pocket-handkerchief

PLURAL.

I, ...		*fazzolétti,*	the handkerchiefs.
Di i .	DEI or DE'	*fazzolétti,*	of the handkerchiefs.
A i .	AI or A'	*fazzolétti,*	to the handkerchiefs.
Da i .	DAI or DA'	*fazzolétti,*	from the handkerchiefs.
In i .	NEI or NE'	*fazzolétti,*	in the handkerchiefs.
Con i .	COI or CO'	*fazzolétti,*	with the handkerchiefs.
Su i .	SUI or SU'	*fazzolétti,*	upon the handkerchiefs.

§ IV. 3d, Contraction of the article *la*, and its plural *le*

SINGULAR.

La.		*saccóccia,*	the pocket.
Di la . .	DELLA	*saccóccia,*	of the pocket.
A la . .	ALLA	*saccóccia,*	to the pocket.
Da la . .	DALLA	*saccóccia,*	from the pocket.
In la . .	NELLA	*saccóccia,*	in the pocket.
Con la .	COLLA	*saccóccia,*	with the pocket.
Su la . .	SULLA	*saccóccia,*	upon the pocket.

Before a vowel, write *dell'*, *all'*, *dull'*, *nell'*, etc.

PLURAL.

Le		*saccócce,*	the pockets.
Di le . .	DELLE	*saccócce,*	of the pockets.
A le . .	ALLE	*saccócce,*	to the pockets.
Da le . .	DALLE	*saccócce,*	from or by the pockets.
In le . .	NELLE	*saccócce,*	in the pockets.
Con le . .	COLLE	*saccócce,*	with the pockets.
Su le . .	SULLE	*saccócce,*	upon the pockets.

Before nouns commencing with *e*, write *dell'*, *all'*, *dull'*, etc.

§ V. The contraction of *con* and of *su* with the articles *lo, gli, la,* and *le,* is used at discretion. We can say, *Con lo stúdio, con la pénna,* or *cóllo stúdio, cólla pénna,* — with the study, with the pen, — according to the harmony of the phrase. Instead of *su,* we can say *sopra* with all the articles, writing them separately; as, *Sul tétto,* or *sopra il tétto; sulla távola,* or *sopra la távola,* — upon the roof, upon the table.

§ VI. The preposition *per* may be united with the articles *il* and *i,* thus: *pel,* plural *pei,* or *pe'.* In speaking, we say, ordinarily, *per il,* to avoid affectation.

The pupil is required to supply the prepositions and articles in the following declensions: —

Il giardíno,	the garden.		*I giardíni,*	the gardens.
„	of the garden.		„	of the gardens.
„	to the garden.		„	to the gardens.
„	from the garden.		„	from the gardens.
Lo spírito,	the spirit.		*Gli spíriti,*	the spirits.
„	of the spirit.		„	of the spirits.
„	to the spirit.		„	to the spirits.
„	from the spirit.		„	from the spirits.
L' álbero,	the tree.		*Gli álberi,*	the trees.
„	of the tree.		„	of the trees.
„	to the tree.		„	to the trees.
„	from the tree.		„	from the trees.
La rósa,	the rose.		*Le róse,*	the roses.
„	of the rose.		„	of the roses.
„	to the rose.		„	to the roses.
„	from the rose.		„	from the roses.
L' ánima,	the soul.		*Le ánime,*	the souls.
„	of the soul.		„	of the souls.
„	to the soul.		„	to the souls.
„	from the soul.		„	from the souls.

UNION OF ARTICLES AND PREPOSITIONS. 25

READING LESSON.

Andiámo nélle stráde délla città. La dónna è partíta. Non
Let us go   streets   city.   woman is departed. Not²

andáte cólla cameriéra. Préndo la chiáve délla cámera. La
go¹   chambermaid. I take   key   room.

primavéra délla víta. Élla morì nel fiór dégli ánni. Non dormíte
spring-time   life. She died in flower years.   Not² sleep¹

all' ária apérta. Il gátto è nélla cámera del padróne. Il
     air open.   cat   master.

lápis non è súlla távola. Léggo con le ragázze. Il calamáio
pencil not is   table.   I read   girls.   inkstand

súlla távola. La chiáve è nell' úscio. Si va álla cúccia nell'
                                door.   One goes chase

autúnno. La pénna è nel calamáio súlla távola. La víta è
autumn.

bréve, e l' árte è lúnga. La moderazióne génera la felicità. L' óro
short   long.   generates happiness.   gold

govérna il móndo. La verità prodúce l' ódio. L' uómo propóne,
governs   world.   truth produces hatred.   man   proposes

e Dío dispóne. La vóce, gli ócchi, il córpo, l' ánima dell' uómo.
  God disposes.   voice   eyes   body   soul

La vóce del pópolo è la vóce di Dío.
              people

EXERCISE FOR TRANSLATION.

Italy is the garden of Europe. The passions are the
Itália   giardíno Európa.   passióni sóno

elements of life. The voice of the people is the voice of God.
eleménti   víta.   vóce   pópolo   Dío.

The whip (is) for the horse, the halter for the ass, and the stick
    frústa (f.)   cavállo   cavézza   ásino   bastóne

for the shoulders of the insolent (one). (The) pride is the
         spálle   impertinénte.   supérbia

daughter of (the) ignorance. An ancient philosopher said, that
fíglia   ignoránza.   Un antíco² filósofo¹ dísse, che

(the) pride breakfasts with (the) abundance, dines with (the)
      orgóglio fa colazione   abbondánza, pránza

poverty, and sups with (the) shame.
povertà   céna   vergógna.

3

Io sóno,	I am.	*Noi siámo,*	we are.
Tu séi,	thou art.	*Voi siéte,*	you are.
Egli è,	he is.	*Eglino sóno,*	they are.

CONVERSATION.

Che còsa avéte? — *Ho il fazzolétto.*
Dov' è? — *Nélla mia saccòccia.*
Són' io póvero (poor)? — *Tu non séi póvero, séi ricco.*
Còsa è l' Itália? — *L' Itália è il giardino dell' Európa.*
Hái tu la pénna del vicíno? — *No, Signóre, mio fratéllo l' ha.*
Qual libro (book) *hái?* — *Ho il libro del sárto.*
Ha súo pádre un cavállo? — *Non ha un cavállo, ha un ásino.*
Che cósa ho io? — *Tu hái il bastóne di mio fratéllo.*
Séi tu filósofo? — *Non sóno filósofo.*
Hái tu il mio temperíno? — *No, è sópra la távola.*
Siéte il mio amíco? — *Sóno il vóstro* (your) *amíco.*
Non hai un (a) *giardíno?* — *Si, ho un giardíno ed* (and) *un cavállo.*

CHAPTER IV.

THE NOUN*—IL NOME.

MNEMONIC EXERCISE.

Il TIMÓRE *di* DIO . . . . . The fear of God.
La CÚPOLA *di* SAN PIÉTRO . . The cupola of St. Peter.
Il DUÓMO *di* FIRÉNZE . . . The cathedral of Florence.
I FIÓRI *délla* PRIMAVÉRA . . . The flowers of spring.
Il COLÓRE *délla* RÓSA . . . . The color of the rose.
Il CAMMINÉTTO *délla* CÁMERA . The small mantelpiece of the chamber.

---

* There are some words in the Italian language which paint so well the character of the nation, that it is impossible to reproduce them in any other language by words strictly analogous. For example, the words *sfógo, smínia, puntíglio, fúria, orgásmo, éstro, sbú- fáre*, etc., representing ideas which are conceived only under a burning sky, cannot be exactly rendered in the calm and misty Northern languages. Being purely euphonic, the rules on the article may be utterly disregarded whenever euphony requires it. The same may also be said respecting the elision and contraction of words.

La cárta è nel cassettíno .	The paper is in the drawer.
Il pózzo è nel cortíle . . .	The well is in the yard.
Lo stúdio è un godiménto .	Study is a pleasure.
Gli ánni fúggono rápidi . . .	Years fly rapidly.
La minéstra è frédda . . .	The soup is cold.
L'ózio è il pádre di ógni vízio,	Idleness is the father of all vices.

THE GENDER OF NOUNS.

There are only two genders in the Italian language, — the masculine and the feminine.

I. All nouns belong either to the masculine or feminine gender.

II. Nouns ending in *a* are feminine. Those expressing dignity, and professions of men, such as *il pápa*, the pope, and the following, derived from the Greek, are masculine: —

Anagrámma,	anagram.	Idióma,	idiom.
Anátema,	anathema.	Pianéta,	planet.
Assióma,	axiom.	Poéma,	poem.
Clima,	climate.	Prísma,	prism.
Diadéma,	diadem.	Probléma,	problem.
Dilémma,	dilemma.	Prográmma,	programme.
Diplóma,	diploma.	Scisma,	schism.
Dógma,	dogma.	Sistéma,	system.
Drámma,	drachm.	Sofísma,	sophism.
Embléma,	emblem.	Stémma,	coat of arms.
Enigma,	enigma.	Stratagémma,	stratagem.
Epigrámma,	epigram.	Téma,	theme.
Fantásma,	spectre.	Teoréma,	theorem.

III. Of the nouns ending in *e*, some are masculine, and others feminine. As no positive rules can be given to indicate their gender, recourse must be had to the dictionary.

IV. Among the nouns ending in *e*, some are of both genders;* as, —

---

* Some masculine nouns ending in *e* take a different termination for the feminine as, *re*, *regína*.

IL or LA *cárcere*,	the prison.	IL or LA *grégge*,	the flock.
IL or LA *cénere*,*	the cinders.	IL or LA *fúne*,	the cord.
IL or LA *fíne*,	the end.	IL or LA *lépre*,	the hare.
IL or LA *fólgore*,	the thunder.	IL or LA *márgine*,	the margin.
IL or LA *fónte*,	the fountain.	IL or LA *sérpe*,	the serpent.
IL or LA *frónte*,†	the forehead.	IL or LA *tígre*,	the tiger.

V. There are some nouns ending in *a* which can end in *e*, without changing the gender; as, *L' árma* or *l' árme*, arms (heraldic); *la sórta*, or *la sórte*, destiny.

VI. Very few nouns terminate in *i*, as this letter is generally the characteristic sign of the plural. Of these few, some are masculine, and some are feminine; as, —

MASCULINE.		FEMININE.	
Il cavadénti,	the dentist.	*La metrópoli*,	the metropolis.
Il lavacéci,	the dunce.	*La sintássi*,	the syntax.
Il Tamigi,	the Thames.	*La tési*,	the thesis.

REMARK. — The noun *dì*, day, and its compounds; as, *Buondì*, good-day; *mezzodì*, noon; *oggidì*, now-a-days; *Lunedì*, Monday; *Martedì*, Tuesday, etc., — are all masculine. So are likewise nouns of dignity; as, *Balì*, bailiff; *pári*, peer; *guardasigílli*, keeper of the seals.

VII. Nouns ending in *o* are of the masculine gender, except *la máno*, hand; and the words whose ending *ágine* is contracted to *ágo*; as, *immágo* for *immágine*. *Éco*, echo, is of either gender.

REMARK. — Several nouns of animate beings, ending in *o*, change *o* into *a* for the feminine; as, *Il ranócchio*, m., *la ranócchia*, f., frog; *il gátto*, m., *la gátta*, f., cat; *cavállo*, horse; *caválla*, mare; *colómbo, colómba*, dove, etc.

VIII. The following nouns ending in *o* become feminine by changing the *o* into *a*: ‡ —

---

* *Il cénere* is used only in poetry.
† *La frónte* is more used than *il frónte*.
‡ *Fanciúllo*, or *ragízzo*, is said of a child who has not yet reached the age of adolescence. *Fanciúlla* and *ragázza*, on the contrary, are used for a person of marriageable age; the first particularly being employed to indicate unmarried women in general, if young.

Ons. — *Lápis*, pencil; *ribes*, currants; *chérmes*, cochineal, and a few foreign nouns end with a consonant.

Il casáto,	the family name.	*Il núvolo,*	the cloud.
Il canéstro,	the basket.	*L' ombréllo,*	the umbrella.
Il cioccoláto,	the chocolate.	*L' orécchio,*	the ear.
Il frútto,*	the fruit.	*Il ranócchio,*	the frog.
Il légno,*	the wood.	*Lo scritto,**	the writing.
Il mattíno,	the morning.	*Il soffítto,*	the ceiling.

Feminine: *La casáta, la canéstra, la frútta, la légna,* etc.

IX. The names of fruit-trees, ending in *o*, become feminine by changing *o* into *a*; and then they serve to express the fruit. Ex.: —

Il pésco, the peach-tree; *La pésca,* the peach.
Il mélo, the apple-tree; *La méla,* the apple.

The words *fíco, pómo, aráncio,* fig-tree and fig, apple-tree and apple, orange-tree and orange, are an exception.

X. Very few nouns end in *u*. These are always marked with a grave accent, and are of the feminine gender; as, *La gioventù,* the youth; *la grù,* the crane, — except *Perù,* m., Peru, *Belzebù,* Belzebub.

GENERAL REMARKS.

All words ending in *ore,* of which there are a great number, are masculine without any exception. Those ending in *zione* or *sione* are feminine without any exception.

Nouns ending in *ge, le, me, re, se,* are generally masculine; as, —

Rége,	king.		*Cuóre,*	heart.
Viále,	path.		*Arnése,*	utensil.
Fiúme,	river.			

---

* Of the words *frutto, légno,* and *scritto,* which are masculine, and become feminine by changing the *o* into *a,* it must be observed that *il frutto* is the fruit in general, properly and figuratively; while *la frutta* or *le frutta* means the dessert. *Légno* means the woods, and *la legna* is the wood to burn. *Scritto* is a writing; and *la scritta,* a contract.

Some names of animate beings denote the feminine by a different word; as, *Uómo,* man; *dónna,* woman; *tóro,* bull; *vácca,* cow.

Nouns ending in *be, ce, pe, te, ve, ie, ine, one, nte,* are generally feminine; as, —

Plébe,	people.		*Árte,*	art.
Siépe,	hedge.		*Ménte,*	mind.
Chiáve,	key.		*Série,*	series.
Fóce,	entry.		*Incúdine,*	anvil.
Immágine,	image.		*Cicatríce,*	scar.
Ragióne,	reason.		*Lezióne,*	lesson.
Páce,	peace.		*Cróce,*	cross.

Nouns ending in *i*, if not of Greek derivation, are masculine. Those of Greek derivation are feminine, except *Génesi* and *Apocalíssi*, which may be masculine when meaning the sacred books bearing that title.

Análisi,	analysis.		*Énfasi,*	emphasis.
Génesi,	Genesis.		*Tési,*	thesis.
Crísi,	crisis.		*Sintássi,*	syntax.

READING LESSON.

Il rispétto per le dónne è l' indízio più sicúro dell' inciviliménto
  respect   women   indication most sure   civilization

di un pópolo. La schiavitù è la vergógna dégli uómini. L' età
              slavery   shame   men.   age

e il sónno inségnano all' uómo la stráda délla mórte. Bisógna
  sleep   teach   death. It is necessary

vedér l' Itália nélla primavéra e nélla státe per potér méglio
to see   summer   to be able better

giudicáre délla serenità del súo ciélo e délla cálma dél máre che
to judge   sky   sea

la circónda. L' árte di regnáre è la mássima di túttc le árti.
it [2] surrounds.[1] art   to reign   greatest   all

La memória dei benefízij è il débito délla gratitúdine. Noi
  memory   benefits   debt   We

vediámo il lámpo príma di sentíre lo scóppio del fúlmine. Il
see   lightning before   to hear   burst   thunder.

filósofo cérca la súa felicità néllo stúdio délla natúra.
  seeks

THE GENDER OF NOUNS. 31

EXERCISE FOR TRANSLATION.

(The) Study is useful to the health of the body. (The)
studio   vantaggióso   salúte   córpo.
Hatred is the want of vengeance.   The loss of liberty is the
ódio   bisógno   vendétta.   pérdita   libertà
greatest of misfortunes.   The philosopher seeks his happiness
prima   disgrázie.   filósofo   cérca   felicità
in the study of (the) nature.   (The) Innocence of life
                      natúra.   innocénza   v .
takes away the fear of death.   (The) Tears are the ta it
tóglie   spavénto   lágrime   tácito ²
language of grief.
linguággio ¹   dolóre.
Datemi dell' óro e dell' argénto.   L' ária délla mattína e un
Give me   gold   silver.   air   morning
bálsamo nélla primavéra.   Non è arriváto óggi il padre del
balm   spring.   Not   arrived to-day
Signór Dúca?

Nói abbiámo,   we have. | *Abbiámo nói?*   have we?
Vói avéte,   you have. | *Avéte vói?*   have you?
Églino hánno, m., they have. | *Hánno églino?* have they?
Élleno hánno, f., they have. | *Hánno élleno?* have they?

CONVERSATION.

Che avéte nel canéstro?   *Ho dell' uóva nel mío canéstro.*
Qual' è il nóme délla lavandáia? *Il súo nóme è Catarína.*
Avéte vedúto (seen) *il cavállo?* *Io l'* (it) *ho vedúto.*
Dóve?   *Nélla stráda.*
Abbiámo nói sigilli?   *Vói non avéte sigilli, avéte cárta.*
Dóve sóno inérti gli uómini?   *Dóve il suólo è mólto fértile.*
Avéte vedúto la cárta?   *Sì, è nel cassettíno.*
Chi è quést' (this) *Italiáno?* *È il cameriére del médico.*
Chi è nel giardíno?   *Il cavadénti.*
Chi è quésta ragázza?   *È mia sorélla.*
Avéte vedúta la mia cása?   *Quále cása?*
La cása nélla stráda del Re?   *No, Signóra, non l' ho vedua.*
Avéte frútta nel vóstro giardíno? *No, ma* (but) *abbiámo un pésco
                                    ed un mélo che ne duránno
                                    l' ánno ventúro*

CHAPTER V.

THE PLURAL OF NOUNS AND ADJECTIVES.

Adjectives agree in gender and number with the nouns they qualify.

After having learned the rules upon the formation of the plural, the scholar will do well to change all the plural nouns of the following exercise into the singular.

MNEMONIC EXERCISE.

I ciéchi hánno buóne orécchie, The blind have good ears.
Le lenzuóla sóno pulíte, The sheets are clean.
Le bélle antichità di Róma, The beautiful antiquities of Rome.
Le bottéghe sóno sótto ai pórtici, The shops are under the porticos.
L' arátro fa i sólchi profóndi, The plough makes deep furrows.
Ecco due páia di stiváli, Here are two pairs of boots.
I fúnghi náscono nei bóschi, Mushrooms grow in the woods.
Mi dólgono le calcágna,* My heels pain me.
Benéfici sóno i rággi del sóle, The rays of the sun are beneficent.
Mi piáce il giuóco dégli scácchi, I like the play of chess.
Le piógge ristórano la térra, The rains refresh the earth.
Altri témpi, áltri costúmi, Other times, other manners.
I malvági non sóno felíci, The wicked are not happy.

GENERAL RULES.

I. The greater proportion of nouns and adjectives in Italian, whatever be their gender, form their plural by changing the last letter into *i;* as,—

MASC. SINGULAR.		MASC. PLURAL.
Il poéta célebre,	the celebrated poet.	*I poéti célebri.*
Il letto mórbido,	the soft bed.	*I létti mórbidi.*
Il máre burrascóso,	the stormy sea.	*I mári burrascósi.*
FEM.		FEM.
La passióne infelíce,	the unhappy passion.	*Le passióni infelíci.*
La máno débole,	the feeble hand.	*Le máni déboli.*

* The letter *i* indicates an idiomatic phrase.

The following are exceptions: —

II. Feminine nouns and adjectives ending in the singular in *a*, make their plural in *e;* as, —

La scárpa strétta, the narrow shoe. Le scárpe strétte.
La bélla dónna, the handsome woman. Le bélle dónne.

III. The nouns ending in *i*, in *ie*, in an accented vowel, and the monosyllables, do not change their termination in the plural; as, *La crísi*, the crisis; *le crísi*, the crises: *la città*, the city; *le città*, the cities: *il re*, the king; *i re*, the kings; etc.

IV. Nouns are also invariable when they immediately follow the ordinal numbers twenty-one, thirty-one, etc.; as, *Ventúno scúdo*, twenty-one crowns; *trentúno dolláro*, thirty-one dollars. But the noun takes the plural when placed before the number; as, *Scúdi ventúno, dollári trentúno*.

V. The words *addío*, adieu; *lóro*, their, are invariable; as, *Gli addío, i lóro amíci*.

EUPHONIC RULES.

VI. All the nouns, masculine or feminine, ending in *ca* or *ga*, insert an *h* in the plural to preserve the hard sound of the *c* or *g;* as, —

Il monárca, the monarch; i monárchi, the monarchs.
La mánica, the sleeve; le mániche, the sleeves.
La stréga, the sorcerer; le stréghe, the sorcerers.

VII. Nouns of two syllables, ending in *co* or *go*, take an *h* in the plural; as, —

Il bósco, the wood; i bóschi, the woods.
Il lágo, the lake; i lághi, the lakes.

Except *pórco, gréco, mágo*, — pig, Greek, magician, — which make, in the plural, *pórci, gréci, mági*.

VIII. Nouns of more than two syllables, ending in *co* or *gc*, also take an *h*, when these terminations are preceded by one or more consonants; as, —

L' albérgo,	the hotel.	*Gli albérghi.*	
Il rinfrésco,	the refreshment.	*I rinfréschi.*	

IX. Nouns ending in *co* or *go*, preceded by a vowel,* form their plural in *ci* or *gi*; as, —

Il médico,	the physician;	*i médici,*	the physicians.
Lo spárago,	the asparagus;	*gli spáragi,*	the asparagus.

X. EXCEPTION. — Several nouns take an *h* in the plural, though preceded by a vowel; as, *Análogo*, analogous; *antíco*, ancient; *decálogo*, decalogue; *demagógo*, demagogue; etc.

XI. Nouns ending in *io* lose the final *o* in all cases where this termination is preceded by a vowel, or by two or three consonants forming a syllable with *io*; as, —

Fornáio,	baker;	*fornái,*	bakers.
Cuóio,	leather;	*cuói,*	leathers.
Fáscio,	bundle;	*fásci,*	bundles.
Máschio,	boy;	*máschi,*	boys.
Artíglio,	claw;	*artígli,*	claws.
Astúccio,	case;	*astúcci,*	cases.
Viággio,	voyage;	*viággi,*	voyages.

XII. The following nouns, although comprehended in the above class, form an exception, by changing the *io* final into *j*: —

Arbítrio,	will.		*Cérchio,*	circle.
Átrio,	vestibule.		*Dóppio,*	double.
Dúbbio,	doubt.		*Próprio,*	proper.
Gráffio,	scratch.		*Sécchio,*	milk-pail.
Impróprio,	improper.		*Sóffio,*	a blow.
Pátrio,	of the country.		*Spicchio,*	a clove of garlic.

* *Mendíco*, beggar: *equívoco*, equivoke; *diálogo*, dialogue; *apólogo*, apologue, — are written with or without the *h*; as, *Mendici* or *mendichi*, beggars.
  Obs. — Some nouns in the singular in *ere* also end in *ero*; as, *Il pensiéro*, the thought; *il pensiéro: il destriere*, the steed; *il destriero: lo scoláre*, the scholar; *lo scoláro. il cónsole*, the consul; *il cónsolo*. When said of bones cleared from the table, *ósso*, bone, makes *óssi*; when of a skeleton, it makes *óssa. Filo*, thread, makes *fila*, threads *Fili* is used when speaking of the edge of cutting instruments.

PLURAL OF NOUNS AND ADJECTIVES.

These nouns make, in the plural, *arbitrj, đtrj, cérchj, dóppj,* etc.

XIII. This same termination, *io*, is changed into *j* whenever it is preceded by a single consonant, or two consonants not forming one syllable; as, —

Giudicio,	judgment;	*giudicj,*	judgments.
Principio,	beginning;	*princ'ipj,*	beginnings.
Provérbio,	proverb;	*proverbj,*	proverbs.

XIV. Except the following nouns, which make their plural by dropping the final *o*, because the *i* is used in the singular only to soften the sound of the *c* or *g* : —

Ágio,	case.	*Frégio,*	ornament.
Aráncio,	orange.	*Grigio,*	gray.
Bácio,	kiss.	*Indúgio,*	delay.
Barbógio,	dotard.	*Malvágio,*	wicked.
Bigio,	gray.	*Palágio,*	palace.
Cácio,	cheese.	*Pertúgio,*	hole.
Céncio,	rag.	*Prégio,*	merit.
Diságio,	disquiet.	*Sórcio,*	mouse.

Plural: *Ági, aránci, báci, cénci,* etc.

XV. The termination *io*, in the syllable *quio*, changes into *j*; as, —

Osséquio,	respect;	*osséquj,*	respects.
Deliquio,	fainting-fit;	*deliquj,*	fainting-fits.

XVI. If, however, the accent falls on the *i* of the syllable *io*, then *io* is changed into *ii* for the plural, and the sound is a little longer than *j*; as, —

Pío, zío, natío, río, } pious, uncle, native, brook.
Píi, zii, natii, rii,

XVII. Proper nouns ending in *io* likewise take *ii* in the plural; * as, —

Dário, Tibério, Cláudio, } Darius, Tiberius, Claudius.
I Dárii, I Tibérii, I Cláudii,

---

* In Italian, as in other languages, some nouns are used only in the singular number; as proper names; and the words *próle,* offspring; *mane,* morning *róba,* luggage; *rosolia,*

XVIII. The terminations *cia* and *gia* drop the *i* of the plural in the words in which this letter is but slightly pronounced; as, —

La cóscia,	the thigh;	le cósce,	the thighs.
La spiággia,	the shore;	le spiágge,	the shores.
La cáccia,	the chase;	le cácce,	the chases.

XIX. But in the words *província*, *ciriégia*, *franchígia*, province, cherries, immunities, and some others, the *i* is retained in the plural, because, being distinctly pronounced in the singular, it is necessary that it should be heard in the plural; as, *Províncie*, *ciriégie*, *franchígie*, etc.

XX. We must also preserve the *i* of *cia* and of *gia* when it is accented, and the accent must be strongly marked by the voice; as, —

La bugía,	the lie;	le bugíe,	the lies.
La farmacía,	the pharmacy;	le farmacíe,	the pharmacies.

IRREGULAR PLURALS.

XXI. The few nouns which have irregular plurals are:

Uómo,	man;	uómini,	men.
Búe,	ox;	búoi,	oxen.
Móglie,	wife;	mógli,	wives.
Mille,	thousand;	míla,	thousands.
Dio,	God;	déi,	gods.

XXII. The possessive adjective pronouns *mío*, *túo*, *súo*, my, thy, his, make *miéi*, *tuói*, *suói*, in the plural; and the adjectives *tále* or *cotále*, such, and *quále*, which, are in the plural *táli* or *tái*, *cotáli* or *cotái*, *quáli* or *quái*.

XXIII. The following nouns form their plural in *a*, and become feminine: —

---

measles. And some are used only in the plura : as, *I calzóni*, the trowsers; *le réni*, the kidneys; *i dólci*, the sweetmeats: *le fórbici*, the scissors; *i víveri*, the victuals; *le ténebre*, darkness. Some nouns have a different signification in the plural; as, *Il céppo*, the trunk of a tree; *i céppi*, the fetters: *il férro*, the iron; *i férri*, the fetters: *la gènte*, the people; *le génti*, the nations: *la grázia*, the favor; *le grázie*, the thanks.

PLURAL OF NOUNS AND ADJECTIVES. 37

Un migliáio,	a thousand.	*Le migliáia.*
Un centináio,	a hundred.	*Le centináia.*
Un uóvo,	an egg.	*Le uóva.*
Un míglio,	a mile.	*Le míglia.*
Un páio,	a pair.	*Le páia.*
Uno stáio,	a bushel.	*Le stáia.*
Un móggio,	a bushel.	*Le móggia.*

XXIV. The following masculine nouns have a masculine plural in *i*, and a feminine plural in *a*. The last is more frequently used.

L' anéllo,	the ring.		*Il fondaménto,*	the base.
Il bráccio,	the arm.		*Il frútto,*	the fruit.
Il budéllo,	the intestine.		*Il fúso,*	the spindle.
Il calcágno,	the heel.		*Il gésto,*	the gesture.
Il castéllo,	the castle.		*Il ginócchio,*	the knee.
Il cíglio,	the eyebrow.		*Il gómito,*	the elbow.
Il coltéllo,	the knife.		*Il grído,*	the cry.
Il córno,	the horn.		*Il lábbro,*	the lip.
Il díto,	the finger.		*Il légno,*	the wood.
Il fílo,	the thread.		*Il lenzuólo,*	the sheet.
Il mémbro,	the member.		*Il ríso,*	the laugh.
Il múro,	the wall.		*Il sácco,*	the sack.
L' ósso,	the bone.		*Lo strído,*	the cry.
Il pómo,	the apple.		*Il vestígio,*	the vestige.
Il quadréllo,	the dart.		*Il vestiménto,*	the garment.

REMARK.—*Córna,* in the plural, signifies horns; *córni,* instruments: *gésta,* exploits; *gésti,* gestures: *gómita,* elbows; *gómiti,* cubits: *mémbra,* members of the body; *mémbri,* members of an assembly: *múra,* ramparts; *múri,* walls.

READING LESSON.

Présso i Románi, i soldáti érano agricoltóri, e le casáte
Among   houses[2]

illústri conserváveno sémpre i cognómi déi frútti e déi legúmi
illustrious[1] preserved always surnames   pulse

che venívano, a preferénza, coltiváti dái lóro an'enáti; táli
came (were)   ancestors

fúrono i Léntuli, i Fábii, i Pisóni. I regáli piácano non sólo gli
presents appease only
uómini ma pur ánco gli déi. 1 pittóri antíchi non usávano nélle
even painters[2] ancient[1] used
lóro pittúre che quáttro colóri. Le dónne sóno fátte per éssere
pictures four colors. women made to be
le compágne e non le schiáve dégli uómini. Un párroco disse
companions slaves curate said
álla prédica, la Doménica délle pálme: Io vi avvérto, fratélli, che
sermon Palm: I you[2] inform[1]
per isfuggíre la cálca, confesserò Lunedì i bugiárdi, Martedì
to avoid confusion, I shall confess liars
gli avári, Mercoledì i mormoratóri, Giovedì i ládri, Venerdì
avaricious slanderers thieves
i díscoli, e Sábato gli ubbriáchi. Non si sa s'égli ébbe mólti
libertines drunkards. We do not know had
peniténti. I fanciúlli ed i pázzi si figúrano che vénti fránchi e
fools imagine francs
vénti ánni ábbiano a durár sémpre. Ho vedúto le óssa di tre
years have last always.
gióvani elefánti.

EXERCISE
ON THE FORMATION OF THE PLURAL OF NOUNS.

[*The singular only is given.*]

The face comprehends the forehead, the eyebrows, the eyelids
vólto comprénde palpébre
the nose, the lips, the mouth, the cheeks, the chin, and the ears.
mento

(The) children ought to obey their parents, scholars their
fanciullo débbono ubbidíre genitóre
teachers, and citizens (to) the laws. When we read certain
maéstro cittadíno legge. Quándo si léggono cérti
historians, we may say that the human species is composed
stórico, si dirébbe umána spécie (consists of) consíste
of only two or three hundreds of individuals decorated with
soltánto di dúe o tre indivíduo decoráto
the title of emperors, kings. popes, generals, and ministers. Men
títolo imperatóre minístro.

PLURAL OF NOUNS AND ADJECTIVES.   39

are generally idle in countries where the soil is very fertile.
sóno   per lo più inérte   paése   dóve   suólo   mólto fértile.
(The) stars, (the) animals, and even plants were (enumerated)
ástro   animále   ánche   fúrono   annoveráte
among   the Egyptian divinities.   The walls of Thebes were
fra   le   egiziáne   Tébe
raised   by the simple sound of the harp; the walls of the city
fabbricáte   sémplice suóno   cétra
of Jericho fell down, on the contrary, at the sound of (the)
   Jérico   cáddero,   in véce
trumpet.   The large sacks are filled with grain.   My sisters
córno.   empiúto   gráno.
have some silver spoons.
      alcúno argénto

    Nói siámo, we are.
    Vói siéte,   you are.
    Eglino sóno, they are.

CONVERSATION.

Chi è quésta dónna? *È la mádre del poéta célebre.*
Avéte vedúto il re?   *Abbiámo vedúto il re.*
È égli Francése?   *No, è Tedésco* (German).
Sóno i poéti felíci (happy)? *Generalménte non sóno felíci.*
Che hánno i ciéchi?   *I ciéchi hánno buóne orécchie*
Dóve náscono i fúnghi? *I fúnghi náscono néi bóschi.*
Quánti anélli avéte? *Ne ho dúe.*
Mangiáte frútti?   *Sì, quándo sóno matúri.*
Quánti (how many) *giórni fa
 úna settimána?*   *Sétte.*
Cóme si chiámano? (How are *Doménica, Lunedì, Martedì,*
 they called?)   *Mercoledì, Giovedì, Venerdì,
          Sábato.*
Ed i mési quánti sóno? *Dódici.*
Cóme si chiámano?   *Gennájo, Febbrájo, Márzo,
          Aprile, Mággio, Giúgno,
          Lúglio, Agósto, Settémbre,
          Ottóbre, Novémbre, Decém-
          bre.*
E le stagióni (seasons)? *Sóno quáttro: Primavéra, Es-
          táte o* (or) *Státe, Autúnno,
          Invérno o Vérno.*

CHAPTER VI.

THE CASES OF NOUNS.

MNEMONIC EXERCISE UPON THE USE OF *DI*, *A*, *DA*.

Vi piáce la città DI *Parigi?*	Does the city of Paris please you?
Il fítto DELLE cáse è cáro,	The rent of the houses is dear.
Vi dico che non ho danári,	I tell you that I have no money.
Spoléto non è lontáno DA *Róma*,	Spoleto is not far from Rome.
Vóglio scrívere DELLE *léttere*,	I wish to write some letters.
Io non vóglio brighe,	I do not wish cares.
Vói non avéte fratélli,	You have no brothers.
L' uómo vive DELLE súe fatiche,	Man lives by (of) his labors.
Io non témo púnto di vói,	I do not fear you at all.
Écco un dizionário DA *tásca*,	Here is a pocket dictionary.
L'Ariósto è il pittóre DELLA *natúra*,	Ariosto is the painter of nature.
L' ócchio del padróne ingrássa il cavállo,	The eye of the master fattens the horse.
Mi è soréllu dal láto DEL *pádre*, e non DAL cánto DELLA *mádre*,	She is a sister on my father's side, but not on the side of my mother.
Égli ha pósto DELLA *pólvere* DA *schióppo* in úna scátola DA *tabácco*,	He has put (some) gunpowder in a tobacco-box.

The several relations of the Italian nouns are expressed by the prepositions *di*, of; *a*, to; *da*, from, or by. The nominative and objective are distinguished by the place they occupy in the sentence.

1. The nominative denotes the relation of a subject to a finite verb; as, *María áma*, Mary loves.

2. The genitive denotes origin, possession, and other relations, which in English are expressed by the preposition *of*, or by the possessive case; as, *I libri di mío fratéllo*, my brother's books.

3. The dative denotes that *to* or *for* which any thing is, or is done; as, *Égli mi dáva il libro*, he gave me the book.

4. The accusative is either the object of an active verb or of certain prepositions, or the subject of an infinitive.

5. The vocative is the form applied to the name of any object addressed.

6. The ablative denotes privation and other relations, expressed in English by the prepositions *with, from, in,* or *by*.

Proper nouns are varied with the prepositions only; common nouns, with the preposition and article.

Variation of the proper noun *Boston:* —

Nominative	*Boston,*	Boston.
Relation of Possession	. *Di Boston,*	of Boston.
„ „ Attribution	. *A Boston,*	to Boston.
„ „ Derivation	. *Da Boston,*	from (or by) Boston.
Accusative	*Boston,*	Boston.

Variation of a common noun in the plural: —

Nominative	*I libri,*	the books.
Relation of Possession	. *Dei libri,*	of the books.
„ „ Attribution	. *Ai libri,*	to the books.
„ „ Derivation	. *Dai libri,*	from (or by) the books.
Accusative	*I libri,*	the books.

I. *Di,* the sign of the genitive, is used, —

1st, When it denotes possession; as, *La cása di mio pádre,* my father's house; *di chi è quésto cappéllo ?* whose hat is this? *è del servitóre,* it is the servant's.

2d, When the noun or verb that follows *di* expresses a quality, limitation, or modification of the noun that precedes it; as, *Cucchiáio d' argénto,* a silver spoon; *è témpo di pranzáre,* it is dinner-time.

II. The preposition *di,* with or without the definite article, translates the words *some* and *any* when they do not express a determinate quantity of a certain thing; as, —

Dátemi del *páne*, Give me *some* bread.
Non bevéte di *quel víno*, Do not drink *any* of that wine.

III. If *some* and *any* have the signification of *a few, various, certain, a little,* &c., they are rendered in Italian by *quálche* before a singular noun; by *un poco di*, or *un po' di*, before a collective noun; and by *cérti, divérsi, alcúni*, and *várii*, or their feminine form, before plural nouns, according to their gender; as,—

Ho pranzáto con quálche *amíco*, I have dined with *some* friend
  or *con* alcúni *amíci*,   or friends.
Prendéte un póco di víno, Take *some* wine.

IV. When there is only a simple designation of the object, without any idea of quantity,—that is to say, when the word *some* or *any* is omitted in English,—generally no article is used in Italian.

Bevéte víno o bírra? Do you drink wine or beer?
Chi ha danári ha amíci, He who has money has friends.

V. The preposition *di* is often used after words requiring a different preposition, and after verbs requiring a direct object. In such cases, the word that governs *di* is understood, and the phrase is elliptical, as may be seen in the following sentences:—

Temére DEL *pópolo*, for *temére* To fear the anger of the peo-
  LO SDÉGNO *del pópolo*,   ple.
Sapér DI *música*, DI *álgebra*, etc., To know a little music, alge-
  for *sapére* UN PÓCO di, etc.   bra, etc.

VI. Sometimes, especially in familiar conversation, the preposition *di* takes the place of the article *il* or *lo* before an infinitive, which, being the subject of a sentence, does not come at the beginning of it; as,—

È fácile DI *studiáre*, DI *parláre*, It is easy to study, to speak.
  for *è fácile* LO *studiáre*, IL
  parláre,

When the preposition *di* is thus substituted for the article, the phrase is elliptical, and stands for *È fácile* L'AZIÓNE *di studiáre*.

VII. It is very common in Italian to use *di* instead of *da* whenever euphony requires it, particularly if the definite article can be omitted after the preposition. This, however, is never done unless *fuóri, via,* or some such word requiring *di,* is easily understood. Thus they say:—

Veníre DI *cása;* that is, *fuóri* or *vía di cása* for *dálla cása,* or *da cása.*   To come out of the house.

VIII. The preposition DI is also frequently translated after verbs by *for,* meaning *on account of;* by *in,* when it does not signify *within;* by *with,* not expressing the idea of *company* or *union;* and occasionally by *on.*

Ella véste DI *néro,*   She dresses *in* black.
Non mi biasimáte DI *quésto,*   Do not blame me *for* this.
Fúrono provvedúti DI *tútto,* or D' *ógni cósa,*   They were provided *with* every thing.
Il bambíno fu nutríto DI *látte,*   The child was fed *on* milk.

IX. *A,* or *ad,* the sign of the dative, expresses direction or aspiration towards some object, and corresponds to the preposition *to.*

Andiámo a Nápoli,   Let us go to Naples.
Scrivéte ad un amíco,   Write to a friend.

X. The preposition A is also translated *in, for, from,* and *of,* after a verb, when it represents an action done against, towards, or to the damage of a person; the direct object of such a verb being easily understood;* as, —

Non pósso crédere a quel che díte,   I cannot believe *in* what you say.
Pensáte a lui e provvedéte ai suoi bisógni,   Think *of* him, and provide *for* his wants.

XI. *Da,* the sign of the ablative, expresses derivation, separation, or dependence, and corresponds principally to the preposition *from,* which in most cases is translated; as, —

---

* REMARK.—The expressions, *little* BY *little, two* BY *two,* etc., are rendered in Italian, *pòco* A *poco, due* A *due,* etc.

Da un giórno all' áltro,   From one day to another.
Non dipéndo da nessúno,   I do not depend on any one.

XII. *Da* is used before a noun which indicates use, employment, or the destination of a thing; as, —

Cavállo da sélla,   saddle-horse.
Cárta da léttere,   letter-paper.

XIII. The English prepositions *at* and *with*, meaning "at the house of;" and *by*, either expressing the relation between a passive verb and its subject, or conveying the idea of solitude and exclusion, — are translated by *da*.

Sta DA *mío pádre,*   He lives *at* my father's.
Lo farà DA *sè,*   He will do it *by* himself.

XIV. *Like* and *as*, when they signify "in the manner of," "as it becomes," and followed by a noun used in an indefinite sense, are generally rendered by *da;* as, —

Portátevi DA *uómo,*   Bear yourself *like* a man.
Fátela DA *padróne,*   Act *as* a master.

Like, followed by the pronouns *himself, herself, ourselves*, etc., is thus translated in Italian: Like himself, DA *quel che è*, or DA *quell' uómo ch' égli è*, etc.

READING LESSON.

Mólte commedióle, compóste dáll' Arósto che le recitáva in
Many little comedies, composed   them recited
compagnía de' suói fratélli e délle súe soréllo, fúrono il prelúdio
    brothers   his sisters, were   prelude
délle immortáli súe ópere. Finalménte l' elegánte orazióne, che
his works.
pronunció   intórno álle régole che si déggiono seguíre, ed
he pronounced concerning   rules   one   ought   to follow
intórno állo scópo che ognún propórre si débbe nei própri stúdi,
    scope   every one proposes   ought   own
féce conóscere álla città di Ferrára, súa pátria, ch' éssa alleváva
made to know   country   reared

THE CASES OF NOUNS. 15

un génio, il quále avrébbela illustráta; ed il pádre súo godéva
genius   who would have (her)   enjoyed
in segréto délla consolazióne d' udíre da' suói concittadíni
                             hearing   fellow-citizens
propórre il próprio figliuólo ái lóro, cóme un modéllo da imitársi.
to propose own   son   as   model   imitate.

EXERCISE.

1. In Italy there are immense plains, majestic rivers, very high mountains, lakes, cascades, forests, volcanoes, and beauty in all varieties.
2. A lady, speaking of a preacher whom she had heard from a great distance, said, "He spoke to me with' his hand, and I listened with' my eyes."
3. It is difficult to satisfy every one's desire in (the) great enterprises.
4. May God send us good princes, and may the devil not give them the fancy of wishing to be heroes!
5. (The) hypocrites cover themselves with the mask of (the) devotion.
6. Never leave flowers in a sleeping-chamber.
7. The greater part of (the) men live like crazy people, and die like fools.
8. One of the miseries of the rich is to be always deceived.

VOCABULARY.

1. There are, *vi sóno;* immense plains, *pianúra stermináta;* majestic rivers, *fiúme maestóso.*
2. A lady, *una Signóra;* speaking, *parlándo;* a preacher whom she had heard, *un predicatóre ch' élla avéa intéso;* far off, *mólto distánte;* said, *disse;* he has spoken to me, *égli mi ha parláto* (with the hands); I have listened to him, *io l' ho ascoltáto* (with the eyes).
3. Great enterprises, *gránd' imprésa;* it is difficult, *è cósa difficile;* to satisfy, *secondáre;* desire, *desidério;* all, *tútti.*
4. May God send us, *Dio ci mándi;* good prince, *buóno príncipe;* devil, *diávolo;* not give them, *non día lóro.*
5. Cover themselves, *si cóprono.*
6. Never leave, *non lasciáte mái.*
7. Live, *vívono;* die, *muóiono.*
8. Always deceived, *sémpre ingannáti.*

Dóve? where? | Chi? who?
Che? what? | Sovénte, often.

CONVERSATION.

Dóve éra la Signóra?
Con che si cóprono gl' ipócriti?
Quánti sénsi avéte?
Cóme si chiámano?
Abbiámo del vino?
È témpo di pranzáre?
Che cáne è quésto?
Che recitáva Ariósto in compagnia de' súoi fratélli e délle súe soréllc?
Dóve sóno maravíglie in ógni génere?
Che sóno ésse (they)?

Che disse úna Signóra d' un predicatóre?
Quáli persóne sóno sovénte ingannáte?
Quáli uómini vívono cóme pázzi?

Mólto distánte dàl predicatóre.
Colla máschera délla divozióne.
Cínque.
Udíto, vísta, odoráto, gústo, tátto.
Avéte úna bótte di vino.
Io ho pranzáto con alcúni amíci.
È un cáne da cáccia.
Mólte commedióle, che fúrono il preludio délle immortáli súe ópere.
In Itália.

Fiúmi maestósi, cascáte, sélve, volcáni, etc.
Egli mi ha parláto cólla máno.

Le persóne rícche.

La maggiór párte degli uómini.

CHAPTER VII.

PRONOUNS.

PERSONAL PRONOUNS IN THE NOMINATIVE.

Io, tu, égli, ésso,   élla, éssa,   nói, vói, églino and éssi, élleno and ésse.
I, thou, he, he or it, she, she or it, we, you, they, m.,   they, f.

MNEMONIC EXERCISE.

Chi bátte? Son io,
Se non vo.... cantár vói, canteró io,
Non dubitáte: pensarémo nói ad ógni cósa,

Who knocks? It is I.
If you do not wish to sing, I will sing.
Do not fear: we will think of every thing.

Così dicéva ancór IO,	I also said so.
Vói faréte quel che vorrò IO,	You will do what I wish.
Io vóglio fáre cóme fáte vói,	I wish to do as you do.
Non ci va EGLI, e non ci andréte nemméno VOI,	He will not go; and you will not go either.
Avéte voi róba? Avéte quattríni?	Have you property? Have you money?
Che bélla cósa il potér dire, Comándo IO!	How beautiful it is to say, I command!
Gli faréte conóscere chi sóno IO e chi siéte VOI,	Let him know who I am, and who you are.
Siéte vói il padróne di quésto albérgo?	Are you the master of this hotel?
Poichè voléte che díca IO, dirò IO,	As you wish that I say it, I will say it.
Vói avéte miglióT vista che non ho IO,	You have better sight than I

PRONOUNS IN THE OBJECTIVE (CLASS I.).

Me, te, lúi, léi, nói, vói, lóro, se.*
Me, thee, him, her, us, you, them; himself, herself, itself, themselves

MNEMONIC EXERCISE.

Che cósa voléte da ME?	What do you wish of me?
Ella è fuóri di SÈ dálla rábbia,	She is beside herself with anger.
Or óra sóno a VOI,	I am with you in a moment.
Fátemi la finézza di pranzár MÉCO,	Do me the pleasure to dine with me.
Io ámo il mio amíco quánto ME STÉSSO,	I love my friend as much as myself.
Sì, fáte voi, io mi rimétto in VOI, mi confído in VOI,	Yes, do what you will, I agree with you, I confide in you.
Egli non sa far núlla du SÈ,	He does not know how to do any thing by himself.
Lasciáte fáre a ME, non dubitáte,	Let me do it: never fear (do not doubt).
Degnáte far colazióne con NÓI,	Have the kindness to breakfast with us.

* These pronouns are called disjunctive.

Égli non dománda VOI,   He does not ask for *you*.
Non dico a VOI, *Signór mío,*   I do not speak to *you*, dear **sir.**
Verrò con VOI *se voléte,*   I will go with *you,* if you wish.
Io non vóglio partíre da VOI,   I do not wish to leave *you.*
Quánto avéte spéso per LEI,   How much have you spent for her.

PRONOUNS* IN THE OBJECTIVE (CLASS II.).

Mi, ti,	gli,	lo,	le,	la,	ci *or* ne,	vi,
Me, thee,	him, *ind.,*	him *or* it.	her, *ind.,*	her *or* it,	us,	you,
Li,	le,		lóro ;	si.		
Thèm, m.,	them, f.,	them, *ind.* ;	himself, herself, itself, themselves.			

MNEMONIC EXERCISE.

Voi VI *siéte dimenticáto* DI ME,   You have forgotten *me.*
Non MI *dimenticherò* DI VOI,   I will not forget *you.*
GLI *è nato un figlio,*   A son is born *to him.*
Che mále VI *ho fátto io?*   What ill have I done *you?*
Davvéro, io non VI *capísco,*   Truly, I do not understand *you.*
MI *piáce la mia libertà,†*   I love my liberty.
Fáte pur quél che VI *páre,*   Do as seems good *to you.*
La fortúna CI *vuól bène,*   Fortune wishes *us* well.
VI *raccomándo di far quésto,*   I recommend *you* to do this.
Che cósa VI *ha egli détto* DI ME?   What has he said to you *of me?*
Potéte dir LORO *che éntrino,*   You can tell *them* to come in.
Io VI *láscio, perchè ho frétta,*   I leave *you,* for I am in a hurry.
Ho scritto una léttera che MI *préme,*   I have written a letter which is important *to me.*
Che MI *cománda il Signor Tizio?*   What does Mr. Tizio wish of me?
Dio dice: Aiútati che TI *aiuterò,*   God says, Help *thyself,* and I will help *thee.*
Dománi GLI *darò da pránzo,*   I will give *him* dinner to-morrow.
Mi ricórdo ciò che MI *avéte détto.* I remember what you have said *to me.*
Amico, CI *rivedrémo staséra,*   Friend, we shall see *each other* this evening.
TI *accérto che non* LE *dirò nulla,*   I assure *you* that I shall say nothing to her.

---

* These pronouns are called conjunctive.
† *Mi piáce,* it pleases me

PERSONAL PRONOUNS IN THE NOMINATIVE.

I. Io,   I ;   Io dórmo,   I sleep.
   Tu,   Thou ;   Tu prànzi,   Thou dinest.
   Égli, ésso,   He, it ;   Égli bálla,   He dances.
   Élla, éssa,   She, it ;   Élla ríde,   She laughs.
   Nói,   We ;   Nói cantiámo,   We sing.
   Vói,   You ;   Vói pensáte,   You think.
   Églino, éssi, They, m. ;   Éssi scrívono,   They write.
   Élleno, ésse, They, f. ;   Ésse párlano,   They speak.

REMARK.—Of these pronouns only *Ésso* in all its forms, *Nói* and *Vói*, can be used as objective.

II. *Égli*, with its feminine and plural forms, can only be used for persons. It translates the subjective pronoun *it* before verbs used impersonally; and it is often, for euphony, contracted to *éi*, or *e'*. Very seldom it is expressed with really impersonal verbs. Ex.: *Égli è difficile*, it is difficult; *Pióve e tuóna*, it rains and thunders.

III. *Élla* may be used to translate *it* before the verbs *éssere*, *parére*, *e sembráre* when followed by a feminine noun; as, *Élla mi sémbra disgrázia inaudíta*, it seems to me a misfortune unheard of. In every other case, *Ésso* and *Éssa* with their plural must be used, as they can represent both persons and things, whilst *Égli* and *Élla* only represent persons.

IV. The use of *gli* for *égli*, of *gli* and *égli* for *églino*, and of *la* or *le* for *élla* or *élleno*, is justified by the example of good writers, ancient and modern, and by the practice of good society. In addressing persons, the Tuscans employ the contractions *la* and *le* for *élla* and *élleno* in the sense of you: as, *La mi perdóni*, I beg your pardon; *Le mi dícano*, (ladies or gentlemen), tell me.

V. If the number of the person is sufficiently indicated, either by the termination of the verb, or by any other circumstance, the subjective pronoun is generally omitted

But when there is antithesis or contrast implied between two or more verbs in different persons, then the pronouns representing the various subjects cannot be suppressed. Ex.: *Essa uscirà e vói staréte in cása,* she will go out and you will stay at home.

VI. The preceding rule must be observed when the stress of the voice is to be laid on the subject of a verb, in which case the pronoun is often put after it. Ex.: *Essa sóla può dir quéste cóse,* or *quéste cóse le può dir essa,* she alone can say such things.

VII. The emphasis often expressed in English by *do* or *did*, and the exclusive meaning given to a pronoun by the word *self*, are rendered in Italian, either by merely placing the subject after the verb, or by the adjectives *stésso* and *medésimo.* Ex.: *Dite óra ciò che pensáte vói,* or *dite ciò che vói stésso pensáte,* say now what you do think; *Lo farà égli,* or *égli medésimo lo farà,* he will do it himself. This rule applies also to nouns, as may be seen in the following examples: *Aspettáte che vénga il padróne,* or *che il padróne stésso vénga,* wait until the master comes himself.

VIII. The words *himself, herself, itself,* and *themselves,* can always be translated by *stésso* and *medésimo,* after a noun or a pronoun, and must agree with it in gender and number. Ex.: *Sáo pádre stésso lo dice,* his father himself says so. After the verbs *éssere* and *parére,* the same pronouns can be translated by *désso, déssa, déssi,* and *désse,* according to the gender of the noun to which they are put in apposition. Ex.: *Non è più désso,* he is no longer himself; *Mi par déssa,* it seems to me it is she, or she herself.

IX. In interrogative phrases, implying the desire and purpose of obtaining information about any thing, the subjective pronoun is either placed after the verb; as, *Anderà égli dománi?* shall he go to-morrow?—or it is suppressed altogether, and the question marked by the inflection of the voice, which is always very distinct in Italian. But if the question is put by persons acquainted already with the fact inquired about, the pronoun should be expressed and placed before the verb. Ex.: *Égli andèrà dománi? Tútti lo aspéttano,* he will go to-morrow? Every one expects him.

X. The subjective pronouns are replaced by the objective in the following cases: 1. After the adverbs *cóme, siccóme,* and *quánto,* when no verb follows them: as, *Érano maliziósi cóme lúi,* they were malicious as he was; *Se égli fósse cóme te,* if he were like thee. 2. When they govern an infinitive: as, *Sapéndo me amar léi,* knowing that I love her; *Udéndo lúi con gli áltri ésser mórto,* hearing that he died with the others 3. After the verb *éssere* preceded by its subject: as, *S' ío fóssi lúi,* if I were he; *Credéva che Piétro fósse te,* I thought Peter was you.

XI. In addressing, the Italians employ either the second person or the third. The second person singular, represented by *Tu,* Thou, denotes affection and familiarity, and always implies that the speaker is equal or superior to the individual thus addressed. Great love can only justify an inferior in using it towards a superior,—children, for instance, towards their parents and grandparents. The second person plural corresponds to it when several persons are spoken to; and it is also used generally with any class of society, correcting its apparent familiarity with some expression of respect when addressing a person entitled to some consideration, as, for instance: *Cóme státe, Signóre?* How do you do, sir? *Che mi commandáte, Signóra?* What can I do for you, my lady? In poetry and elevated prose the rules are the same as in English.

XII. The third person singular is used in addressing any one that does not belong to the low classes; and it is expressed by the feminine pronoun *Ella,* representing the words *Vóstra Signoría,* or their contraction Vossignoría (V.S.), which would sound too formal if used very frequently in conversation. The same feminine pronoun precedes the verb in the third person when the individual addressed is entitled to be treated as *Eccellénza, Altézza, Grandézza,* or with some other feminine word. If many are to be addressed in this way, the third person plural is substituted for the singular.

PERSONAL PRONOUNS IN THE OBJECTIVE.

XIII. The pronouns of the first class may be used as direct or indirect regimen; that is, they may be governed by the verb, or by a preposition, as the following examples will show: —

Cercáte me?　　　Are you looking for me?
Pensáte a me?　　Do you think of me?

When the pronouns *me*, *te*, and *se* are governed by the preposition *con*, they may be prefixed and joined to it, thus; *méco*, *téco*, *séco*. *Nósco* and *vósco*, for *con nói* and *con vói*, are now entirely left to poetry.

XIV. The pronouns of the second class are employed either as direct or indirect regimen of the verb; but they can never be governed by a preposition. They serve to conjugate pronominal or reflective verbs, and in such case *mi, ti si, ci, vi, si*, mean respectively *myself, thyself, himself;* or, *herself, ourselves, yourself;* or, *yourselves* and *themselves*. Ex.: —

Io mi ricórdo,　　　I remember.
Mi mandò déi fióri,　He sent me some flowers.

The pronoun *lóro* belongs to both classes; it can therefore be used for the direct or the indirect object, with a preposition or without, as the case may require.

XV. When the objective pronoun is emphatic, when the preposition cannot be suppressed, and when there is antithesis between two pronouns, a pronoun of the first class must be used; in other cases, one of the second class is to be preferred.

READING LESSON.

L' uómo scioperáto è l' uómo più affaccendáte Égli ha
　　　　idle　　　　　　　　most　occupied.
cinquánta amíci　　che　　si créde in óbbligo di coltiváre.
　fifty　friends whose (friendship)　believes　obliged

Vi dirà il nóme di tútti i ricamatóri, di tútti gli speziáli délla
 will give (tell)   embroiderers   apothecaries
città. Égli vi provvederà il sárto, il calzoláio, la lavandáia; so
       will procure
siéte ammaláto, condurrà da vói un médico; siéte addoloráto,
       sick,   will conduct   afflicted
égli non vi láscia, fintantochè non vi ábbia vedúto rídere.
           leaves, until   have   seen   to laugh.
S' incaricherà di tútte le vóstre cómpre, e finirà coll' andáre a
 will take charge   purchases   will finish   going
létto strácco di avér lavoráto tánto. L' allegrézza ci consóla e
bed   tired   worked   so much.   joy
ci tiéne in sanità; le cúre váne ci opprímono, distúrbano l' ánimo
   keeps   health   cares   oppress
nóstro e ci tràggono tósto nélla tómba.
           drag   quickly

EXERCISE FOR TRANSLATION.

1. When Paulus Emilius repudiated Papiria, his wife, some persons were astonished that he should separate himself from so modest and so handsome a woman; but Emilius, showing them his shoe, said, "You see that it is well made, but none of you know where it hurts me."

2. It was reported to Frederick the Great, that some one had spoken ill of him. He asked if this person had a hundred thousand men. He was answered, "No."—"Ah! well," added the king, "I can do nothing with him: if he had a hundred thousand men, I would declare war against him."

3. A young man who passed for rich, but who was laden with debts, sat very pensive, the evening before his betrothal, in his future mother-in-law's parlor. Several times she said to him, "*Che cósa avéte?*" "What have you?" (meaning, "What is the matter with you?") To which he continually answered, "*Non ho niénte,*" "I have nothing," (meaning, "Nothing is the matter with me.") Eight days after his marriage, his mother-in-law, seeing a crowd of creditors, said to him, "Sir, you have deceived me."—"Madam," added he, "I well informed you that I had nothing; and I repeated the same thing to you more than ten times in your parlor before my betrothal."

VOCABULARY.

1. Repudiated, *ripudiò;* some persons, *alcúni;* were astonished, *si maravigliávano;* should separate himself, *si separásse,* so pretty a woman, *úna dónna così vezzósa;* modest, *modésta,* showing, *mostrándo;* his, *la súa;* said, *dísse;* you see, *vói vedéte;* well made, *ben fátta;* however, *però;* no one, *nessúno,* knows where, *sa dóve;* hurts, *offénda.*

2. It was reported, *fu riferíto;* Frederick the Great, *Federico il Gránde;* had spoken ill, *sparláto;* if this person, *se costúi;* a hundred thousand, *cénto míla;* he was, *gli fu;* no, *di no;* well, *béne;* added, *soggiúnse;* I cannot, *non pósso;* nothing, *núlla;* had, *avésse;* would declare war, *muoveréi guérra.*

3. A young man, *un giovinótto;* who passed for, *tenúto per;* laden, *cárico;* debt, *débito;* was pensive, *stáva tútto pensieróso;* evening before, *vigília;* of his betrothal, *déi suói sponsáli;* parlor, *salótto;* of his future mother-in-law, *délla súa futúra suócera;* many times, *parécchie vólte;* sir, *signóre;* always, *sémpre;* eight days after, *ótto giórni dópo;* seeing arrive, *vedéndo capitáre;* a crowd, *úna túrba;* deceived, *ingannáta;* I well informed you, *vi féci pur avvertíta;* repeated, *ripetéi;* more than, *più di;* ten, *diéci;* in your, *nel vóstro;* before, *príma de'.*

CONVERSAZIONE.

Chi bátte? — *Son io.*
Che cósa voléte da me? — *Vóglio far colazióne con vói.*
Che cósa mi avéte détto? — *Non me ne ricórdo.*
Pagáte vói il pránzo? — *Sì, lo págo io.*
Mi aspettáte? — *Non vi aspétto.*
Di chi párla égli? — *Égli párla di nói.*
Cóme si chiáma quésta ragázza? — *Élla si chiáma Carolína.*
A chi scriverò io? — *Al pádre di María.*
Ti pénti tu? — *Io mi pénto.*
Ci divertiámo nói? — *Nói non ci divertiámo.*
Chi vi dirà il nóme di tútti gli speziáli délla città? — *L' uómo scioperáto vi dirà il nóme di tútti.*
Siéte vói il padróne di quésta cása? — *Sóno il padróne di quésto albérgo.*
Avéte il bastóne di mio fratéllo? — *Io non ho il súo bastóne, vói l' avéte.*
Voléte dármi un anéllo? — *Non vóglio dárvi un anéllo, vi darò* (will give) *un libro.*

CHAPTER VIII.

PRONOUNS, PERSONAL AND CONJUNCTIVE.

[*Continuation of Preceding Lesson.*]

To avoid several monosyllables, and for the sake of euphony, the Italians unite several words together. This union constitutes one of the chief beauties of the language. For example: the imperative *dátemelo* is composed of *date me lo*, give it to me; and, because the accent falls on the first syllable, the word has all the strength of the imperative, the desire of prompt obedience.

MNEMONIC EXERCISE.

LA *riverisco divotaménte,*	I have the honor to salute you.
*In che pósso servir*LA?	How can I serve you?
Cóme VE LA *passáte?*	How do you do?
Io ME LA *pásso benóne,*	I am very well.
VI *do la buóna nótte,*	I wish you good night.
Non VI *vóglio incomodáre,*	I do not wish to trouble you.
*Tornátev*ENE *indiétro,*	Turn back.
GLIÉLO *pósso dir* 10,	I can tell it to him myself.
*Andáte*GLIELO *a dir* VOI,	Go tell it to him yourself.
*Léva*MITI *dinánzi, temerário,*	Go out of my sight, insolent one.
Non MI *comparíte più dinánzi,*	Never appear before me again.
Che VE NE *páre?*	How does it seem to you?
*Ragioniámo*LA *qui fra di* NOI,	Let us reason here together.
*Facciámo*LA *da buóni amíci,*	Let us act like good friends.
Vói non ME LA *daréte ad inténdere,*	You will not make me believe it.

I. A pronoun stands for a person or thing: —

Lo or *il,*	him, it;	*Io* LO *védo,*	I see it *or* him.
La,	her, it;	*Tu* LA *conósci,*	Thou knowest her.
Li,	them *m.*;	*Noi* LI *vediámo,*	We see them.
Le,	them, *f.*;	*Io le aspétto,*	I expect them.
Ne,	of it;	*Voi* NE *rideréte,*	You will laugh about it.
Ci or *vi,*	of it;	*Io* CI or VI *pénso,*	I think of it.

II. The pronoun *il* or *lo* may be contracted and blended with the negative *non* into the monosyllable *nol:* as. *Nol so*, I do not know it; *Nol védo*, I do not see him. When not thus contracted, *lo* is used, as it always is before verbs beginning with *s* impure, or a vowel. Before other verbs *lo* is generally preferred to *il*, unless euphony should otherwise require. Ex.: *Lo riconóbbi súbito che'l vídi*, I recognized him as soon as I saw him; *Nol vídi e per conseguénza non lo salutái*, I did not see him, and consequently I saluted him not; *Il chiése e lo spédi a súo fratéllo*, he asked for him and sent him to his brother.

III. It is also by euphony that we should be guided in the elision of pronouns before verbs, whenever the meaning allows it. The rules that govern the elision of the article apply also to pronouns, with the exceptions that may result from the verbs having no gender. *Lo víde e l' amó* is properly said, because the gender of the pronoun elided is already determined by the object of *víde*. *L' amó quánto úna mádre può amáre* would not be correct, owing to the double meaning that the pronoun thus elided assumes; viz., *She loved him* or *her as much as a mother can love*.

IV. Though the pronoun *gli* signifies *to him*, it is also used for the feminine *le* when prefixed to and blended with *lo*, *la*, *li*, *le*, *ne*. In such case, the letter *e* is inserted between the two pronouns; thus:—

Gliélo;	Vói gliélo daréte,	You will give it to him *or* her.
Gliéla;	Io gliéli manderò,	I will send them to her *or* him.
Gliéle;	Gliéle venderà,	He will sell them to him *or* her.
Gliéne;	Vói gliéne compreréte,	You will buy her *or* him some.

Léne instead of *gliéne* is occasionally used for the feminine.

V. In a great number of Italian phrases, the pronoun *la* refers to a feminine noun which is not expressed, but it is easily supplied by the reader or listener. Ex.:—

Io ve LA *díco schiétta,*	I tell *it* to you frankly (the truth).
Vói ve LA *godéte,*	You enjoy it (life).
Io me LA *bátto,*	I beat it (retreat); I run away.

The words *veritá*, *víta*, and *ritiráta* are understood.

PRONOUNS, PERSONAL AND CONJUNCTIVE. 57

VI. Euphony requires that the *i* of the pronouns *mi*, *ti*, *si*, *vi*, *ci*, should change the *i* into *e* when they are followed by the pronouns *lo*, *la*, *li*, *ne;* as,—

Me lo,	it to me;	*Tu me lo dài*,	Thou givest it to me.	
Te la,	it to thee;	*Io te la do*,	I give it to thee.	
Se li,	them to him;	*Egli se li farà dàre*,	He will cause them to be given to himself.	
Ce ne,	us of it;	*Noi ce ne occupiàmo*,	We occupy ourselves with it.	
Ve le,	them to you;	*Io ve le prèsto*,	I lend them to you.	

VII. *Mel*, *tel*, *sel*, *cel*, *vel*, are written before a word which commences with a consonant, instead of *me lo*, *te lo*, etc.; as, *Egli sel figùra*, or *se lo figùra*, he figures it to himself; *io vel dicéva*, or *ve lo dicéva*, I said it to you.

VIII. Some ancient authors have often placed the pronouns *lo*, *la*, *li*, *le*, before *mi*, *ti*, *si*, *ci*, *vi*, when euphony permitted. Thus, instead of saying, *Dio te lo perdóni*, may God pardon you; they have said, *Dio il ti perdóni*.

IX. All the pronouns *mi*, *ti*, *si*, *ci*, *vi*, *lo*, *la*, *gli*, *le*, *ne*, *me lo*, *te lo*, *se lo*, etc., whether simple or compound, are generally placed before the verb, except when used with an infinitive, a gerund, the second person singular, and the first and second plural of the imperative; in which cases they are placed after the verb to which they are joined, so as to make one word; thus,—

*Parlàr*MI,	To speak to me.		*Cercàndo*LO,	Seeking him.
*Parlàr*MENE,	To speak to me of it.		*Vendéndo*GLIELA,	Selling it to him.
*Scrivéte*LE,	Write to her.		*Mostràte*CENE,	Show us some.
*Ricordiàmo*CI,	Let us remember.		*Dàte*MELO,	Give it to me.
*Compràte*GLIELO,	Buy it for him.		*Levàte*GLIELA,	Take it from her.
*Guardàte*LO,	Look at him.		*Pensiàmo*CI,	Let us think of it.

Observe that the infinitive loses the final *e* when the pronoun is joined to it; and if the infinitive terminates in *rre*, as *condùrre*, it loses the syllable *re*, and we say, *Condùrmi*, conduct me.

X. To express "give it to me," "give it to us," etc., the conjunctive pronoun is placed after the personal in this way: *Dàte*MELA *dàte*CELO.

XI. The pronoun is likewise placed after the word *écco*, to which it is joined; as, *Eccómi*, *éccolo*, behold me, behold him.

XII. With the negation *non*, these pronouns are placed before the verb, except when the verb is in the infinitive; as, —

Non GLIÉLO *domándate*,	Do not ask it of him.
Non ME NE *dáte*,	Do not give me any.
Non LO *facciámo*,	Let us not make it.
Non LO *facéndo*, or *non facéndolo*,	Not making it.

XIII. These pronouns are also joined to the past participle when the auxiliary is understood; as, *Rallegrátosi*, having rejoiced.

REMARK.—These pronouns admit of other transpositions, and very much assist in expressing an energetic, rapid, or gentle sentiment. For example, the phrase "I say it" may be constructed thus: —

Lo díco, to express a grave sentiment.
Il díco, to give a mild form to the phrase.
Dícolo, to impress with the rapidity of the thought.
Dícol, to join rapidity with sweetness.

The learner should, however, be careful not to place the pronoun after any other than the imperative, infinitive, and gerund.

XIV. The first consonant of the pronoun should be doubled whenever it is joined to a verb of one syllable, or one which has the grave accent upon the final vowel; as, *Díllo*, *dámmi*, *fállo*, tell it, give me, do it.

XV. The position of the pronoun can be changed for the sake of euphony; as, —

Io lo vóglio vedére, or *io vóglio vedérlo*,	I wish to see him.
Io gliéne pósso parláre, or *io pósso parlárgliene*,	I can speak to him of it.

PRONOUNS, PERSONAL AND CONJUNCTIVE.

XVI. In certain cases, the personal pronoun is changed into the possessive; as, *Mío malgrádo*, in spite of me: and, on the contrary, the possessive is sometimes changed into the personal; as, *Cavátevi il vestíto*, take off your coat.

READING LESSON.

Tra le várie nazióni del móndo la <s>politeness</s> *cortesía* ha introdótto
                                  politeness   introduced

infiníti úsi di salutáre. Pláuto párla di pópoli che si salutávano
modes salutation.   Plautus speaks

tirándosi fórte l' orécchia. I Fránchi sí strappávano un
pulling strong (hard)   car.   pulled out

capéllo, e lo presentávano álla persóna che volévano salutáre.
hair   presented   they wished

Al Giappóne un conoscénte vi salúta togliéndosi dal piéde úna
Japan   acquaintance   taking   foot

pantófola; e nélle Indie, égli viéne a préndervi per la bárba
slipper   comes   to take   beard;

áltri si salútano voltándosi la schiéna. Gl' isoláni del gránde
others   turning   back.   islanders

océano frégano il lóro náso con quéllo délla persóna salutáta,
rub   nose   that

oppúre gli sófiano nell' orécchio. Gli abitánti di Horn si
or   blow   inhabitants

córicano col véntre a térra, e la maggiór párte dei négri si
lie down   belly   greater   negroes

préndono a vicénda le díta e le fánno schricchioláre. L' Inglése
take turn   make   crack.   Englishman

in un eccésso d' amicízia vi affèrra per la máno e ve la scuóte
fit   friendship seizes   shakes

vigorosaménte cóme se volésse strappárvi il bráccio. Quésta
                if he wished to pull out   arm.   This

gentilézza fa la véci dégli abbrácci dei Francési e degl' Italiáni.
courtesy takes the place   embraces

EXERCISE.

1. A thoughtless wag saw three blind people in the street, who, keeping together, went begging. "Stop," said he to them; "take this crown, divide it between you, and pray God for me."

As to the crown, he gave it to ~~neither~~ *none* of them   The blind men all thanked him at once, and ran quickly into a tavern, where they ordered a breakfast. When they were well satisfied, one said to the others, "Let him who has the crown pay the fare;" but each one answered, "I have it not: thou hast it." From hard words they came to blows; and gave so many blows with their sticks, that they broke every thing that was on the table, to the great detriment of the host.

2. The authors of the century of Louis XIV. have expressed great thoughts in simple words.

VOCABULARY.

1. Humorist, *burlóne;* thoughtless, *spensieráto;* saw in, *víde per;* keeping together, *strétti insiéme;* went begging, *se ne andávano accattándo;* stop, *fermátevi;* take, *togliéte;* divide it, *spartítelo;* neither of them, *nessúno;* thanked, *ringraziárono;* all at once, *concordeménte;* they ran, *córsero;* a breakfast, *da colazióne;* well satisfied, *ben satólli;* let him who, *chi;* pay, *pághi;* but each one answered, *al che ciascúno rispondéndo;* thou hast it, *tu l' hái;* they came, *vénnero;* they gave, *diédero;* so many, *tánte;* blows with a stick, *bastonáte;* everything that was, *tútto ció che si trováva;* to the great detriment, etc., *con gran dánno dell' óste.*

2. Have expressed, *hánno espresso.*

CONVERSAZIÓNE.

Che è l' Itália?	Il giardíno d' Európa.
Che avéte?	Ho úna rósa.
Avéte il libro?	Non ho il libro, ho la pénna.
È gióvane la sorélla del Signóre?	Sì, élla è gióvane.
Che fánno gl' isoláni del gránde océano quándo salútano?	Églino frégano il lóro náso con quéllo délla persóna salutáta.
E gli abitánti di Horn?	Si córicano véntre a térra.
Che vide un burlóne?	Égli vide tre ciéchi.
Che disse il burlóne?	Pregáte Dio per me.
A chi diéde égli úno scúdo?	Égli non lo diéde a nessúno.
Cóme salútano gli Inglési?	Vi affèrrano per la máno e ve la scuótano.
Quál' è la príma légge?	La légge di Dio è la príma légge.
Triónfa éssa sémpre?	Sì, tósto o tárdi

CHAPTER IX.

THE ADJECTIVE — L' ADDIETTIVO.

MNEMONIC EXERCISE.

Gódo di vedérvi in buóna salúte,	I am glad to see you well.
Passerémo per la più córta,	We will take the shortest.
Parliámoci schiétto,	Let us speak clearly.
Perchè avéte tánta premúra?	Why are you so hurried?
Quánti ánni avéte?	How old are you?
I ricchi hánno mólti amíci,	The rich have many friends.
Il béllo piáce a tútti,	The beautiful pleases all.
Mólti póchi fánno un assái,¹ *	A little repeated makes much.
Gl' ingráti hánno póca memória,	Ungrateful people have short memories.
Chi perdóna ai cattívi, nuóce ai buóni,	He who pardons the wicked injures the good.
Buon dì, buóna séra, felíce nótte,	Good day, good evening, good night.
Per mólti la fatíca è póco sána,	Labor is not healthy for many people.
È úno che ha póchi pári,	He is a man who has few equals.

ADJECTIVES: THEIR NUMBER, GENDER, ETC.

I. Italian adjectives all end in *o* or *e*. Those ending in *o* change the *o* into *a* for the feminine: those in *e* preserve the same form in both genders. The plural of adjectives is formed like that of nouns; as, —

SINGULAR.

Pópolo líbero ed indipendénte,	Free and independent people.
Nazióne líbera ed indipendénte,	Free and independent nation.

PLURAL.

Pópoli líberi ed indipendénti,	Free and independent peoples.
Nazióni líbere ed indipendénti,	Free and independent nations.

---

* Idioms and proverbs are marked *i*

II. Some adjectives end either in *e* or in *o;* as, *Violente* or *violénto*. In this case one might say, *Un uómo violénte, una dónna violénte,* or *un uómo violénto, úna dónna violénta,* a violent man, a violent woman.

III. The only adjectives terminating in *i* are *pári,* equal, and *dispári* or *impári,* unequal. These are invariable, whatever be the gender or the number of the noun to which they belong.

IV. The word *pári* is often used as a noun. It then has a possessive adjective after it; as, *Un pári mío, un pári vóstro, dei pári nóstri,* a man like me, like you, persons like us; *così si trátta cón un pári mío?* is it thus that one acts with a person of my rank?

V. Substantives used as adjectives, ending in *tóre,* change *tóre* into *trice* for the feminine; as, *Autóre,* author; *autrice,* authoress, — except *dottóre, fattóre,* doctor, farmer; which make *dottoréssa, fattoréssa.* Other substantives used as adjectives form their feminine in *éssa.* Such are, *Poéta,* poet; *poetéssa,* poetess; *baróne,* baron; *baronéssa,* etc.

VI. Adjectives of quantity, — as, *Quánto,* how much; *tánto,* so much; *altrettánto,* as much; *tróppo,* too much; *póco,* little; *mólto,* much, — agree with their nouns; as, —

Tánto orgóglio; tánta paúra,	So much pride; so much fear.
Tánti sciócchi; tánte vólte,	So many fools; so many times.
Póco sángue; póca cárne,	Little blood; little meat.
Mólti disgústi,	Much (or many) chagrins.
Altrettánti soldáti; altrettánte dónne,	As many soldiers; as many women.
Tróppo vénto; tróppe ceremónie,	Too much wind; too many ceremonies.
Quánto vino? quánte bontà?	How much wine? how much kindness?

VII. The word "such" is sometimes translated by *così fátto, a; si fátto, a;* as, —

Guardátevi da cosi fátta ribal-   Guard yourself against such a
dáglia,   rabble.

VIII. The adjective *alquánto* (singular) signifies a little; *alquánti* (plural), some. *Parécchi, parécchie,* signify also many, and can be replaced by the word *più, more*; as, *Vi érano* PARECCHIE *ballerine,* or PIÙ *ballerine,* there were many dancers.

IX. The adjective *mézzo* always precedes and agrees with the noun which it limits; but it may be invariable when the noun is understood: as, *Una mézza bottíglia,* half a bottle; *una bottíglia e mézza* or *mézzo,* a bottle and a half. If the noun is not expressed, the adjective *mézzo* takes no article.

X. The last syllable of the words *béllo, sánto, quéllo,* must be suppressed before masculine nouns commencing with a consonant. The adjective *gránde,* great, is written *gran* before masculine and feminine nouns, both in the singular and plural; as,—

SINGULAR.		PLURAL.
Bel giardíno,	fine garden.	*Béi* or *be' giardíni.*
Quél palázzo,	this palace.	*Quéi* or *que' palázzi.*
San Piétro,	Saint Peter.	*Sánti Piétri.*
Gran birbóne,	great villain.	*Gran birbóni.*
Gran regína,	great queen.	*Gran regíne.*

XI. *Buóno,* good, loses the *o* before a consonant; as, *Il buón víno fa buón sángue,* good wine makes good blood.

XII. To avoid the union of too many consonants, the last syllable of these adjectives is *not* retrenched before nouns commencing with *s,* when followed by another consonant; as,—

SINGULAR.		PLURAL.
Béllo spóso,	handsome spouse.	*Bégli spósi.*
Quéllo straniéro,	that stranger.	*Quélli straniéri.*
Gránde strépito,	great noise.	*Grándi strepiti.*
Gránde spáda,	great sword.	*Grándi spáde.*
Sánto Stéfano,	Saint Stephen.	*Sánti Stéfani.*
Buóno scólare,	good scholar.	*Buóni scolári.*

XIII. The final vowel of the preceding adjectives is retrenched before a vowel, and replaced by an apostrophe; as, *Bell' òcchio,* fine eye; *quell' àsino,* that ass; *grànd' impéro,* great empire; etc.

XIV. No fixed rules can be given to determine the place of the adjective, the Italians being guided by the ear. Usage generally places the adjectives expressive of form, color, and savor, after the noun; as, —

Tàvola quadràta,	square table.
Àbito turchìno,	blue coat.
Colór giàllo,	yellow color.
Un Signóre italiàno,	an Italian gentleman.
Àcqua inzuccheràta,	sugared water.
Una rósa biànca,	a white rose.

REMARKS.

The following observations will assist the student: —

The Italian adjective can be placed before or after the noun, and must agree with it in gender and number: euphony determines its position. Adjectives denoting materials, nations, dignity, color, taste, etc., are placed after the nouns; as, *Cappéllo biànco,* white hat; *un uómo ciéco,* a blind man.

Participles and adjectives, preceded by an adverb, may be placed after the noun; as, *Una càsa tróppo píccola,* too small a house.

The position of some adjectives alters their signification: as, —

Una cérta còsa,	a certain (that is any) thing.
Una còsa cérta,	a certain (sure) thing.
Grán còsa,	something important.
Una còsa grànde,	a great thing.
Un galantuómo,	an honest man.
Un uómo galànte,	a polite man.
La sóla mìa fìglia,	my only daughter.
Mìa fìglia sóla,	my daughter alone.
Un fiér uómo,	a savage man.
Un uómo fiéro,	a proud man.
Un póvero uómo,	an unhappy man.
Un uómo póvero,	a poor man.

THE ADJECTIVE.

READING LESSON.

Giambattísta Pígna, scrittóre célebre del fortunáto sécolo
        writer   century
décimo sésto ci ha tramandáto il ritrátto seguénte dell' Ariósto.
sixteenth   transmitted   portrait following
L' Ariósto,* in quánto álla fórma e all' aspétto del córpo avéa la
                                                                had
statúra álta, la testa cálva, i capélli néri e créspi, la frónte
       tall   bald   black   curly
spaziósa, le cíglia álte e sottíli, gli ócchi in déntro, néri, vivácí,
broad eyes   thin
e giocóndi, il náso aquilíno gránde e cúrvo, le lábbra raccólte,
lively   lips   contracted
i dénti biánchi ed equáli, le guánce scárne e di colóre quási
                                      cheeks hollow   almost
olivástro, la bárba un póco rára che non cingéa il ménto infíno
olive-colored   thin   covered   chin
álle orécchie, il cóllo ben proporzionáto, le spálle lárghe e
                 neck well   shoulders
alquánto piegáte, quáli sógliono   avére quási tútti quélli che,
somewhat curved,   as   are accustomed to have   those
da fanciúlli, hánno cominciáto a státe inchiodáti in súi líbri: Le
young girls   began   nailed
máni asciútte, i fiánchi strétti. Égli dipínto dálla máno dell'
       thin   hips   narrow.   painted
eccellénte Tiziáno, páre che ancór sía vívo. Un pópolo fanático
                   seems   still   alive.
e superstizióso è un árma terríbile nélle máni d' un déspota.
Ove la pélle del leóne non básta bisógna aggiúngervi quélla
When   skin   lion   sufficient   to add
délla vólpe.

EXERCISE FOR TRANSLATION.

1. Osley, a famous beggar of London, made a fortune by using the following stratagem. He placed himself in streets where there was the greatest concourse of fashionable people; and, when he saw elegant ladies, he asked charity of them. If they refused,

---

* A few proper nouns of very remarkable people take the definite article in Italian as, *Il Dánte, l' Ariósto*, etc.

"Madam," said he to one, "in the name of your beautiful black eyes;" to another, "in the name of your fine hair;" to this one, "in the name of your rosy lips;" and, to that one, "in the name of your admirable figure." Finally came the divine legs, the charming feet, the majestic carriage: nothing was forgotten, and he returned home with his purse well filled.

2. A drunkard, who wished to excuse himself to his confessor for his too great love of wine, reasoned thus singularly: "My father, good wine makes good blood, good blood produces good humor, good humor creates good thoughts, good thoughts produce good works, and good works conduct man to heaven: then (the) good wine leads man to heaven."

VOCABULARY.

1. Made, *féce*; following, *seguénte*; he placed himself, *égli si appostáva*; where there was, *óve éra*; fashionable people, *bel móndo*; when he saw, *allorchè vedéva*; refused, *ricusaváno*; admirable, *mirábile*; came, *venívano*; forgotten, *dimenticáto*.

2. Drunkard, *bevitóre*; wished, *voléa*; too great love of wine, *tróppo gránde amóre del víno*; reasoned thus singularly, *facéa quésto curióso argoménto*; makes, *fa*; produces, *prodúce*; creates, *fa náscere*; conduct, *ménano*.

CONVERSAZIÓNE.

Sóno gli Americáni líberi?
Che proclamazióne è quélla di cùi si párla?
Che predicatóre avéte?
Come si chiáma (called)?
Dov' è la vóstra Signóra mádre?
Cósa è il vóstro Signór pádre?
E súa móglie (wife)?
Quánti ánni ha María?
Che statúra ha élla?
Di che cólore è il súo ábito?
Che buóna cósa ha egli fátto?

Chi è quésta cára fanciullína?
Che ócchi celésti!

Si sóno líberi ed indipendénti.
Si párla mólto dell' emancipazióne dei póveri* néri.
Abbiámo un brávo predicatóre.
L' amíco dei póveri.
È nélla chiésa di San Páolo.
È autóre.
È dottoréssa.
Ha nóve ánni.
Ha la statúra piccola.
Il súo nuóvo ábito è turchíno.
Non pósso (I cannot) dírvelo (tell you).
Luisína. Ella è mia nipóte.
Si, élla ha l' ária d' un angiolétta.

---

* The repetition of the objective strengthens its expression; as, *Póvero*, poor; *pòvere póvero*, very poor.

CHAPTER X.

ADJECTIVES: THEIR COMPARATIVES.

MNEMONIC EXERCISE.

Vi sóno più póveri che ricchi,	There are more poor than rich.
Le dónne sóno più compassio-	Women are more compassion-
névoli degli uómini,	ate than men.
È méglio morire che temér sém-	It is better to die than always
pre,	to fear.
Quánto più vi pénso, tánto più	The more I think of it, the
mi vién rábbia,	more I am enraged.
Táli dobbiámo éssere quáli vo-	We ought to be such as we
gliámo comparire,	wish to appear.
Il sóle è più gránde della térra,	The sun is larger than the earth.
La térra non è così piccola	The earth is not as small as the
cóme la lúna,	moon.
La fáma di sua bellézza è mi-	The renown of her beauty is
nóre assái della verità,	much below the truth.
I creditóri miglióa memória	Creditors have a better memo-
hánno che i debitóri,	ry than debtors.
È méglio fáre invídia che pietà,	It is better to cause envy than pity.
L' usuráio è peggióre del ládro,	The usurer is worse than the thief.
Il víno è il mio maggiór ne-	Wine is my greatest enemy.
mico,	

THE COMPARISONS OF ADJECTIVES.

I. A comparison can only be made between two objects. An object may be more beautiful, less beautiful, and as beautiful as another. There are, therefore, three degrees of comparison, — the degrees of superiority, of inferiority, and of equality.

II. The comparative of superiority is indicated by the words *più*, more; *mólto più* or *assái più* or *víe più*, much more; *miglióre*, better (a.); *maggióre*, greater *méglio*, better (ad.).

ITALIAN GRAMMAR.

III. The comparative of inferiority is expressed by the words *méno* or *mánco*, less; *mólto méno* or *assái méno* or *vie méno*, much less; *peggióre*, worse (a.); *minóre*, smaller; *péggio*, worse (ad.).

IV. The conjunction *than*, which joins the two terms of comparison, is translated by *di* when it is followed by a pronoun or a possessive or demonstrative adjective.

He is much happier than you,	È mólto più felice di vói.
Your sister is prettier than mine,	Vóstra soréllla è più bélla délla mía.
There are no people more credulous than those who have an interest in being deceived,	Non v'è génte più crédule di quélla che ha interésse di éssere ingannáta.

V. *Than* is sometimes translated by *che*, especially if the phrase is elliptical. *Di*, however, may always be used.

VI. If *than* is followed by any other word, and there is a complement of the phrase understood, it can be translated by *di* or by *che;* as in the following examples:—

Is man more happy than woman (is happy)?	È l'uómo più felice délla dónna? or che la dónna?
The stomach digests water more easily than wine,	Lo stómaco digerisce più facilménte l'ácqua che il vino.

VII. It is better to use *che* for *than*, when the comparison is made between two verbs, two adjectives, or two adverbs; as,—

There are more poor than rich,	Vi sóno più póveri che ricchi.
It is better late than never,	È méglio tárdi che mái.
It is better to save a culpable person, than to condemn an innocent one,	È méglio salváre un colpévole, che condannáre un innocénte.

VIII. If the natural order of the words is inverted,—that is to say, if the verb is placed before the subject,—it is better to use *che*. This rule may be applied to phrases where *than* is followed by a demonstrative adjective; as,—

ADJECTIVES: THEIR COMPARATIVES.

He who attacks, always has more courage than he who defends himself,	Più ánimo ha sémpre colúi che assálta, che colúi che si diféude.

IX. To translate "more than three years," "more than twenty thousand men," etc., we say, Three years and more, twenty thousand men and more, *tre ánni e più; vénti míla uómini e più*, or *più di tre anni*, etc., *più che tre anni*.

X. The comparative of equality is indicated by *così* or *tánto:* and the conjunction ~~than~~ as is translated by *cóme*, if *così* has been used; and by *quánto*, if *tánto* has been used; as, —

The eye of the domestic never sees as well as the eye of the master,	L' ócchio del servitóre non véde mái così béne cóme l' ócchio del padróne; or, non véde mái tánto béne quánto l' ócchio, etc.

XI. Sometimes the word *così* or *tánto* is suppressed; as, —

A skin as white as snow,	Una pélle biánca cóme or quánto la néve.

XII. When the words *as many* and *as* refer to a noun, *as many* must be rendered by *tánto*, and *as* by *quánto*, making them agree in gender and number with the noun; as, —

He has as many debts as there are stars in the sky,	Égli ha tánti; or, altrettanti débiti quánte sóno le stélle nel cièlo.
See the strawberries. Take as many as you wish,	Écco délle frágole. Prendétene quánte voléte.

XIII. In English we say (with the complement understood), —

I have as much money as you (have).	Naples is not as populous as Paris (is).

In Italian, the complement is generally expressed in similar phrases; as, —

Io ho tánti danári quánti ne aréte voi.	Nápoli non ha tánta popolazióne quánta ne ha Parigi.

XIV. Sometimes *tánto* or *quánto* is placed before *more* or *less*, so as to give more energy to the expression; as in the following phrases: —

Quánto più úno è ignoránte,   The more ignorant a person
tánto più égli è prónto nel   is, the more ready he is to
giudicáre,   judge.
L' aria è tánto più dénsa quán-   The air is much more dense as
to è più propínqua álla térra,   it is nearer the earth.

XV. *As well as*, and *as much as*, signifying *as*, are translated by *così*, *cóme*, or *quánto*, and are invariable; as, I know him as well as you, *io lo conósco cóme* or *quánto vói.* One can say, also, *io lo conósco al par di vói.*

READING LESSON.

I Románi, nei lóro stravízzi, bevévano tánti bicchiéri di víno
                           banquets,   drank
quánte érano le léttere del nóme déi lóro amíci ai quáli facé-
                                                         they
vano   brindisi.   Catóne, il censóre, che vedéa (sórgere)
made (drank) honor (health).   saw   to come
la pómpa délla ménsa, dísse, che éra assái malagévole il salváre
                                          difficult   save
úna città dóve un pésce si vendéva più cáro di un búe. Di
              fish   was sold
dúe negoziatóri in política vínce sémpre il più scáltro; cioè chi
                          conquers always   sharp; that is
sa méglio ingannáre l' áltro. Il diávolo non è così brútto come
     to cheat
si dipínge. Non è cósa nel móndo più preziósa del témpo. La
painted.
nója è fórse il maggiór mále che sía uscíto dal vaséllo di Pan-
ennui   went
dóra. I sógni sóno le immágini del dì, guáste e corrótte. L' óro,
                                    spoiled corrupted.
come il fuóco, e buón servitóre ma cattívo padróne. Gli déste una
                                                                 gave
líbbra, dátemene altrettánto.

ADJECTIVES: THEIR COMPARATIVES. 71

EXERCISE FOR TRANSLATION.

1. It is difficult to decide if irresolution renders man more unhappy than despicable, and if it is more inconvenient to take a bad part than not to take any.
2. Usage is always introduced by the ignorant, who form the greatest number (in society).
3. Two consolations solace the heart of the unhappy: one is, to recall the time when he lived more happily; and the other, to see that there are some in the world more unhappy than he.
4. The city of Naples is more beautiful in darkness than London is when the sun shines.
5. The fatter the kitchen, the leaner the testament.
6. Since we cannot make men what we would have them, it is necessary to bear with them as they are, and make the best of them.

VOCABULARY.

1. Man, *se;* renders, *fa;* unhappy, *infelíce;* despicable, *dispregévole;* if there are, *se vi sóno;* to take a bad part, *appigliársi ad un cattivo partíto;* not to take any, *non appigliársi ad alcúno.*
2. Usage, *úso;* introduced by, *introdótto da.*
3. Solace, *sollévano;* is to recall, *il rimembrársi;* when (in which), *in cúi;* he lived, *visse;* to see (to think), *pensáre;* more unhappy, *con maggiór dóglia.*
6. Since, *poichè;* we can, *possiámo;* we would, *vorrémmo;* we must, *conviéne;* bear with, *tolleráre.*

CONVERSAZIÓNE.

Chi è più felíce, l' uómo o la dónna?

L' úno non è più felíce che l' áltra.

Quál è méglio per lo stómaco, l' ácqua o il víno?

Per i gióvani l' ácqua è méglio che il víno.

Vi sóno mólti rícchi in Lóndra?

Si, ma vi sóno più póveri che rícchi.

Pensáte (do you think) che io sóno infelíce?

Siéte mólto più infelíce di me.

È bélla la Signorína Rósa?

Si, ma vóstra sorélla è più bélla ancóra.

È brútta la lóro zia?

Non è cósi brútta cóme si dice (they say).

Hánno i creditóri buóna memó-
ria?
Avéte nemíci?
Qual è la cósa più preziósa nel
móndo?
Quánte bráccia (yards) di qués-
to pánno vólete?
Luigi, siéte studióso?

Éssi hánno miglior memória
che i debitóri.
Il víno è il mio maggiór nemíco.
Nel móndo non è cósa più pre-
ziósa del témpo.
Ne ho quánte ne vóglio (I wish)

Sì, ma quánto più stúdio (I
study) tánto méno imparo
(I learn).

CHAPTER XI.

THE ADJECTIVES: SUPERLATIVES.

MNEMONIC EXERCISE.

Parígi è úna bellíssima cittá,
Avéte pochíssimi riguárdi,
Fu uómo integérrimo,
Di cattívo égli diventò péssimo,
Gódo un' óttima salúte,
È uómo di pochíssime paróle,
Ho vedúto úna bellíssima ragáz-
za,
Vi servirò puntualissimamén-
te,
Infelicíssimo è l' uómo che nón
ha amíci,
Mi rincrésce assaíssimo ch' égli
parta,
Quélla génte è di óttimo cúore,

Notáte ógni mínima cósa,

A tútti il ríso è gratíssimo,

Vénne úna dirottíssima pióggia,

Paris is a most beautiful city.
You have very little regard.
He was an upright man.
From bad he has become worse.
I enjoy excellent health.
He is a man of very few words.
I have seen a very beautiful
girl.
I will serve you most punctu-
ally.
Very unhappy is the man who
has no friends.
I am very sorry that he is
going away.
These people have an excel-
lent heart.
Take notice of the smallest
thing.
A smile is very agreeable to
everybody.
There was a pouring rain.

THE ADJECTIVES: SUPERLATIVES.

THE SUPERLATIVE ABSOLUTE.

1. *Cattivíssimo,* mólto cattivo, assái cattivo, very bad.
2. *Savíssimo,* mólto sávio, assái sávio, very wise.
3. *Freschíssimo,* mólto frésco, assái frésco, very fresh.
4. *Larghíssimo,* mólto lárgo, assái lárgo, very large.

I. We see, by the above examples, that the superlative is formed by *íssimo*, *mólto*, or *assái*. *Issimo*, taken from the Latin, is united to the adjective, the final vowel of which is retrenched. When the adjective ends in *io*, both vowels are dropped. If the adjective ends in *co* or *go*, the letter *h* is placed after the *c* or *g*, to preserve the hard sound of these letters. The words *amíco* and *nemíco*, friend and enemy, are exceptions: they make *amicíssimo*, *nemicíssimo*.

II. *Very*, before a past participle, is rendered by *mólto* or *assái;* as, He is very much esteemed by every one, *égli è mólto stimáto da tútti.* We cannot say, *Égli è stimatíssimo da tútti.* But, if the past participle is used simply as a qualificative adjective, then it receives the superlative *íssimo;* and we say, *Mío stimatíssimo signóre.*

III. The following words express the superlative of themselves:—

Óttimo,	very good.	Ínfimo,	very low.
Péssimo,	very bad.	Egrégio,	very noble.
Sómmo,	highest.	Mássimo,	supreme.
Estrémo,	extreme.	Misérrimo,	very unhappy.
Stupéndo,	wonderful.	Acérrimo,	very bitter.
Insígne,	renowned.	Integérrimo,	entirely honest.

IV. The particle *stra* (extra) is prefixed to a few words, giving them a superlative signification; as, *Straricco,* very rich; *stracótto,* very much cooked.

V. The adverbs terminating in *mente* (corresponding to *ly* in English), from the Latin *mens*, which is feminine, form their superlative in *íssima;* as, *grandíssimaménte.*

REMARK. — The termination *íssimo* serves in Italian for the superlative absolute, and can never be translated in English by those superlatives ending in *st* or *est*, which are of the relative kind. The latter must be rendered by the adjective, preceded by *il più, la più*, etc.; as, *Il più córto poéma* (not *cortíssimo poéma*), the shortest poem.

THE SUPERLATIVE RELATIVE.

VI. This superlative is formed by the words *il più* or *il méno*, suppressing the article when *più* or *méno* comes after the noun; as, *Demóstene fu l' oratóre più eloquénte délla Grécia*, Demosthenes was the most eloquent orator of Greece. But, if the adjective is placed before the noun, then the article is used; as, *Demóstene fu il più eloquénte oratóre délla Grécia*.

The words *mássimo, ínfimo*, are also superlative relatives, and signify *the greatest, the lowest;* as, —

Io lo vedrò col mássimo piacére.	I shall see him with the greatest pleasure.

READING LESSON.

Il Dúca d'Épernon, príma di moríre, scrísse al cardinále di
                before   dying, wrote
Richelieu, e terminò la léttera col "vóstro umilíssimo ed obbidientíssimo sérvo," ma ricordándosi che il cardinále non gli avéa
                               remembering
dáto che dell' affezionatíssimo, mandò úno   appósta   per
given   sent   on purpose (an express)
trattenére la léttera che éra già partíta, la principiò da cápo,
to retain   recommenced
sottoscrísse affezionatíssimo, e morì conténto.
subscribed   died

Un cattivíssimo autóre   diéde   in lúce un líbro, che avéa
                        gave (brought) light
per títolo, "dell' ánima délle béstie:" Voltaire, avéndolo létto, dísse ad un amíco che glie ne chiedéva il súo paréte, l' autóre è un
                                  asked

óttimo cittadíno, ma non è abbastánza informáto délla stória del
súo paése.
                          sufficiently   informed

Io non conósco miglió*r* preservatívo cóntro la nója che di
        know   against   ennui
adempíre esattissimaménte i próprj dovéri.
to fulfil   own   duties.

EXERCISE FOR TRANSLATION.

1. Louis XI. and Ferdinand of Arragon were both cruel and perfidious, notwithstanding the first took the title of Very Christian, and the second that of Catholic.

2. The study of languages is very useful and very agreeable.

3. It has been said, that a nation of wise men would be the most foolish people in the world, as an army of captains would be the worst army.

4. When there was an eclipse of the moon, the Romans were accustomed to recall its light by beating upon copper vases in a very noisy manner, and by raising towards heaven a great number of flambeaus and lighted firebrands.

5. A three days' fast would make a coward of the bravest man on earth.

6. The language of a people is the most important monument of its history.

VOCABULARY.

1. Louis XI., *Ludovíco undécimo;* Ferdinand of Arragon, *Ferdinándo d' Arragóna ;* notwithstanding, *nonostánte ;* took, *prése ;* that, *quéllo.*

2. Agreeable, *piacévole.*

3. It has been said, *fu détto ;* foolish, *pázzo ;* as, *cóme ;* worst, *il più cattívo.*

4. There was, *succedéva* (succeeded) ; were accustomed, *solévano ;* recall, *richiamáre ;* light, *chiaróre ;* by beating, *col báttere ;* very noisy, *strepitosaménte ;* copper, *ráme ;* to raise, *sollevúre*, flambeau, *fáce ;* lighted, *accéso.*

5. Three, *tre ;* would make, *farébbe ;* coward, *poltróne ;* brave, *valoróso.*

CONVERSAZIÓNE.

Cóme avéte dormíto?
È il Sig. D. buón cittadíno?
L' avéte vedúto?
Fu crudéle Ludovíco XI.?
Prése égli un títolo?
Siéte conténto?
Non è quést' elefánte mólto gránde?
Qual mése è il più fréddo (cold) dell' ánno?
Che stúdio è utilíssimo?

È il vóstro generále valoróso?

Quáli sóno i metálli più pesánti?

Qual animále è il più crudéle?

Ho dormíto saporitissimaménte.
È un óttimo cittadíno.
Sì, spessíssime vólte.
Sì, crudéle e pérfido.
Prése il títolo di cristianíssimo.
Sóno contentíssimo.
Égli è grandíssimo e fortíssimo.
Il mése di Febbráio è ordinariaménte freddíssimo.
Lo stúdio délle língue è utilíssimo e piacevolíssimo.
Sì, è l' uómo più valoróso délla térra.
Il plátino e l' óro sóno i più pesánti metálli.
La tigre è un animále crudelíssimo; è più crudéle di tútti gli altri animáli.

CHAPTER XII.

AUGMENTATIVES AND DIMINUTIVES.

The signification of many words, both nouns and adjectives, may be either increased or diminished by the addition of certain syllables to their termination.

I. The augmentatives, reducible to rules, are formed in *óne* (m.), *óna* (f.), *ótto* (m.), *ótta* (f.), to signify bigness and stoutness, in a good sense.

Likewise in *áccio* (m.), *áccia* (f.), to signify something of a disgusting or contemptible bulk.

The addition *áme* expresses a great abundance of any thing of the same species, but differing in form and qualities; sometimes for things not very agreeable.

AUGMENTATIVES AND DIMINUTIVES.

EXAMPLES.

Líbro,	book;	*libróne,*	a very large book.
Ragázza,	a girl;	*ragazzóna,*	a stout jolly girl.
Cása,	a house;	*casótto, casótta,*	a good roomy house.
Sála,	a hall;	*salóne,*	a large hall.
Cavállo,	a horse;	*cavalláccio,*	a great ugly horse.
Cása,	a house;	*casáccia,*	an ugly large house.
Béstia,	beast;	*bestiáme,*	cattle.

Observe that many nouns have a natural ending in *áccia, áccio,* and *áme,* without being augmentatives. Observe, also, that masculine augmentatives often come from feminine nouns, as *cásone* (m.), from *cása* (f.).

II. The diminutives reducible to rules are formed in *íno, éllo, étto,* with the variations incident to adjectives and substantives in *o;* as, —

Caríno (m. s.), *carína* (f. s.), *caríni* (m. p.), *caríne* (f. p.), dear pretty little creature, or creatures; from *cáro.*

Poveréllo, poverélla, poverélli, poverélle, poor little creature, or creatures; from *póvero.*

Librétto, a pretty little book; from *líbro. Acquétta,* a clear small stream; from *ácqua.* Such diminutives generally denote endearment and smallness.

Other diminutives, ending chiefly in *úccio, úccia,* and *úzzo, úzza,* indicate something small or contemptible; as,

Casúccia, a small mean-looking house; from *cása,* house.
Uomúzzo, a puny little fellow; from *uómo,* man.

Yet all these rules are liable to exceptions, which nothing but practice can teach; for, besides the terminations which we have just given for augmentatives and diminutives, many others are freely used in familiar conversation, and in books on trivial subjects. Thus, from *dónna,* a woman, *cása,* house, *líbro,* a book, may be formed the following augmentatives and diminutives: —

Donnóne, a tall, stout, masculine woman	. . .	from *dónna*
Donnóna, a tall, strong, healthful woman	. . .	,, ,,
Donnáccia, an impudent, shameful virago	. . .	,, ,,

7*

Donnétta, a pretty little, smart woman . . . . from *dónna*
Donniciuóla, a mean-looking woman . . . . . „ „
Donnina, a pretty little woman . . . . . . „ „
Donnáccia, a vulgar woman . . . . „ „
Donnaccióne, a bold, impudent, stout woman . . „ „
Casóne, a very large house; a mansion . . . . from *cása*.
Casáccia, a large, ill-contrived house . . . . . „ „
Casaménto, a well-built, roomy house . . . . . „ „
Casípola and *casúpola*, a small, despicable house . „ „
Casucciáccia, a small, wretched house . . . . „ „
Casile, a poor, thatched cottage . . . . „ „
Casélla, a small, low-built house . . . . . . „ „
Casótta, a snug, comfortable house . . . . . . „ „
Casétta, a snug house; also, a neat kennel . . . „ „
Casellína, a very little but genteel house . . . . „ „
Casettíno (m.), *casettína* (f.), a neat, pretty cottage, „ „
Casina, a very small house . . . . „ „
Casíno, a small, neat, summer house . . . . . „ „
Libróne, a bulky, heavy book . . . . from *líbro*.
Libráccio, an ugly, large book . . . . „ „
Librícolo and *libercólo*, a small, contemptible book . „ „
Librétto, a pretty, neat, little book . . . . . . „ „
Libréttino, a very little and pretty book . . . . „ „
Libriccino, a very small pamphlet . . . . . . „ „

And so on, with thousands of other words, in all the range of humor and whims. But few augmentatives and diminutives are admitted in a style strictly correct, beyond those in *óne*, *áme*, *áccio*, for increasing; and those in *íno*, *étto*, *éllo*, for diminishing.

The termination *áglia* indicates an indeterminate number, and can be applied only to individuals, and always in a bad sense; as, *Ragázza*, child; *ragazzáglia*, a great number of wicked children; *plebáglia*, *gentáglia*, from *plébe*, *génte*, meaning a great number of low people, vulgar persons. This termination is feminine.

Ástro gives a bad qualification, and is applicable only to professions; as, *Médico*, a physician; *medicástro*, a bad physician; *filosofástro*, *poetástro*, a bad philosopher, a bad poet. However, we can say *giovinástro*, for a naughty boy; *verdástro, olivástro, biancástro*, etc., of a greenish, olive, whitish color, etc.

Besides this quantity of augmentatives and diminutives which modify the nouns in so many different ways, there are still several others which are called irregular, because they only belong to a few words. Such are —

Mediconzolo, a bad physician; from *médico* and *ónzolo*.
Leprátto, small hare; from *lépre* and *átto*.
Cagnuolino, little dog; from *cáne, nólo, íno*.
Omiciátto, poor little man; from *uómo, iccio, átto*.
Tristanzuólo, unwholesome; from *tristo* and *anzuólo*.

A diminutive syllable may also be added to some verbs, such as *vivacchiáre*, to live poorly; from *vívere: leggichiáre*, to read carelessly; from *léggere: innamoracchiársi*, to be slightly in love; from *innamorársi*.

We can join together the augmentative terminations, and thus form a double augmentative; as, *Omáccio*, bad man; *omaccióne*, a very bad man: from *uómo, áccio, óne*.

MNEMONIC EXERCISE.

Mangiáte un bocconcíno di páne,	Eat a little mouthful of bread.
Dátegli un' occhiatína,	Give him a slight glance.
È úna fanciullétta semplicína,	She is a very simple little girl.
Égli ha un póco del goffótto,	He is a little foolish.
Siéte un cattivéllo,	You are a naughty little one.
Che ventaréllo che tráe!	What a pleasant little wind!
Abbiáte un tantíno di giudízio,	Have a little sense.
È un pézzo di volpóne,¹	He is a sly-boots.
Égli è un béllo zerbinótto,	He is an elegant young man.
Com' è bellína e leggiadrétta!	How pretty she is! how graceful!
Vorréi dírvi dúe parolíne,	I wish to say two brief words to you.
Ha úna brútta linguáccia,	He has a very wicked tongue.
Égli ha céra d' úno scimiottíno,	He has the face of a little monkey.
È un ragazzáccio ignorantóne,	He is a very ignorant ugly child.

Státe zitta, sfacciatélla!	Be quiet, impudent little one
Che visíno graziosétto!	What a pretty little face!
Intratteneteví un momentíno,	Stop only a little moment.
Vói státe benóne,	You are very well.
Fa cón tútti il dottoréllo,¹	He plays the wise man.
Ma guardáte che amoríno!	See the little darling!
Quél gonnellíno è gentíle,	That little skirt is very nice.
Dov' è il mío berrettíno da nótte?	Where is my small night-cap?
È nel cassettíno délla távola,	It is in the little drawer of the table.
Mi rispóse con úna scrollatína di cápo,	He answered me by a little shake of the head.
Quélla vóstra nipotína è un angiolétta,	Your little niece is a little angel.
Bélla facciótta ha quésta ragázza!	What a beautiful face this girl has!
Va vía, asináccio, sénza creánza!	Go away, great ass, without education!
Quéi pasticcétti mi consólano il cuóre,	These little cakes rejoice my heart.
In Lóndra le cáse non hánno portóni,	In London the houses have not coach-doors.
Dátemi úna spazzolatína al tabárro,	Give a little stroke of the brush to my cloak.
Ho già fátto un migliaréllo,	I have already gone a short mile.
È ricciúto, biondétto, e bassótto,	He is little curly-headed, pretty blonde, and rather small.
Mi vuói tu fáre un servigétto?	Will you do me a little service?
Ho fátto alcúne speserélle,	I have made some trifling expenses.
Aspettátemi un quarticéllo d'óra,	Wait for me a brief quarter of an hour.
Quél birbantéllo me l' ha fátta,	This little rogue has tricked me.
Le seráte d' invérno són lunghétte,	Winter evenings are rather long.
Ha un bocchíno che innamóra,	She has a ravishing small mouth.
Guardátevi da quélla ribaldáglia,	Mistrust that rabble.

AUGMENTATIVES AND DIMINUTIVES. 81

Gli ho tiráto úna sassáta,	I have thrown a stone at him.
Le mattináte són freschétte,	The mornings are a little cool.
Si è fátta úna corpacciáta,	He has eaten to satiety.
Siéte un bel ribaldonáccio,	You are a great villain.
Il poverétto è magricciuólo,	The poor fellow is rather thin.
Venite nél mio salottíno,	Come into my little parlor.
Élla ha un bél bracciótto,	She has a plump fine arm.
Che tempáccio fa quest' oggi!	What bad weather it is to-day!
Che spallácce da facchíno!	What great shoulders for a porter!
Oh! cára la mía gioiétta!	O my dear little jewel *of a woman!*

REMARK. — It will be seen by the above examples, that the Italian language admits of the frequent use of augmentative and diminutive terminations. These last modify the signification of words in much the same way as the terminations *kin, ling, ing, ock, en, el,* in English; as, lamb-*kin,* duck-*ling,* hill-*ock,* chick-*en,* cock-*erel,* etc. Augmentative terminations have no corresponding meaning in English.

Augmentatives and diminutives form one of the striking beauties of the Italian language; but, as no strict rules can be given concerning them, the student is cautioned not to venture upon their use until familiar with the language.

CONVERSAZIÓNE.

Chi è fanciullíno?	*Mio fratéllo è fanciullíno.*
Dóve dimóra (lives) *égli?*	*In un casíno.*
Che avéte?	*Ho un canino.*
Di che colóre?	*Biancástro.*
Che uómo è égli?	*È úna cattíva linguáccia.*
Chi è quésto cattivéllo?	*È fíglio del medicónzolo.*
Avéte vedúto (seen) *mia cugína?*	*Sì! Com' è bellína e leggiadrétta!*
Dátemi úna canzóne, se vi piáce.	*Non ho che quésta canzoncína, prendétela* (take it).
Abbiáte ún tantíno di giudízio nel parláre?	*L' ho, non vi páre, quándo vi dico* (I say) *che siéte un bél zerbinótto?*

CHAPTER XIII.

THE NUMERAL ADJECTIVES.

MNEMONIC EXERCISE.

Vo a létto álle úndici in púnto,	I go to bed precisely at eleven.
Mi álzo álle diéci precíse,	I rise precisely at ten.
Vi andrémo úna vólta per úno,	We will each go there once.
Vi són tórti d' ámbo le párti,	There are wrongs on both sides.
Gli ho détto a quáttr' ócchi le míe ragióni,'	I told him my way of thinking, face to face.
Il capitále mi frútta il séi per cénto,	The capital yields me six per cent.
Quánto impórtano dúe ánni di frútti, al cinque per cénto, di un capitále di mílle sétte cénto novánta dúe fránchi?	What is the interest of one thousand seven hundred and ninety-two francs for two years, at five per cent?
Cárlo ottávo scése in Itália nel mílle quáttro cénto novánta quáttro,	Charles VIII. went into Italy in one thousand four hundred and ninety-four.
Mi par mílle ánni di rivedére la mía pátria,'	I am impatient to see my country again.
Égli non sa nemméno che dúe vía dúe fan quáttro,	He does not even know that twice two make four.

NUMERAL ADJECTIVES.

The numeral adjectives* are divided into cardinal and ordinal.

I. — CARDINAL NUMBERS.

Úno,	one.	Cínque,	five.
Dúe,	two.	Séi,	six.
Tre,	three.	Sétte,	seven.
Quáttro,	four.	Ótto,	eight.

---

* Numbers may be divided into cardinal, ordinal, collective, distributive, and proportional.

THE NUMERAL ADJECTIVES. 83

Nòve,	nine.	Cinquánta,	fifty.
Dièci,	ten.		
Úndici,	eleven.	Sessánta,	sixty.
Dódici,	twelve.		
Trédici,	thirteen.	Settánta,	seventy.
Quattórdici,	fourteen.		
Quíndici,	fifteen.	Ottánta,	eighty.
Sédici,	sixteen.		
Diciassétte,	seventeen.	Novánta,	ninety.
Diciótto,	eighteen.		
Diciannóve,	nineteen.	Cénto,†	hundred.
Vénti,	twenty.	Duecénto,	
Vent'úno, or Ventúno,*	twenty-one.	Ducénto, or Dugénto,	two hundred.
Ventidúe,	twenty-two.	Trecénto,	three hundred.
Ventitrè,	twenty-three.	Quattrocénto,	four hundred.
Ventiquáltro,	twenty-four.		
Venticínque,	twenty-five.	Mille,†	thousand.
Ventiséi,	twenty-six.	Duemíla, or Dumíla,	two thousand.
Ventisétte,	twenty-seven.		
Vent'otto, or Ventótto,	twenty-eight.	Tremíla,	three thousand.
Ventinóve,	twenty-nine.	Millecénto, or Mille e cénto,	eleven hundred.
Trénta,	thirty.		
Trentúno,*	thirty-one.		
. . . .		Diecimíla,	ten thousand.
Trentótto,	thirty-eight.		
. . . .		Centomíla,	hundred thousand
Quaránta,	forty.		
. . . .		Milióne,	million. ‡

* When a noun follows the numbers twenty-one, thirty-one, forty-one, etc., it remains in the singular; as, Vent' úno libro, twenty-one books. But, when the noun precedes the number, it is put in the plural; as, Libri trent' úno.

† The numerals cénto and mille are never accompanied by the indefinite article as in English,—a hundred, or a thousand. Cénto is invariable.

‡ When the numerals are used to indicate the hour of the day, they are preceded by the feminine article la, le: but then the word óra, hour, óre, hours, is not expressed.

ITALIANISMS.

Vérso le sèi,	at about six o'clock.	Di dúe giórni l' úno,	every other day.
Suóna un' óra,	it has struck one.	Quíndici giórni fa, or Sóno quíndici giorni,	a fortnight ago.
È l' úna, or é un óra,	it is one o'clock.		
Ad un' óra, or al tócco,	at one o'clock.	Dománi a quíndici,	to-morrow fortnight.

II. — ORDINAL NUMBERS.

Prímo	first.
Secóndo	second.
Térzo	third.
Quárto	fourth.
Quínto	fifth.
Sésto	sixth.
Séttimo	seventh.
Ottávo	eighth.
Nóno	ninth.
Décimo	tenth.
Undécimo, or décimo prímo	eleventh.
Duodécimo, or décimo secóndo	twelfth.
Tredécimo, or décimo térzo	thirteenth.
Décimo quárto	fourteenth.
Décimo quínto	fifteenth.
Décimo sésto	sixteenth.
Décimo séttimo	seventeenth.
Décimo ottávo	eighteenth.
Décimo nóno	nineteenth.
Ventésimo, or vigésimo	twentieth.
Ventésimo prímo, etc.	twenty-first.
Trentésimo	thirtieth.
Quarantésimo	fortieth.
Cinquantésimo	fiftieth.
Sessantésimo	sixtieth.
Settantésimo	seventieth.
Ottantésimo	eightieth.
Novantésimo	ninetieth.
Centésimo	one hundredth.
Millésimo	one thousandth.

These adjectives agree with their nouns. (See Chapter IX.)

III. Fractional and collective numbers are —

Mézzo,	half.		Una dozzína,	a dozen.
Una metà,	a half (moiety).		Una quindicína,	a fifteenth.
Un térzo,	a third.		Una ventína,	a score.
Un quárto,	a fourth.		Un centináio,	a hundred.
Una décima,	a ten (half-score).		Un migliáio,	a thousand

THE NUMERAL ADJECTIVES.

IV. *Úno*, numeral adjective, like the indefinite article *un*, agrees with its noun; but the final *o* is suppressed, unless the noun begins with *s* followed by another consonant; as, *Un gállo*, one or a cock; *un autóre*, one or an author; *úno spíllo*, a pin. The feminine is *úna;* as, *Una dónna*, a woman. We write *un'* before a feminine noun beginning with a vowel; as, *Un' ánitra*, a duck.

V. There are a great many phrases in Italian in which the noun after *úno* is suppressed; as, *È úno che díce mále di tútti*, he is a man (one) who speaks ill of everybody.

VI. On the contrary, *úno* is often suppressed before nouns which express an indefinite sense; as, *È uómo di buóna fáma*, he is a man of good repute.

VII. *Per úno* signifies per head; as, *Il pránzo ci è costáto cínque fránchi per úno*, the dinner cost us five francs per head.

VIII. The expression *in un*, often employed by the poets, is an abridgment, signifying *in un sólo moménto*, *in un medésimo témpo*, in a single moment, in an even time; and the expression *ad úna vóce*, signifies *unanimously*.

IX. To translate "one by one," "two by two," "three by three," etc., the preposition is repeated; and we say, *ad úno ad úno, a dúe a dúe, a tre a tre*. "Both," "all three," etc., are translated *tútti e dúe, tútti e tre*.

X. "Firstly" and "secondly" are expressed by *premieraménte, secondariaménte:* afterwards we say, *in térzo luógo, in quárto luógo*, for "in the third place," "in the fourth place," etc.

XI. In multiplication, *via* expresses *times;* as, Twice or two times two are four, *dúe vía dúe fan quáttro;* or, by abbreviation, *dúe vía dúe quáttro*.

8

XII. In dating letters, the article may be used either in the singular or plural; as, The 21st May, *li 21 Mággio*, or *ai 21 di Mággio*, or *il 21° Mággio*, etc.

XIII. In speaking of years,* in Italian we use *in the;* as, *Nel 1500, nel 1862.*

XIV. For the knowledge of epochs, it is important to know that the Italians sometimes call the thirteenth century *il 200*, because it goes from 1200 to 1299; and, for the same reason, they say *il 300, il 400, il 500*, etc., for the fourteenth, fifteenth, sixteenth centuries: hence the words *un trecentísta, cinquecentísta, un seicentísta*, etc., for "an author of the fourteenth, sixteenth, seventeenth centuries." Generally, however, they say, as in English, *il décimo térzo sécolo, il décimo nóno sécolo*, the thirteenth century, the nineteenth century.

XV. "Both" is translated by *ámbo* or *ambedúe;* as, *Ámbo i piédi, ámbe le gámbe, ambedúe le famíglie,* Both feet, both legs, both families.

XVI. In speaking of sovereigns, the ordinal number is used, as in English; as, *Enríco quárto*, Henry the Fourth; *Gregório décimo sésto*, Gregory the Sixteenth.

READING LESSON.

Ludóvico Arrósto nácque addì ótto di Settémbre, dell' ánno mílle quattrocénto settánta quáttro.

Dánte nácque in Firénze nel Márzo dell' ánno mílle ducénto sessánta cínque da Alighiéro e da Bélla. Il súo primiéro nóme di Duránte fu cangiáto per vézzo in quéllo di Dánte. Nell' ánno mílle trecénto ventúno, nel mése di Settémbre, morì il gránde e valénte poéta Dánte Alighiéri nélla città di Ravénna.

Petrárca nácque addì vénti di Lúglio néll' ánno mílle trecénto quáttro nélla città d'Arézzo. Morì d' apoplessía nélla nótte del diciótto di Lúglio déll' ánno mílle trecénto settánta tre.

---

* I am twenty, thirty, fifty years old, cannot be rendered literally; but is expressed thus: I have twenty, thirty, fifty years, *Io ho cént' ánni, trént' ánni, cinquánt' ánni.*

THE NUMERAL ADJECTIVES. 87

Torquáto Tásso nácque in Sorrénto ágli úndici Márzo dell' ánno mille cinquecénto quaránta quáttro. Spirò ai venticinque d'Aprile mille cinquecénto novánta cínque.

Giovánni Boccáccio nácque nell' ánno 1313; e morì addì 21 di Dicémbre, 1374.

Machiavéllo vénne álla lúce in Firénze ai 3 di Mággio dell' ánno 1467, e morì ai 22 di Giúgno 1527.

Leonárdo Salviati il più illústre grammático di Firénze vide il giórno nel 1540.

Leonárdo da Vinci nácque nel 1452.

Michelágnolo Buonarróti ébbe víta nel 1475; e morì in età di quási 89 ánni.

Benvenúto Cellíni vénne al móndo il dì d' ognissánti 1500.

Nácque il Galiléo nel 1564, néllo stésso giórno e quási álla stéssa óra, in cúi morì Michelángelo.

Francésco Soáve, autóre délle "Novélle Moráli," vide la lúce nel 1743 e morì in età di 63.

EXERCISE FOR TRANSLATION.

1. It is more difficult to make five francs with six sous than to gain a million with ten thousand francs.

2. An inhabitant of Padua invented paper in the twelfth century, and a Florentine invented spectacles at the commencement of the fourteenth.

3. Man has commonly but twenty-two years to live: during these twenty-two years, he is subject to twenty-two sicknesses, of which many are incurable. In this horrible state, man still struts: he loves (makes love), he wars (makes war), he forms projects, as if he would live a thousand centuries in his delights.

4. A regimen to be followed by every man who wishes to live a hundred years: first repast, — a glass of pure water at nine o'clock in the morning; second repast, — soup, roast meat, stewed fruit, a glass of old wine, at two o'clock in the afternoon; third repast, — a walk, without fatigue, at four o'clock; fourth repast, — a glass of sugared water at nine o'clock at night, on going to bed.

5. A very brave soldier had lost both his arms in battle. His colonel offered him a crown. "You think, without doubt," said the grenadier, with vivacity, "that I have lost only a pair of gloves."

VOCABULARY.

1. Sou, *sóldo;* franc, *fránco.*
2. Padua, *Pádova;* Florentine, *Fiorentíno;* at the commencement, *nel princípio.*
3. During these, *nel decórso di quésti;* is subject, *va soggétto,* would, *dovésse.*
4. To follow by every one who would wish, *da tenérsi da chiúnque vorrà;* stewed fruits, *consérva;* afternoon, *dópo mézzogiórno;* walk, *passeggiáta;* fatigue, *stancársi;* sugared, *zuccheráto;* on going to bed, *nell' andáre a létto.*
5. Lost, *perdúto;* offered him, *gli offérse;* you think, *credéte*

CONVERSAZIÓNE.

Quánti ánni avéte?
È vóstro fratéllo?
Avéte danáro in tásca?
In che clásse è Luígi?
In che ánno nácque Galiléo?
Quánti ánni vísse Adámo?
Che óra è?
A che óra pranziámo óggi?
Quánti ne abbiámo del mése?
Quánti ócchi hái?
Quánte díta (fingers) *abbiámo a ciascúna máno?*
E le díta dei piédi (feet) *quánte sóno?*
E le díta délle máni e déi piédi quánte sóno?
Quánti abitánti ha la città di Lóndra?
Che età ha il Signór S——?

Quánti sénsi avéte?

Quándo morì Napoleóne?

In che pósso servírvi?

Adésso (now) *ho trént'ótto ánni.*
Diciótto ánni.
Sì, ho cénto cinquánta scúdi.
È nélla secónda clásse.
Nel 1564.
Égli vísse nóve cénto trénta.
È un quárto dópo mezzodì.
Pranzerémo álle dúe.
Ne abbiámo venticínque.
Dúe.
Ne abbiámo cínque.

Diéci.

Sóno vénti.

Lóndra ha tre millióni d' abitánti.
È nel súo sessantésimo secóndo ánno.
Cínque: udíto, vísta, odoráto, gústo, tátto.
Nel mággio del mille ottocénto ventúno.
Nel prestármi cinquemíla fránchi.

CHAPTER XIV.

RELATIVE PRONOUNS.

MNEMONIC EXERCISE.

Chi è che bátte? or *chi bátte?*	Who knocks?
Chi è? Chi chiáma?	Who is it? Who calls?
Che cósa è successo?	What has happened?
Che nuóve abbiámo?	What news have we?
Sapéte vói chi sóno?	Do you know who I am?
Che rázza di pensáre?	What manner of thinking?
Non so che dire, davvéro,	Truly, I know not what to say.
Che mále vi ho fátto io?	What harm have I done you?
Che giórno è óggi?	What day is it to-day?
Di chi è la cólpa?	Whose fault is it?
Che età avéte?	How old are you?
Che cósa siéte venúto a fáre?	What are you come to do?
Che vále avére ricchézze sénza salúte?	What are riches worth without health?
Che bélla cósa è il giráre il móndo!	What a pleasure to travel over the world!
Che cósa mi daréte da mangiáre?	What will you give me to eat?
Quál è la minéstra che più vi piáce?	What soup do you like best?
Che cósa sénto? che cósa védo?	What do I hear? what do I see?
Che cósa fáte di béllo, amíco?	What good thing are you doing, friend?
Che? Cóme? Che díte?	What? How? What do you say?
In quál concétto mái mi tenéte?	What opinion have you, then, of me?
Sapéte quál sía l'ánimo súo?	Do you know what is his intention?
Quánti pázzi vi sóno nel móndo!	How many fools there are in the world!
È · a uómo cúi niúno piáce,	He is a man who likes no one.

RELATIVE PRONOUNS.

I. These pronouns are *chi, che, quále, cúi*, who, which, what.*

II. "Who," *chi*, when it has no antecedent expressed; as,—

Who loves, fears,	*Chi áma, téme.*
Of whom do you speak?	*Di chi parláte?*
See who knocks,	*Guardáte chi picchia.*

III. "He who," "some one who," "no one who," "those who," or "the one," "the other," may be translated by *chi*, whenever they do not relate to an antecedent; as,—

Distrust those who flatter you,	*Diffidátevi di chi vi adúla.*
Those who live on hope will die of hunger,	*Chi vive di speránza morrà di fáme.*
In the world, some are rich, others poor,	*Nel móndo, chi è rícco, chi è póvero.*

The word *chi*,† used only for persons, and representing an individual in the singular, requires the verb of which it is the subject to agree with it in the singular.

IV. "Who," relating to an antecedent expressed, is translated by *che* when it is the subject, and by *cui* when it is the object; ‡ as,—

The woman to whom I speak,	*La dónna a cúi párlo.*
The master for whom I labor,	*Il padróne § per cúi lavóro.*
Man is the only animal who weeps and who laughs,	*L' uómo è il sólo animále che piánge e che ride.*

---

* *Chi*, not interrogative, is always singular; *che, cúi*, which, singular and plural; *quále*, who, which, singular; *quáli*, plural.

† *Chi* refers to persons only: *che, cúi, quále*, refer both to persons and things.

‡ *Che* is chiefly used in the nominative: *cúi*, in all other relations: *chi, quále*, are used in all their relations. *Che*, when it relates to a person, must be translated in English by *who* or *whom*; when it relates to an animal, by *which*. In English, the relative pronouns, though understood, are often left out after the noun. In Italian, they must always be expressed: as, *Chi si umílía, si es'ltu*, who humbles himself, etc.; *qu*'*i gióvani che voi vi-déte, those* young men whom you see; *il c:ne che vedete,* the dog which you see; *la lettera che avéte scritta,* the letter you have written; *il ragazzo ch' io ho vedúto,* the boy I have seen.

§ The master who teaches is *maéstro*; the master who commands is *padróne*.

V. The preposition *a*, to, can be understood before *cúi;* and we may say, *La dónna cúi párlo.*

VI. "I who write," "thou who writest," etc., are translated, *Io che scrívo, tu che scrívi,* etc. In similar phrases, the verb agrees with the personal pronoun, as in English.

VII. "Which," as the regimen of a verb, is translated by *che* or by *cúi;* as, —

The bread which you eat,   *Il páne che mangiáte.*
The wall which the house con-   *Il múro cúi nascónde la cása.*
ceals,

In the last phrase, *cúi* (*nascónde*) is better than *che,* because *che* serves either for subject or object. Petrarch says, *Quélla dónna gentíl cúi piánge amóre.*

VIII. *Che,* or *quále* (*quáli, quái,* in the plural), is used in exclamatory phrases; as, —

What a misfortune!   *Che disgrázia!*
What a pity!   *Che peccáto!*
What beauties!   *Quái* (or *che*) *bellézze!*

IX. *Quále* is used in doubtful phrases, or when followed by a verb; as, Which of these two books do you wish? *quál voléte di quésti dúe líbri?*

X. *Che* is generally used in interrogative phrases; as, —

What book is this?   *Che líbro è?*
What man is that?   *Che uómo è?*
What house is that?   *Che cása è?*
What business have you?   *Che affári avéte?*

XI. "Which" in the genitive, signifying "of which," "for which," is rendered in Italian by *di cúi,* or *del quále,* etc.; as, It is a favor for which I thank you, *è un favóre di cúi,* or *del quále io vi ringrázio.*

XII. When the noun following *which* designates something belonging to that which precedes it, then *cúi* (whose) is used with the article; as, The hero whose exploits have astonished the world, *l' eróe le cúi gésta hánno fátto maravigliáre il móndo.*

XIII. The word "which" in the ablative case, signifying "by which," "from which," indicating the origin, the derivation, the point of departure of an action or thing, is rendered in Italian by *da cúi*, or *dal quále*, etc.; as, —

There is no evil from which good does not arise,   *Non c' è mále da cúi non násca un béne,*
The army by which the city is besieged,   *L' armáta da cúi è assediáta la città.*

XIV. "What," interrogative, is translated by *che* or *che cósa;* as, —

Upon what shall we dine?   *Con che pranzerémo?*
What is the use of merit without fortune?   *A che gióva il mérito sénza fortúna?*

XV. "To which," relating to an entire phrase, is translated by *al che;* relating to a single word, by *a cúi*, or *al quále*, or *álla quále;* as, —

To which I answered,   *Al che rispósi.*
That of which the miser thinks the least is to succor the poor,   *La cósa a cúi méno pénsa l' aváro, è il sovvenire i míseri.*

XVI. We translate such phrases as the following, thus: —

What are politics?   *Che cósa è,* or *cos è la política?*
What do you say?   *Che cósa díte? che díte?*
What is it?   *Che cos' è?*
What is there?   *Che cósa c' è? che c' è?*
What do I hear?   *Che cósa sénto? che sénto?*
What are you doing?   *Che cósa fáte? che fáte?*
Who is going?   *Chi párte?*
In what manner?   *In che módo? in quál módo?*

OBSERVATIONS.

XVII. The word *ónde* is often used in Italian poetry in lieu of *di cúi*, or *del quále*, *dal quále*, either in the singular or plural, masculine or feminine; as, *Di quéi sospíri ond' io nudríva il córe* (Petrárca), those sighs with which I nourished my heart. In this line the word *ónde* is in place of *cói quáli*, with which.

XVIII. In poetry particularly, the word *che*, relative, is sometimes employed as an indirect object, in place of *cúi* or *quáli*; as, *Gli ócchi di ch' io parlái si caldaménte* (Petrárca), the eyes of which I spoke so warmly. Here the word *che* is in place of *cúi*.

XIX. In using *che* as an indirect object, the Italian authors sometimes omit the preposition which ought to precede it, and which is the sign of the regimen; as, *Ed io són un di quéi che 'l piánger gióva* (Petrárca), and I am one of those to whom weeping helps. Here the preposition *a* (to) before *che* is understood.

XX. It often happens that *che* is used in Italian in place of *núlla*, nothing; as, *È un dúro péso il non avér che fáre*, it is a heavy burden to have nothing to do.

XXI. *Non che* is elegantly used for "not only." But, in this case, the *non che* is placed in the second part of the phrase; as in the line from Petrárca, — *Spéro trovár pietà, non che perdóno*, I hope to find, not only pardon, but pity.

XXII. Finally, *che* is often connected with other words; thus forming adverbs and conjunctions at pleasure. In these cases, the final letter is accented, which renders the sound more striking, as in the words *primachè*, *benchè*, *fuorchè*, *perciocchè*, *avvegnachè*, *contuttochè*, etc.

XXIII. In the subjunctive mood of the verb, *che* may be understood; as, *Vóglio mi diciáte*, I wish that you would say it to me.

READING LESSON.

I Románi avéndo scélti per mandáre in Bitínia tre ambascia-
     chosen to send

tóri, uno déi quáli patíva di podágra, l' áltro éra státo trapanáto
     suffered   trapanned

e l' último éra tenúto per uómo scémpio, Catóne dísse ridéndo,
                      laughing

che i Románi mandávano un' ambascería che non avéva nè
      sent   neither

piédi, nè cápo, nè ménte. Dío ci día buóni príncipi, perchè,
  nor   May God send us

úna vólta che s' hánno, è fórza soffrírli táli quáli sóno. L'
           to bear with them

egoísta è un uómo che appiccherébbe fuóco ad úna cása per far
       would set   to make

cuócere un uóvo. Ógni língua è piacévole all' orécchio del
to cook

pópolo per cúi è fátta. Ciceróne fu assassináto da Popélio Léna,
     made.

a cúi avéva già salváto la víta in úna cáusa in cúi éra accusáto
     saved

d' áver uccíso il próprio pádre. Síbari éra úna città délla
  killed

Mágna Grécia, i cúi abitánti érano mólto dáti all' effeminatézza;
               given

dónde viéne il nóme di sibaríta per dinotáre un uómo effemináto.
 comes   denote

EXERCISE FOR TRANSLATION.

1. I have seen this Italy which Corinne calls "the empire of the sun." What a fertile soil! What a delightful climate! What superb cities! What noble antiquities! What more sublime than the genius of the man who emulates nature, and erects eternal monuments everywhere (in all parts)!

2. Who can love repose before having experienced the pain of weariness? Who is he that finds pleasure in eating, drinking, and sleeping, before having suffered from hunger, thirst, and sleepiness?

3. "I have three sorts of friends," said Voltaire; 'the friends who love me, the friends to whom I am indifferent, and the friends who detest me."

4. It is a very glorious thing for Italy, that the three powers between whom almost all America was divided, owed their first conquests to the Italians: the Spaniards, to Christopher Columbus; the English, to the two Cabots of Venice; and the French, to Florentine Verazzani.

VOCABULARY.

1. Calls, *chiáma*; what, *che áltro v' ha*; genius, *ingégno*; erects, *innálza*; in all parts, *da ógni párte*.

2. Can love, *può avér cáro*; before, etc., *se príma non ha sentito*.

3. Detest, *detéstano*.

4. Divided, *divíso*; almost, *quási*; owed, *dovesséro*; their first conquests, *le príme lóro conquíste*; *Spagnuóli*; *Cristóforo Colómbo*; *Inglési*; *Cabótti Veneziáni*.

CONVERSAZIÓNE.

Che avéte vedúto?
Come è élla chiamáta?
E del clíma che díte?
E che? Siéte vói?
Che cercáte?
Dov' éra?
Che dicéva Voltáire déi suói amíci?
Quál differénza v' è fra óggi e iéri?
A chi piáce úna língua qualúnque?
Che si (one) díce délle città d' Itália?
Che abbiámo per pránzo?

Che disse Catóne déi tre ambasciatóri mandáti in Bitínia?

Cósa è assái glorióso per l' Itália?

Ho vedúto la bélla Itália.
È chiamáta l' impéro del sóle.
Che è deliziósó!
Io, in persóna.
Il mío líbro.
Sópra la távola.
Egli dicéva, "io ho tre spécie d' amíci."
Óggi non è tánto cáldo.

Al pópolo per cúi è fátta.

Che són supérbe.

Avrémo (we shall have) uóva o frútti.
Che éra un' ambascería che non avéva nè piédi, nè cápo, nè ménte.
Che le poténza d' Európa débbono ágl' Italiáni le lóro príme conquíste in América.

CHAPTER XV.

POSSESSIVE ADJECTIVE PRONOUNS.

MNEMONIC EXERCISE.

Che intenzióne è la vóstra?	What is your intention?
Vóglio la róba mía,	I wish my property.
Partiréte con vóstro cómodo,	You will depart at your ease.
Mio pádre ha da vivere,	My father has enough to live upon
Égli è un po' scárso del súo,	He is a little short of money.
Andátemi lontáno dágli ócchi,	Go far from my sight.
Ho gettáto via il mío danáro,	I have thrown my money away.
Non ho danári in tásca,	I have no money in my pocket.
Ho quálche cosétta del mío,	I possess something.
Vi són sérvo,	I am your servant.
So che mi siéte amico,	I know that you are my friend.
Ógni mía cósa è vóstra,	All I have is yours.
Andátevi in mía véce,	Go in my stead.
Io attèndo ái fátti miéi,	I attend to my affairs.
Vóglio far a módo mio,	I wish to do as I please.
Égli ha pósto in sicúro la víta,	He has put his life in security.
Vói siéte del mío paróre,	You are of my opinion.
Sentiámo il súo parére,	Let us listen to his advice.
Io aspetterò il vóstro padróne,	I expect your master.
Ognúno vuol béne ái súoi,	Every one loves his own.
Io non ci vóglio andár di mézzo per cáusa vóstra,	I do not wish to be compromised on your account.
Vi ringrázio di tánte vóstre bontà,	I thank you for so much kindness.
Oggi metterò il mío bel vestíto,	To-day I shall put on my best coat.
Se siéte ciéco, vóstro dánno,	If you are blind, so much the worse for you.
Che vi dice il cúore di tútto ciò?	What says your heart to all that?
Ognúno amár die la pátria,	Every man should love his country.

POSSESSIVE ADJECTIVE PRONOUNS.

I. The possessive pronouns* are —

Mío,	mía,	my or mine.
Túo,	túa,	thy or thine.
Súo,	súa,	his, her or hers, its.
Nóstro,	nóstra,	our or ours.
Vóstro,	vóstra,	your or yours.
Lóro,	lóro,	their or theirs.

Mío, túo, súo, nóstro, vóstro, are masculine; and are changed in the plural into —

Miéi,	my or mine.
Tuói,	thy or thine.
Suói,	his, her or hers, its.
Nóstri,	our or ours.
Vóstri,	your or yours.

Mía, túa, súa, nóstra, vóstra, are feminine; and form their plural thus: —

Míe,	my or mine.
Túe,	thy or thine.
Súe.	his, her or hers, its.
Nóstre,	our or ours.
Vóstre,	your or yours.

II. *Lóro;* their or theirs, is of both genders, and of both numbers, and takes the article agreeing with the noun to which it belongs.

III. Possessive pronouns are generally varied with the prepositions and articles.

---

* REMARK.—Galignani divides the possessive pronouns into three classes; viz., conjunctive, disjunctive, and relative.
    The conjunctive are those which are united to nouns; as, *Il mio libro,* my book; *i miéi parénti,* my relations.
    The disjunctive are those which are not united to nouns; as, *La vóstra cása, e la mia,* your house and mine; *i miéi cavalli, e i vóstri,* my horses and yours. *La mia* and *i vóstri* are disjunctive, as they stand in place of the noun.
    The relative are those which have relation to a person or a thing already spoken of; as, *È mio* or *mia,* it is mine; *sóno tuói* or *túe,* they are thine.

Variation of a masculine possessive pronoun: —

SINGULAR.

Subjective	Il mio,	my *or* mine.
Relation of Possession .	Del mio,	of my *or* mine.
„ „ Attribution .	Al mio,	to my *or* mine.
„ „ Derivation .	Dal mio,	from *or* by my *or* mine.
Objective	Il mio,	my *or* mine, etc.

IV. *Mío, túo, súo, nóstro, vóstro*, and *lóro* are sometimes used with the article substantively, — *il mío, il túo, súo*, etc. In this case, the word *avére*, property, is understood; and the pronouns are equivalent to "my property," "thy property," etc. ; as, —

Mángi del súo,   Let him eat of his own [property]
Non mangerà del nóstro,   He will not eat of ours.

V. *Miéi, tuói, nóstri*, and *lóro*, are also used substantively, — *i miéi, i tuói, i suói, i nóstri, i lóro*. Then the word *parénti*, relations, *amíci*, friends, *compágni*, companions, *familiári*, domestics, *soldáti*, soldiers, or *seguáci*, followers, is understood; and these pronouns are equivalent to "my relations," "thy friends," "his companions," "our domestics," "your soldiers," "their followers;" as, —

Incóntra á' miéi,   Against my relations.
Pregáto da' suói,   Requested by his friends.

VI. To avoid the ambiguity which in many instances would arise, in Italian,* from the indiscriminate use of

---

* REMARK. — The English language, for want of a sufficient variety of personal pronouns of the third person and their possessives, often labors under an ambiguity which is unknown in Italian. Observe the example, "He sent him to kill his own father." Nothing but the sense of that which precedes can determine whose father is meant; whereas, in Italian, the pronouns *súa* and *di lúi* mark the sense.

OBSERVATION. — *Próprio* adds emphasis to the possessive pronoun, as *own* in English: it is considered by some grammarians a real possessive pronoun.

In Italian, the possessive pronoun agrees in gender and number with the thing possessed, and not with the possessor as in English; as, —

POSSESSOR (sing.).   POSSESSED OBJECT (*f.* sing.).

Il padre áma (loves) *súa figlia* 'his daughter).
La madre áma (loves) *súa figlia* 'her daughter)

the possessive pronouns *súo*, *súa*, *suói*, *súe*, when these pronouns do not relate to the subject of the proposition, they are changed for the personal pronouns *di lúi*, *di léi*, of him, of her. Thus, in the phrase "John loves Peter and his children," if the pronoun "his" relates to "John," the subject of the proposition, it is expressed by *i suói;* as, *Giovánni áma Piétro ed i suói figliuóli*, John loves Peter and his [John's] children; but if "his" does not relate to "John," but to "Peter," the object of the proposition, then it is expressed by *i di lúi;* as, *Giovánni áma Piétro ed i di lúi figliuóli*, John loves Peter and his [Peter's] children.

Mandò ad uccídere súo pádre,	He sent to kill his father [the father of him who sent].
Súa soréla e i fígli di léi,	Her sister and her children [the children of her sister].

VII. The article is used, first, when titles, or the names of relationship, are in the plural; as, My brothers, *i miéi fratélli;* your majesties, *le vóstre Maestà:* second, when the possessive is placed after them; as, *Il fratéllo mio, la Maestà súa:* third, when they are accompanied by another adjective; as, *Il mio cáro pádre*, or *il cáro pádre mio*, my dear father: fourth, when the name of the relation is a diminutive; as, My little sister, *la mía sorellína*, or *la sorellína mía*.

VIII. There are a number of expressions where the possessive pronoun does not receive an article; as, *È mio parére, a súo sénno, di súa tésta,* etc., it is my advice, at his pleasure, of his head. Such phrases are easily learned by practice.

IX. Politeness requires the Italians to say, *Il vóstro Signór pádre, la vóstra Signóra zía,* your father, your aunt, etc.

X. To translate "it is one of my cousins," "there are three of our domestics," "there are many of our friends," the Italians say, without the article, *È un mio cugíno, sóno tre nóstri servitóri, sóno parécchi nóstri amíci,* or *è un déi miéi cugíni, son tre déi nóstri servitóri, sóno parécchi dei nóstri amíci.* The same is the case in such phrases as, It is my fault, *è un mío erróre.*

XI. To translate "these are my children," "these are my sisters," "these are my parents," etc., we say, *Sóno miéi fígli, sóno míe sorélle, sóno miéi parénti.*

XII. The possessive forms an Italianism in many phrases; as, —

Mío dánno,	So much the worse for me.
Ogni mío pensiére,	My every thought.

XIII. The possessive pronouns, referring to parts of the body or dress, are rendered by the pronouns *mi, ti, si, gli, ci,* and *vi,* particularly when they follow the verb.

Take off your hat,	*Levátevi il cappéllo.*
We shall put it in our pocket,	*Ce lo metterémo in tásca.*
He put it upon his knees,	*Se lo póse súlle ginócchia.*
I put it upon his head,	*Io gliélo pósi in cápo.*

XIV. We say in the same manner, —

He is not my father,	*Égli non mi è pádre.*
I am not his friend,	*Io non gli sóno amico.*
Remember that he is thy son,	*Ricórdati ch' égli ti è fíglio.*
Call my domestic,	*Chiamátemi il cameriére.*

READING LESSON.

IL CAVÁLLO RUBÁTO.
STOLEN.

Il piú bel cavállo d' un contadíno vénne di nótte rubáto nélla
        paysan came
súa stálla. Alcúni giórni dópo il paesáno si recò al mercáto de'
              went
caválli che si ténne nélla città vicína, per comprárne un áltro
   one held   to buy

Quále fu la súa sorprésa, allorchè tra i caválli in véndita égli riconóbbe il súo. Súbito lo prése per la bríglia, sclamándo: "Quésto cavállo è mío. Sóno tre giórni che mi fu rubáto." —

"Vói v' ingannáte, galantuómo," rispóse tranquillaménte il padróne del cavállo, "è più d' un ánno che quésto cavállo mi appartiéne; dúnque non è il vóstro: può éssere, però, che gli rassomígli quálche póco."

Il contadíno copérse súbito gli ócchi del cavállo cólle súe máni, e dísse: "Ebbéne, se l' animále vi appartiéne da tánto témpo, dítemi un póco, di qual ócchio égli è ciéco?"

L' áltro, il quále infátti avéva rubáto il cavállo sénza esaminárlo da présso, rimáse sbigottíto un moménto. Dovéndo però díre quálche cósa, égli rispóse all' avventúra: "Dell' ócchio sinístro!"

"V' ingannáte," rispóse il contadíno, "il cavállo non è ciéco dell' ócchio sinístro!" — "Eh!" sclamò il fúrbo, "ho fátto úno sbáglio di língua; il cavállo è ciéco dell' ócchio déstro."

Allóra il contadíno scopérse gli ócchi del cavállo e dísse: "È evidénte óra che séi ládro e bugiárdo. Guardáte tútti! Il cavállo non è ciéco nè póco nè púnto. Gli ho fátto le dománde soltánto per iscopríre il fúrto."

Tútti gli astánti si mísero a rídere ed a báttere le máni,
bystanders   put   laugh   clap
gridándo: "È cólto, il fúrbo, è cólto."
crying: caught

EXERCISE FOR TRANSLATION.

1. If the best man was obliged to wear his faults written on his forehead, he would never dare to raise his hat.

2. A woman of Sparta said to her son, who had returned lame from battle, "At every step which you take, you will now remember your valor and your glory."

3. A man, who had dissipated his property, complained of the injury the hail had caused to his farms. A person, who knew the boaster well, said, "It is your own fault; for, if you had had the precaution to open your umbrella when it hailed, your farms would not have been injured.

4. The great Condé — tired of hearing a certain fop continually speak of monsieur, his father; madam, his mother; misses, his sisters — called one of his servants, and said to him, "Mister, my lackey, tell mister my coachman to harness messrs. my horses to madam my carriage."

5. A superstitious prince once dreamed that he saw three mice, — a fat one, a poor one, and a blind one. The prince consulted a sibyl, who said to him, "My prince, the fat mouse is your minister, the poor mouse is your people, and the blind mouse is your portrait."

VOCABULARY.

1. If he was obliged, *se dovésse;* written, *scrítti;* upon, *in;* to dare, *ardíre*.

2. Of Sparta, *Spartána;* return from, *tornáre da;* at every step, *ad ógni pásso;* you will remember, *rammenteréte*.

3. A man (a spendthrift), *úno spiantáto;* complained, *lagnávasi;* caused, *fátto;* farms, *podére;* boaster, *millantatóre;* it is your own fault, *la cólpa è vóstra;* it hailed, *si míse a grandináre;* injured, *danneggiáti*.

4. Tired of hearing, *annojáto d' inténdere;* fop, *sciócco vanaéllo;* Miss, *Signorína;* called, *chiamáva;* lackey, *staffiére;* tell, *díte;* harness, *attaccáre*.

5. Once, *úna vólta;* that he saw, *che víde;* consulted, *consultò*.

DEMONSTRATIVE ADJECTIVE PRONOUNS. 103

CONVERSAZIÓNE.

Chi è quésta dónna?
Dov' è il di léi ritrátto (picture)?
Chi avéte vedúto?
A chi scrivéte (write) *vói?*
Di chi è quésto cavállo?
Cóme viággia il Cónte?
María dórme ancóra?
Perchè tiéne élla gli ócchi chiúsi?
Si díce che il Signór E., è mórto, ha fátto un testaménto?

Avéte vedúto le míe sorélle?

Che voléte da me?

Signór Maéstro, desidereréi (I should like) *di avére da léi quálche lezióne di bállo,*

Úna cérta mía amíca.
Io lo pósi nélla súa cámera.
Ho vedúto la sorellína vóstra.
Álla mía cára fíglia.
Del mío staffiére.
Cólla própria carrózza.
Non dórme, no.
Tien (she keeps) *gli ócchi chiúsi* (closed) *per célia* (sport).
Sì, ha fátto di gran lásciti állo spédale; résta però al fíglio un bel património.
No Signóre, ho vedúto solaménte (only) *vóstro fratéllo.*
Non vóglio (wish) *niénte* (nothing) *da vói.*
Sóno prónto a servírla.

CHAPTER XVI.

DEMONSTRATIVE ADJECTIVE PRONOUNS.

MNEMONIC EXERCISE.

Sérvo di quésti, Signóri,	Your servant, gentlemen.
È capitáto quést' óggi,	He has arrived to-day.
Dite quánto vi páre,	Say all that you please.
Che maniére son quéste?	What manners are these?
Non è tútt' óro quél che lúce,	All is not gold that glitters.
Compráte quésto mío cavállo,	Buy my horse.
Quésto pánno è tróppo cáro,	This cloth is too dear.
Il mio débole parére è quésto,	That is my weak advice.
*Che vuól dir quésto?*¹	What does this mean?
Quésto si sa da tútti,	Everybody knows that.

È un seccatóre costúi,	This man is importunate.
Mandáte vía colóro,	Send those people away.
Scuotétevi da cotésta tristézza,	Shake off this sadness.
Quésto è quánto mi dísse,	This is all he said to me.
Chi è costúi?	Who is he?
L' uómo ascólta volentiéri quél che gli piáce,	A man willingly listens to what pleases him.
Quésto è quéllo che più di tútto m' affligge,	This is what afflicts me the most.
Mi renderéte ragióne di cotésti ingánni,	You shall account for having thus deceived me.
Quánti vívono in quésto móndo álle spése di quésto e di quéllo!	How many people in this world live at the expense of this one and that!
Non mi parláte più di colúi,	Speak no more to me of this man.
Costúi v' ingannerà di cérto,	This man will certainly cheat you.
Staséra vi aspetterò a cása,	This evening I shall expect you.
Maladétta sía quésta mía curiosità!	Cursed be my curiosity!
Quésta cása non è più vóstra,	This house no longer belongs to you.

DEMONSTRATIVE ADJECTIVE PRONOUNS.

I. *Quésto* and *quésta*, with their plurals *quésti* and *quéste*, signify <u>this</u> and <u>these</u>, or <u>this here</u> and <u>these here</u>, and indicate an object near to the person who speaks.

<u>Cotésto, cotésta</u>, with their plurals *cotésti, cotéste*, <u>this</u>, <u>these</u>, are used to point out an object near the person to whom we speak.

Quéllo, quélla, with their plurals *quélli, quélle*, that, those, that there, those there, indicate an object distant from the person who speaks;* as, —

---

* <u>In English</u>, we use the personal pronoun before the relative "who," "whom," or "that;" and, in Italian, we use the demonstrative instead; as, *Quélla che mi piácque tánto*, she whom I so much admired; *colúi che accatáva pélle strade*, he that begged in the streets. *Quésto, cotésto, quéllo*, are frequently represented by *ciò*; as, *Ciò è véro*, that is true.

Take this book, and give me that,	Pigliáte quésto libro, e dátemi quéllo,
I see that thief who has stolen from me,	Védo quél ládro che m' ha rubáto.
This dress becomes you very well,	Cotésto vestito vi sta benóne.
I prefer this room to that,	Preferisco quésta cámera a quélla.

II. *Quésto* refers to the object last named in a phrase, and *quéllo* to that first mentioned; as,—

Riches and poverty are alike injurious: the former creates too many wants; the latter hardly permits the knowledge of them,	La ricchézza e la povertà son del pári nocévoli: quélla fa náscere tróppi bisógni; quésta non permétte di conoscérne quási alcúno.

III. "In the mean while," "during this time," is expressed by *in quésto méntre, in quésto mézzo,* or, abridged, *in quésto, in quésta;* and in the same sense, but referring to a more distant epoch, the Italians say, *in quél mézzo, in quél méntre,* or *in quéllo*.

IV. "That which" is translated by *ciò che* or *quél che;* as,—

He will do what (that which) I tell him,	Égli farà quél che gli dirò or ciò che gli dirò io.
All that (that which) pleases the eyes pleases the heart,	Tútto ciò che piáce, or quánt piáce ágli ócchi, piáce al cuóre.

V. The demonstrative adjective may be added to the possessive pronoun in Italian; as, *Lasciáte stáre quésta mía pénna, e scrivéte con cotésta vóstra.* This, literally translated, signifies, "Leave this pen which is near me, and which belongs to me, and write with that which is near you, and which belongs to you."

VI. Instead of saying *quésta mattína, quésta séra, quésta nótte,* this morning, this evening, this night, the Italians say, for abbreviation, *stamattína* or *stamáne, staséra, stanótte*.

VI. *Tále*, such, often replaces the demonstrative pronoun *quésto* or *quéllo*. Thus we can say, *tále considerazióne*, instead of *quésta considerazióne*, provided that the idea has been specified in the anterior phrase.

VIII. Speaking of persons in an absolute sense, the Italians say, —

Costúi, this man here; *Colúi*, that man there.
Costéi, this woman here; *Coléi*, that woman there.
Costóro, these men or women here; *Colóro*, those women there.

Sometimes these pronouns are transposed, and the preposition omitted.

Per lo colúi consíglio,   By the advice of that man.
Per la costúi dappocággine,   By the stupidity of this man.

Instead of *Pel consíglio di colúi, per la dappocággine di costúi.*

IX. *Quésti, quégli, quéi, cotésti*, are also used in speaking of a man; as, *Quésti fu dótto; quégli, ignoránte*, this man was learned; that, ignorant. These words are used only in the singular, and may likewise be applied to animals and inanimate things personified; as in this quotation from Boccaccio: *Dáll' úna párte mi tráe l' amóre, e dáll' áltra, mi tráe giustíssimo sdégno; quégli vuóle ch' io ti perdóni, e quésti vuóle, che cóntro a mía natúra in te incrudelísca,* On one side love influences me; and, on the other, a just anger: that wishes that I would pardon thee; and this, that I, contrary to my nature, should be cruel to thee.

READING LESSON.

La política di un príncipe è l' árte di conserváre quéllo che ha, o di usurpáre quéllo che non ha.

Diógene un giórno víde un giovinétto che arrosíva: "ánimo,
           youth   blushed:
figliuólo mío," díss' égli, "cotésto è il colóre délla virtù."

Non v' è pópolo cólto che créda di cédere ágli áltri in génere
         cultivated   to cede

DEMONSTRATIVE ADJECTIVE PRONOUNS.

di língua, benchè tútti convéngano nélle qualità che ne fórmano
     although   agree
la perfezióne, il che è un ségno che ognúno ha quél che gli
básta, no sente quel che gli mánca.
 sufficient   feels   is wanting.
Un contadíno tagliáva un álbero álla ríva d' un fiúme; per
    was cutting   margin   river
mála sórte la scúre gli cádde nell' ácqua, nè potè ritrovárla.
 ill luck axe   fell   could he
Mercúrio gli appárve: "È quésta la túa scúre, galantuómo?"
     appeared
mostrándogliene úna d' óro. "No, cotésta scúre non è la mía."—
 showing him
"È fórse quésta," porgéndogliene úna d' argénto. "No, cotésta
      presenting
non è áncora quélla che mi appartiéne."—"È quésta dúnque?"
         belongs.
mostrándogliene úna di férro, che éra veraménte quélla che avéa
       iron
perdúta. "Ecco veraménte quélla scúre la cúi pérdita mi afflig-
ge."—"Préndi quésta e ancóra le dúe príme che ti ho mostráte;
    take
ricévile in prémio délla túa sincerità. La probità è la migliórc
receive them   honesty
política."
policy.

EXERCISE FOR TRANSLATION.

1. Merit depends on neither titles nor manners: these depend on ourselves; those, on chance.

2. An English banker was accused of having plotted a conspiracy to carry off George III., and conduct him to Philadelphia. "I know very well," said he to the judges, "what a king can make of a banker; but I do not know what a banker can make of a king."

3. A considerable sum of money had been stolen from a lord. He, suspecting that it was one of his domestics, called them all one morning, and said to them, "My friends, the Angel Gabriel appeared to me last night, and told me that the thief should have a parrot's feather on the end of his nose." At these words,

the guilty man immediately put his hand to his nose. "It is you, villain, who have stolen from me!" said the master: "the Angel Gabriel came to tell me of it." In this manner he recovered his money.

4. Lent is never long to him who is obliged to pay at Easter.

VOCABULARY.

1. Depends on, *dipénde da*.
2. Was accused, *vénne accusáto*; plotted, *tramáto*; to carry off, *rapíre*; *Giórgio*; a *Filadélfia*; I know, so, *so*; can, *può*; I do not know, *non so*.
3. Considerable, *ragguardévole*; suspecting, *sospettándo*; domestic, *servitóre*; called, *chiamò*; end, *púnta*; guilty, *réo*; put his hand on his nose, *si tócca il náso*; villain, *mariuólo*; recovered, *riébbe*.
4. Is obliged (has) to pay, *ha da pagáre*; Easter, *pásqua*.

CONVERSAZIÓNE.

Che víde Diógene un giórno?
Cósa díss' égli?
Dóve tagliáva un contadíno un álbero?
Avéa égli dúe scúri?
Che gli accádde?

La ritrovò?
Chi gli appárve?
Che dísse égli?

Che rispóse il contadíno?
"Fórse è quésta d' argénto?"

"È dúnque quésta di férro?"
Che dísse Mercúrio allóra?

Qual' è la política di un príncipe?

Un giovinétto che arrosíva.
"Ánimo, figliuólo mío."
Alla ríva d' un fiúme.

No, non ne avéa che úna.
Per mála sórte gli cádde la scúre nell' ácqua.
Non potéva ritrovárla.
Mercúrio.
"È quésta la túa?" mostrándogli úna scúre d' óro.
"No, cotésta scúre non è la mía."
"No, cotésta non è ancóra quélla che mi appartiéne."
"Veraménte, quésta è la mia."
"La probità è la miglióre política."
È l' árte di conserváre quéllo che ha, o di usurpáre quéllo che non ha.

CHAPTER XVII.

INDEFINITE ADJECTIVE PRONOUNS.

MNEMONIC EXERCISE.

Ógni rósa ha la súa spína, — Every rose has its thorns.
Andáte con TÚTTA frétta, — Go with all haste.
La fortúna govérna ÓGNI cósa, — Fortune governs every thing.
Véngo da párte di TÚTTI lóro, — I come from them all.
QUALÚNQUE fática mérita prémio, — Every exertion deserves reward.
La pósta párte ÓGNI dì per l' Itália, — The mail leaves every day for Italy.
Mi vi tratténni ALCÚNE settimáne, — I stopped there some weeks.
Spendéte il témpo in QUÁLCHE útile occupazióne, — Spend your time in some useful occupation.
La mórte è il fíne di TÚTTE le sciagúre, — Death is the end of all our misfortunes.
QUALÚNQUE síano le míe ragióni, — Whatsoever be my reasons.
Starò in cása per TÚTTO quést' óggi, — I shall be at home all day.
TÚTTO il mále non víen per nuócere, — All is for the best.
È pazzía il volér sapére TÚTTO, — It is a folly to wish to know (all) every thing.
Lo sapréte in TÚTT' ÁLTRA guísa, — You will know it in a very different way.

I. Of indefinite pronouns, the following are used only in the singular, and cannot be put before nouns in the plural number: —

Quálche, m. and f. . . . . some, any.
Ógni,* m. and f. . . . . all, every.
Chiúnque, m. and f. . . . . . . whoever, whosoever.

---

* With ógni are formed the words ognidì, every day; ognóra, always; ognúno, every one. Ógni, before numeral adjectives, as in the phrases, ógni dúe mési, every two months; ógni sèi págine, every six pages; ógni diéci soldáti, every ten soldiers; and in the word ognissánti, the day of All-saints, — is used with nouns in the plural.

Chisivóglia, m. and f.		whoever, whosoever.
Chi che, m. and f.		,, ,,
Chicchessía, m. and f.		,, ,,
Che che, m. and f.		whatever, whatsoever.
Checchessía, m. and f.		,, ,,
Qualúnque, m. and f.		whosoever, whatsoever.
Qualsivóglia, m. and f.		,, ,,
Qualsisía, m. and f.		,, ,,
Núlla, m. and f.		nothing.
Niénte, m. and f.		,,
Úno, m.	*úna*, f.	one.
Un'áltro, m.	*un'áltra*, f. . .	another.
Qualcúno, m.	*qualcúna*, f. . . .	some, some one, somebody
Qualchedúno, m.	*qualchedúna*, f. .	,, ,, ,, ,,
Ognúno, m.	*ognúna*, f.	every one, everybody.
Ciascúno, m.	*ciascúna*, f. . .	,, ,, ,,
Ciaschedúno, m.	*ciaschedúna*, f. . .	,, ,, ,,
Verúno, m.	*verúna*, f. . . .	no one, nobody.
Nessúno, m.	*nessúna*, f. . . .	,, ,, ,,
or *Nissúno*, m.	*nissúna*, f. . . .	,, ,, ,,
Neúno, m.	*neúna*, f. . . .	,, ,, ,,
or *Niúno*, m.	*niúna*, f. . . .	,, ,, ,,
Núllo, m.	*núlla*, f. . . .	,, ,, ,,

II. The following are used in both numbers: —

SINGULAR.

Tále, m. and f.		such.
Cotále, m. and f.		such, such a one.
Alcúno, m.	*alcúna*, f. . . .	some, some one, somebody
Talúno, m.	*talúna*, f. . . .	,, ,, ,, ,,
Cérto, m.	*cérta*, f. . . .	certain.
Stésso, m.	*stéssa*, f. . . .	same.
Medésimo, m.	*medésima*, f. . .	,,
Áltro, m.	*áltra*, f.	other.
Tutto, m.	*tútta*, f.	all.
Alquánto, m.	*alquánta*, f. . .	a little, somewhat.
Tánto, m.	*tánta*, f. . . .	so much.
Cotánto, m.	*cotánta*, f. . . .	,, ,,
Altrettánto, m.	*altrettánta*, f. . .	as much, as much **more.**
Póco, m.	*póca*, f. . . .	a little, a few.
Mólto, m.	*mólta*, f. . . .	much,
Tróppo, m	*tróppa*, f. . . .	too much.

INDEFINITE ADJECTIVE PRONOUNS. 111

PLURAL.

Táli, m. and f.		such.
Cotáli, m. and f.		such, such ones.
Alcúni, m.	alcúne, f.	some, some ones.
Talúni, m.	talúne, f.	,, ,, ,,
Cérti, m.	cérte, f.	certain.
Stéssi, m.	stésse, f.	same.
Medésimi, m.	medésime, f.	,,
Altri, m.	áltre, f.	others.
Tútti, m.	tútte, f.	all, every one, everybody.
Alquánti, m.	alquánte, f.	a few, not many.
Tánti, m.	tánte, f.	as many.
Cotánti, m.	cotánte, f.	,, ,,
Altrettánti, m.	altrettánte, f.	as many, as many more.
Póchi, m.	póche, f.	few.
Mólti, m.	mólte, f.	many.
Tróppi, m.	tróppe, f.	too many.

III. *Chiúnque, chisivóglia, chi che, chicchessía, qualcúno, qualchedúno, ognúno, talúno*, are applied to persons only: the others may be applied both to persons and things.

IV. "Every," and the word "all" meaning "every," are translated by *ógni* or *qualúnque*, which are always in the singular, and serve for the masculine and feminine; as,—

Every king, every queen,   *Ógni re, ógni regína.*
Every merit, every pain,   *Ógni mérito, ógni péna.*

Or *qualúnque re, qualúnque regína, qualúnque mérito, qualúnque péna*, etc. We can also say, *ciascúno re, ciascúna regína*, etc.; *ciascúno* agreeing in gender with its noun.

V. "All," and "the whole," expressing a collective sense, are rendered by *tútto*, and agree with the noun; as,—

All the people, the whole city,   *Tútto il pópolo, tútta la città.*
All hearts, all nations,   *Tútti i cuori, tútte le naziόni.*

The inversion, *il pópolo tútto, la città tútta*, etc., is much used, and is very pretty.

VI. The Italianisms *tútto quánto, tútta quánta,* with their plurals, express collectively all the parts of a whole; as, —

La cósa è brucciáta tútta quánta,	The entire house is burned.
Oggi vi aspétto a pránzo tútti quánti,	To-day I expect you all (as many as you are) to dinner.
Trémo tútto quánto,	I tremble all over (from head to foot).

VII. "All," when it means "every thing," may be translated by *tútto,* or by *ógni cósa,* according to euphony; as, —

Idleness renders all (every thing) difficult,	*La pigrízia fa parér diffícile ógni cósa,* or *fa parér tútto diffícile.*

VIII. "All," used as an adverb, and signifying "entirely," is often rendered thus: *La faccénda è bélla e finíta, la cósa è bélla e fátta, le návi sóno bélle e apparecchiáte,* the affair is entirely finished, the thing is all done, the vessels are all ready.

IX. "No," "no one," is translated by *nessúno, niúno, verúno,* or by *alcúno* employed only as the object (*alcúno* as the subject signifies "some one"). Any of these Italian words, when put after the verb, requires *non* before it; as, —

No country is more beautiful than Tuscany,	*Verún paése è più béllo délla Toscána.*
I never saw that anywhere,	*Non ho vedúto quésto in alcúna párte.*

X. "Some" is translated by *quálche* or *alcúno* (plural *alcúni* or *alquánti*), and not by *quálchi;* as, —

He has been gone some time,	*È partíto già da quálche témpo.*
We have some books,	*Abbiámo alcúni líbri.*
I have some of them,	*Ne ho alquánti.*

XI. "Such" is rendered by *tále* or *cotále;* as, —

I have seen such a person,	*Ho vedúto quél tále.*
He has such a face as does not please me,	*Égli ha úna tál céra che non mi piáce.*

INDEFINITE ADJECTIVE PRONOUNS.

READING LESSON.

Ógni sécolo, ógni época, ógni età, ógni paése, divién célebre
                                                                                  becomes
per quálche nuóva scopérta; il témpo presénte aggiúnge
                    discovery   adds
sémpre quálche cósa al témpo passáto.

Se la pazzía fósse un dolóre, si sentirébbero laménti in tútto
                         were   should hear
le cáse.

Ógni língua, per se stéssa, è intraducíbile, per motívo del súo
                                  untranslatable
caráttere particoláre, che è il frútto del clíma, del govérno, del
génio, dégli stúdj e délle occupazióni dei pópoli.

Pope asserísce francaménte che dópo la língua gréca, verúna
     declares
língua ha un' armonía così imitatíva cóme la língua ingléso:
comúnque sía, nessúno è obbligáto a crédergli.
however that may be

L' educazióne vária quási in ógni paése; ógni uómo assennáto
procúra di adattársi álle usánze esisténti nel sito in cúi si
endeavors   adapt   existing
tróva.
finds himself.

Sénza úna buóna educazióne, il dótto non è áltri che un pedánte, il filósofo un cínico, il soldáto un brúto, e ógni uómo
qualsisía sarà spiacevolíssimo.

Non v'è pazzía la quále, per quánto stravagánte éssere póssa,
                                                                   it may be
non sía córsa per la ménte a quálche filósofo.
may be passed

EXERCISE FOR TRANSLATION.

1. No farmer is pleased to have grain cheap, no soldier is pleased with peace in his country, nor an architect with the solidity of houses, nor a doctor with the health of his friends.

2. After the defeat of Perseus, king of Macedon, Paulus Emilius poured such a quantity of silver into the public treasury, that the people were not obliged to pay any tribute during the space of a hundred and five years. Useful and glorious victories!

3. Newton was born on the same day that Galileo died; as if Nature had not wished to have any interval between these two philosophers.

4. A philosopher, who had the misfortune to live under a tyrant, was in the habit of feeling his neck every morning on awaking, to see if his body was still attached to it.

VOCABULARY.

1. Is pleased, *si compiáce di;* nor, *nè.*
2. *Pérseo; Macedónia; Paólo Emílio;* poured, *versò;* such, *tánta;* during, *per.*
3. As if, *quási;* had not wished to have, *non avésse volúto lasciáre.*
4. To live, *vívere;* under, *sótto;* was in the habit, *soléva;* of feeling, *di tastársi;* on awaking, *destándosi;* was still attached, *vi stáva ancóra attaccáto.*

CONVERSAZIÓNE.

È ógni língua traducíbile?
Che disse Pope della língua inglése?
Cóme i divérsi paési divéntano célebri?
Aggiúnge il témpo presénte al témpo passáto?
Che è il dótto sénza úna buóna educazióne?
Cósa è il filósofo sénza educazióne?
Perchè?

In che giórno nácque Newton?

Di che è frútto il caráttere d' úna lingua?

No, per se stéssa è intraducíbile.
Verúna língua ha un' armonía così imitatíva.
Diventáno célebri per quálche nuóva scopérta.
Il témpo presénte vi aggiunge sémpre quálche cósa.
Égli non è áltro che un pedánte.

È un cínico.

Perchè ha un caráttere particoláre.

Néllo stésso giórno in cúi morì il Galiléo.

È il frútto del clíma, del govérno, dégli stúdj e délle occupazióni déi pópoli.

CHAPTER XVIII.

INDEFINITE ADJECTIVE PRONOUNS.
(*Continued.*)

MNEMONIC EXERCISE.

Non bisógna rubáre l' ALTRÚI,	We must not rob the property of *others*.
NIÉNTE facéndo, s' impára a fár mále,	Doing *nothing*, one learns to do evil.
Dópo il fátto, OGNÚNO è buón consigliére,	After the deed, *every one* is a good adviser.
Schiávo ALTRÚI si fa chi díce il súo segréto,	He who reveals his secret becomes the slave of *others*.
Ha da ésser prívo di ógni difétto chi vuól censuráre gli ALTRÚI,	He who wishes to criticise the defects of *others* should himself be free from them.
È padróne délla víta ALTRÚI chi sprézza la súa,	He is master of the lives of others who despises his own.
Gli farò parláre da QUALCHEDÚNO,	I will have him spoken to by *some one*.
OGNÚNO è l' amíco dell' uómo che regála,	*Every one* is the friend of the man who makes presents.
V' è in CIASCÚN di nói quálche séme di pazzía,	In *every one* of us there is some germ of folly.
NIÚNO è proféta nélla sua pátria,	*No one* is a prophet in his own country.
Un malvágio felíce non fa invídia a NESSÚNO,	*Nobody* envies a happy wicked person.
Il péggio che póssa fársi è il nón fár NÚLLA,	The worst thing that one can do, is to do *nothing*.
Il páne d' ÁLTRI sémpre sa di sále,	The bread of *others* is always bitter.
Non mi sénto NIÉNTE affátto béne,	I do not feel well at *all*.
Non conviéne beffársi di NESSÚNO,	We should make fun of *no one*
Non fáte ingiúrie a CHICCHESSÍA,	Injure *no one* whosoever.

I. *Altrúi*, with the article, signifies "the property of others;" as, —

È un ladronéccio l' usurpáre l' altrúi,   It is a theft to usurp the goods of others.

II. "One" and "another" are translated by *gli úni, gli áltri;* as, Fortune humbles one, and exalts another, *la fortúna abbássa gli úni, e innálza gli áltri.*

III. The above sentence may be differently constructed; as, Some ascend, others descend: thus go the wheels of fortune, *Chi sále, chi scénde,* or *áltri sále, áltri scénde,* or *quál sále, quál scénde,* or *quésti sále, quégli scénde: così va la ruóta délla fortúna.*

IV. For the correct use of all these forms, the choice of which depends on taste guided by the ear, we must remember, first, that *chi*, and sometimes *quále*, may be repeated many times; second, that the word *áltri** and *quégli,* without an article, are pronouns in the singular, indicating a person.

V. "Nothing" is rendered by *niénte* or *núlla*. The negation *non* is used when one of these words comes after the verb; as, —

It is better to labor without an object than to do nothing,   È méglio lavoráre sénza scópo che il non fár núlla.

He who observes nothing, learns nothing,   Chi núlla ossérva, núlla impára; or, chi non ossérva núlla, non impára núlla.

VI. *Niénte* or *núlla* without *non*, expressed or understood, means "something," "any thing:" in which case it is generally placed after the verb, if governed by it; as,

S' io pósso far núlla per vói, comandátemi,   If I can do any thing for you, command me.

---

* *Altri* is a word very much used in elegant style, and must not be confounded with *gli áltri*, which means "the others."

This word, as well as *chi*, belongs to persons: *quále* refers to persons and things; as in this verse of Petrarca: "*Quál si posáva in térra, e quál su l' ónde,*" some (flowers) were on the earth, others upon the waves. These words all require the verb in the singular.

VII. The word "nothing," employed negatively, may sometimes be translated by *che;* the verb being preceded by *non,* and sometimes by *cósa.*

The idle have nothing to do,	*I pígri non hánno che fáre.*
He who is innocent has nothing to fear,	*Chi è innocénte non ha che temére.*

VIII. *Núlla* and *niénte* are sometimes used with an article; as, Sempronio rose from nothing, *Semprónio è sórto dal núlla.* The following phrases are thus translated: —

He is a man of nothing,	*È un uómo di niénte.*
A man good for nothing,	*Un uómo da niénte.*
He has quarrelled with us for a trifle,	*S'è corrucciáto con nói per un nulla,* or *per úna bagattélla.*
This man is nothing to me,	*Non ho alcúna affinitù,* or *relazióne con lúi.*

IX. *Si* is generally considered as an indefinite pronoun, and is used both for the masculine and feminine gender, singular and plural: it is equivalent to the English words "one," "we," "people," "they;" as, —

Cóme si è détto,	As we have said.
Si parláva di guérra,	People talked of war.
Si loderà mólto il súo corággio,	They will praise his courage very much.
Si véde che siéte un galantuómo,	One sees that you are a gentleman.

But, in these and similar phrases, *si* holds the place of a passive proposition, and may be equally well rendered in English by "it is," "it was," "it will be;" as, —

Si credévi così generalménte,	It was generally so believed.
Si dice che la páce è già fermáta,	It is said that the peace is already concluded.

X. *Non,* when used in a sentence expressing an indefinite meaning, is always placed at the commencement; as, *Non si può fár núlla,* one can do nothing.

XI. "To us," "to you," is rendered by *ci, vi,* and is placed before the indefinite pronoun *si;* but "of it," "of him," "of her," "of them," is translated by *ne,* and is placed after *si,* which is changed into *se;* as,—

    They do not speak to you,   *Non vi si párla.*
    They do not speak of it,   *Non se ne párla.*

XII. The indefinite pronoun cannot be translated by *si* when it is followed by the reflective pronoun *si,* as *si si* would not be euphonious. It is then necessary to adopt another form, according to the sense of the phrase. Thus, to translate "Man believes himself happy when he lives in opulence, but he deceives himself," we can say, *Úno* or *tále* or *áltri* or *l' uómo si créde felíce quándo víve néll' opulénza, ma s' ingánna;* or *gli uómini,* or *alcúni si crédono felíci quándo éssi vívono nell' opulénza;* or *nói ci crediámo felíci quándo viviámo néll' opulénza, ma c' inganniámo.*

READING LESSON.

O vói, chiúnque siáte, povéri o rícchi, pópoli o príncipi,
               you may be
ricordátevi che la fálce délla mórte miéte néll' úmile capánna
remember   harvests
cóme néi supérbi palági.

   Un gentiluómo éra travagliáto dálla podágra. Tútti gli
                           tormented
consigliávano di lasciár l' úso délle cárni saláte, ma égli rispon
advised   leave off   salted
déva che néi dolóri délla súa malattía éra assái conténto di
potérsela pigliáre con quálche cósa, e che arrabbiándosi quándo
to be able   to blame   getting angry
col presciútto e quándo col salúme si sentíva béllo e confortáto.
                                            felt

   Néi paési dispótici si sóffre mólto e si grída póco; néi paési
                           suffers   complains
úberi, si sóffre póco e si grída mólto.

INDEFINITE ADJECTIVE PRONOUNS.

I grándi sóno cóme quéi mulíni erétti súlle montágne, i quáli
<small>erected</small>
non dánno farína se non quándo si dà lóro del vénto.
<small>give   gives</small>
Alcúni si divertívano in cása di úna signóra a trovàre délle differénze ingegnóse da un oggétto ad un áltro. "Quál differénza," dísse la Signóra, "si potrébbe fáre fra me ed un oriuólo."—
<small>could   make</small>
"Signóra," égli le rispóse, "un oriuólo índica le óre, e apprésso
<small>near</small>
di vói, si diménticano."
<small>forgets.</small>

EXERCISE FOR TRANSLATION.

1. There is not a man who can say, I have need of no one.
2. There is nothing more dangerous than to have for enemies those whom we have laden with benefits.
3. Every man may presume with reason, that no one can ever attain to a perfect knowledge of all the secrets and all the riches of nature.
4. The same deed, the same word, awakens remembrances agreeable to some, and sad to others. Whosoever looked at Caligula's forehead, excited in him sudden anger, because this action reminded him of his baldness, which he wished to conceal from everybody; but he who looked at the forehead of Scipio Africanus, gave him great pleasure, because he had a warlike wound there, — a witness of his valor and his glory.
5. Some one, in speaking of a tyrant who enjoyed the reputation of liberality, said, "Judge how much liberality dominates in this man; who gives not only his own spoils, but even those of others."
6. Envy is certainly the basest and the most cruel of all the passions, since there is hardly any person who may not have in himself something to excite the passion of the envious.
7. Never do to others that which you would not wish others should do to you.
8. One day a lady wrote to her husband this letter, which may serve for a perfect model of laconism: "Having nothing to do, I write to you: having nothing to say to you, I finish."

VOCABULARY.

1. There is not, *non v' è;* can, *póssa;* need, *bisógno.*
2. Laden with benefits, *beneficáto.*
3. May, *può;* presume, *presúmere;* attain, *perveníre.*
4. Same deed, *stésso, fátto;* awakens, *svéglia;* looked at, *guardáva;* excited in him sudden anger, *suscitáva in lúi súbito sdégno;* reminded him of, *gli rammentáva;* to conceal, *nascóndere; Scipióne l' Africáno;* great pleasure, *magnánimo piacére;* warlike, *marziále.*
5. Judge, *pensáte;* dominates, *régna;* not only, *non solaménte*, gives, *dóna;* his own spoils, *la róba súa;* even, *ancóra.*
6. There is hardly, *v' è quási;* to excite, *da suscitáre;* envious, *invidióso.*
7. Never do, *non fáte;* wish, *vorréste.*
8. Wrote, *scrísse;* may serve, *può servíre;* I write, *scrívo.*

CONVERSAZIÓNE.

Con chi siéte venúto?
Con nessúno.

Avéte áltre amiche?
Non ne ho áltre.

Chi ha détto ciò?
Ognúno lo díce.

Sóno le vóstre dúe sorélle rícche?
L' úna è rícca, l' áltra e póvera.

Cóme sóno i commandánti?
Gelósi gli úni dégli áltri.

Voléte (will you) *avér quálche cósa?*
No, vi ringrázio (thank you), *non vóglio niénte.*

Qualcúno pícchia, andáte a vedére chi è?
È la Signora K.

Non crédesi che avrémo (shall have) *la páce?*
Non è probábile.

Avéte ritrováto le léttere perdúte?
Ne ho ritrováte alcúne, ma la maggiór párte sóno perdúte.

Sóno fratélli quésti dúe uómini?
Non so (I do not know); *si rassomigliano* (resemble) *l' úno all' áltro.*

Che si díce (say) *di nuóvo?*
Non ho létto (read) *néssun giornále óggi, ma si díce che ci sóno cattíve núove.*

Dóve l' avéte intéso?
In cása d' un amíco e per via d' úna léttera priváta.

CHAPTER XIX.

THE PREPOSITIONS *DI, A, DA.*

A thorough acquaintance with these prepositions is absolutely necessary, and therefore requires the attention of the pupil: first, because the English and Italians differ somewhat in the use of them; and, second, because they are the signs which establish the connection between our ideas, and the slightest error in their interpretation would entirely change the sense of a phrase.*

MNEMONIC EXERCISE.

Io són DEL vóstro parére,	I am of your opinion.
Vói mi pagáte DI cattiva monéta,	You pay me with ingratitude.
Il móndo va DA sè stésso,	The world goes by itself.
Si è cacciáto A rídere,	He burst out laughing.
Le Álpi separano l'Itália DÁLLA Fráncia,	The Alps separate Italy from France.
La pólvere da cannóne fu inventáta DA un fráte,	Gunpowder was invented by a friar.
Vói non avéte ragióne DA far valére,	You have no good reason to give.
Andáte A vedére che cósa c' è,	Go, see what it is.
Vói mi trattáte per DA piú che sóno,	You do me more honor than I deserve.
Io ho détto DA schérzo e vói fáte davvéro,	I said it in joke, and you took it in earnest.
Dátemi la mía véste DA cámera e il berrettíno DA nótte,	Give me my night-gown and night-cap.
DÁLL' ópera si conósce il maéstro,	We know the master by the work.
Siéte vói maritáta o DA maritáre?	Are you married, or to be married?
È venúto nessúno A domandáre di me?	Has no one come to ask for me?

---

* Observe that some of the prepositions govern one, two, or three cases.

PREPOSITIONS IN COMMON USE.

*Di,**	of.	*Accánto,*	aside, about, near, by.
A,†	to, in, at.	*Alláto,*	,, ,, ,, ,,
Da,‡	from, by, on, at.	*Attórno,*	about, around.
In,§	in, on, upon.	*Dattórno,*	,, ,,
Con,	with.	*Addósso,*	on, upon, about.
Per,	through, by, on account of, in order to, for.	*Présso,*	near, almost.
		Apprésso,	,, ,,
		Vicíno,	,, ,,
Su,	on, upon.	*Lúngi,*	far, from.
Sópra,	,, ,,	*Lontáno,*	,, ,,
Sotto,	under.	*Áppo,‖*	at, with, in comparison with.
Fra,	amongst, within.		
Tra,	,, ,,	*Vérso,¶*	towards.
Ínfra,	in, in about.	*Óltra,*	beyond, besides.
Íntra,	,, ,, ,,	*Óltre,*	,, ,,
Príma,	before.	*Lúngo,*	along.
Dópo,	after.	*Fíno,*	till, until, as far as
Ánzi,	before, in presence of.	*Síno,*	,, ,, ,, ,, ,,
Innánzi,	,, ,, ,, ,,	*Infíno,*	,, ,, ,, ,, ,,
Dinánzi,	,, ,, ,, ,,	*Insíno,*	,, ,, ,, ,, ,,
Avánti,	,, ,, ,, ,,	*Cóntra,***	against.
Davánti,	,, ,, ,, ,,	*Cóntro,*	,,
Diétro,	behind.	*A-frónte,††*	opposite.
Didiétro,	,,	*Rimpétto,*	,,
Éntro,	in, within.	*Dirimpétto,*	,,
Déntro,	,, ,,	*Sénza,‡‡*	without.
Fuóra,	out of, without, besides.	*Sálvo,*	except, excepted.
Fuóri,	,, ,, ,, ,,	*Eccétto,*	,, ,,
Infuóri,	except, excepted.	*Tránne,*	,, ,,

The pupil is requested to commit to memory the phrases given under the various prepositions.

---

* From the Celtic *de*, a sign of qualification.
† From the Celtic *a*, near, joining with.
‡ From the Celtic *da*, at.
§ From the Celtic *en*, in.
∥ From the Latin *apud*, Celtic *ap*, joint, attached.
¶ From the Latin *versus*, Celtic *gwero*, to turn.
** From the Celtic *con*, a sign of opposition; and *track,* side.
†† From the Latin *frons*, Celtic *fron*, before.
‡‡ And *sánza* and *san* (used by old writers). From the Latin *sine*, Celtic *sy*, want privation. — *Bachi*.

DI.*

I. *Domandáre di úno, domandáre la presénza di úno*, to ask the presence of some one; *fár d'ócchio, fáre un cénno d'ócchio*, to make a sign of the eye; *far di cappéllo, fáre un salúto di cappéllo*, to salute with the hat; *dáre di pénna, dáre un cólpo di pénna*, to efface with the pen; *dáre del briccóne, dáre il títolo di briccóne*, to treat as a villain; *puníre di mórte, puníre cólla péna di mórte*, to punish with penalty of death; *accusáre di fúrto, accusáre per delítto di fúrto*, to accuse of theft.

II. Many adverbial phrases are formed with the preposition *di*; such as *di ráro*, rarely; *di soppiátto, di nascósto*, in secret; *di cérto*, certainly; *di frésco, di nuóvo*, newly; etc.

A.

III. The preposition *a*, in Italian, is a sign of the dative: it is used to mark the object towards which the action or the intention of the subject is directed. It expresses the idea of tendency of action, of attribution, or of proximity to a place or person; as,—

Égli vénne A trovármi,	He came to me.
Mandáre A vedére, A cercáre,	To send to see, to find.
Avvicinársi AD úno,	To approach some one.
Appoggiársi AD úno,	To lean upon some one.
Appoggiársi AL múro,	To lean against the wall.
Vicíno AL fuóco, AL létto,	Near the fire, the bed.
AL témpo di Noè,	At the time of Noah.
Voltársi AD úno,	To turn to a person.
Andáre ALLA vólta di Miláno,	To go towards Milan.
Pórre ménte AD ógni cósa,	To pay attention to every thing.
Passáre ALL' áltra párte délla stráda,	To go on the other side of the street.

It will be seen that all the verbs of motion, which express a direction towards some object, are followed by the preposition *a*.

---

* The preposition *di* may express a relation of possession, of extraction, or of qualification, as in English.

IV. There are many other expressions in Italian in which the preposition *a* is likewise employed; such as—

Tagliáre A *fétte,*	To cut in slices.
Andáre A *dúe a dúe,*	To go two by two.
Morívano A *migliáia,*	They died by thousands.
Imparáre A *ménte,*	To learn by heart.
Stáre ALL' *érta,**	To be upon one's guard.
Andáre, parláre AL *búio,*	To walk, to speak in the dark.
Tenéte le máni A *vói,*	Keep your hands off.
Stáre A *cápo chíno,* A *bócca apérta,*	To be with the head down, and mouth open.

V. The Italians say, adverbially, *álla sfuggíta,* by stealth; *all' impazzáta,* foolishly; *all' impensáta,* suddenly; *álla rinfúsa,* pell-mell; *álla peggío,* at the worst; *álla méglio,* at the best; ~~álla grósso,~~ nearly.

DA.

VI. *Da* is the sign of the ablative: it is used to express the point from which persons or things depart; as,—

Allontanársi DA *Parígi,*	To go from Paris.
Liberársi DA *un impégno,*	To get out of a difficulty.
I piacéri náscono DAI *bisógni,*	Pleasures spring from wants.
Separársi DÁLLA *famíglia,*	To separate from one's family.
Astenérsi DAL *rídere,* DAL *parláre,*	To abstain from laughing, from talking.
Riparársi DAL *vénto,* DÁLLA *pióggia,*	To shelter one's self from the wind and from the rain.
DALL' *ánno* or *sin* DÁLL' *ánno scórso,*	Since last year.
La carità comíncia DA *sè medésimo,*	Charity begins at home.
La móglie dipénde DAL *maríto,*	The wife depends on her husband.
Staccáre úna còsa DA *un áltra,*	To detach one thing from another.
Veníre DAL *teátro,* DA *cása,*	To come from the theatre, from the house.

---

* *All' érta.* This *all' érta* has given rise to the English word "alert."

Éssere incalzáto DAL *nemíco,*	To be pursued by the enemy.
Giudicáre DÁLLE *apparénze,*	To judge by appearances.
Andáte DA *quélla parte,*	Go on that side.
Che voléte DA *me?*	What do you wish of me?
Fáre úna cósa DA *sè,* or DA *per sè,*	To do a thing alone, or by one's self.
Guardársi DA *úno,*	To be on one's guard against one.
Distinguére il véro DAL *fálso,*	To distinguish the true from the false.
Cadér DA *cavállo,* DALL' *álbero,*	To fall from a horse, from a tree.
Diféndersi DÁGLI *ipócriti,* DÁI *ládri,* DAL *nemíco,*	To defend one's self against hypocrites, thieves, and enemies.

VII. The verbs *uscíre, veníre, muovére, levársi,* to go out, to come, to move, to rise, etc., sometimes take *di* for the sake of euphony, particularly when the article is not used; as, *Ésco di chiésa, si levò di távola,* I go out of church, he rose from the table. With the verb *cadére,* the Italians say, *Cadér di máno,** *di bócca,* to fall from the hand, from the mouth; but with the article, and, above all, in the plural, they say, *Uscír dálla chiésa, cadér dálle máni,* to go out of the church, to let fall from the hands.

VIII. "Out of" is translated by *fuór di,* because it sounds better than *fuór da;* as, *Fuóri di perícolo,* out of danger.

IX. *Da* is likewise used before words marking the **use, employment,** or **distinction** of a thing; as, —

Cárta DA *scrívere,*	writing-paper.
Cárta DA *léttere,*	letter-paper.
Ácqua DA *bére,*	water to drink.
Cása DA *véndere,*	house to sell.
Bótte DA *ólio,*	oil-cask.
Cámera DA *létto,*	bed-chamber.
Ragázza DA *maritáre,*	a marriageable girl.

---

* *Máno* admits of various significations in idiomatic phrases. (See list of idioms.)

X. *Da* is employed to express the idea of **aptitude**, etc.; as, —

Ármi DA difendérsi,	Arms proper for defence.
Non sóno cóse DA dírsi,	They are not things to be said.
L' erráre è DA uómo,	It is human to err.
Uómo DA mólto, DA póco, DA niénte, DA sténto,	A man fit for many things, for few things, for nothing, for fatigue.
Son cóse DA rídere,	They are things to cause laughter.
Non è cósa DA un pári vóstro,	It is not proper for such a man as you.
È una ragázza DA maríto,	A young lady of marriageable age.

XI. *Da* may be used in various other ways; as, —

Avéte DA fáre?	Have you something to do?
Dátemi DA lavoráre,	Give me something to do.
Veníte quà DA me,	Come here near me.
Díte DA búrla?	Do you say it in jest?
Díte DA véro, or DAvvéro?	Do you speak seriously?
Uómo DA béne, or DABbéne,	An honest man.
Andúte DAL fornáio,	Go to the baker's.
Andrò DA mia mádre,	I shall go to my mother's.
Víve DA Signóre,	He lives like a lord.
Ha trattáto DA birbánte,	He has behaved like a rogue.
Égli fa DA dottóre, da médico,	He plays the doctor, the physician.
Vi giúro DA galantuómo,	I swear to you upon the faith of a gentleman.

READING LESSON.

Napoleóne andáto a Miláno a fársi incoronáre re d' Itália,
          gone

visitò l' Università di Pávia. Égli si féce presentáre i professóri,
                                            made

e domandò di Scárpa. Gli fu détto che era státo depósto
                                    was said   was (had) been deposed

dálla súa cáttedra per non avér volúto prestáre giuraménto
                                  to have wished to take

al nuóvo govérno. Eh! che impórta, riprése Buonapárte, il
                                                          replied
giuraménto e le opinióni polítiche! Scárpa onóra l' Università
ed il mío státo.

Il nóme sólo di Róma è una stória di maravíglie che scálda il
                                                                                      warms
pétto ad ógni mortále. Térra dégli éroi, cápo del móndo
innánzi a léi sparírono nazióni, pópoli e città famóse, ed élla
before   disappeared
stétte e stà onóre e glória d' Itália, aspettándo che suóni l' óra
stood   stands   awaiting   may sound
d' úna nuóva grandézza.

Un giórno Brásidas trovò tra alcúni fíchi sécchi un sórcio, che
                           found
lo mórse si fattaménte che lo lasciò andár vía. Voi vedéte,
   bit   let   see
dísse a chi gli stáva intórno, che non v' è animalétto, il quále
                 stood
per píccolo che sía, non póssa scampár la víta óve ábbia il
              may be   can   save   may have
cuóre di difénders da chi l' assále.

EXERCISE FOR TRANSLATION.

1. If you wish to have a faithful servant, serve yourself.
2. "Deliver me from my friends," said a philosopher; "because I can defend myself against my enemies."
3. We should abstain from such truths as have the appearance of falsehood.
4. Amerigo Vespúcci, of Florence, made many discoveries in the New World in the year one thousand four hundred ninety-seven. Hence it was called America, from this navigator.
5. Princes ought to punish as princes, and not as executioners.
6. The knowledge of foreign languages serves to correct and perfect our own.
7. The changes of states, far from injuring, often aid in the rapid progress of civilization and the arts.
8. "From the evils which the barbarians brought into Italy," said Varchi, "two good things have come forth, — our Italian language, and the city of Venice."

VOCABULARY.

1. If you wish, *se voléte;* serve yourself, *servitevi da voi.*
2. Deliver me, *liberátemi;* I can (shall) defend, *difenderò.*
3. We should abstain, *conviéne astenérsi;* appearance, *fáccia.*
4. Made, *féce;* hence it was called, *che vénne quíndi chiamáto.*
5. Ought, *débbono.*
6. Our own, *la própria.*
7. Injuring (to injure), *nuócere;* aid, *gióvano.*
8. Brought, *portáti;* have come forth, *nácquero.*

CONVERSAZIÓNE.

Dóve andáte?	*Vádo al teátro.*
Con chi andáte?	*Con mio marito* (husband).
Che avéte da fáre,	*Non ho niénte da fáre.*
Dóve va il Dóttore?	*Égli va in campágna.*
Che avéte?	*Ho del caffè e úna focáccia.* cake
A chi sarà dedicáto quésto monuménto?	*Sarà dedicáto a Mozart.*
Dóve trováste voi (did you find) *i libri?*	*Io li trovái súlla távola.*
Cóme andávano (went) *i fanciúlli?*	*A dúe a dúe.*
Sóno le távole e le sédie nélla cámera?	*Si, sóno nélla cámera.*
Veníte da me óggi?	*Non pósso; non ésco* (go out) *di cása.*
Che cása avéte?	*Úna buóna cása a tre piáni* (floors).
Dátemi di grázia dúe uóva.	*Non ne abbiámo, ma abbiámo páne e butírro.*
Ha égli del pépe?	*Si, Signóre, ha del pépe, e del sále.*
Che voléte fáre?	*Ho intenzióne di andáre al bállo, ma andrò prima da mia mádre.*

CHAPTER XX.

THE PREPOSITIONS *CON, IN, PER.*

MNEMONIC EXERCISE.

Io lo vídi CO' *miéi próprj ócchi,*	I saw him *with* my own eyes.
Assistétemi CÓI *vóstri consígli,*	Assist me *with* your counsels.
La Sénna métte fóce IN *máre,*	The Seine flows *into* the sea.
Léggo PER *divertírmi,*	I read (*for*) to amuse myself.
Io appúnto ho mandáto PER *vói,*	I have just sent *for* you.
Égli ha dáto in lúce un' ópera,	He has published a work.
È famóso PER *le súe imprése,*	He is famous *by* his exploits.
Tútti parlávano IN *úna vólta,*	They all spoke *at* once.
Diéde un' occhiáta IN *gíro,*	He cast a glance *around* him.
Io véngo a bélla pósta per vói,	I come expressly *for* you.
Lo faréte con vóstro cómodo,	You will do it at your leisure.
È virtù il dir mólto IN *póchi détti,*	It is a talent to say much *in* few words.
È cósa che non gli può capír in tésta,	It is something which he cannot understand.
Le sélle non son fátte PER *gli ásini,*	Saddles are not made *for* asses.
Díce quéllo che gli viéne IN *bócca,*	He says what comes *into* his head.
Quélla dónna si adíra CON *tútti,*	This woman gets angry *with* everybody.
PER *carità, non mi precipitáte!*	For pity's sake, do not ruin me!
È un uómo chiáro PER *nobiltà,*	He is a man illustrious *by* his nobility.
Vádo ad aspettárvi IN *giardíno,*	I shall wait for you *in* the garden.
Vói cercáte d' ingarbugliármi CON *paróle che non inténdo,*	You try to confuse me *with* words which I do not understand.
Ognún per sè e Dío per tútti,	Every one for himself, and God for us all.

CON (with).

I. *Con* is used as in English in such sentences as the following:—

Strígnere amicízia CON *alcúno,*	To make friends *with* some one.
Eglí párla CÓGLI *ócchi chiúsi,*	He speaks *with* his eyes shut.
Dórme CÓLLA *bócca apérta,*	He sleeps *with* his mouth open.
Parlársi CÓGLI *ócchi,*	To speak *with* the eyes.
Percuótere COL *piéde,*	To stamp *with* the feet.
Far cénno CON LA *máno,* COL *cápo,*	To make a sign *with* the hand, *with* the head.
Díre CON *vóce bássa,* CON *vóce sonóra,*	To speak *in* a low voice, *in* a sonorous voice.
Lavoráre COL *pennéllo,* CÓLLO *scalpéllo,*	To work *with* pincers, *with* a chisel.
Fáre úna cósa CON *piacére,* CON *facilitá,* CON *difficoltá,* CON *destrézza,*	To do a thing *with* pleasure, *with* facility, *with* difficulty, *with* dexterity.
Parláre COL *cúore in máno,*	To speak *in* an open-hearted manner.
È uscíto COL *servitóre,*	He has gone out *with* his servant.

II. In some phrases, the Italians use *con* where the English use *by;* as, *Illustrársi* COL *súo mérito,* to make himself illustrious *by* his merit.

IN (*in*).

III. *In* follows a verb when it expresses the existence of an object in or upon another; as will be seen by the following:—

Il pránzo è IN *távola,*	The dinner is *upon* the table.
Ponéte víno IN *távola,*	Put the wine *upon* the table.
Andáre IN *villeggiatúra,*	To go *into* the country.
Éssere IN *máre,*	To be *upon* the sea.
Cadére IN *térra,*	To fall *to* the earth.
Non ho denári IN*dósso,**	I have no money about me.
Io non éntro NÉI *fátti vóstri,*	I do not meddle *in* your affairs.
Alzársi IN *púnta di piéde,*	To stand *on* tiptoe.

---

* *Indósso* is from *in* and *dósso,* back.

In *mía,* in *súa véce,*	*In* my, *in* his place.
Éssere in *potére di,* éssere nel- la *cúna,*	To be at the power of, to be *in* the cradle.
Stáre in *piédi* in *mézzo álla piázza,*	To stand up *in* the middle of the place.
Tútti gli sguardi érano físsi in *lúi,*	Every look was fixed *upon* him.
Stáre in *città,* in *villa,* in *cása,*	To live *in* the city, *in* the town, *in* the house.
Io l' ho gettáto in *máre,*	I have thrown him *into* the sea.
Moríre in *età di cénto ánni,*	To die *at* the age of one hundred.

IV. In elegant style, *in* is sometimes used instead of *cóntro* (against); as, *Vendicársi* in *úno,* to avenge one's self *against* another; *incrudelíre* ne' *súoi schiávi,* to be cruel *to* (against) his slaves.

V. It is difficult to know when to use the article with *in,* and when to suppress it; and there can be no positive rules given on this point. We must, however, observe that *in* is generally used without an article for any thing which is, or seems to be, on the surface; as, *Il vascéllo che éra* in *máre si è rótto* negli *scógli,* the vessel which was *upon* the sea is broken *on* the rocks; *i pésci vívono* nel *máre,* fish live *in* the sea.

PER (*for, by, through, etc.*).

VI. The preposition *per* indicates two distinct connections: —

1. It denotes the idea of passage; as, — —

Scrívere per *la pósta,*	To write *by* post.
Éssere crudéle per *natúra,*	To be cruel *by* nature.
Operáre per *interésse,*	To work *for* interest.
Préndere pel *bráccio,*	To take *by* the arm.
Pagáre cínque fránchi per *giórno,*	To pay five francs *a* day.
Per *pádre égli è nóbile,*	*Through* his father, he is of noble birth.

PER *un sécolo,* PER *un ánno,* During (for) a year, a century,
Una vóce córre PER *la città,* A rumor runs *through* the city.
Viaggiáre PER *la Fráncia,* To travel *through* France.
Passáre PER *la Fráncia,* PER *la* To pass *through* France, *through*
cámera, PER *la pórta,* the chamber, *through* the door.

2. *Per* serves also to mark the aim or object of a person; as, —

Egli è mórto PER *la pátria,* He died *for* his country.
Io lavóro PER *i miéi scolári,* I work *for* my pupils.
Fúrono lasciáti PER *mórti,* They were left *for* dead.

VII. We can also say, *nélla città, nélla stráda, in Fráncia;* but the idea of motion is better expressed by the word *per,* rendering the phrase more forcible.

VIII. We also say, —

PER *verità, io non lo crédo,* In truth, I do not believe it.
Égli è venúto PER *párte di úno,* He came from some one.
Éssere PER, or *stáre* PER, To be about to.
PER *me vi assicúro che,* As for me, I assure you that.
Io ho quél che díte più che PER I perfectly believe all that you
véro, say.
Andáte PE' *fátti vóstri,* Let me alone; *or,* mind your business.
PER *quánto si affatichi, tútto gli* He may tire himself as much
va a vóto, as he will, nothing succeeds with him.

READING LESSON.

Un giovinótto avéva i capélli néri e la bárba biánca. Tútti domandávano la cáusa di un tal fenómeno. Un motteggiatóre rispóse: " Perchè fórse quel Signóre ha lavoráto più cólla ma-
                   labored
scélla che col cervéllo.

Giúlio secóndo, in età di 70 ánni, con un élmo in cápo montò, all' assálto délla mirándola. Si díce che un giórno quésto pápa guerriéro buttásse nel Tévere le chiávi di San Piétro, per non
      threw
aver più ad usáre, dicéva égli, che la spáda di San Páolo.

Un buón vécchio párroco di villa, che éra débole di vista, e
avéa le dita póco elástiche, stáva leggéndo in púlpito un cápo
 was reading
délla génesi. A quéste paróle: "Il Signóre diéde ad Adámo
 gave
úna móglie," voltò dúe págine in úna vólta, e sénza abbadárvi
 he turned perceiving it
lésse tuttavía con vóce fórte e chiára: "Ed élla éra incatramáta
read pitched
per di déntro e per di fuóri." Quel buón piováno si éra
 without. parson
disgraziataménte imbattúto nella descrizióne dell' árca di Noé.
unfortunately lighted upon
Bisógna che l'uómo ábbia tánto sénno da sapérsi accomodáre
álle costumánze délle nazióni nelle quáli si tróva. Per mancánza
 is. want
di un chiódo si pérde il férro ad un cavállo; per mancánza di
 lost shoe (iron)
un férro si pérde il cavállo, e per mancánza di un cavállo, ánche
il cavaliére è perdúto, perchè il nemíco lo sopraggiúnge, l'
 succeeded
ammázza, e tútto quésto per non avér pósto ménte ad un chiódo
killed put
d' un férro del súo cavállo.

EXERCISE FOR TRANSLATION.

1. It is a great misfortune not to have wit enough to speak well, nor judgment enough to keep silent.
2. In this world, we ought to be born either a king or a fool: a king, to be able to avenge injuries, and punish the vices of men; a fool, so as not to perceive injuries, or be troubled by any thing.
3. A caricature represented George III. with a very large sleeve, from which Napoleon wished to come out; but, as soon as he put out his nose, George gave him a push to force him back into the sleeve.
4. We shall be measured by the same measure as we measure others.

5. We should be careful not to lose time and words in refuting things evidently false. Zeno denied motion, and Diogenes began to walk without saying a word: Zeno persisted in his paradox, and Diogenes continued to walk.

VOCABULARY.

1. To speak, *parláre;* to keep silent, *stáre zítto.*
2. We ought to be born, *converrébbe nascére;* to be able, *po tére;* to avenge, *vendicáre;* to punish, *castigáre;* to perceive (to know), *conóscere;* or to be troubled, *nè dársi pensiéro.*
3. Represented, *figuráva; Giórgio;* wished to come out, *voléva uscíre;* put out, *sporgéva;* gave, *dáva;* to force him back, *per fárlo tornár déntro.*
4. Measured, *misuráti;* we measure, *misuriámo.*
5. We should be, etc., *bisógna guardársi dal pérdere;* in refuting, *nel confutáre;* denied, *negáva;* began to walk, *si mise a passeggiáre;* persisted, *persistétte;* continued, *continuò.*

CONVERSAZIÓNE.

Che fa il vóstro sérvo?
Che vuol (wishes) díre?
Dov' è la vóstra amíca?
Che è cadúto in térra?
Perchè è il Signór M. famóso?
Che cósa ha égli fátto?
L' avéte létte?
Cóme ha égli parláto?
Dóve státe óra?
Prestátemi un dóllaro.
Che si díce del fù Capitáno?
Perchè lavóra il Signór B.?
Voléte andáre in véce mía?
Che chiedéte (demand) vói?
È crudéle quést' animále?
Ha égli compráto úna carrózza?

Égli fa un cénno col cápo.
Che il pránzo è in távola.
È uscíta col servitóre.
Lo scalpéllo con cúi lavóro.
Per le súe ópere letterárie.
Ha dáto in lúce mólte ópere.
Sì, le ho létte con piacére.
Ha parláto col cuóre.
Sto in città.
Non ne ho in dósso.
Che égli è mórto per la pátria
Lavóra pei suói scolári.
Sì, andrò in véce vóstra.
Chiédo danáro in préstito.
Per natúra non è crudéle.
No, è tróppo aváro per far quésta spésa.

CHAPTER XXI.

THE PREPOSITIONS.
(Continued.)

MNEMONIC EXERCISE.

Ciò sía détto FRA di nói,
Égli verrà FRA diéci giórni,
Che c' è quì DÉNTRO?
Facciámocegli INCÓNTRO
Ío le sedéva ACCÁNTO,
Égli stétte alquánto SÓPRA di se,'
Noè nácque PRÍMA del dilúvio, e morì DÓPO il dilúvio,
Vénni quésta máne A cása vóstra,
Non v' è cósa nuóva SÓTTO il sóle,
Élla ha trováto un maríto SECÓNDO il súo génio,
Nell' invérno si sta béne ACCÁNTO al fuóco.
Bisógna vívere SECÓNDO le léggi délla natúra,
Non vo mái a létto PRÍMA dell' álba,
Il sónno IN SUL mattíno è salutévole,
Ánimo, Signorína; viùn tárdi; leváievi su, ci alzi
Che avéte fátto INFÍNO ad óra?

Ciascúno è padróne IN cása súa,

Quándo avrò CÁSA MÍA, invite:ò tútti i miéi amíci,

That may be said among us.
He will arrive in ten days.
What is that within?
Let us go to meet him.
I was seated beside her.
He stopped some time to reflect
Noah was born before the flood, and died after it.
This morning I went to your house.
There is nothing new under the sun.
She has found a husband according to her taste.
In winter, one is well near the fireside.
We ought to live according to the laws of Nature.
I never go to bed before daybreak.
Sleep in the morning is healthy,
Come, miss; it is late; get up.

What have you done up to the present moment?

Every one is master in his own house.

When I have a house of my own, I will invite all my friends.

UPON.

I. "Upon" is often translated by *in;* as, —

I will wait for you on the piazza,	V'aspetterò IN *piázza.*
Ungrateful people write benefits upon the sand,	*Gl' ingráti scrívono i benefízi* NELL' *aréna.*
To have no money upon (or about) you,	*Non avére danári* IN *dósso.*

BETWEEN, AMONG.

II. These prepositions are rendered by *fra* or *tra*, and occasionally by *infra* or *intra;* as, —

Among the people,	FRA (or TRA) *il pópolo.*
Among men,	FRA (or TRA) *gli uómini.*
Between these two cities you find three villages,	FRA *quéste dúe città s' incóntrano tre paesétti.*

III. *Fra* (or *tra*) sometimes expresses "in" or "within;" as, —

I said within myself,	*Io dicéva* FRA *me.*
God has created the world in six days,	*Dío ha creáto il móndo* IN *séi giórni.*
He will arrive within two months,	*Égli arriverà* FRA *dúe mési.*
To live in pleasure, in pain,	*Vivére* FRA *i piacéri,* FRA *le péne.*

UNTIL.

IV. "Until" is translated by *fíno* or *síno;* also *insíno* or *infíno.*

TO or AT.

V. "To" or "at" is rendered by *da* when it signifies going to some one; as, —

I go to my banker's,	*Io vo* DAL *mío banchiére.*
You go to your uncle's,	*Vói andáte* DA *vóstro zio.*
He will send to the baker,	*Manderà* DAL *fornáio.*
Yesterday I went to your house to beg you to call upon me to-day,	*Iéri vénni* DA *vói per pregárvi di passáre óggi* DA *me.*

PREPOSITIONS.

A casa di, a *cása mía,* a *cása vóstra,* etc., are also used when we refer more particularly to the house; as, *Vói andáte a cása di vóstro zío; iéri vénni a cása vóstra per pregárvi di passáre óggi a cása mía.*

VI. The following examples illustrate the use of various prepositions : —

At the fireside,	ACCÁNTO *al fuóco.*
After dinner,	DÓPO *pránzo.*
After me,	DÓPO *di me.*
About the table,	INTÓRNO *álla távola.*
Against me, him,	CÓNTRO *di me, di lúi.*
Against the enemy,	CÓNTRO *al nemíco.*
About 3,000 francs,	CÍRCA *a tre mila fránchi.*
About three feet high,	*Álto* CÍRCA, or *álto* INTÓRNO *a tre piédi.*
Along the river,	LÚNGO *il fiúme.*
According to your opinion,	SECÓNDO, or GIÚSTA *il vóstro parére.*
Before all, before me,	PRÍMA *di tútto,* PRÍMA *di me.*
Before speaking,	PRÍMA *di,* or AVÁNTI *di párlare.*
Before daylight,	INNÁNZI *l' álba,* or PRÍMA *dell' álba.*
Beyond the sea,	AL DI LÀ *dal máre.*
Behind the door,	DIÉTRO *la pórta,* or *álla pórta.*
Before the chimney,	DAVÁNTI *il,* or *al cammíno.*
Beyond the Rhine,	DI LÀ *dal Réno.*
Beside that,	ÓLTRE *a ciò.*
Far from the truth,	LÚNGI, or LONTÁNO *dal véro.*
In the middle of the street,	IN MÉZZO *álla,* or *délla stráda.*
In face of, *or* opposite to,	DIRIMPÉTTO A, OR IN FÁCCIA A.
Near the bed,	ACCÁNTO, or VICÍNO *al létto.*
Near the sea,	VICÍNO, or PRÉSSO *al* or *del máre.*
Outside,	PER DI FUÓRI, or AL DI FUÓRI.
Out of the house,	FUÓRI or FUÓRA *di cása.*
Towards me, thee,	VÉRSO or INVÉRSO *a me, a te,* or *di me.*
Towards spring,	VÉRSO *primavéra.*
Without money,	SÉNZA *danáro.*
Within him,	DÉNTRO, or PER DI DÉNTRO, *di lúi.*

VII. When the above prepositions are followed by a personal pronoun, the pronoun is often placed before the verb, and the preposition terminates the phrase; as, *Non mi comparíte più dinánzi,* appear no more before me.

READING LESSON.

Tasso's last Letter

Che dirà il mio Signór António, quándo udirà la mórte del
<small>will say   will hear</small>

súo Tásso? e per mío avvíso nón tarderà mólto la novélla, perchè
<small>   will not delay</small>

io mi sénto al fíne délla mía víta, non esséndosi potúto trovár
<small>   feel   being able</small>

mái rimédio a quésta mía fastidiósa indisposizióne sopravvenúta

álle mólte áltre míe sólite, quási rápido torrénte, dal quále sénza
<small>   accustomed</small>

potére avér alcún ritégno védo chiaraménte ésser rapíto. Non è
<small>   defence   taken away.</small>

témpo che io párli délla mía ostináta fortúna, per non díre dell'
<small>   speak</small>

ingratitúdine del móndo, la quále ha pur volúto avér la vittória

di condúrmi álla sepoltúra mendíco; quánd'io pensáva, che quélla

glória, che, mal grádo di chi non vuóle, avrà quésto sécolo da miéi

scrítti, non fósse per lasciármi in alcún módo sénza guiderdóne.

Mi son fatto condúrre in quésto Monastéro di Sant' Onófrio, non
<small>   to conduct</small>

sólo perchè l' ária è lodáta da' médici, più che d' alcún' áltra
<small>   praised</small>

párte di Róma, ma quási per cominciáre da quésto luógo emi

nénte, e cólla conversazióne di quésti divóti Pádri, la mía con-

versazióne in Ciélo. Pregáte Iddío per me: e siáte sicúro che

siccóme vi ho amáto, ed onoráto sémpre nélla presénte víta, cosı

farò per voi nell' áltra più véra, ciò che álla non fínta, ma ve-
<small>will do   feigned</small>

ráce carità s' appartiéne; ed álla Divína grázia raccomándo vói,
<small>   belongs</small>

e me stésso. Di Róma in Sant' Onófrio.

EXERCISE FOR TRANSLATION.

1. The tears of an inheritor are smiles concealed under a mask.
2. Distrust those who love you very much on short acquaintance.
3. Private thieves spend their lives in chains and prisons; public thieves, in the midst of purple and gold.
4. With many people, love of country is none other than to kill and despoil other men.
5. There are some country towns in France where societies meet at six o'clock in the evening, in winter. They seat themselves around the fireplace; and, after the usual compliments, each one goes to sleep. At eight o'clock, one of them sneezes. Then, there is a general movement of surprise. "What is it?" — "Nothing." One of the company takes out his watch, and announces that it is eight o'clock. "Ah! it is not late: we can amuse ourselves a little longer." They sleep again till nine o'clock, when the mistress of the house gives a signal. They rise; they congratulate each other at having been much amused; and each one goes to his own home.
6. "Wit and judgment," says Pope, "are always in opposition to each other, as the husband and wife; although made to live together, and mutually help each other."
7. A preacher displayed all his eloquence in a panegyric upon St. Antonio; and, among the figures of rhetoric with which he embellished his style, there was one wherein he said, "Among what inhabitants of heaven shall I place our saint? Shall it be with angels or archangels? shall it be with cherubims or seraphims? No! Shall I place him among patriarchs, among prophets? No! Neither shall I place him among apostles, nor doctors, nor evangelists." One of his auditors, who was tired of this long declamation, said to him, in rising, "My father, if you do not know where to place your saint, you can put him here; because I am going away."

VOCABULARY.

1. Concealed, *nascosti*.
2. Distrust, *difidátevi* ; love very much, *vógliono gran béne*.
3. Private, *priváto* ; spend (pass), *pássano*.
4. Is none other than, *non è áltro che* ; kill, *ammazzáre* ; despoil, *spogliáre*.
5. There are, *vi sóno* ; societies meet, *si va in conversazióne* ; at six o'clock, P.M., *álle séi pomeridiáne* ; usual, *sóliti* ; there is

a general movement, *insórge un móto generále;* takes out, *cáva,* it is not late, *non è tárdi;* to amuse, *trattenére;* they sleep again, *ognúno tórna ad adormentársi;* they rise *tútti si álzano;* they congratulate each other, *si rallégrano.*

6. Although made, *benchè fátti;* to live together, *tenérsi compagnía;* to help, *ajutáre.*

7. Displayed, *sfoggiáva;* to embellish, *ornáre;* to place, *collocáre;* neither, *neppúre;* declamation, *filastrócca;* if you do not know, *se non sapéte;* you can put him here, *ponételo pur quì;* because, *chè;* I am going away, *io vádo vía.*

CONVERSAZIÓNE.

Che cósa avéte?
Díte da véro, o díte da búrla?
Dov' è il mío páne (roll) *imbutirráto* (buttered)?
Che fécero (do) *quéi poveríni cólle lágrime in súgli ócchi?*
Fra quáli déi celésti abitatóri fu collocáto Sant' António?
Ho io lasciáto (left) *il mío bastóne quì?*
Chi è felíce?

Qual è quéll' animále, che va (goes) *con quáttro piédi, pói con dúe, ed in último con tre?*

Úna bottíglia di víno.
Da véro; non ischérzo.
Non so, vádo nélla cucína per cercárlo.
Chiésero aiúto col piánto e cólle strída.
Amíco mío, non è importánte di sapérlo.
Vói lo lasciáste da mía sorélla.

Vói ed ío, perchè non ci mánca (fails) *un amíco sincéro.*
È l' uómo, che da bambíno va carpóni con le máni e cói piédi, e cósi con quáttro piédi, pói rítto su dúe piédi, ed in vecchiája con tre, perchè va col bastóne.

CHAPTER XXII.

THE VERBS *ÉSSERE* AND *AVÉRE*.

MNEMONIC EXERCISE.

Non c' è témpo da pérdere, — There is no time to lose.
Non c' è cárne senz' óssa, — There is no meat without bones.
Avéte vói in prónto la monéta? — Have you the money ready?
Non bisógna avérsela a mále, — You must not take it ill.
Io v' ho cára quánto soréllla, — I cherish you as a sister.
Perchè avéte così frétta? — Why are you in such a hurry?
Compráte délla légna; perchè in cantína non ce n' è più, — Buy more wood; for there is no more in the cellar.
Se non avéte che fáre, veníte méco, — If you have nothing to do, come with me.
Tócca a vói a copríre i miéi difétti, — It is for you to conceal my faults.
Óra toccherà a me a racconciárla, — Now it is my turn to adjust the affair.
Non ho piacére di viaggiáre di nótte, — I feel no pleasure travelling by night.
Con chi l' avéte? Io non l' ho con nessúno, — With whom are you displeased? I am displeased with no one.
Vi sóno gran ribáldi in quésto móndo, — There are great villains in this world.
Non si può dáre un cuóre più pérfido, — There cannot be a more perfidious heart.
Abbiámo a discórrere a quáttro ócchi, — We must speak of that together tete-a-tete.
Ho incontráto dúe giórni fa vóstro cugíno, — Two days ago I met your cousin.
I béni del móndo sóno in máno délla sórte, — The riches of this world are in the hands of fate.
A vói tócca il dir príma il vóstro parére, — It is for you to give your advice first.
Égli non è in grádo di far quésta spésa, — He is not in a position to incur this expense.

ÉSSERE, TO BE.

I. This verb is very much used in Italian, by its forming the passive, which predominates in that language. 1st, It is its own auxiliary in compound tenses; as, *Io sóno státo*, I have been: 2d, The past participle *státo* agrees in gender and number with its subject; as, *Élla è* STÁTA, she has been; *nói siámo* STÁTI, we have been.

II. When *éssere* is used impersonally, it agrees with the subject which follows it; as, *È un óra*, it is one o'clock; *sóno le úndici*, it is eleven o'clock.

III. The verb *veníre* is very often used for *éssere*.

IV. The Italian expression *éssere per*, or *stáre per*, signifies "to be upon the point of;" as, *Io sóno*, or *io stò per ammogliármi*, I am about to marry.

V. In the phrases "there is," "there are," "there was," etc., the Italians use *ci* and *vi* (there), abridged from *quínci* and *quívi*. *Ci* denotes proximity, and *vi* a more distant place; as, —

There is, was, etc.,	*V'è*, or *c'è; v'éra*, or *c'éra*, etc.
There are many people who wish to learn much without study,	*Vi sóno mólti che vorrébbero imparáre mólto sénza studiáre.*

VI. *Ci* and *vi* are changed into *ce* and *ve* when it is necessary to use the indefinite pronoun *ne* (of it, of them), etc.; as, —

Non ce n'è più, or *non ve n'è più*,	There are no more of them.
Non ce n'è più, etc.,	There is no more of it.

VII. To express "it is ten years since," etc., the Italians say, "*Diéci ánni fa*, or *diéci ánni sóno*; and for "it is an hour," "a week," "a month," "two centuries," etc., they say *un' óra fa, una settimána fa, un mése fa, dúe sécoli fa.* "There is," "there are," is occasionally rendered by *vi ha*, or *hávvi*.

VERBS.

VIII. *Avére* (to have), besides being the auxiliary of active verbs as in English, is used idiomatically in the following phrases:—

To be judicious,	Avér giudízio, avér cervéllo.
To be ready,	Avére in prónto; avére a máno.
To be thirsty,	Avér séte.
To be hungry,	Avér fáme.
To be hot,	Avér cáldo.
To be satisfied with,	Avér cáro di.
To cherish some one,	Avér cáro úno.
To remember,	Avére a ménte.
To be in a hurry,	Avér frétta.
To be cold,	Avér fréddo.
To be ill,	Avér mále.
To be ashamed,	Avér vergógna.
To take a thing ill,	Avér per mále.
To be afraid,	Avér paúra.
To be charmed,	Avér gústo; avér piacére.
To be in possession of,	Avére in máno.
To have knowledge of,	Avére conoscénza.

READING LESSON.

Sedúta un po' in dispárte, cólla frónte bássa e le máni intrecciá·te súlle ginócchia, stáva piangéndo chéta, la póvera Laudómia. Le súe guánce in quésti mési s'éran affiláte e fátte pállide, che quél vivér sémpre in agitazióne, quél dovér ad ógni óra temére le giungésse l'avvíso che Lambérto éra rimásto ucciso, esauríva in léi a póco a póco la víta. Ed óra, dópo quésta rótta, délla quále s'ignoraváno i particolári, ed in cúi si sapéva però quási 3,000 persóne avér perdúta la víta, rimanér col treméndo dúbbio s'égli fósse vívo o mórto! Non avér módo di uscírne, non sapére a chi domandárne! "Oh! pensiámo," dicéva, "s'égli non si sarà gettáto nel maggiór pericólo! s'égli avrà volúto staccársi dal fiánco del Ferrúccio! Oimè! Oimè! ch'io non ábbia próprio a vedérlo mái più?"

Le cognáte, le nipóti e gli áltri tútti di quélle tre cáse che formávano úna sóla famíglia, la veneráva no più che soréllae zía, e la chiamávano l'Améda, nóme antíco, venúto dal latíno Amita (che vuól dír zía), e tuttóra vívo nel contádo délla Briánza.

EXERCISE FOR TRANSLATION.

1. There was in Athens a very opulent miser, who troubled himself very little about being the talk of his fellow-citizens. "People may hiss me," said he; "but I am not angry: for, when I am at home, I rejoice at the sight of my crowns."

2. Wherever there are tears to be dried up, you will be sure to meet a woman.'

3. There are men on whom is imprinted the whole character of their nation.

4. Unhappily, it is but too true, that no nation can flourish without vices. If it were not for ambition or cupidity, there would not be a single man who would wish to take charge of the government of others. Take vanity away from women, and the fine manufactures of silk and lace, which furnish labor (cause to live) to so many thousands of artisans, would cease (would be no more). If there were no thieves, lock-makers would die of hunger. Thus good and evil are always found together.

5. Always live as if you were old, in order that you may never repent having been young.

6. There are men who know neither how to speak nor to be silent.

7. An old woman asked Mahomet what it was necessary to do so as to go to Paradise. "My dear," said he, "Paradise is not for old women." The good woman began to weep; and the prophet said, to console her, "There are no old women there, because they all become young again."

8. Dolabella said to Cicero, "Do you know that I am only thirty years old?"—"I ought to know it," said Cicero; "because you have been telling it to me these ten years."

9. If princes were obliged to combat hand to hand, there would be no more wars.

VOCABULARY.

1. *Aténe;* who troubled himself very little, *che si dáva póca briga;* hiss, *fa le fischiáte;* I rejoice, *mi rallégro.*

2. Wherever, *dovúnque;* to dry, *asciugáre.*

3. Imprinted, *imprésso.*

4. Unhappily, etc., *è cósa disgraziataménte pur véra;* can flourish, *può ésser flórida;* if it were not, *se non fósse;* would wish, *avésse vóglia di;* to take charge, *incaricársi;* take away, *togliéte vía;* manufacture, *fábbrica;* cause to live, *dánno da vivere a;* would die, *morirébbero.*

VERBS. 145

5. If you were, *se fóste* ; may never repent, *non vi abbiáte a pentíre mái.*
6. To be silent, *stáre zítti.*
7. Old woman, *vécchia* ; asked, *domandáva* ; *Maométto* ; it was necessary, *convenísse* ; to go, *per andáre* ; *paradíso* ; my dear, *cára mía* ; began to weep, *si cacciò a piángere* ; to console, *racconsoláre* ; become young, *ritorneránno gióvani.*
8. *Dolabélla* ; *Ceróne* ; only, *solaménte* ; I ought to know it, *lo débbo sapére* ; because, *perchè* ; telling, *andáte dicéndo.*
9. Were obliged to, *dovéssero* ; combat, *pugnáre* ; hand to hand, *córpo a córpo.*

CONVERSAZIÓNE.

Dov' è la Luísa?
Perchè?
Louísa, che hai?
Che cósa ha?
Bevéte (drink). *È dólce abbastánza?*
Che cos' è quésta nóstra vita!
Quánti ánni sóno che siéte fuóri di pátria?
Figliuóli miéi, avéte appetíto?
Voléte (will you) *bére* (drink)?

È mórta la Signóra?
È la Giuliétta?

Avéte studiáto la vóstra lezióne di música? L' avéte praticáta perbéne?

Potréi (could I) *vedérla?*

È rimásta a casa.
Perchè è un póco infreddáta.
La mámma stà (is) *male.*
Ha úna gróssa fébbre.
Sì, è buoníssimo.

Un sógno, sogniámo in páce.
Sóno ormái quíndici ánni?

No, cára mádre.
Prenderémo (we will take) *úna limonáta.*
Sì, la Signóra María è mórta.
È desoláta. Il súo vivo dolóre mi lácera (pierces) *l' ánimo.*
Mi son leváto quésta mattína álle sétte, e non mi sóno più móssa (moved) *dal pianofórte.*
Sì; se voléte entráre un moménto, ma non le díte (say) *núlla.*

CHAPTER XXIII.

THE VERBS AND THEIR SYNTAX.

MNEMONIC EXERCISE.

Cóme ve la passáte, carino?'	How goes it with you, dear?
Io sto ascoltándo: non mi muóvo,	I listen: I do not move.
Amico, gettáte via la fatica,	Friend, you lose your labor.
Venite púre avánti,	You can likewise enter.
Che cósa dite?	What do you say?
Tiráte via, gocciolóne!	Go away, great fool!
Io stáva scrivéndo úna léttera,	I was writing a letter.
Comportátevi béne, e saréte ben volúto da tútti,	Behave well, and everybody will love you.
Da alcúni filósofi si créde che la vita sía un sógno,	Some philosophers believe that life is a dream.
Vi sóno talúni che vánno sémpre macchinándo délle novità,	There are people who are always thinking of something new.
Che cósa impedísce all' uómo di esser felíce?	What prevents man from being happy?
Pióve, tuóna, e baléna, in un púnto,	It rains, thunders, and lightens, all at once.
Méntre státe pranzándo scriveró állo zio,	While you dine, I will write to my uncle.
Che andáte facéndo cosi per témpo?	What are you doing so early?
Non parlár mái sénza avér pensáto,	Never speak without reflection
È cósa che si díce da alcúni,	There are some persons who speak of it.
Muóve più l'interésse próprio che l' altrúi,	One's own interest is always more touching than that of others.
Non ho godúto un' óra di béne,	I have never enjoyed a moment's happiness.
Appéna mi víde tiró via súbito,'	He no sooner saw me than he ran away.

The verbs in the infinitive are easily recognized in Italian by their terminations, namely, in ARE, ERE, IRE; as, *amáre*,* to love; *vedére*, to see; *finíre*, to finish. Many verbs have two terminations for the infinitive: some end in *ere* or *íre*.

In Italian, the infinitive, when preceded by the definite article, has the nature of a noun; as, *È proibíto il far mále*, it is forbidden to do evil.

GENERAL RULES.

I. The word *vía* (which signifies "way," "street") is placed after certain verbs of motion; as, —

Levár vía,	to take away.
Portár vía,	to carry away.
Andár vía,	to go away, etc.

II. The passive form of the verb, as we have already stated, is much used in Italian; particularly in didactic, poetic, and historic styles. The active form becomes passive by changing the construction of the phrase: the subject becomes the regimen, and takes the preposition *da:* the verb takes the addition of *si*, which is a sign of the passive; or it is conjugated through all its tenses with the verbs *éssere* or *veníre;* as, Everybody says, *si díce da tútti, è détto da tútti*, or *vién détto da tútti;* the people fear war, *la guérra è temúta dal pópolo.*

III. There are many impersonal verbs † in Italian; among which are the following: —

Albéggia,	the day appears.	Piovíggina,	it drizzles it
Raggiórna,	„ „ „	Lámica,	rains in small
Annótta,	it is growing dark.	Sprúzzola,	drops.

---

* The verbs of the first conjugation — which ends in ARE — amount to more than four thousand: among them, only about thirty are irregular.

† The impersonal verbs may be divided into proper and improper. The proper are those which have only the third person singular throughout all their moods and tenses; as, *Si fa oscúro*, it grows dark; *tempésta*, it hails. The improper are those which are not impersonal by themselves, but only occasionally used in an impersonal signification; as *Conviéne*, it is proper; *bisógna*, it must.

Baléna,	it lightens.	*Accáde,*	it happens.
Lampéggia,	„ „	*Avviéne,*	„ „
Pióve,	it rains.	*Interviéne,*	„ „
Névica,	it snows.	*Páre,*	it appears.
Tuóna,	it thunders.	*Sémbra,*	it seems.
Grándina,	it hails.	*Disdíce,*	it does not become.
Géla,	it freezes.	*Bisógna,*	it is necessary.

IV. Impersonal verbs are used in the plural when the noun which follows them is plural; as, —

Accádono stráne cóse,   Strange things happen.
Sóno le séi,   It is six o'clock.

V. All the impersonal verbs are conjugated in their compound tenses with *éssere;* as, *È tonáto, è piováto.*

VI. Many of these verbs are conjugated with the personal pronouns; as, *Mi páre,* it seems to me; *mi dispiáce,* I am sorry.

REMARK. — In most languages, many verbs are used with an idiomatic turn very different from their proper signification.

VII. The verbs *veníre* and *volére,* for instance, do not always answer to the English verbs "to come" and "to be willing:" but the former is sometimes used instead of the verb *éssere* (to be); and the latter, being preceded by the particles *ci, vi,* and unipersonally employed, has the same meaning as the verb *bisognáre* (must or to be necessary); as, —

Mi vién détto così,   I am told so.
Ci vuól paziénza,   We must have patience.

VIII. The verb *dovére* is expressed in English by the verb "to owe" when it means *to be a debtor,* and by the verb "to be obliged" when it signifies *duty* or the necessity of doing an action. It is also used instead of the verb *bisognáre,* in the signification of "must;" as *E' gli dovéva trecénto fioríni,* he owed him three hundred florins.

IX. The English verb "to be," used in the sense of "to be one's turn," "business," or "duty," is rendered in Italian by the verb *toccáre*, in the signification of "to belong;" as, —

Tócca a me a giuocáre,   It is for me to play.
Tócca a lúi a léggere,   It is for him to read.

X. The verb "to think," used in English in the sense of "to believe" or "to suppose," is translated into Italian by the verb *crédere;* and, when in the sense of "to reflect" or "meditate," by the verb *pensáre*.

XI. The verb "to know" is translated by the verb *sapére* when intellectual knowledge is meant, and by the verb *conóscere* when personal knowledge derived from the evidence of one of our senses is intended.

XII. The pronouns *mi, ti, ci, ne*, etc., are often used as expletives* with certain verbs; as, *Ío mi son présa la libertà di scrívervi*, I have taken the liberty to write to you.

XIII. The verbs *dovére, potére, sapére, volére*, sometimes form their compound tenses with *éssere* when followed by an infinitive; as, *Ío non son potúto veníre*.

XIV. The verb *suonáre*, or *sonáre*, is used in the sense of to play on an instrument; as, *Suóna il violíno, suóna il córno da cáccia*.

XV. The verbs *avvertíre* and *badáre* (to take care) are followed by a negation; as, *Avvertíte* or *badáte di non ingannárvi*, take care not to deceive yourself.

XVI. The verb may be placed before or after the subject, according to the dominant idea of either verb or

---

* Expletives are particles which give strength and energy. They are *béne, si béne, vúre, tútto, mi, ti, pói, altriménti, ci, già, via, vi, mai, égli, si, béllo, non, ne;* as, —

Il vóstro vestíto e béll' e fátto,   Your suit of clothes is finished.
Son tútto stánco.   I am quite tired.
Che témpo fa égli?   What is the weather?
Egli è più dótto ch' io non credéva,   He is more learned than I thought.

subject. This inversion sometimes gives great effect, particularly to poetry. We may see it in Tasso : —

GIÁCE *l' álta Cartágo; appéna i ségni
Dell' álte súe ruíne il lído sérba,*
MUÓIONO *le città ; muóiono i régni,* etc.

REMARKS.

1. The verbs ending in CARE and GARE, as *predicáre, spiegáre,* take *h* in those tenses in which *c* and *g* would precede *e* or *i,* so as to preserve the hard sound of the infinitive. (See conjugation of *cercáre.*)

2. Students should be careful to notice the difference between the imperfect and perfect-definite tenses of Italian verbs. The *imperfect* expresses an action not accomplished during the time of another past action, or the repetition of an action, and may be known by its making sense with the auxiliary *was.* The *perfect-definite* expresses an action entirely past; as, I *was going* to your sister when I *saw* you, ío me ne (imp.) ANDÁVA *da vóstra sorélla, quándo ío vi* (perfect) VÍDI ; I *went* almost every night to pay a visit to the famous Schiller, ío ANDÁVA *quási ógni séra a far visíta al célebre Schiller.*

READING LESSON.

Éra intánto compársa la Caterína con quálche cosarélla per céna : e chi non avésse sapúto che la cása éra andáta a sácco, l' avrébbe indovináto vedéndo quéll' imbandigióne, che tútta consistéva in un' insaláta, un pézzo di cácio, e dúe pan néri, che l' úno neppúr éra intéro. La póvera dónna, scúra e macilénta in víso, cógli ócchi gónfi e róssi, apparecchiáva sénza parláre, e mettéva ógni tánto, lúnghi sóspiri ; e dópo quélle príme e brévi paróle, nessúno aprì più bócca, e rimasér pensósi, sedéndo su úna pánca che éra tútt' in gíro confítta nel múro : e quésto silénzio paréa tánto più mésto, che nessúna vóce, nessúno strépito s' udíva neppúre, al di fuóri, benchè fóssero nel cuór délla térra, póco lontáni di piázza. Il cánto d' un gállo o l' abbaiár d' un cáne avrébber alméno dáto ségno di cósa víva ; ma quel desoláto bórgo avéva aspétto di cimitéro. — D'AZÉLIO.

VERBS AND THEIR SYNTAX. 151

EXERCISE FOR TRANSLATION.

The Stranger and the Guide (seated on the top of the Coliseum).

1. *S.* — As I just now observed, as we climbed up here, the name of Rome awakens the most agreeable sensations.
2. *G.* — It is because you have read so much, sir: besides, you know Latin, and then you have travelled much.
3. *S.* — Two years of travel have profited me much more than eight years of Latin. I have studied nature: I have freed myself from my prejudices, and from the false national love which makes us so unjust towards our fellow-creatures.
4. *G.* — What think you, then, of Italy?
5. *S.* — Italy has conquered the world by her arms; she has enlightened it by her sciences; civilized us by her fine arts; governed by her genius; and, far from succumbing under the redoubtable blows of barbarians, she has triumphed over them, forcing them to lay down their ensanguined arms at her feet.
6. *G.* — Very true; and you cannot mention another nation which has held its conquests so long as Italy.

VOCABULARY.

1. We climbed, *salivámo;* awakens, *désta.*
2. Read, *létto;* travelled, *viaggiáto.*
3. Profited, *giováto;* studied, *studiáto;* have (am) freed, *sóno spogliáto;* fellow-creatures, *símile.*
4. Think, *pensáte.*
5. Conquered, *conquistáto;* enlightened, *illumináto;* civilized, *ingentilíto;* governed, *governáto;* far from succumbing, *non che soggiacére;* triumphed, *trionfáto;* forcing (constraining them), *costringéndoli;* ensanguined, *insanguináti.*
6. You cannot mention (cite), *vossignoría non può citáre.*

CONVERSAZIÓNE.

Avéte cámere da affittáre (to let)?
Vorréi un appartaménto.
Lo vorréi (should like) smobigliáto.
Non più che l' invérno.
Al partíre rivenderò (I will sell again) la mobíglia.

Sì, Signóre, ne ho várie.
Con móbili o sénza móbili?
Pensáte di trattenérvi (to remain) mólto?
E al partíre?
Non ne caveréte un térzo del cósto.

Allora è méglio trováre úna buóna padróna ed un bell' appartaménto.
Andiámo a vedére.
Che móbili ha élla?

Il létto è la cósa principalíssima.
La cámera rispónde súlla stráda?
Desídera vedére un' áltra stánza?

Che si dice dell' ostinazióne?

Che ci vuóle in tútte le cóse?

Quándo è il sóle più risplendénte?
Che voléte amíco mío?

Che bisógna fáre per godére buóna salúte?
Che sta facéndo quést' uómo?

Che cósa è pazzía?

Vi condurrò io dálla Signora Biánca; élla è persóna gentilíssima e discréta.
La situazióne è bellíssima.
Ha móbili di mógano (mahogany), *e tappéti di lússo.*
Non potéte desiderárne un miglióre.
No Signóre, da nel giardíno.

No, crédo che il létto sia buóno. Non si trátta adésso che del prézzo.
Si dice che l' ostinazióne è peggiór di tútti i peccáti.
In tútte le cóse ci vuóle la moderazióne.
Dópo úna burrásca è sémpre più risplendénte il sóle.
Vóglio più che vói potéte dármi.

Bisógna vívere parcaménte.

Sta ragionándo per passáre t. témpo.
Lo sperár sémpre nell' avvenír e pazzía.

CHAPTER XXIV.

THE VERB: THE SUBJUNCTIVE MOOD.

MNEMONIC EXERCISE.

Gli comandò che parlásse,	He ordered him to speak.
Dúbito che l' óra sia tárda,	I fear that it is late.
Dítegli ch' égli fáccia cóme vuóle,	Tell him to do as he likes.
Non so se ío débba dír di si o di no,	I do not know if I ought to say yes or no.
Quánd' ánche io lo sapéssi, non ve lo diréi,	Even if I knew it, I would not tell you.
Si dà per sicúro che la páce sía fátta,	We are assured that peace is made.
Bisógna che gli scriviáte vói stésso,	It is necessary that you write to him yourself.
È il più brávo uómo ch' ío ábbia mái conosciúto,	He is the most honest man that I have ever known.
Benchè sía difficile, bisógna però vincere se stésso,	Although it is difficult, we must conquer ourselves.
Égli lo díce perchè non diáte a me la cólpa,	He says it that you may not blame me.
Io gli dissi che cóme gli piacésse le rispondésse,	I told him that he might answer her as he pleased.
Púre ch' élla si fáccia ognór più bélla,	She seems to be continually growing handsomer.
Gli dissi che facésse cóme volesse,	I told him to do as he pleased.
Se ío avéssi studiáto, saréi dótto,	If I had studied, I should be learned.
Può éssere ch' ío párta dománi,	It is possible that I may leave to-morrow.
Se tu sapéssi quánto ío t'ámo!	If thou knewest how much I love thee!
Vénne da me e mi domandò chi fóssi, e dóve andássi,	He came to me, and asked me who I was, and where I was going.

THE SUBJUNCTIVE MOOD.

Every proposition is either positive or doubtful.

I. The positive indicates that the thing positively exists; that the action is done in an absolute manner. This proposition is expressed by the *indicative* mood; as, *ìo párlo*, I speak; *ìo parláva*, I was speaking.

II. The doubtful proposition, on the contrary, is expressed by the subjunctive mood, and serves to indicate the possibility or doubt of a thing existing: it shows that the existence of the action is conditional and relative, because it depends on an antecedent proposition, expressed or understood; as, I wish to write, *ìo vóglio scrívere*, is positive, and in the indicative mood; I wish that you would write, *ìo vóglio che vói scriviáte*, is doubtful, depending on the will of another, and therefore put in the subjunctive.

III. The verb is used in the subjunctive after all verbs that signify *asking, entreating, suspecting, wondering, rejoicing, grudging, supposing, hoping, imagining, conjecturing, intimating;* after all verbs expressive of *desire, will, command, permission, prohibition, fear, belief;* after all verbs implying *doubt, ignorance, uncertainty,* or *future action;* and after all verbs used with a negative; as, —

Per amór di te ti prégo (che) te ne rimánghi,	For your sake, I beseech you to desist.
Che vuói tu ch' ìo sáppia?	What do you think that I know?

IV. Some of these verbs, however, appear sometimes to be used indiscriminately, either in the indicative or in the subjunctive mood: but it is not so in fact; for, when they are so used, each mood expresses the action in a different manner, as may be seen in the following examples: —

THE SUBJUNCTIVE MOOD.

Vóglio sposáre úna dónna che mi piáce,	I wish to marry a woman whom I like.
Vóglio sposáre úna dónna che mi piáccia,	I wish to marry a woman whom I may like.
Vádo cercándo úno che mi vuól béne,	I am seeking one who is fond of me.
Vádo cercándo úno che mi vóglia béne.	I am seeking one who may be fond of me.

In which, in the first instance, being certain of the existence of the action expressed, we use the indicative; and, in the second, we use the subjunctive, because the existence of the action is not certain, but doubted or desired.

V. After *sembráre, parére, bisognáre*, or any other impersonal verb, the subjunctive is always used; as,—

Bisógna che vói partiáte dománi,	You must go away to-morrow.
Mi sembráva che avésse vóglia di rídere,	He appeared as if he had a wish to laugh.
Parévami che élla fósse più biánca che la néve,	She appeared to me to be whiter than snow.

VI. The verb is also used in the subjunctive after the relative pronoun *che*, following a comparative or a superlative; as,—

Bélla quánt' áltra dónna (che) fósse mái in Firénze,	As handsome as any other lady in Florence ever was.
È la miglióre ópera che sía compársa,	It is the best work which ever appeared.

VII. And after the relative *quále*, not used in an interrogative manner; as,—

Úna párte quále volésse ne reggerébbe,	He might govern such a part as he should wish.

OF THE TENSES OF THE DEPENDENT VERBS IN A COMPOUND SENTENCE.

VIII. When, in a compound sentence, the principal verb is in the present of the indicative, or in the future, the dependent verb must be put in the *present of the* subjunctive, if we mean to imply the present or future time; and in the *imperfect* of the subjunctive, if we mean to imply the past; as, —

Crédo mi portásse amóre, — I believe that he loved me.
Io crédo omái che mónti e piágge sáppian di che témpra sia la mía víta, — I believe, that, by this time, mountains and plains know what is the condition of my life.

IX. When the dependent verb expresses an action which may be done at all times, it may be put either in the *imperfect* or the *present* of the *subjunctive*, although the principal verb be in the perfect-indefinite of the indicative; as, —

Iddio ci à dáto la ragióne affinchè ci distinguiámo, or *ci distinguéssimo, dágli animáli,* — God gave us reason in order that we might distinguish ourselves from animals.

X. In suppositive or conditional phrases, the *imperfect* of the *indicative* in English — *had, was,* or *were* — is rendered in Italian by the *imperfect of the subjunctive;* as, —

Se io avéssi quésti denári, gliéli presteréi incontanénte, — If I had this money, I would lend it to you immediately.
Chi starébbe méglio di me, se quéi denári fósser miéi? — Who would be more happy than I, if that money was mine?

REMARK. — Some conjunctions require the subjunctive mood; as, *Affinchè,* in order that; *benchè,* though; *senza chè,* without; *dato chè,* suppose.

READING LESSON.

È cósa rára che s'incóntri un giureconsúlto che lítighi, un médico che prénda medicína, e un teólogo che sía buón cristiáno.

Flechier éra fíglio d'un droghiére. Dícono che in un moménto di malavóglia, un véscovo gli rimproverásse la viltà dei suói natáli, e che Flechier gli rispondésse: Monsignóre, v'e quésta differénza fra vói e me, che se vói fóste náto nélla bottéga di mio pádre vi saréste ancóra.

Tre giórni dópo la mórte di Caterína di Fráncia, il predicatóre Lincestre cosi dall'álto del pérgamo la raccomandava agli astánti: "La Regína mádre è mórta, la quále, vivéndo, féce mólto mále, e per me crédo mólto più mále che béne. In quést' óggi si presénta úna difficoltà, che consiste in sapére se la chiésa cattólica déva pregáre per léi che vísse tánto mále, e così spésse sosténne la eresía, quantúnque si díca che in último sía státa con nói, e non ábbia acconsentíto álla mórte déi nóstri príncipi. Su di che ío dévo dírvi, che se voléte recitárle un páter ed áve così casáccio, fáte vói; varrà per quéllo che può valére: e lo rimétto alla vóstra libertà."

EXERCISE FOR TRANSLATION.

1. As a countryman was one day walking in the streets of Paris, he passed by a broker's shop; and, not seeing any thing but a man occupied in writing, he was anxious to know what business he did. He entered, and asked what they sold. "Asses' heads," answered the money-changer. "You must do good business," immediately replied the countryman, "since you have only your own left."

2. Semiramis ordered the following inscription to be engraved upon her tomb: "Let the king who has need of money demolish this tomb, and he will find a treasure." Darius caused the tomb to be opened: instead of money, he found this other inscription: "If thou hadst not been a bad man, and of insatiable avarice, thou wouldst not have disturbed the ashes of the dead."

3. A Turkish ambassador asked Lorenzo de Medecis why they did not see as many fools in Florence as in Cairo. Lorenzo pointed to a monastery, and said, "See where we shut them up."

4. A man having consulted the philosopher Bias, to know if he should marry, or lead a life of celibacy, he answered, "The woman you marry will be pretty or homely: if she is pretty, you will marry a Helen; if she is homely, you will marry a Fury: so you would do better not to marry."

VOCABULARY.

1. As a countryman was walking in, *girándo un paesáno per;* was anxious to know, *ébbe vóglia di,* etc.; did, *facésse;* entered, *entrò;* sold, *vendésse;* you must do, etc., *ne abbiáte un gran consúmo;* you have left, *rimáne.*

2. Demolish (make to demolish), *fáccia demolíre;* will find, *troverà.*

3. Did see, *vedéssero;* pointed, *addítò;* we shut, *rinchiudiámo.*

4. Should marry (if he had to take a wife); will marry, *meneréte.*

CONVERSAZIÓNE.

Che cósa domandò égli?
Che dicéste vói?
Che voléte sapére?
Quándo ritorneréte?
Chi sarébbe státo generóso se fósse náto rícco?
Che dísse María?

Che cósa è rára?

Perchè vi maravigliáte vói?

E se ìo avéssi bisógno di danáro?

Se ìo avévo ben studiáto.
Non so s' ìo débba dir di sì o di nò
Vóglio sapére chi élla sía.
Può éssere ch' ìo ritórni dománi.
Il póvero che si móstra riconoscénte di un benefízio.
Se ìo fóssi rícca, so ben ìo quél che avréi a fáre.
È cósa rára che s' incóntri un médico che prénda medicína.
Perchè vói avéte vendúto quel cavállo.
Se sapéste quánt' ìo v' ámo, m' avréste domandáto di **prestárvene**.

CHAPTER XXV.

THE INFINITIVE, GERUND, PRESENT AND PAST PARTICIPLES.

MNEMONIC EXERCISE.

Spésso la verità sta occúlta,	Truth is often concealed.
Che cósa avéte sentíto díre?	What have you heard said?
Ho sémpre odiáto l' adulazióne,	I have always hated flattery.
Il fuóco è spárso in tútta la natúra,	Fire is spread throughout all nature.
Bisógna andáre cáuto nel parláre,	It is necessary to be careful in speaking.
Giúnto álla pórta, la trovái chiúsa,	When I arrived at the door, I found it shut.
I Toscáni sóno acutíssimi nel motteggiáre,	The Tuscans are very sharp at raillery.
Al prímo vedérla la sorprésa mi ha tradíto,	Surprise betrayed me when I first saw her.
Lo speráre nell' avveníre è pazzía,	It is foolish to place one's hopes on the future.
La fólla crescénte sboccáva da ógni párte,	The swelling crowd poured in from all parts.
Il parlár póco, il fáre assái, e 'l non laudáre sè stésso, sóno virtù ráre,	To speak little, to do much, and not to praise one's self, are rare virtues.
Guardáti dal vantáre le cóse túe,	Abstain from praising what belongs to thee.
Una búrla per éssere détta fuóri di témpo può diventáre un' offésa,	An untimely joke may become an offence.
Si può díre quélla éssere véra árte che non appáre éssere árte,	It may be said, that true art is that which does not appear to be so.
Non il cominciáre, ma il perseveráre, è dégno di lóde,	It is not the commencing, but the persevering, which merits praise.

I. The infinitive takes the place of the third person when the phrase is composed of a principal proposition and a subordinate one, connected by the conjunction "that;" as, He said that the people *ought* not to be deceived, *égli díce il pópolo non* DOVER *éssere ingannáto;* it is said that time *is* the father of all truth, *dícono il témpo* ÉSSERE *pádre di ógni veritá*. This style, though very elegant and much used, is not adapted for common conversation. The above phrases may be translated word for word; as, *Égli díce che il pópolo non dée éssere ingannáto.*

II. The pronouns *lúi* and *léi* are used instead of *égli* and *élla* with the infinitive; as, *Sa ognúno lúi éssere státo maéstro di bel díre,* everybody knows that he was a model of eloquence.

III. The infinitive is used for the second person singular of the imperative mood, when preceded by the negative particle *non;* as, —

Non fáre strépito,	Do not make a noise.
Non ti lusingáre,	Do not flatter thyself.
Ció non temére,	Do not fear that.
Non mi toccáre, ribáldo!	Do not touch me, rascal!

IV. The infinitive may be used as a noun in the nominative case, or as regimen of the verb; as, —

Mi piáce mólto il súo fáre,	His manners please me much.
Nel danzáre, élla non ha pári nel móndo,	In dancing, she has no equal anywhere.
Dal parláre si conósce l' intérno dégli uómini,	We know the hearts of men by their speech.

V. The infinitive is used as follows by an able historian, in describing the movements of a camp preparing for an assault: *Quíndi éra nel cámpo un andáre,** *un*

---

* The Italians make frequent use of *andáre, veníre,* and *státe:* the first two convey an idea of movement; the latter, that of rest.

veníre, un urtársi d' uómini e di cárri un forbír d' ármi, un apparecchiáre di mácchine murdli, che l' ácre ne éra a mólta distánza intronáto.

VI. Many English phrases may be translated literally; as, —

It is a great folly to live poor, in order to die rich,	È *gran pazzía il vivér póvero, per morír rícco.*
It is a virtue to say much in few words,	È *virtù di dir mólto in póchi détti.*

THE PARTICIPLES.

VII. When the past participle * is joined to the verb *éssere* (to be), or to such verbs as *veníre, restáre* or *rimanére, vedérsi,* etc., used in the signification of "to be," it should agree with the subject of the verb with which it is joined, in gender and number; as, —

Éssi éran di fróndi di quércia inghirlandáti,	They were garlanded with oak-leaves.
Nè érano le fálte de' Vitelliáni punite, ma ben pagáte,	Nor were the faults of Vitellius' troops punished, but well paid.

VIII. But when the past participle is joined to the verb *avére* (to have), — if this verb is used, instead of *éssere,* in the signification of "to be," or is used in the signification of "to hold," "to possess," etc., as an active and not an auxiliary verb, — the participle agrees with the object of the verb in gender and number; as, —

S' avéa (for *s' éra*) *mésse alcúne petrúzze in bócca,*	He had put some small stones in his mouth.
Per non potérti vedére t' avrísti (for *ti sarésti*) *caváti gli ócchi,*	Thou wouldst have torn out thy eyes, not to see thyself.
Uno che foráta avéa (for *tenéa, posseđéa*) *la góla,*	One who had his throat pierced.

---

* There are many participles in *áto, áta,* which are contracted by suppressing the *a;* these are —

Accétto — a	for	*accettáto — a,*	accepted.
Adátto — a	for	*adattáto — a,*	adapted.
Cárico — a	for	*caricáto — a,*	loaded, etc.

IX. If the verb *avére*, to which the past participle is joined, is used as an auxiliary verb in order to represent the idea of past time, which could be equally expressed by a single form of the verb to which the participle belongs, then this participle remains invariable; as, —

Cóme io avrò dáto (or *darò*) *lóro ógni cósa*,	As soon as I shall have given every thing to them.
Cercáto ho (or *cercái*) *sémpre solitária via*,	I have always sought a solitary way.
Chi quéste cóse ha manifestáto (or *manifestò*) *al maéstro?*	Who has told these things to the master?

X. When the past participle is preceded by one of the pronouns *mi, ti, ci, vi, si, il, lo, la, li, gli, le, ne, che, cúi, quále, quáli, quánti*, as objects of the verb, the participle agrees with the pronouns, or the objects represented by them, in gender and number; as, —

Élla medésima me le ha détte (or *mi ha détte quéste cóse*),	She herself has told them to me.
Il libérto icéva avérla ésso uccísa (or *avére ésso uccísa la dónna*),	The freedman said that he had killed her himself.

XI. The English present participle may be expressed in Italian, —

1. By the gerund of the corresponding verb; as, —

Veggéndolo consumáre cóme la néve al sóle,	Seeing him waste away like snow in the sun.
Dorméndo gli párve di vedére la dónna sua,	(Sleeping, *or*) whilst he was asleep, it seemed to him that he saw his lady.

2. By the conjunction *che*, or the adverb *quándo*, and a tense of the indicative mood; as, —

Pói ch' ébbi riposáto il córpo lásso,	Having rested my weary body.
Quánd' ébbe détto ciò, riprése il téschio mísero có' dénti,	Having said this, he took up once more that miserable skull with his teeth.

3. By a preposition and the verb in the infinitive; as,—

Consumò quélla mattína in cercárli,	He spent that morning in looking after them.
Crédo che le suóre sién tútte a dormíre,	I believe that the nuns are all (sleeping *or*) asleep.

XII. When the English present participle has before it a preposition, such as "of," "from," "on," "in," etc., it is always rendered in Italian by the corresponding verb in the infinitive with a preposition.

XIII. If the participle is preceded by the prepositions "of," "from," "with," they are expressed in Italian by the preposition *di*, attended by the infinitive; as, *Ébbi il piacére di vedérlo*, I had the pleasure of seeing him.

XIV. The preposition "on," before the participle, may be expressed by the prepositions *di* or *in*; as,—

Si vánta d' avér la lóro conoscénza,	He values himself on being acquainted with them.
Nel partíre gli sovvénne di léi,	On his leaving, he recollected her.

The preposition "in" is rendered by *a* or *in*; as,—

Avéa nel quetár pópolo autorità ed árte,	In appeasing the people, he had both authority and art.
Che a far ciò volésse aitárlo,	That he would assist him in doing that.

XV. The prepositions "for," "without," "before," "after," etc., are literally translated.

XVI. If the participle is preceded by the preposition "by," this preposition is generally omitted in Italian, and the participle rendered by the gerund of the corresponding verb; as,—

Gli scolári impárano le régole di úna língua studiándole,	Scholars learn the rules of a language by studying them.

XVII. But if we wish to express the preposition, then the verb must be put in the infinitive, and "by" rendered by *con;* as, —

Il divíno Giúlio rintuzzò la sedizióne del súo esército col dir sólo, " Ah, Quiríti ! "

The divine Julius checked the sedition of his army by only saying, " Ah, Romans ! "

READING LESSON.

Dío mi creò per amáre; ío mi ricórdo di un fanciúllo sensitívo, vágo di solitúdine, abbandonáre il trambústo délla città, e lontáno nei cámpi voltársi indiétro a contemplárla, cóme l'Alghiéri descríve il naúfrago che uscíto fuóri dal pélago álla ríva, si vólge all' ácqua perigliósa, e guáta; égli si avvolgéva péi bóschi, udíva la vóce arcána che par che mándi la natúra al súo Creatóre, ascoltáva commósso l'armonía dégli uccélli, ed inviliáva la vóce lóro per cantáre anch'égli un ínno di glória, e le áli per accostársi al firmaménto, perchè gli avévano détto il Pádre del creáto abitáre nei ciéli: quánto tesóro di affétto éra nell'ánima di quel fanciúllo! Appéna la campána délla séra indicáva l'óra déi mórti, prosternáto davánti álla immágine di Gesù Crísto non sénza lácrime la supplicáva per le ánime dei suói defúnti . . . per tútti quélli che purgándosi aspéttano di sollevársi álle gióie divíne: égli avéva úna paróla di confórto per qualúnque sconsoláto. Ah! quel fanciúllo fúi ío. — GUERRÁZZI.

EXERCISE FOR TRANSLATION.

1. The ancients pretended that the greatest happiness was not to be born; and the next, to die young.

2. The Epicureans denied the existence of the soul, and recognized only physical principles: they said the gods did not enter into worldly things.

3. The philosopher Cleánte earned his living by drawing water during the night, so that he might study by day (to attend to study).

4. Apelles painted a bunch of grapes so natural, that several birds, seeing it, came to peck at it.

5. At Rome, a father emancipated his son by giving him a box on the ear.

6. In Paris, various academies are seen aiming at very different ends. There is the Academy of Music, which excites (moves)

PARTICIPLES.

the passions; and the School of Philosophy, to quiet them: the Fencing Academy, which teaches how to kill men; and the Medical Academy, to preserve life.

7. The painter Carácci, having been despoiled by certain thieves, knew so well how to delineate their physiognomy, and paint their faces, that they were discovered and arrested.

VOCABULARY.

1. Pretended, *pretendévano;* to be born, *náscere;* to die, *morire*.
2. To deny, *negáre;* recognized, *riconóbbero;* they said, *dicévano*.
3. Earned, *guadagnáva*.
4. Painted, *dipínse;* came, *vénnero*.
5. To emancipate, *emancipáre;* box on the ear, *schiáffo*.
6. Are seen, *védonsi;* moves, *muóve;* to quiet, *acchetáre;* to teach, *insegnáre;* to kill, *ammazzáre*.
7. To despoil, *spogliáre;* to designate, *disegnáre;* discovered, *scopérti*.

CONVERSAZIÓNE.

Che negárono gli epicuréi?
L' esisténza dell' ánima.

Che riconóbbero éssi?
Soltánto i princípj físici.

Che dicévano?
Dicévano gli déi non entráre nélle cóse di quésto móndo.

Di chi éra Bellíni maéstro?
Di Tiziáno.

Che féce il pittóre Bellíni per Maométto secóndo?
Égli dipínse la decollazióne di San Giovánni Battísta.

Ne fu conténto il sultáno?
Lodándo la pittúra, avvertì l' artísta d' un erróre.

Cóme guadagnáva la vita il filósofo Cleánte?
Col cavár ácqua in témpo di nótte per atténdere állo stúdio di giórno.

A chi somígliano gli uómini in generále?
A un miserábile príncipe dominánte sulle cóste délla Guinéa.

Perchè?
Perchè dicéva ad alcúni Francési: "Si párla mólto di me in Fráncia?"

Che pretendévano gli antíchi?
Pretendévano, la príma felicità éssere il non náscere, la secónda, il morír présto.

CHAPTER XXVI.

THE VERBS *ANDÁRE, DÁRE, FÁRE* AND *STÁRE*.*

MNEMONIC EXERCISE.

Mi rincrésce di dárvi distúrbo,	I am sorry to disturb you.
Fece vista di non inténdere,	He pretended not to hear.
Veníte a stáre con nói,	Come to live with us.
Cóme státe d' appetíto?	How is your appetite?
A che óra siéte sólito far colazióne?	At what hour do you generally breakfast?
È un ragázzo che non puo stár férmo,	He is a child who cannot keep still.
Siámo cosí stánche che nón possiámo più stáre in piédi,	We are so tired that we can no longer stand.
Ditegli ch' égli fáccia cóme vuóle,	Tell him that he may do as he likes.
Il gústo dégli uómini va soggétto a mólte vicénde,	The taste of men is liable to many changes.
Égli non póse gran fátto cúra a quéllo ch' ío dissi,	He did not pay much attention to what I said.
Io scélsi úna móglie secóndo il cuór mío,	I took a wife after my own heart.
Non fáte capitále délla súa paróla,	Do not depend upon his word.
Da nói si dà in távola álle cínque,	We dine at five at our house.
Vi darò contézza del súo státo,	I will inform you of his situation.
Io l' indúco quánto so e pósso, a stáre allégro e a fársi ánimo,	I will induce him, as much as I can, to drive away melancholy, and take courage.

---

* *Andáre, dáre, stáre*, are the only irregular verbs of the first conjugation. In some of their compounds, they become regular; as *riandáre, trasandáre*, etc., which are varied like *amáre*. *Fáre* is a contraction of *facére* (now obsolete), of which it retains many forms. It is considered by some grammarians as belonging to the second conjugation, and is irregular in its compounds.

ITALIANISMS WITH ANDÁRE (TO GO).

Quésta cósa non va fátta,	This thing ought not to be done.
Andár diétro ad úno,	To follow some one.
Andáre a vóto, in váno,	Not to succeed.
Andáre álla ventúra,	To go at random.
Andáre in cóllera,	To get angry.
Andár sicúro,	To be sure.
Lasciámo andáre quésto,	Do not speak of that.
A lúngo andáre,	In the long-run.
Andáre altéro,	To be proud.
Ío so quél che va détto,	I know what I must say.
Il sóle va sótto,	The sun sets.
Andáre béne,	To succeed.
Andárne la víta,	To have one's life at stake.
Il mérito va congiúnto cólla modéstia,	Merit is accompanied by modesty.
Le dónne vánno trattáte con gentilézza,	Women ought to be treated with courtesy.

WITH DÁRE (TO GIVE).

Dáre a cámbio,	To put out money at interest.
Dáre compiménto,	To finish.
Dar da dormíre,	To lodge.
Dar da rídere,	To give cause for laughter.
Dáre de' cálci,	To kick.
Dar féde,	To believe.
Dar luógo,	To give an opportunity.
Dar le véle a' vénti,	To set sail.
Dar il buón ánno,	To wish a merry new-year.
Dáre il mótto,	To give the word.
Dar la máno,	To marry, to shake hands.
Avére a dáre,	To be in debt.
Dársi buón témpo,	To live a merry life.
Dársi l' acqúa ai piédi,	To praise one's self.
Dársi a gámbe,	To run away.
Dársi pensiére,	To care for.
Dar che díre,	To give occasion to talk.
Dar giù,	To subside, to decline.
Dáre úna vóce ad úno,	To call some one.
Dáre in távola,	To serve the dinner.
Dáre vóce,	To spread a report.

WITH *FÁRE* (TO DO).

Fáte che vénga da me,	Bid him come to me.
Fáre le cárte,	To deal at cards.
Quésto non fa per me,	This will not do for me.
Avér mólto a fáre,	To be very busy.
Nón ne ho a fáre,	I have no need of it.
Fátevi a me,	Come near me.
Fársi álla finéstra,	To look out of the window
Tre mési fa,	Three months ago.
Úna settimána fa,	A week ago.
Al far del giórno,	At the break of day.
Far béllo,	To set off.
Non fa fórza,	It is no matter.
Far cérto,	To assure.
Fátevi indiétro,	Go back.
Far cápo ad úno,	To address some one.
Far del gránde,	To be self-important.
Far stáre úno,	To restrain some one.
Fáre una prédica,	To admonish.
Far víta strétta,	To live niggardly.
Far súa vóglia,	To do as one pleases.
Che vi fa égli che vénga o non vénga?	What is it to you if he comes or not?

WITH *STÁRE* (TO BE).

Sto per partíre,	I am on the point of leaving.
Qui sta il púnto,	This is the question.
Státe quánto vi piáce,	Stay as long as you please.
Dóve státe di cása?	Where do you live?
Il tútto sta, s' égli sía buóno o no,	The point is, if it be good or not.
La cósa sta cóme vi dico,	The thing is as I tell you.
Stáre a páne ed ácqua,	To live upon bread and water.
Cóme státe vói?	How do you do?
Égli sta béne,	He is well.
Star chéto,	To be quiet.
Stándo álla finéstra lo vídi passáre,	Whilst I was at the window, I saw him going by.
Sta cóme úna státua di mármo sénza parláre,	He stands like a marble statue, without speaking.
Ditémi in che módo sta che égli sía vóstro fratéllo?	Tell me, how comes it that he is your brother?

READING LESSON.

Il fuóco, l' àcqua e l' onóre.

Il fuóco, l' àcqua e l' onóre, fécero un témpo comunélla insième. Il fuóco non può mài stáre in un luógo, e l' àcqua ánche sémpre si muóve; ónde tràtti dàlla lóro inclinazióne, indússero l' onóre a far viàggio in compagnía. Príma dúnque di partírsi, tútti e tre dissero che bisognàva dàrsi fra lóro un ségno da potérsi ritrováre, se mài si fóssero scostàti e smarríti l' úno dall' áltro. Dísse il fuóco : " E se mi avvenísse mài quésto cáso che ío mi segregàssi da vói, ponéte ben ménte colà dóve vói vedéte fúmo; quésto è il mío segnále e quivi mi troveréte certamènte." — " E me," dísse l' àcqua," se vói non mi vedéte, non mi cercáte colà dóve vedréte seccàra o spaccatúre di térra, ma dóve vedréte sálci, ontáni, cannúcce o èrba mólto álta e vérde; andáte costà in tràccia di me, e quivi sarò io." — " Quánto a me," dísse l' onóre, "spalancáte ben gli ócchi, e ficcátemegli béne addósso e tenétemi sáldo, perchè se la mála ventúra mi guída fuóri di cammíno, sicchè io mi pérda úna vólta, non mi troveréste più."

EXERCISE FOR TRANSLATION.

1. A drop of water complained of remaining unknown in the ocean. Moved to compassion, a genius caused an oyster to swallow it. It became the most beautiful pearl of the East, and was the most splendid ornament of the Great Mogul's throne.

2. Milton, after he became blind, married, for his third wife, a woman who was very beautiful, but of a furious temper. A friend once said to him, that his wife was like a rose. " I cannot judge so by its color," he replied, " but I do by the thorns."

3. Who would believe that smoking tobacco was in fashion with the English ladies in the sixteenth century? Every day, when Queen Elizabeth rose, there were (one saw) thirty ladies seated in a circle around her, smoking pipes. The queen set (gave) them the example; but one day she broke the pipe, saying, " We will renounce a pleasure that evaporates in smoke."

4. A doctor was translating a work. They came to tell him that his wife was very sick, and desired to speak with him. " I have only one page to translate," said he ; " when I will come immediately." A second messenger came, and informed him that she was dying. " Two words more, and I have done," said the translator. " Go, return to her." A moment after, they came to tell him that she was dead. " I am very sorry for it," said he ; " she was a good woman:" and he continued his work.

VOCABULARY.

1. Complained, *si dólse;* moved, *mósso;* caused, *féce che;* became, *divénne.*
2. Become, *divenúto;* furious, *furibóndo;* can, *pósso;* judge, *giudicáre.*
3. Would believe, *crederébbe;* one saw, *si vedévano;* seated, *sedúto;* smoking pipes, *pipávano;* gave, *dáva;* broke, *spezzò;* we will renounce, *rinunzierémo;* evaporates, *svapóra.*
4. Was translating, *stáva tracucéndo;* they came, *vénnero;* will come, *verrò;* came, *vénne;* she was dying, *éra ágli estrémi;* go, *andáte;* return, *tornáte;* I am sorry, *me ne rincrésce;* continued, *continuò.*

CONVERSAZIÓNE.

A chi sóno cári i nómi del Sárpi, del Parúta e dell' Algarótti?

Son tánto cári all' Európa quánto all' Itália.

Che bisógna fáre per l' infortúnio?

Bisógna compiángerlo e soccórrerlo se si può.

Per réggere all' ingiustízia dégli uómini che è necessário?

Un gran coraggio.

Chi fu Áldo Manuzio?

Il primo célebre stampatóre che sia státo in Európa.

E il Zéno ed il Goldóni?

Sóno i pádri del drámma e délla commédia italiána.

Chi fu Bémbo?

Il primo legislatóre della lingua italiána.

Cóme si chiamáva anticaménte Nápoli?

Parténope, nóme di una Siréna che credési ábbia fondáta la città.

Che si dice délla poténza Veneziána?

Élla ha arricchíta l' Itália e l' ha difésa gran témpo dái Bárbari.

CHAPTER XXVII.

ADVERBS.

MNEMONIC EXERCISE.

Vi racconterò la cósa per minúto,	I will relate the affair minutely.
Osservate minutaménte ógni cósa,	Observe every thing minutely.
Per óra non pósso dírvi di più,	I cannot tell you any more now.
Dóve andáte cosí per témpo?	Where do you go so early?
Díte da véro, oppúre burláte?	Are you in earnest, or joking?
Dóve si va cosí in frétta?	Where are you going so quickly?
Cattíva érba násce dappertútto,	Weeds grow everywhere.
Il témpo pássa présto,	Time passes quickly.
Mi préme assái di parlárgli,	I much need to speak to him.
Veníte quánto più présto potéte,	Come as soon as possible.
V' ingannáte di grán lúnga,	You are greatly mistaken.
Quésta non è già cólpa vóstra,	This is not your fault.
Gli uómini ímitano mólto, e riflèttono póco,	Men imitate much, and reflect little.
Chi obbedísce álla cíéca, spésso si pénte,	He who obeys blindly, often repents.
Chi sémpre ríde, spésso ingánna,	He who always laughs, often deceives.
Le súe cóse vánno di béne in méglio,	His affairs become better and better.
Io non vi vóglio neppúr guardáre!	I do not wish even to look at you!
Gli ho réso cónto appuntíno di ógni cósa,	I have rendered an exact account of every thing.
Di ráro il médico píglia medicíne,	The physician rarely takes medicine.
Non bisógna mái parláre a cáso,	We should never speak at random.
Me ne ricorderò per un pézzo,	I shall remember it for a long time.
Dónde veníte? Dóve andáte?	Whence do you come? Where are you going?

ADVERBS.

I. The greater portion of the Italian adverbs are formed of a feminine adjective and the noun *ménte*, manner (from the Latin *mens*); as, *Dótta*, learned; *dotta-ménte*, learnedly; *sávia*, wise; *savia-ménte*, wisely; *dólce*, sweet; *dolce-ménte*, sweetly.

If the adjective ends in *le* or *re*, the final *e* is dropped, for the sake of euphony, in the formation of the adverb: as, *Fedéle*, faithful; *fedel-ménte*, faithfully; *maggióre*, greater; *maggior-ménte*, greatly.

II. These adverbs have their comparatives and superlatives formed from the comparatives and superlatives of the adjectives; as, *Più sincéra*, more sincere; *più sinceraménte*, more sincerely; *méno felíce*, less happy; *méno feliceménte*, less happily; *prudentíssima*, very prudent; *prudentissimaménte*, very prudently.

III. Some adverbs are mere adjectives, and are used also in their comparatives and superlatives; as, *Chiáro* (*chiaraménte*), clearly; *più chiáro*, more clearly; *schiétta* (*schiettaménte*), candidly; *méno schiétta*, less candidly; *tríste* (*tristaménte*), sadly; *tristíssimo*, very sadly.

IV. The following are the other adverbs most in use in Italian: —

ADVERBS OF TIME.

Adésso,	now.	*Avantiéri,*	the day before yester
Mò,	„	*Iér l' áltro,*	the other day. [day
Óra,	„	*L' altriéri,*	„ „ „
Allóra,	then.	*Iermattína,*	yesterday morning.
Ancóra,	still.	*Ierséra,*	last evening.
Tuttóra,	„	*Óggi,*	to-day.
Talóra,	sometimes. (*talvolta*)	*Oggidì,*	in our days.
Ognóra,	always.	*Stamáne,*	this morning.
Sémpre,	„	*Staséra,*	this evening.
Sovénte,	often. (*spesso.*)	*Stanótte,*	to-night.
Testéso,	just now.	*Domattína,*	to-morrow morning
Testè,	„	*Dimáni,*	to-morrow.
Iéri,	yesterday	*Dománe,*	„

ADVERBS.

Posdimáni,	the day after to-morrow.	Non mai,	never.
Posdománe,	,, ,, ,, ,,	Ománi,	now.
Innánzi,	before.	Oramái,	,,
Diánzi,	,,	Oggimái,	,,
Prima,	,,	Quási,	almost.
Diétro,	afterward.	Circa,	about.
Dópo,	,,	Incirca,	,,
Pói,	then, since, afterward.	Intórno,	,,
Dipói,	,, ,, ,,	Tárdi,	late.
Dappói,	,, ,, ,,	Pertémpo,	soon.
Póscia,	,, ,, ,,	Présto,	quick.
Indi,	then, afterward.	Adágio,	slow.
Quíndi,	,, ,,	Méntre,	whilst.
Apprésso,	,, ,,	Intánto,	in the mean time.
Infine,	in fine.	Frattánto,	,, ,, ,, ,,
Da capo,	once more.	Trattánto,	,, ,, ,, ,,
Già,	already.	Dacchè,	since.
Di giù,	,,	Finchè,	until.
Mái,	never.	Quándo,	when.
Giammái,	,,	Tuttavía,	still.

OF PLACE.

Quì,	here, hither.	Ovúnque,	wherever.
Quà,	,,	Dovúnque,	,,
Lì,	there, thither.	Ógni dóve,	everywhere.
Là,	,, ,,	Altróve,	elsewhere.
Costì,	there near you.	Altrónde,	,,
Costà,	,, ,, ,,	Avánti,	before.
Colì,	there, thither.	Davánti,	,,
Colà,	,, ,,	Diétro,	behind.
Sù,	up.	Didiétro,	,,
Giù,	down.	Indiétro,	back.
Quívi,	there.	Addiétro,	,,
Gli,	,,	Sópra,	upon, above.
Ivi,	,,	Sótto,	under, below.
Indi,	thence.	Abbásso,	below.
Quínci,	from hence.	Éntro,	within.
Quíndi,	from thence.	Déntro,	,,
Quassù,	here above.	Fuóri,	without.
Quaggiù,	here below.	Fuóra,	,,
Insù,	upward.	Difuóri,	from without.
Ingiù,	downward.	Difuóra,	,, ,,
Lassù,	there above.	Alláto,	aside.
Laggiù,	there below.	Accánto,	,,
Colassù,	there above.	Attórno,	around.
Colaggiù,	there below.	Dattórno,	,,
Costaggiù,	there below near you.	Rimpétto,	opposite.
Costínci,	from thence.	Dirimpétto,	,,
Óve,	where.	Lúngi,	far.
Dóve,	,,	Óltre,	beyond.
Dónde,	whence.		

15*

OF ORDER.

Príma,	first.	Assiéme,	together.
Dipói,	then.	Insiéme,	,,
Quíndi,	afterward.	A vicénda,	by turns.
Infíne,	finally.	Al tútto,	altogether.
In gíro,	by turns.	Al rovéscio,	the reverse.
Alla fíla,	in a row.	Sossópra,	topsy-turvy.

OF QUANTITY.

Più,	more.	Niénte,	nothing.
Méno,	less.	Non guári,	not much.
Mánco,	,,	Davantággio,	more.
Assái,	much.	Alpiù,	at the most.
Abbastánza,	enough.	Alméno,	at least.
A sufficiénza,	,,	Almánco,	,, ,,

OF QUALITY.

Béne,	well.	Brancolóne,	crawlingly.
Mále,	badly.	Inginocchióne,	on one's knees.
Appéna,	hardly.	Carpóne,	upon all fours.
Appósta,	purposely.	A cavalcióne,	astride over.
A gára,	emulously.	Tentóne,	gropingly.
A cáso,	by chance.	Boccóne,	with one's face downward.
A tórto,	wrongly.		

OF AFFIRMATION.

Sì,	yes.	Maisì,	yes, indeed.
Già,	yes, certainly.	Sì, béne,	yes, truly.
Béne,	well.	Affè,	in faith.
Invéro,	indeed, truly, in truth.	Appúnto,	just.
Davvéro,	,, ,, ,,	Volentiéri,	willingly.
Da dovéro,	,, ,, ,,	Benvolentiéri,	very willingly.
In verità,	,, ,, ,,	Malvolentiéri,	unwillingly.

OF NEGATION.

No,	no, not.	Nonmái,	never.
Mái,	never.	Míca,	not.
Mainò,	no, indeed.	Nonmíca,	not at all.
Cérto no,	certainly not.	Per nulla,	by no means.
Nongià,	not, not at all.	Niénte affátto,	nothing at all.

OF DOUBT.

Fórse,	perhaps.	Per accidénte,	perchance
Forsechè,	,,	Per sórte,	,,
Può éssere,	may be.	Per avventúra,	,,
Può dársi,	,,		

ADVERBS.

OF COMPARISON.

Sì,	so, thus.	*Viappiù,*	a great deal more
Così,	,, ,,	*Vieppiù,*	,, ,, ,, ,,
Cóme,	as.	*Viamméno,*	a great deal less.
Siccóme,	so, as.	*Viemméno,*	,, ,, ,, ,
Più,	more.	*A guísa,*	like.
Méno,	less.	*A módo,*	,,
Assái,	much.	*Al pári,*	,,

OF INTERROGATION.

Óve?	where?	*Chè?*	how?
Dóve?	where? whither?	*Cóme?*	how?
Dónde?	whence?	*Perchè?*	why?
Quándo?	when?	*Quánto?*	how much?

OF CHOICE.

Ánzi,	rather, sooner.	*Piuprésto,*	rather, sooner.
Príma,	,, ,,	*Piuttósto,*	,, ,,

OF DEMONSTRATION.

Écco,	here or there is; lo! behold!	*Eccoli,*	there is, there are.
Eccoquí,	here is, here are.	*Eccolà,*	,, ,, ,, ,,
Eccoquà,	,, ,, ,, ,,	*Quánd' écco,*	when, lo!

V. A list of the adjectives which are used in Italian as adverbs:—

Fórte,	very much.	*Ráro,*	rarely.
Spésso,	often.	*Sólo,*	only.
Sódo,	fast, hard.	*Tútto,*	all.
Álto,	softly.	*Póco,*	little.
Cérto,	certainly.	*Mólto,*	much.
Tríste,	sadly.	*Tróppo,*	too much.
Dólce,	sweetly.	*Béllo,*	handsomely.
Chiáro,	clearly.	*Buóno,*	very well.
Schiétto,	candidly.	*Méglio,*	better.
Piáno,	low, softly.	*Péggio,*	worse.
Tárdo,	late.	*Apérto,*	openly.
Lénto,	slowly.	*Súbito,*	immediately.
Présto,	soon.	*Sicúro,*	surely.
Prónto,	readily.	*Dimésso,*	lowly.
Tósto,	speedily.	*Somésso,*	humbly.
Rátto,	,,	*Vicíno,*	near.
Tánto,	so much.	*Lontáno,*	far.

In order to know when these words are adjectives, and when adverbs, it is sufficient to observe, whether they stand by themselves, or are added to or used for a noun: for, in the former case, they are always adverbs; and, in the latter, adjectives.

VI. Besides the above adverbs, there are some expressions called *adverbial phrases;* chiefly the following:—

Di súbito,	suddenly.	*Di rádo,*	seldom, rarely.
Di bótto,	presently.	*Di ráro,*	,, ,,
In un baléno,	in an instant.	*Infátti,*	in fact.
In un bátter d' ócchio,	in the twinkling of an eye.	*Difátti,* *Di gran lúnga,*	,, ,, by far.
Póco fa,	a little while ago.	*A lúngo andáre,*	in the long-run,
Fra póco,	in a short time.		in time.
Un pézzo fa,	some time ago.	*A più potére,*	with all one's
Délle vólte,	at times.		might.
All' improvvíso,	unexpectedly.	*Di mála vóglia,*	unwillingly.
All' avveníre,	in future.	*A un di présso,*	almost.
A minúto,	in detail.	*D' allóra in quà,*	since that time.
Di frésco,	newly.	*D' óra innánzi,*	henceforth.
Di buón grádo,	willingly.	*In quél méntre,*	in or at that
Mío malgrádo,	against my will.		time.
Sénza méno,	positively.	*Di púnto in púnto,*	exactly.
Quánto príma,	very soon.	*Di púnto in biánco,*	point-blank.
A béllo stúdio,	designedly.	*Di quándo in quándo,*	now and then.
A bélla pósta,	,,	*Di trátto in trátto,*	,, ,, ,,
A méno che,	unless.	*Di tánto in tánto,*	,, ,, ,,
Da per tútto,	everywhere.	*Il più,*	the utmost.
Per ógni dóve,	,,	*Per lo più,*	for the most part,
Ad un trátto,	at once.		generally.

READING LESSON.

La Póvera Ciéca.

È brúna l' ária — per le contráde,
A fiócche a fiócche la néve cáde;
E là in ginócchio présso la chiésa,
Géme una vécchia dónna prostésa:
Órba dégli ócchi, la poverétta
Atténde il páne, che a léi si gétta ...
Fáte limósina, pietósa génte,
Fáte limósina álla dolénte!

Vói non sapéte che quélla dónna,
Mácero il víso, lórda la gónna,
De' suói concénti cóll' armonía
Di cénto pópoli l' álme rapía;

Oh quánta invídia ai fortunáti
Che d' un sorríso rendéa beáti!
Fáte limósina, pietósa génte,
Fate limósina álla dolénte!

Oh quánte vólte fuór de' teátri
L' imménsa fólla dégl' idolátri
Fra mille plaúsi le féa codázzo
Fíno álla pórta del súo palázzo,
E riveránte stendéa il ginócchio
Perchè scendésse dáll' auréo cócchio!
Fáte limósina, pietósa génte,
Fáte limósina álla dolénte!

Quánte dovízie spandéva intórno
Il súo magnífico vásto soggiórno!
Brónzi, colónne, vási, cristálli,
Argénto ed óro, cócchi e caválli ...
Di fióri e gémme da tútte bánde,
Sóvra i súoi pássi piovéan ghirlánde ...
Fáte limósina, pietósa génte,
Fáte limósina álla dolénte!

Ma un dì fra l' ánsie d' un dúolo atróce
Perdè la vísta, perdè la vóce —
Ahi sventuráta! or per le stráde
Va mendicándo l' altrúi pietáde,
Élla che un giórno per chi geméa
De' suói tesóri l' árche schiudéa!
Fáte limósina, pietósa génte,
Fáte limósina álla dolénte!

Ma il fréddo addóppia — gélida e spéssa
La néve cópre la genufléssa,
Che, pur pregándo, intirizzíta
Strínge il Rosário fra le súe díta —
Perchè la mísera confídi ancóra
Nélla pietáde del ciel, chè implóra,
Fáte limósina, pietósa génte,
Fáte limósina álla dolénte!

A. Fusinato

EXERCISE FOR TRANSLATION.

1. A truly courageous man is he who has a knowledge of danger. We often see men who neither fear nor are afraid of death: yet we cannot call them courageous; because (being), ignorant of danger, they rush forward foolishly.

2. Francis I., going out from the council which had determined upon war with Italy, met his buffoon, who said to him, " Sire, it seems to me that your councillors are fools."—" Why?" asked the king. " Because," he replied, " they have been so long discussing what part of Italy they intend to enter, and have never said a word about the part to go out. Therefore, O sire! take care not to go there at all." A month after this, Francis was a prisoner in Pavia.

3. There are many people who think that they can learn the Italian language in three months; and (these people), after six months' study, do not know how to say, "I have just written; the clock has just struck ten; I should like to know it for certain."

VOCABULARY.

1. We see, *si védono*; they rush, *spíngono*.
2. Going, *uscéndo*; met, *incontrò*; have (been discussing) discussed, *hánno discússo*; said, *détto*; take care, *avvertíte*.
3. Think, *stímano*; do know, *sánno*; I should like, *vorréi*.

CONVERSAZIÓNE.

Che cósa dimandò égli?
Che óra è?
Perchè non siéte venúto?
È quélla dúnque la vóstra amíca?
Avéte vino, páne, formággio, quálche cósa?
Non avéte neppúre úna scodélla di látte?
È dúnque un ánno e mézzo ch' élla è partíta?
Dóve dimóra il súo Signór pádre?
Che effétto fa la medicína?
Quándo conósce úno il valóre dell' ácqua?

Il perchè.
Sóno appéna battúte le diéci.
Perchè sóno státo alla villa.
È ben léi.
Non ho próprio núlla da dárvi?
Non ho núlla in verità.
No, non sóno ancóra quíndici mési?
Dimóra quì vicíno.
Guarísce talvólta e consóla spésso.
Quándo è asciútto (dry) il pózzo.

CHAPTER XXVIII.

CONJUNCTIONS AND INTERJECTIONS.

MNEMONIC EXERCISE.

Via, via; méno ciárle!
Oimè! che védo mái?
Deh! non lo fáte,
Oh bélla! son venúto per quésto,
Quándo è così, vádo via,
Così díco; ancór ío,
La cósa andò pur così,
Éhi, quél gióvine!
Ánimo, ánimo básta così!
Éhi, quélla gióvine,
Evvíva, il nóstro Semprónio!
Io ve l' ho pur détto.
Non ha púre mostráto di conóscermi,
Oh! se potéssi rídere, rideréi pur di cuóre,
Al cán che fúgge, ognún grída, dágli, dágli,
Per Bácco, più ci pénso, e méno so comprèndere il motívo,
Quésto partito è il miglióre; ánzi, il sólo cúi débba appigliármi,
E così, che cósa facciámo?

Addío, cáro: dóve si va?

Vía, non lo sgridáte: poveríno!

Io vi ámo, perchè lo meritáte,

Come, come; less talk!
Alas! what do I see?
Do not do it, I beg of you.
Indeed! I came on purpose.
Since it is so, I shall go.
I say so; even I.
It certainly went off so.
Here, young man!
Courage! that will do.
Well, miss.
Bravo, our Sempronio!
I have, however, told you.
He did not even appear to know me.
Oh! if I could laugh, I would laugh willingly.
When a dog runs, people cry after him, after him.
Truly, the more I think of it, the less I understand the motive.
This part is the best; nay, the only one which I ought to take.
Well, what are we going to do?

Adieu, my dear: where are you going?

There, don't scold him: poor boy!

I love you, because you deserve it.

CONJUNCTIONS IN COMMON USE.

E,	and.	*Nonostánte,*	
O,	or, either.	*Nondi.neno,*	
Nè,	nor, neither.	*Nientedimeno,*	
Se,	if, whether.	*Con tútto ciò,*	still, nevertheless,
Ma,	but.	*Non per tánto,*	notwithstanding,
Però,	,,	*Non per quésto,*	for all that.
Che,	that.	*Ciò non ostánte,*	
Púre,	yet, nevertheless.	*Ciò non di méno,*	
Già,	yet, already.	*Tuttavía,*	
Anzi,	nay, rather, on the contrary.	*Non giù,*	not at all, not indeed.
Anche,	also, even.	*Non sólo,* }	not only, not merely.
Anco,	,, ,,	*Non che,* }	
Eziandío	,, ,,	*Purchè,*	provided.
Altresì,	,, ,,	*A méno chè,*	unless.
Ancóra,	also, even, again.	*Anzi che,*	rather, sooner.
Eppúre,	yet, nevertheless.	*Anzi che no,*	rather than not, rather so than otherwise.
Ossìa,	or, either.		
Ovvéro,	,, ,,		
Oppúre,	,, ,,	*Sì,*	so, thus.
Nemméno,	neither, not even.	*Così,*	,, ,,
Nemmánco,	,, ,, ,,	*Cóme,*	as, like.
Neppúre,	,, ,, ,,	*Siccóme,*	,, ,,
Neánche,	,, ,, ,,	*Sicchè,*	so, thus, wherefore.
Tampóco,	,, ,, ,,	*Così che,*	,, ,, ,,
Se mái,	if ever, if indeed.	*Talchè,*	so, so that.
Se púre,	,, ,,	*Giacchè,*	since.
Se però,	if however.	*Cioè,*	that is.
Se non,	unless, except, but.	*Cioè a díre,*	that is to say. ——
Se non che,	,, ,, ,,	*Vále a díre,*	,, ,,
Acciò,		*Alméno,*	at least.
Acciocchè, }	in order that, to the end that.	*Ahndnco,*	,,
Affine, }		*Di più,*	moreover.
Affinchè, }		*Inóltre,*	besides, besides this
Ancorchè,	even that.	*Oltrecchè,*	,, ,, ,,
Contuttochè,	,, ,,	*Oltracciò,*	,, ,, ,,
Chè,	for, why, because.	*D' altrónde,*	,, ,, ,,
Perchè,	,, ,, ,,	*Dúnque,*	then, therefore.
Poichè, }	because, since, as, after.	*Adúnque,*	,, ,,
Posciachè, }		*Ónde,*	wherefore, whereupon.
Perocchè, }		*Laónde,* }	
Imperocchè, }	because, whereas, as, since.	*Quíndi,* }	
Perciocchè, }		*Perciò,*	therefore, for which reason.
Imperciocchè, }			
Conciosiacchè, }		*In sómma,* }	in short, in conclusion.
Quantúnque,	although.	*In fíne,* }	
Sebbéne,	,,	*Sía che,*	whether, or, either
Benchè,	,,	*Vuói,*	,, ,, ,,
Comechè,	,,	*Del résto,*	otherwise, besides
Avvegnachè,	,,	*Per áltro,*	,, ,,

CONJUNCTIONS.

Tánto,	as.	Intánto,	in the mean time, mean
Quánto,	„	Frattánto,	while, whilst.
Quándo,	when.	Méntre,	whilst, whilst that.
Quánd' ánche,	even when.	Mentrecchè,	„ „ „
In guísa che,		Sálvo,	save, saving, except.
In módo che,	so that, in such a manner.	Eccètto,	„ „ „
In maniéra che,		Tránne,	„ „ „
Di módo che,		Fuorchè,	„ „ „
Di maniéra che,		Fórse,	perhaps.
		Óra,	now.

I. *Púre* is often used in the sense of *ancóra* (even), and *sólo* (only).

II. *Perchè* has four significations: 1. In an interrogative phrase, it has the meaning of "why;" as, *Perchè andáte viá?* why do you go away? 2. Followed by a verb in the subjunctive, it signifies "in order that;" as, *Non vi ho dáto il danáro perchè lo spendiáte súbito*, I did not give you the money that (in order that) you should immediately spend it. 3. It is used for "though;" as in the phrase of Dante, *Non lasciávam l' andár, perchè e' dicésse*, We did not cease walking, although he spoke. 4. It also signifies "because;" as, *Perchè ridéte? Perchè ho vóglia di rídere*, Why do you laugh? Because I wish to laugh.

III. *Anzi* is sometimes used for "before;" as, *Ánzi témpo, ánzi l' óra, ánzi la mía mórte*, before the time, before the hour, before my death.

IV. *Méntre, nel méntre che* or *méntre che, in témpo che*, signifies "whilst" or "whilst that;" as, *Méntr' égli cantáva, ío balláva*, whilst he sung, I danced.

V. Many conjunctions, as *nondiméno, ciò non ostánte*, etc., contain in themselves a pronoun, a preposition, an adverb, etc.; but, from their office of joining sentences together, they are commonly reckoned amongst conjunctions, though in fact they are but *conjunctive phrases*.

INTERJECTIONS IN COMMON USE.

Ah!	ah! ha! alas!	Ahimè! aimè!	alas (me)!
Eh! eh!	eh!	Ehimè! eimè!	,,
Ih!	ih!	Ohimè! oimè!	,,
Oh! o!	oh! ho!	Omè!	,,
Uh!	uh!	Oilè!	alas (thee)!
Ahi!	ah! alas! [there!	Oisè!	alas (him *or* her)!
Ehi!	here! ho hey! ho	Guai!	woe!
Ohi! oi!	ah! oh!	Aiùto!	help!
Uhi!	ah! alas!	O Dio!	O Heavens!
Deh!	ah! alas! pray! prithee!	Lásso!	alas!
		Lásso me!	,,
Doh!	oh! pshaw!	Ahi lásso!	,,
Ah, ah!	ah, ah!	Póvero me!	wretched that I am! unfortunate that I am! wretched me! poor me!
Eh, eh!	eh, eh!	Mísero me!	
Oh, oh!	oh, oh!	Meschíno me!	
Poh!	poh!	Dolénte me!	
Puh! pu!	pu! pooh!		
Eia!	halloo!	O me beáto!	happy that I am! happy me!
Olà!	holla! ho there!	O me felíce!	
Così!	so! thus!	Beáto me!	
Sì!	yes, certainly!	Felíce me!	
Già!	,, ,,	Alto!	halt!
Pure!	yet!	Sta!	stop!
Come!	how! how then! why! why so!	Ohè!	take care! have care! beware!
		Guárda!	
		Lárgo!	
Su!	up, up! come! come then!	Piáno,	softly! gently! slowly!
Orsù!		Adágio,	
Su, su!		Zi! zitto!	whist! hush!
Via!		Chéto!	quiet! still!
Via, via!	away!	Non più!	enough!
Eh via!	fie! fie upon!	Básta!	,,
Vergógna!	for shame!	Silénzio!	silence!
Oibò!	oh, fie! oh, fough!	Tacéte!	,,
Animo!	courage! cheer up!	Andáte!	away!
Corággio!	,, ,,	Badáte!	mind! have care! beware!
Fáte cuóre!		All' érta!	
Bène!	well!	State all' érta!	
Brávo!	bravo! very well!	Di grázia!	pray!
Buóno!	good!	Per carità!	for charity's sake!
Viva!	long live!	Per amór del cielo!	for heaven's sake!
Eh viva! evviva!	huzza!	Mercè,	mercy! mercy upon us!
Cánperi!	ay! heyday! marry!	Misericórdia,	
Cáppita!		Possíbile!	is it possible!
Poffáre!		Appúnto!	exactly! just!
Oh bella!	fine!	Pensáte!	just think!*
Ecco!	lo! behold!		

* It is important to observe, that, as some of these interjections are used to expr different and even contrary emotions or affections of the mind, their exact significati can only be determined by the sense of the words which accompany them, or give rise the exclamation.

INTERJECTIONS.

The interjections *lásso, póvero, mísero, meschíno, beáto* (*me!*), are mere adjectives; and, when used by a female, take the feminine termination, — *lássa, póvera, mísera* (*me!*), etc.; and in the plural make *lássi, póveri* (*nói!*), etc., for the masculine; and *lásse, póvere* (*nói!*), etc., for the feminine; as, —

Lássa me! in che mal' óra nácqui?	Alas! in what evil hour was I born?
Míseri nói! che siám, se Iddio ci láscia?	Miserable that we are! what becomes of us, if God forsakes us?

Brávo, zítto, chéto, are also adjectives; and when used in speaking to a female, or to more than one male or female, follow the same rule; as, —

Bráva! cóme quándo?	Bravo! as when?
Zítti, un pó'!	Hush, a little!

Brávo is also used in its superlative, and makes *bravíssimo, bravíssima, bravíssimi, bravíssime,* "bravissimo."

READING LESSON.

La Rondinélla.

Rondinélla pellegrína
Che ti pósi in sul veróne
Ricantándo ógni mattína
Quélla flébile canzóne,
Che vuói dírmi in túa favélla
Pellegrína rondinélla?

Solitária nell' oblío,
Dal túo spóso abbandonáta,
Piángi fórse al piánto mío
Vedovélla sconsoláta?
Piángi, piángi in tua favélla,
Pellegrína rondinélla.

Pur di me mánco infelíce
Tu álle pénne almén t' affídi,

Scórri il lágo e la pendíce,
Émpi l' ária de' tuói grídi,
Tútto il giórno in túa favélla,
Lúi chiamándo, o rondinélla!

Oh, se anch' io! Ma lo conténde
Quésta bássa angústa vólta,
Dóve sólo non risplénde,
Dóve l' ária ancór m' è tólta,
D' ónde a te la mía favélla
Giúnge appéna, o rondinélla!

Il settémbre innánzi viéne,
E a lasciármi ti prepári:
Tu vedrái lontáne aréne,
Nuóvi mónti, nuóvi mári,
Salutándo in túa favélla,
Pellegrína rondinélla.

Ed ío tútte le mattíne
Riapréndo gli ócchi al piánto
Fra le névi e fra le brine
Crederò d' údir quél cánto,
Ónde par che in túa favélla
Mi compiánga, o rondinélla.

Una cróce a primavéra
Troverái su quésto suólo;
Rondinélla iu su la séra
Sóvra a léi raccógli il vólo:
Dílle páce in túa favélla,
Pellegrína rondinélla!

EXERCISE FOR TRANSLATION.

1. Lycurgus prohibited those who returned from a feast taking a light. in order that the fear of not being able to find their homes might prevent their becoming intoxicated.

2. There is nothing meaner than to see hypocrites launching their thunders against the weaknesses of humanity, whilst their heart is the sink of every vice.

3. Vespasian incurred the danger of being condemned to death, because he gaped while the fool Nero was singing on the stage in Rome.

CONJUNCTIONS AND INTERJECTIONS.

4. During summer evenings, Dante was accustomed to sit upon a stone, which is still religiously preserved in Florence. One evening, a man unknown to him passed before him, and said, "Sir, I have promised to give an answer, and know not how to get myself out of the difficulty: you, who are so learned, can suggest it to me. What is the best mouthful?" Dante immediately answered, "An egg." A year after, at the same hour, Dante being seated on the same stone, the same man, whom he had not since seen, returned, and asked, "With what?" Dante, without hesitation, answered, "With salt."

VOCABULARY.

1. Prohibited, *vietò*; returned, *tornávano*; might prevent, *impedísse*; intoxicated, *ubbriacáte*.
2. Launching thunders, *scagliáre i fúlmini*; sink, *sentína*.
3. Incurred (ran), *córse*; gaped, *sbadigliáva*.
4. Was accustomed, *soléva*; unknown, *sconosciúto*; to get out, etc., *trármi d' affáre*; can suggest, *potréste suggeríre*; mouthful, *boccóne*; without hesitation, *sénza métter témpo in mézzo*.

CONVERSAZIÓNE.

Quál fu il regálo che féce un colonnéllo ad uno de suói granatiéri che pugnándo valorosissimaménte avéva perdúte ámbe le bráccia?

Uno scúdo, credéndo fórse con ciò di ricompensárlo di tánta pérdita.

Tále meschinità non eccitò éssa lo sdégno del brávo soldáto?

Certaménte, e con ragióne dísse al súo Colonnéllo — Credéte fórse ch' ío non ábbia perdúto che un páio di guánti?

Quále fáma hánno lasciáta Ludovíco XI. e Ferdinándo d' Arragóna?

Una tristíssima fáma, perchè fúrono entrámbi crudéli e pérfidi.

Non si chiamárono, il primo cristianíssimo e l' áltro cattólico?

Sì, e ciò próva che l' ómbra del tróno può coprire imménsi delítti.

Che rispóse Dánte a chi gli domandáva qual fósse il migliór boccóne?

Un uóvo con sále.

Auxiliary Verbs.

Avére, to have.

INFINITIVE MOOD.—*Avére*, to have.

INDICATIVE MOOD.

PRESENT TENSE.

ho or ò,	I have.	*abbiámo (avémo),*	we have.
hai or ái,	thou hast.	*avéte,*	you have.
ha or á (áve),	he has.	*hánno or ánno,*	they have.

IMPERFECT TENSE.

io avéva or avéa,	I had.	*avevámo,*	we had.
tu avévi,	thou hadst.	*avevâte,*	you had.
égli avéva or avéa,	he had.	*avévano (avíeno),*	they had

PERFECT TENSE.

ébbi,	I had.	*avémmo,*	we had.
avésti,	thou hadst.	*avéste,*	you had.
ébbe,	he had.	*ébbero,*	they had.

FUTURE TENSE.

avrò,	I shall have.	*avrémo,*	we shall have.
avrái,	thou wilt have.	*avréte,*	you will have.
avrà,	he will have.	*avránno,*	they will have.

CONDITIONAL MOOD.

PRESENT TENSE.

avréi (avría),	I should have.	*avrémmo,*	we could have.
avrésti,	thou wouldst have.	*avréste,*	you should have.
avrébbe (avría),	he would have.	*avrébbero (avríano),*	they would have.

SUBJUNCTIVE MOOD.

PRESENT TENSE.

che io àbbia,	if I may have.	*che abbiámo,*	if we may have.
che tu àbbia or àbbi,	if thou mayst have.	*che abbiáte,*	if you may have.
che égli àbbia,	if he may have.	*che abbiano,*	if they may have.

IMPERFECT TENSE.

che io avéssi,	if I might have.	*che avéssimo,*	if we should have.
che tu avéssi,	if thou couldst have.	*che avéste,*	if you might have.
che égli avésse,	if he would have.	*che avéssero (-ino),*	if they might have.

IMPERATIVE MOOD.

		abbiámo nói,	let us have.
àbbi tu,	have thou.	*abbiáte vói,*	have ye.
àbbia égli,	let him have.	*àbbiano églino,*	let them have

GERUND.

avéndo, having.

PARTICIPLES.

avénte, having.
avúto, avúta (s.), } had.
avúti, avúte (p.), }
avéndo avúto, having had.

COMPOUND TENSES

io ho avúto,	I have had.
io avéva avúto,	I had had.
io ébbi avúto,	I had had.
io avrò avúto,	I shall have had.
io avréi avúto,	I should have had
che io àbbia avúto,	if I may have had.
che io avéssi avúto,	if I might have had.

AUXILIARY VERBS.

Éssere, to be.

INFINITIVE MOOD.—*Éssere*, to be

INDICATIVE MOOD.

PRESENT TENSE.

io sóno,	I am.	siámo (sémo),	we are.
téi or sé',	thou art.	siéte (séte),	you are.
é,	he is.	sóno,	they are.

IMPERFECT TENSE.

io éra,	I was.	eraváwo (éramo),	we were.
éri,	thou wast.	eraváte,	you were.
éra,	he was.	érano,	they were.

PERFECT TENSE.

fúi,	I was.	fúmmo,	we were.
fósti,	thou wast.	fóste,	you were.
fu (fúe),	he was.	fúrono (fúnno),	they were.

FUTURE TENSE.

saró (fia),	I shall be.	sarémo,	we shall be.
sarái,	thou wilt be.	saréte,	you will be.
sard (fia, fie),	he will be.	saránno (fiano),	they will be.

CONDITIONAL MOOD.

PRESENT TENSE.

saréi (saria, fóra),	I should be.	sarémmo,	we should be.
sarésti,	thou wouldst be.	saréste,	you should be.
sarébbe (saria, fóra),	he would be.	sarébbero (sariano),	they should be.

SUBJUNCTIVE MOOD.

PRESENT TENSE.

che io sia,	if I may be.	che siámo,	if we may be.
che tu sia, or sii,	if thou mayst be.	che siáte,	if you may be.
che égli sia,	if he may be.	che siano, or sieno,	if they may be.

IMPERFECT TENSE.

che io fóssi (fússi),	if I were, or should be.	che fóssimo,	if we were.
che tu fóssi,	if thou wert.	che fóste,	if you were.
che égli fósse,	if he were.	che fóssero (fóssino),	if they were.

IMPERATIVE MOOD.

		siámo nói,	let us be.
sia, or sii tu,	be thou.	siáte vói,	be ye.
sia égli,	let him be.	siano, or sieno églino,	let them be.

GERUND.

esséndo,	being.

PARTICIPLES.

státo, státa *(s.),	
státi, státe (p.),	been.
esséndo stato,	having been.

COMPOUND TENSES.

io sóno státo,	I have been.
io éra státo,	I had been.
io saró státo,	I shall have been.
io saréi státo,	I should have been.
che io sia státo,	if I may have been.
che io fóssi státo,	if I might have been.

* The past participle of the verb *éssere* always agrees with the subject in gender and number: thus we say, *io sóno státo*, if the subject is masculine singular; *io sóno státa*, if feminine singular; *nói siamo státi*, if masculine plural; *nói siamo státe*, if feminine plural; and so on.

Regular Verbs.

VARIATION OF ACTIVE VERBS.

Active verbs, in the compound tenses, are varied with the auxiliary verb *avére*, to have.

FIRST CONJUGATION.
Amáre, to love.

PARADIGM OF THE VERBS ENDING IN *áre*.

INFINITIVE MOOD.

Present.		Past.	
am-áre,	to love.	avére amáto,	to have loved.

GERUND.

Present.		Past.	
am-ándo,	loving.	avéndo amáto,	having loved.

PARTICIPLE.

Present.		Past.	
am-ánte (s.), am-ánti (p.),* loving.		am-áto (m. s.), am-áti (p.), loved. am-áta (f s.), am-áte (p.),* loved.	

INDICATIVE MOOD.
SIMPLE TENSES.
Present.

ám-o,	I love, or do love.	am-iámo,	we love.
ám-i,	thou lovest.	am-áte,	you love.
ám-a,	he loves.	ám-ano,	they love.

Imperfect.

io am-áva,	I loved, or did love.	am-avámo,	we loved.
am-ávi,	thou lovedst.	am-aváte,	you loved.
égli am-áva,	he loved.	am-ávano,	they loved.

Perfect.

am-ái,	I loved, or did love.	am-ámmo,	we loved.
am-ásti,	thou lovedst.	am-áste,	you loved.
am-ò,	he loved.	am-árono (am-áro), they loved.	

Future.

am-eró,†	I shall or will love.	am-erémo,	we shall or will love.
am-erái,	thou wilt love.	am-eréte,	you will love.
am-erá,	he will love.	am-eránno,	they will love.

---

* The present participle of active verbs, like that of *avére*, agrees with the subject of the preposition in gender and number. The past participle agrees, sometimes, with the object in gender and number.

† The verbs of this conjugation in the future and the conditional change the *a* of their terminations for *e*, and make *am-eró*, instead of *am-aró*, etc.

REGULAR VERBS.

COMPOUND TENSES.
Second Perfect.

ho amáto,	I have loved.	abbiámo amáto,	we have loved.
hái amáto,	thou hast loved.	avéte amáto,	you have loved.
ha amáto,	he, she, *or* it has loved.	hánno amáto,	they have loved.

Pluperfect.

lo avéva amáto,	I had loved.	avevámo amáto,	we had loved.

Second Pluperfect.
Future Anterior.

ébbi amáto,	I had loved.	avrò amáto,	I shall have loved

SUBJUNCTIVE MOOD.
SIMPLE TENSES.
Present.

che io ám-i (ám-e),	that I love, or may love.	che am-iámo,	that we love.
che tu ám-i,	that thou lovest.	che am-iáte,	that you love.
che égli ám-i (ám-e),	that he loves.	che ám-ino,	that they love.

Imperfect.

che io am-ássi,	If I loved, *or* should love.	che am-ássimo,	if we loved.
che tu am-ássi,	if thou lovedst.	che am-áste,	if you loved.
che égli am-ásse,	if he loved.	che am-ássero (-ino),	if they loved.

COMPOUND TENSES.
Perfect.
Pluperfect.

che io ábbia amáto,	that I have loved, *or* may have loved.	che io avéssi amáto,	if I had loved.

CONDITIONAL MOOD.
SIMPLE TENSE.
Present.

am-eréi (am-eria),	I should love.	am-erémmo,	we should love.
am-erésti,	thou wouldst love.	am-eréste,	you would love.
am-erébbe (am-eria),	he would love.	am-erébbero (ameriano),	they would love

COMPOUND TENSE.
Past.

avréi amáto, I should, would, *or* could have loved, *or* might have loved.

IMPERATIVE MOOD.

		am-iámo nói,	let us love.
ám-a tu,	love thou.	am-áte vói,	love ye.
ám-i égli,	let him love.	ám-ino églino,	let them love.

Besides the foregoing changes of termination, there are some verbs of the first conjugation which undergo in some persons and tenses a change of orthography.

Verbs ending in *ciáre*, *giáre*, drop the *i*, which follows *c*, *g*, whenever *ci*, *gi*, precede *e*, *i*; as, *Baciáre*, to kiss; *fregiáre*, to adorn.

Verbs ending in *iáre*, in which *ia* form one syllable, drop the *i* whenever it is followed by another *i*; as, *Noiáre*, to annoy.

Verbs ending in *iáre*, in which *ia* form two syllables, drop the *i* only when it would be followed by the vowels *ia*; as, *Inviáre*, to send.

Variation of the Verb Cercáre.

PARADIGM OF THE VERBS ENDING IN cáre.

INDICATIVE MOOD.
Present.

cérc-o,	I search, or do search.	cercH-iámo,	we search.
cércH-i,	thou searchest.	cerc-áte,	you search.
cérc-a,	he searches.	cérc-ano,	they search.

Future.

cercH-eró,	I shall or will search.	cercH-erémo,	we shall search.
cercH-erái,	thou wilt search.	cercH-eréte,	you will search.
cercH-erá,	he will search.	cercH-eránno,	they will search.

SUBJUNCTIVE MOOD.
Present.

che io cercH-i (-e),	that I search.	che cercH-iámo,	that we search.
che tu cércH-i,	that thou search.	che cercH-iáte,	that you search.
che égli cércH-i (-e),	that he search.	che cércH-ino,	that they search.

CONDITIONAL MOOD.
Present.

cercH-eréi (-ería),	I should search.	cercH-erémmo,	we should search.
cercH-erésti,	thou wouldst search.	cercH-eréste,	you would search.
cercH-erébbe,	he would search.	cercH-erébbero,	they would search.

IMPERATIVE MOOD.

		cercH-iámo nói,	let us search.
cérc-a tu,	search thou.	cerc-áte vói,	search ye.
cércH-i égli,	let him search.	cércH-ino églino,	let them search.

Tenses conjugated like those of the regular verb are omitted.

Variation of the Verb Pregáre.

PARADIGM OF THE VERBS ENDING IN *gáre.*

INDICATIVE MOOD.
Present.

preg-o,	I entreat, *or* do entreat.	pregh-iámo,	we entreat.
prégh-i,	thou entreatest.	preg-áte,	you entreat.
prég-a,	he entreats.	prég-ano,	they entreat.

Future.

pregh-eró,	I shall *or* will entreat.	pregh-erémo,	we shall entreat.
pregh-erái,	thou wilt entreat.	pregh-eréte,	you will entreat
pregh-erá,	he will entreat.	pregh-eránno,	they will entreat.

SUBJUNCTIVE MOOD.
Present.

che io prégh-i (-e),	that I entreat.	che pregh-iámo,	that we entreat.
che tu prégh-i,	that thou entreat.	che pregh-iáte,	that you entreat.
che égli prégh-i (-e),	that he entreat.	che prégh-ino,	that they entreat.

CONDITIONAL MOOD.
Present.

pregh-eréi,	I should entreat.	pregh-erémmo,	we should entreat.
pregh-erésti,	thou wouldst entreat.	pregh-eréste,	you would entreat.
pregh-erébbe,	he would entreat.	pregh-erébbero,	they would entreat

IMPERATIVE MOOD.

		pregh-iámo nói,	let us entreat.
preg-a tu,	entreat thou.	preg-áte vói,	entreat ye.
prégh-i égli,	let him entreat	prégh-ino églino,	let them entreat

SECOND CONJUGATION.

The verbs of this conjugation are commonly divided into two classes, — those ending in *ēre* (long), accented, and those ending in *ĕre* (short), unaccented: both of these in the perfect have two terminations, *éi* and *étti*, except a few which have the termination *éi* only.

Variation of the Verb Temére.

PARADIGM OF THE VERBS ENDING IN *ēre* (LONG), ACCENTED, AND OF THOSE WHICH, IN THE PERFECT, END IN *éi* AND *étti*.

INFINITIVE MOOD.

Present.		*Past.*	
em-ére,	to fear	*avére temúto,*	to have feared.

GERUND.

Present.		*Past.*	
tem-éndo,	fearing.	*avéndo temúto,*	having feared.

PARTICIPLE.

Present.		*Past.*
tem-énte (s.), *tem-énti* (p.), fearing.		*tem-úto* (m. s.), *temúti* (p.), feared.
		tem-úta (f. s.), *temúte* (p.), feared.

INDICATIVE MOOD.
SIMPLE TENSES.

Present.

tém-o,	I fear, *or* do fear.	*tem-iámo,*	we fear.
tém-i,	thou fearest.	*tem-éte,*	you fear.
tém-e,	he fears.	*tém-ono,*	they fear.

Imperfect.

Io *tem-éva* or *tem-éa,*	I feared, *or* did fear.	*tem-evámo,*	we feared.
tem-évi,	thou fearedst.	*tem-eváte,*	you feared.
égli tem-éva,	he feared.	*tem-évano,*	they feared.

Perfect.

tem-éi or *tem-étti,*	I feared, *or* did fear.	*tem-émmo,*	we feared.
tem-ésti,	thou fearedst.	*tem-éste,*	you feared.
tem-é or *tem-étte,*	he feared.	*tem-érono,*	they feared.

REGULAR VERBS.

Future.

tem-erò,	I shall *or* will fear.	tem-éremo,	we shall *or* will fear.
tem-erài,	thou wilt fear.	tem-eréte,	you will fear.
tem-erà,	he will fear.	tem-erànno,	they will fear.

COMPOUND TENSES.

Second Perfect.

ho temúto,	I have feared.	abbiámo temúto,	we have feared.

Pluperfect

io avéva temúto, I had feared, etc.

SUBJUNCTIVE MOOD.

SIMPLE TENSES.

Present.

che io tém-a,	that I fear.	che tem-iámo,	that we fear.
che tu tém-a or -i,	that thou fear	che tem-iáte,	that you fear.
che égli tém-a,	that he fear.	che tém-ano,	that they fear.

Imperfect.

che io tem-éssi,	if I feared.	che tem-éssimo,	if we feared.
che tu tem-éssi,	if thou fearedst.	che tem-éste,	if you feared.
che égli tem-ésse,	if he feared.	che tem-éssero,	if they feared.

COMPOUND TENSES.

Perfect.		Pluperfect.	
che io àbbia temúto,	that I have feared.	che io avéssi temúto,	if I had feared.

CONDITIONAL MOOD.

SIMPLE TENSE.

Present.

tem-eréi (-erìa),	I should fear.	tem-erémmo,	we should fear.
tem-erésti,	thou wouldst fear.	tem-eréste,	you would fear.
tem-erèbbe (-erìa),	he would fear.	tem-erèbbero,	they would fear.

COMPOUND TENSE.

Past.

avréi temúto, I should, would, *or* could have feared, *or* might have feared.

IMPERATIVE MOOD.

tém-i tu,	fear thou.	tem-iámo nói,	let us fear.
tém-a égli,	let him fear.	tem-éte vói,	fear ye
		tém-ano églino,	let them fear.

Variation of the Verb Téssere.

PARADIGM OF THE VERBS ENDING IN ĕre (SHORT), UNACCENTED AND OF THOSE WHICH, IN THE PERFECT, END IN éi ONLY.

INFINITIVE MOOD.

Present.
téss-ere, to weave.

Past.
avére tessúto, to have woven.

GERUND.

Present.
tess-éndo. weaving.

Past.
avéndo tessúto, having woven.

PARTICIPLE.

Present.
tess-énte (s.), tess-énti (p.), weaving.

Past.
tess-úto (m. s.), tess-úti (p.), woven.
tess-úta (f. s.), tess-úte (p.), woven.

INDICATIVE MOOD.
SIMPLE TENSES.
Present.

téss-o, I weave, *or* do weave, *or* am weaving. | tess-iámo (tess-émo), we weave.

Imperfect.

Io tess-éva or tess-éa, I wove, *or* did weave, *or* was weaving.

Perfect.

tess-éi, I wove, *or* did weave.
tess-ésti, thou wovest.
tess-è (tess-éo), he wove.

tess-émmo, we wove.
tess-éste, you wove.
tess-ÉRONO, they wove.

Future.

tess-erò, I shall *or* will weave.

COMPOUND TENSES

Second Perfect.
ào tessúto, I have woven

Pluperfect.
io avéva tessúto, I had woven, etc

SUBJUNCTIVE MOOD.
SIMPLE TENSE.

Present.
che io téss-a, that I weave.

Imperfect.
che io tess-éssi, that I wove.

COMPOUND TENSES.

Perfect.
che io àbbia tessúto, that I may have woven.

Pluperfect.
che io avéssi tessúto, if I might have woven

CONDITIONAL MOOD.
SIMPLE TENSE.
Present.
tess-eréi (tess-eria), I should, would, *or* could weave, *or* might weave.

COMPOUND TENSE.
Past.
avréi tessúto, I should, would, *or* could have woven, *or* might have woven.

IMPERATIVE MOOD.
téss-i tu, weave thou.

Verbs ending in *cére* (long), accented, in order to preserve the soft sound of *c* in all their inflections, take an *i* after that consonant, whenever it is followed by *a*, *o*, *u*; as, *Tacére*, to be silent.

Verbs ending in *iere* drop the *i* whenever it is followed by another *i*; as *Empiere*, to fill.

THIRD CONJUGATION.

The verbs of this conjugation are divided into three classes, — those which, in the present of the indicative, end in *o;* those which end in *isco;* and those which have both of these terminations.

Variation of the Verb Sentíre.

PARADIGM OF THE VERBS OF THE THIRD CONJUGATION, WHICH, IN THE PRESENT OF THE INDICATIVE, END IN *O* ONLY.

INFINITIVE MOOD.

Present.		*Past.*	
sent-íre,	to hear.	avére sentíto,	to have heard.

GERUND.

Present.		*Past.*	
sent-éndo,	hearing.	avéndo sentito,	having heard.

PARTICIPLE.

Present.		*Past.*	
sent-énte (s.), sent-énti (p.), hearing.		sent-íto (m. s.), sent-íti (p.), heard.	
		sent-íta (f. s.), sent-íte (p.), heard.	

INDICATIVE MOOD.

SIMPLE TENSES.

Present.

sent-o,	I hear, *or* do hear	sent-iámo,	we hear
sent-i,	thou hearest.	sent-íte,	you hear.
sent-e,	he hears.	sent-ono,	they hear

Imperfect.

io sent-íva *or* sent-ía,	I heard, *or* did hear.	sent-ivámo,	we heard.
sent-ívi,	thou heardst.	sent-ivátte,	you heard.
égli sent-íva *or* sent-ía,	he heard.	sent-ivano,	they heard.

Perfect.

sent-íi,	I heard, *or* did hear.	sent-ímmo,	we heard.
sent-ísti,	thou heardst.	sent-íste,	you heard.
sent-ì (sent-io),	he heard.	sent-írono,	they heard.

REGULAR VERBS.

Future.

sent-iró,	I shall or will hear.	sent-irémo,	we will hear.
sent-irai,	thou wilt hear.	sent-iréte,	you will hear.
sent-irá,	he will hear.	sent-iránno,	they will hear.

COMPOUND TENSES.

Second Perfect.   *Pluperfect.*

ho sentito,	I have heard.	to avéva sentito,	I had heard, etc

SUBJUNCTIVE MOOD.

SIMPLE TENSES.

Present.

che io sént-A,	that I hear.	che sent-iámo,	that we hear.
che tu sént-A or -I,	that thou hear.	che sent-iáte,	that you hear.
che égli sént-A,	that he hear.	che sént-ANO,	that they hear

Imperfect.

che io sent-íssi,	that I heard.	che sent-íssimo,	if we heard.
che tu sent-íssi,	that thou heardst.	che sent-íste,	if you heard.
che sent-ísse,	that he heard.	che sent-íssero,	if they heard.

COMPOUND TENSES.

Perfect.   *Pluperfect.*

to ábbia sentito,	that I may have heard.	to avéssi sentito,	if I had heard.

CONDITIONAL MOOD.

SIMPLE TENSE.

Present.

sent-iréi (-iria),	I should hear.	sent-irémmo,	we should hear.
sent-irésti,	thou wouldst hear.	sent-iréste,	you would hear.
sent-irébbe (-iria),	he would hear.	sent-irébbero,	they would hear.

COMPOUND TENSE.

Past.

avréi sentito, I should, would, or could have heard, or might have heard.

IMPERATIVE MOOD.

sént-I tu,	hear thou.	sent-iámo nói,	let us hear.
sént-A égli,	let him hear.	sent-íte vói,	hear ye.
		sént-ANO églino,	let them hear.

Variation of the Verb Esibíre.

PARADIGM OF THOSE VERBS OF THE THIRD CONJUGATION, WHICH IN THE PRESENT OF THE INDICATIVE, HAVE THE TERMINATION *ísco* ONLY.

INFINITIVE MOOD.

	Present.		*Past.*	
Esib-íre,	to offer.	avére esibíto,	to have offered.

GERUND.

	Present.		*Past.*	
esib-éndo,	offering.	avéndo esibíto,	having offered.

PARTICIPLE.

Present.	*Past.*
esib-énte (s.), esibénti (p.), offering.	esib-íto (m. s.), esib-íti (p.), offered. esibíta (f. s.), esib-íte (p.), offered.

INDICATIVE MOOD.
SIMPLE TENSES.
Present.

esib-ÍSCO,	I offer, *or* do offer.	esib-iámo,	we offer.
esib-ÍSCI,	thou offerest.	esib-íte,	you offer.
esib-ÍSCE,	he offers.	esib-ÍSCONO,	they offer.

Imperfect.

io esib-iva *or* -ía,	I offered, *or* did offer.	esib-ivámo,	we offered.
esib-ivi,	thou offeredst.	esib-ivàte,	you offered.
esib-iva *or* -ía,	he offered.	esib-ivano,	they offered.

Perfect.

esib-ii,	I offered, *or* did offer.	esib-immo,	we offered.
esib-isti,	thou offeredst.	esib-iste,	you offered.
esib-í (esib-ìo),	he offered.	esib-irono (esib-ir:),	they offered.

Future.

esib-iró,	I shall *or* will offer.	esib-irémo,	we will offer.
esib-irái,	thou wilt offer.	esib-iréte,	you will offer.
·ib-irá,	he will offer.	esib-iránno,	they will offer

REGULAR VERBS. 199

COMPOUND TENSES.

Second Perfect. | Pluperfect.
ao esibito, I have offered, etc. | *to avéva esibito,* I had offered, etc.

SUBJUNCTIVE MOOD.
SIMPLE TENSES.
Present.

che to esib-ÍSCA,	that I offer.	*che esib-iámo,*	that we offer.
che tu esib-ÍSCA,	that thou offer.	*che esib-iáte,*	that you offer.
che égli esib-ÍSCA,	that he offer.	*che esib-ÍSCANO,*	that they offer.

Imperfect.

che to esib-issi,	if I offered.	*che esib-íssimo,*	if we offered.
che tu esib-issi,	if thou offeredst.	*che esib-iste,*	if you offered.
che égli esib-isse,	if he offered.	*che esib-íssero,*	if they offered.

COMPOUND TENSES.
Perfect. | Pluperfect.
te io ábbia esibíto, that I have offered. | *che io avéssi esibito,* if I had offered.

CONDITIONAL MOOD.
SIMPLE TENSE.
Present.

esib-iréi (esib-iría),	I should offer.	*esib-irémmo,*	we should offer.
esib-irésti,	thou wouldst offer.	*esib-iréste,*	you would offer.
esib-irébbe (esib-iría),	he would offer.	*esib-irébbero,*	they would offer

COMPOUND TENSE.
Past.

avréi esibíto, I should, would, *or* could have offered, *or* might have offered.

IMPERATIVE MOOD.

		esib-iámo,	let us offer.
sib-ÍSCI,	offer thou.	*esib-íte,*	offer ye.
sib-ÍSCA,	let him offer.	*esib-ÍSCANO,*	let them offer.

Cucíre, to sew.

Verbs ending in *círe*, in order to preserve the soft sound of the *c* in all their inflections, take an *i* after that consonant, whenever it is followed by *a*, *o*; as, *Cucíre*, to sew.

PARADIGM OF THE VERBS ENDING IN *círe*.

INDICATIVE MOOD.
Present.

cúci-o,	I sew, *or* do sew.	cuc-iámo (-imo),	we sew.
cúc-i,	thou sewest.	cuc-íte,	you sew.
cúc-e,	he sews.	cúci-ono,	they sew.

SUBJUNCTIVE MOOD.
Present.

che io cúci-a,	that I sew *or* may sew.	che cuc-iámo,	that we sew.
che tu cúci-a *or* cúc-i,	that thou sew.	che cuc-iáte,	that you sew.
che égli cúci-a,	that he sew.	che cúci-ano,	that they sew.

IMPERATIVE MOOD.

cúci tu,	sew thou.	cuciámo-noi,	let us sew.
cúcia égli,	let him sew	cuc-íte voi,	sew ye.
		cúciano eglino,	let them sew.

Abborríre, to abhor.

PARADIGM OF THOSE VERBS OF THE THIRD CONJUGATION, **WHICH**, IN THE PRESENT OF THE INDICATIVE, END BOTH IN *o* AND *ísco*.

INDICATIVE MOOD.

Present.

abbórr-o or abborr-ísco, I abhor, *or* do abhor.
abbórr-i or aborr-ísci, thou abhorrest.
abbórr-e or abborr-ísce, he or she abhors.

abborr-iámo, we abhor.
abborr-íte, you abhor.
abbórr-ono or -íscono, they abhor.

SUBJUNCTIVE MOOD.

Present.

che abbórr-a or -ísca, that I abhor.
che abbórr-a,-i,or -ísca, that thou abhor.
che abborr-a or ísca, that he abhor.

che abborr-iámo, that we abhor.
che abborr-iáte, that you abhor.
che abbórr-ano or -íscano, that they abhor.

IMPERATIVE MOOD.

abbórr-i or abbórr-ísci, abhor thou.
abbórr-a or -ísca, let him abhor.

abborr-iámo, let us abhor.
abborr-íte, abhor ye.
abbórr-ano or -íscano, let them abhor.

A Synoptical Table

OF THE
VARIATIONS OF THE REGULAR VERBS,

Showing their different Terminations in their Simple Tenses.

FIRST CONJUGATION.	SECOND CONJUGATION.	THIRD CONJUGATION.

INFINITIVE MOOD.
PRESENT.

[Am-] áre.	[Tem-] ére. [Créd-] ere.	[Abborr-] íre.

GERUND.
PRESENT.

[Am-] ándo.	[Tem-] éndo.	[Abborr-] éndo.

PARTICIPLES.
PRESENT.

[Am-] ánte.	[Tem-] énte.	[Abborr-] énte.

PAST.

[Am-] áto, -a, áti, -e.	[Tem-] úto, -a, úti, -e.	[Abborr-] íto, -a, íti, -e.

INDICATIVE MOOD.
PRESENT.

[Am-] o, i, a; iámo áte, ano.	[Tem-] o, i, e; iámo, éte, ono.	[Abborr-] o, isco. i, isci, e, isce; iámo, íte, ono, íscono.

IMPERFECT.

[Am-] áva, ávi, áva; avámo, aváte, ávano.	[Tem] éva, éa (ía), évi, éva, éa; evámo, eváte, évano, éano.	[Abborr-] íva, ía, ívi, íva, ía; ivámo, iváte, ívano, íano

PERFECT DEFINITE.

[Am-] ái, ásti, ò; ámmo, áste, árono (áro, ár).	[Tem-] éi, étti, ésti, è, étte (eo); émmo, éste, érono, éttero (éro).	[Abborr-] íi, ísti, ì (ío); ímmo, íste, írono.

FIRST CONJUGATION.	SECOND CONJUGATION.	THIRD CONJUGATION.
	FUTURE INDEFINITE.	

[Am-] erò,	[Tem-] erò,	[Abborr-] irò,
erài,	erài,	iràì,
erà ;	erà ;	irà ;
erèmo,	erèmo,	irèmo,
eréte,	eréte,	iréte,
eránno.	eránno.	iránno.

CONDITIONAL MOOD.

PRESENT.

[Am-] eréi (eria),	[Tem-] erèi (eria),	[Abborr-] iréi (iria),
erésti,	erésti,	irésti,
erèbbe (eria);	erèbbe (eria) ;	irèbbe (iria);
erémmo,	erémmo,	irémmo,
eréste,	eréste,	iréste,
erèbbero eriano)	erèbbero (eriano).	irèbbero (iriano)

IMPERATIVE MOOD.

[Am-] a,	[Tem-] i,	[Abborr-] i,	isci,
i;	a,	a,	isca ;
iàmo,	iàmo,	iàmo,	
àte,	éte,	ìte,	
ino.	ano.	ano,	iscano

SUBJUNCTIVE MOOD.

PRESENT.

-Am] i (e),	[Tem-] a,	[Abborr-] a,	isca,
i,	a, i,	a, i,	isca, ischi,
i (e) ;	a ;	a,	isca ;
iamo,	iàmo,	iàmo,	
iàte,	iàte,	iàte,	
ino.	ano.	ano,	iscano.

IMPERFECT.

[Am-] àssi,	[Tem-] éssi,	[Abborr-] issi,
àssi,	éssi,	issi,
àsse ;	ésse ;	isse ;
àssimo,	éssimo,	issimo,
àste,	éste,	iste,
àssero.	éssero.	isseru.

VARIATION OF PASSIVE VERBS.

Passive verbs are formed by joining the verb *éssere*, to be, to the past participle of active verbs. They are, therefore, through all their tenses, varied with the auxiliary verb *éssere*.

Variation of the Verb Éssere amáto.

PARADIGM OF THE PASSIVE VERBS.

INFINITIVE MOOD.
Present.
éssere amáto (m. s.), amáti (p.), to be loved.
éssere amáta (f. s.), amáte (p.), to be loved.

Past.
éssere státo amáto (m. s.), státi amáti * (p.), to have been loved.
éssere státa amáta (f. s.), státe amáte (p.), to have been loved.

PARTICIPLE.
Present.
esséndo amáto (m. s.), amáti (p.), being loved.
esséndo amáta (f. s.), amáte (p.), being loved.

Past.
esséndo státo amáto (m. s.), státi amáti (p.), having been loved.
esséndo státa amáta (f. s.), státe amáte (p.), having been loved.

INDICATIVE MOOD.
SIMPLE TENSES.
Present.

io sóno amáto (m.),-a (f.),	I am loved.	siámo amáti (m.),-e (f.),	we are loved.
séi amáto, -a,	thou art loved.	siéte amáti, -e,	you are loved.
é amáto, a,	he is loved.	églino sóno amáti,	they are loved.

Imperfect.

io éra amáto, -a,	I was loved.	eravámo amáti, -e,	we were loved.
éri amáto, -a,	thou wast loved.	eraváte amáti, -e,	you were loved.
éra amáto, -a,	he was loved.	érano amáti, -e,	they were loved

Perfect.

fúi amáto, -a,	I was loved.	fúmmo amáti, -e,	we were loved.
fósti amáto, -a,	thou wast loved.	fóste amáti, -e,	you were loved.
fu amáto, -a,	he was loved.	fúrono amáti, -e,	they were loved.

Future.

saró amáto, -a,	I shall be loved.	sarémo amáti, -e,	we shall be loved.
sarái amáto, -a,	thou wilt be loved.	saréte amáti, -e,	you will be loved.
sará amáto, -a,	he will be loved.	saránno amáti, -é,	they will be loved

---

* The past participle of passive verbs, like that of *éssere*, agrees with the subject of the verb in gender and number.

PASSIVE VERBS.

COMPOUND TENSES.

Second Perfect.
io sóno stàto amato, stàta amàta, I have been loved.
siàmo stàti amàti, stàte amàte, we have been loved.

Pluperfect.
io éra stàto amato, stàta amata, I had been loved.

Future Anterior.
sarò stàto amàto, stàta amàta, I shall or will have been loved.

SUBJUNCTIVE MOOD.

SIMPLE TENSES.

Present.

io sia amàto, -a,	that I be loved.	siàmo amàti, -e,	that we be loved.
tu sia amàto, -a,	that thou be loved.	siàte amàti, -e,	that you be loved.
ég'i sia amàto, -a,	that he be loved.	siano amàti, -e,	that they be loved.

Imperfect.

io fóssi amàto, -a,	if I were loved.	fóssimo amàti, -e,	if we were loved.
tu fóssi amàto, -a,	if thou wert loved.	fóste amàti, -e,	if you were loved.
fósse amàto, -a,	if he were loved.	fóssero amàti, -e,	if they were loved.

COMPOUND TENSES.

Perfect.
io sia stàto amàto, stàta amàta, that I have been loved.

Pluperfect.
io fóssi stàto amàto, stàta amàta, if I had been loved.

CONDITIONAL MOOD.

SIMPLE TENSE.

Present.

sarèi amàto, -a,	I should be loved.	sarémmo amàti, -e,	we should be loved.
sarésti amàto, -a,	thou wouldst be loved.	saréste amàti, -e,	you would be loved.
sarèbbe amàto, -a,	he would be loved.	sarébbero amàti, -e,	they would be loved

COMPOUND TENSE.

Past.
sarèi stàto amàto, stàta amàta, I should, would, or could have been loved.

IMPERATIVE MOOD.

		siàmo amàti, amàte,	let us be loved.
sii amàto, amàta,	be thou loved.	siàte amàti, amàte,	be ye loved.
sia amàto, égli,	let him be loved.	siano amàti églino,	let them be loved.

Many active verbs become passive by taking the particle si as, *Domandàrsi*, to be asked: but then they are used in the third person only; as, Si domànda, it is asked; si è domandàto, it has been asked; etc.

VARIATION OF NEUTER VERBS.

Neuter verbs are generally varied with the auxiliary verb *éssere*, to be, according to the conjugation to which they belong

Variation of the Verb Partíre.

PARADIGM OF THE NEUTER VERBS.

INFINITIVE MOOD.

Present.
partíre, to depart.

Past.
éssere partíto (m. s.), partíti (p.), partíta (f s.), partíte (p.),* to have departed

GERUND.

Present.		*Past.*	
parténdo,	departing.	esséndo partíto,	having departed.

PARTICIPLE.

Present.

parténte (m. s.),	departing.	parténti (p.),	departing.

Past.

partíto (m. s.),	departed.	partíti (p.),	departed.
partíta (f. s.),	departed.	partíte (p.),	departed.

INDICATIVE MOOD.
SIMPLE TENSES.

Present.		*Imperfect.*	
párto,	I depart.	io partíva,	I departed.
Perfect.		*Future.*	
partíi,	I departed.	partiró,	I shall *or* will depart.

---

* The past participle of the neuter verbs that are varied with *éssere*, **agrees with the subject** of the verb in gender and number.

COMPOUND TENSES.

Second Perfect.
io sóno partito, -a, I have departed.

Pluperfect.
Io éra partito, -a, I had departed.

Second Pluperfect.
fùi partito, -a, I had departed.

Future Anterior.
saró partito, -a, I shall have departed

SUBJUNCTIVE MOOD.

SIMPLE TENSES.

Present.
che io párta, that I depart.

Imperfect.
che io partíssi, if I departed.

COMPOUND TENSES.

Perfect.
che io sia partito, -a, that I have departed.

Pluperfect.
che io fóssi partito, -a, if I had departed

CONDITIONAL MOOD.

SIMPLE TENSE.

Past.
partirèi, I should, would, *or* could depart, *or* might depart.

COMPOUND TENSE.

Present.
saréi partito, I should, would, *or* could have departed, *or* might have departed.

IMPERATIVE MOOD.

párti tu, depart thou.

VARIATION OF PRONOMINAL VERBS.

Pronominal verbs are varied with the auxiliary *éssere*, to be, according to the conjugation to which their termination belongs.

Variation of the Reflective Verb Pentírsi.

PARADIGM OF THE PRONOMINAL VERBS.

INFINITIVE MOOD.

	Present.		*Past.*	
pentir-si,	to repent one's self.	ésser-si pentito,	to have repented one's self.

GERUND.

	Present.		*Past.*	
penténdo-si,	repenting one's self.	esséndo-si pentito,	having repented one's self.

PARTICIPLE.

Present.

penténte-si (s.), repenting one's self.

Past.

pentito-si (m. s.), pentiti-si (p.), having repented one's self.
pentita-si (f. s.), pentite-si (p.), having repented one's self.

INDICATIVE MOOD.

SIMPLE TENSES.

Present.

io mi pento,	I repent myself.	nói ci pentiámo,	we repent ourselves.
ti pénti,	thou repentest thyself.	vi pentite,	you repent yourselves.
si pente,	he repents himself.	si péntono,	they repent themselves.

Imperfect.

mi pentíva, I repented myself.

	Perfect.		*Future.*
mi pentii,	I repented myself.	mi pentirò,	I shall repent myself

PRONOMINAL VERBS.

COMPOUND TENSES.

Second Perfect.
mi sóno pentíto, -a, I have repented myself.

Pluperfect.
mi éra pentíto, -a, I had repented myself

Second Pluperfect.
mi fúi pentíto, -a, I had repented myself.

Future Anterior.
mi sarò pentíto, -a, I shall *or* will have repented myself.

SUBJUNCTIVE MOOD.

SIMPLE TENSES.

Present.
che mi pénta, that I repent myself.

Imperfect.
che mi pentíssi, if I repented myself.

COMPOUND TENSES.

Perfect.
che mi sia pentíto, -a, that I have repented myself.

Pluperfect.
che mi fóssi pentíto, -a, if I had repented myself.

CONDITIONAL MOOD.

SIMPLE TENSE.
Present.
mi pentiréi, I should, would, *or* could repent myself.

COMPOUND TENSE.
Past.
mi saréi pentíto, -a, I should, would, *or* could have repented myself.

IMPERATIVE MOOD.

pénti-ti,	repent thyself.	
si pénta *or* pénta-si,	let him repent himself.	
	pentiámo-ci,	let us repent ourselves
	pentíte-vi,	repent yourselves.
	si péntano, *or* péntan-si,	let them repent themselves.

A great number of active and neuter verbs may become pronominal by the addition of the conjunctive pronouns *mi, ti, si,* &c., either in the objective or in the relation of attribution: and then these verbs are varied with the auxiliary *èssere*, to be; as, *Lodáre,* to praise; *dáre,* to give; *tacére,* to keep silent:—

mi sóno dáto un cólpo, I have given [to] myself a blow.
ti séi dáto per vínto, thou hast given thyself up as conquered.
si è lodáto, he has praised himself.
ci siámo taciúti, we have kept ourselves silent.

Usage, however, in some instances, allows us also to employ the auxiliary *avére,* to have: but then the conjunctive pronouns *mi, ti, si,* are always in the relation of attribution; as,—

mélo sóno *or* méi' ho godúto, I have enjoyed it.
télo séi *or* tel' hai credúto, thou hast believed it.
sel' è *or* sel' ha bevúto, he has drunk it.

VARIATION OF UNIPERSONAL VERBS.

Unipersonal verbs are generally varied with the auxiliary *avére*, to have, according to the conjugation to which they belong.

Variation of the Verb Pióvere.

PARADIGM OF THE UNIPERSONAL VERBS.

INFINITIVE MOOD.

	Present.		*Past.*
piócere,	to rain.	avére piovúto,	to have rained.

GERUND.

	Present.		*Past.*
piovendo,	raining.	avéndo piovúto,	having rained.

PARTICIPLE.

Past.
piovúto, rained.

INDICATIVE MOOD.

SIMPLE TENSES.

	Present.		*Imperfect.*
pióve,	it rains.	piovéva,	it rained
	Perfect.		*Future.*
piové, piovette,	it rained.	pioverá,	it will rain

COMPOUND TENSES.

	Second Perfect.		*Pluperfect.*
ha piovuto,	it has rained.	avéva piovúto,	it had rained.
	Second Pluperfect.		*Future Anterior.*
ebbe piovúto,	it had rained.	avrá piovúto,	it will have rained

SUBJUNCTIVE MOOD.

SIMPLE TENSES.

	Present.		*Imperfect.*
che pióva,	that it rains.	*che piovésse,*	if it rained.

COMPOUND TENSES.

	Perfect.		*Pluperfect.*
che àbbia piovúto,	that it has rained.	*che avésse piovúto,*	if it had rained

CONDITIONAL MOOD.

SIMPLE TENSE.
Present.

pioverébbe (pioveria), it would *or* could rain, *or* might rain.

COMPOUND TENSE.
Past.

avrébbe piovúto, it would *or* could have rained, *or* might have rained.

IMPERATIVE MOOD.

pióva, let it rain.

The following are the unipersonal verbs most in use:—

aggiornáre,	to be day.	*geláre,*	to freeze.
annottáre,	to grow night.	*ghiacciáre,*	„ „
balenáre,	to lighten.	*dighiacciáre,*	to thaw.
lampeggiáre,	„ „	*far fréddo,*	to be cold
tuonáre,	to thunder.	*far chiáro,*	to be light.
nevicáre,	to snow.	*far búio,*	to be dark.
grandináre,	to hail.	*far cáldo,*	to be hot.
tempestáre,	„ „	*far vénto,*	to be windy.
pióvere,	to rain.	*far buón témpo,*	to be good weather
diluviáre,	to rain very hard, to deluge.	*far cattivo témpo,*	to be bad weather.

Éssere, to be, is also used unipersonally, both in the singular and plural, when it is joined to the particles *ci* or *vi;* as, *Ésserci* or *ésservi,* to be here, *or* to be there. It is varied as follows:—

Variation of the Verb Éssere, *unipersonally used*.

INFINITIVE MOOD.

Present.
ésser-ci or *ésser-vi*, to be here, *or* to be there.
Past.
ésser-ci or *ésser-vi státo* (m. s.), (*státi* (p.), *státa* (f. s.), *státe* (p.), to have been there

GERUND.

Present.
esséndo-ci, or *esséndo-vi*, there being.
Past.
esséndo-ci or *esséndo-vi státo* (m. s.), *státi* (p.), *státa* (f. s.), *státe* (p.), there having been

INDICATIVE MOOD.

SIMPLE TENSES.

Present.

c' é or *v' é*,	here is, *or* there is.	*ci sóno* or *vi sóno*,	there are.

Imperfect.

c' éra or *v' éra*,	there was.	*c' érano* or *v' érano*,	there were.

Perfect.

ci fu or *vi fu*,	there was.	*ci fúrono* or *vi fúrono*,	there were.

Future.

ci sarà or *vi sarà*,	there shall be.	*ci saránno* or *vi saránno*,	there shall be.

COMPOUND TENSES.

Second Perfect.

c' é or *v' é státo* (m.), -*a* (f.),	there has been.
ci sóno or *vi sóno*, *státi* (m.), -*e* (f.),	there have been.

Pluperfect.

c' éra or *v' éra státo*, -*a*,	there had been.
c' érano or *v' érano státi* -*e*,	there had been.

Future Anterior.

ci sarà or *vi sarà státo*, -*a*,	there will have been.
ci saranno or *vi saranno státi*, -*e*,	there will have been.

SUBJUNCTIVE MOOD.

SIMPLE TENSES.
Present.

che ci sia or *vi sia,*	that there be *or* may be.
che ci siano, vi siano or *ci sieno, vi sieno,*	that there be *or* may be.

Imperfect.

ci fósse or *vi fósse,*	if there were *or* should be.
ci fóssero or *vi fóssero,*	if there were *or* should be.

COMPOUND TENSES.
Perfect.

ci sia or *vi sia státo, -a,*	that there has been.
ci siano or *vi siano státi, -e,*	that there have been *or* may have been.

Pluperfect.

ci fósse or *vi fósse státo, -a,*	if there had been.
ci fóssero or *vi fóssero státi, -e,*	if there had been

CONDITIONAL MOOD.

SIMPLE TENSE.
Present.

ci sarébbe or *vi sarébbe,*	there should, would, *or* could be, *or* might be
ci sarébbero or *vi sarébbero,*	there should, would, *or* could be, *or* might be

COMPOUND TENSE.
Past.

ci sarébbe or *vi sarébbe státo, -a,*	there should, would, *or* could have been.
ci sarébbero or *vi sarébbero státi, -e,*	there should, would, *or* could have been.

IMPERATIVE MOOD.

ci sia, vi sia, or *sia-ci, sia-vi,*	let there be.
ci siano, vi sieno, or *sian-ci, sien-vi,*	let there be.

The verb *avére,* to have, is often substituted for the verb *éssere* when unipersonally used, and then it is varied after the same manner; as, *Avérci* or *avérvi,* to be here *or* to be there; *ci ha* or *vi ha,* here is *or* there is; *ci hánno* or *vi hánno,* there are; etc.

The verb *avére* not only may be used with propriety for the verb *éssere,* but it is also elegantly used in the singular, although the noun to which it is joined is in the plural; as, *Quánte míglia ci* HA? how many miles is it? ÉBBEVI *mólti uómini,* there were a great many men there; etc.

To express in Italian "here or there is some of it," "here or there are some of them," we join the particle *ne,* of it, of them, to *ci* or *vi,* and say, *éssercene or éssercene.*

Irregular Verbs.

The irregularities of Italian Verbs are chiefly confined to the perfect tense of the indicative mood, and to the past participle.

Some verbs, however, are also irregular in the present of the indicative; and then they are irregular likewise in the present of the subjunctive and in the imperative.

When verbs are contracted in the infinitive mood, they are contracted also in the future tense and in the conditional mood.

In those tenses in which verbs are irregular, the irregularity, generally, does not extend to all the persons. Thus, with very few exceptions, in the perfect of the indicative, the second person singular, and the first and second persons plural; and in the present of the indicative and subjunctive, and in the imperative, the first and second persons plural, — are regular.

In the variation of these verbs, we will give only those tenses in which they depart from the paradigms already given, to which we must refer for the formation of the other tenses. The persons which are irregular are here printed in small capitals.

For the assistance of learners, we have added to each verb the auxiliary with which it is varied in its compound tenses.

VARIATION OF THE IRREGULAR VERBS OF THE FIRST CONJUGATION.

There are but four simple verbs in the first conjugation, which are not varied like *amáre*; viz.: —

andáre,	to go.	fáre,	to do, *or* to make.
dáre,	to give	stáre,	to be, to dwell, to stand, *or* to stay

Andáre (*varied with* Éssere).

INFINITIVE MOOD.
andáre, to go.

GERUND.
andándo, going.

PARTICIPLE.
andáto, gone.

INDICATIVE MOOD.
Present.

vo or vádo,*	I go or am going.	andiámo,	we go.
vái,	thou goest.	andáte,	you go.
va,	he goes.	vánno,	they go.

Future.
andró (by contraction for anderó), I shall or will go.

SUBJUNCTIVE MOOD.
Present.

ío váda,	that I go or may go.	andiámo,	that we go.
tu váda (vádi),	that thou go.	andiáte,	that you go.
égli váda,	that he go.	vádano,	that they go.

CONDITIONAL MOOD.
Present.

andréi (andría), by contraction for anderéi (anderia), I should, would, or could go.

IMPERATIVE MOOD.

		andiámo nói,	let us go.
va (vá') tu,	go thou.	andáte vói,	go ye.
váda égli,	let him go.	vádano églino,	let them go.

Andáre is sometimes varied with the conjunctive pronouns *mi, ti, si, ci, vi,* and the particle *ne;* thus, ME NE vo, I go hence TE NE vái, thou goest hence; etc. *Me, te,* etc., are then mere expletives.

Riandáre, signifying to examine, or to go over again; and *trasandáre,* to go beyond, — are regular and varied like *amáre.*

---

* *Andáre* is also a defective verb, and borrows these forms from the Latin verb *vádere.*

Dáre (*varied with* Avére).

INFINITIVE MOOD.
dáre, to give.

GERUND.
dándo, giving.

PARTICIPLE.
dáto, given.

INDICATIVE MOOD.
Present.

do,	I give *or* am giving.	diámo,	we give.
DÁI,	thou givest.	dáte,	you give.
dá,	he gives.	DÁNNO,	they give.

Perfect.

DÉTTI *or* DIÉDI,	I gave *or* did give.	DÉMMO,	we gave.
DÉSTI,	thou gavest.	DÉSTE,	you gave.
DÉTTE *or* DIÉDE,	he gave.	DÉTTERO *or* DIÉDERO,	they gave.

Future.
DARÓ, I shall *or* will give

SUBJUNCTIVE MOOD.
Present.

to DÍA,	that I give.	diámo,	that we give.
tu DÍA *or* DÍI,	that thou give.	diáte,	that you give.
égli DÍA,	that he give.	DÍANO *or* DÍENO,	that they give.

Imperfect.
io DÉSSI, if I gave *or* should give.

CONDITIONAL MOOD.
Present.
DARÉI (*daria*), I should, would, *or* could give, *or* might give.

IMPERATIVE MOOD.

dá (dá') tu,	give thou.	diámo nói,	let us give.
DÍA égli,	let him give.	dáte vói,	give ye.
		DÍANO,	let them give.

The compounds of *dáre* — as, *ridáre,* to give again; *addársi,* to devote one's self; etc. — have the same irregularities.

IRREGULAR VERBS.

Fáre (*varied with* Avére).

INFINITIVE MOOD.
FÁRE (*fácere*),* to do, *or* to make

GERUND.
facéndo, doing.

PARTICIPLE.
FÁTTO, done.

INDICATIVE MOOD.
Present.

FÒ (*fáccio*),	I do *or* am doing.	FACCIÁMO,	we do.
FÁI (*fári*),	thou doest.	FÁTE,	you do.
FA (*fáce*),	he does.	FÁNNO (*fán*),	they do.

Imperfect.
io *facéva* or *facéa* (*féa*), I did *or* was doing

Perfect.

FÉCI (*féi*),	I did.	facémmo (*fémmo*),	we did.
FACÉSTI (*fésti*),	thou didst.	facéste (*féstr*),	you did.
FÉCE (*fe'*, *féo*),	he did.	FÉCERO (*féreno*),	they did

Future.
FARÒ, I shall *or* will do.

SUBJUNCTIVE MOOD.
Present.

io FÁCCIA,	that I do *or* may do.	FACCIÁMO,	that we do.
tu FÁCCIA,	that thou do.	FACCIÁTE,	that you do.
égli FÁCCIA,	that he do.	FÁCCIANO,	that they do.

Imperfect.
io *facéssi* (*féssi*), if I did *or* should do.

CONDITIONAL MOOD.
Present.
FARÉI (*faria*, *faré'*), I should, would, *or* could do, *or* might do

IMPERATIVE MOOD.

		FACCIÁMO,	let us do
fa (*fà*) tu,	do thou.	FÁTE,	do ye.
FÁCCIA égli,	let him do.	FÁCCIANO,	let them do.

The compounds of *fáre* — as, *assuefáre*, to accustom; *confáre*, to suit, to agree; *contraffáre*, to mimic, to imitate; *disfáre*, to undo; *misfáre*, to do wrong; etc. — have the same irregularities. *Sodisfáre*, or *soddisfáre*. to satisfy, is both regular and irregular

---

* This verb belongs properly to the second conjugation; it being but a contraction of *fácere*, now become obsolete, of which it retains many of the forms

Stáre (*varied with* Éssere).

INFINITIVE MOOD.
Present.
Stáre, to stand, to stay, to dwell, *or* to be.

GERUND.
stándo, standing.

PARTICIPLE.
státo, stood.

INDICATIVE MOOD.
Present.

sto,	I stand.	*stiámo,*	we stand.
STÁI,	thou standest.	*státe,*	you stand.
sta,	he stands.	**STÁNNO,**	they stand

Perfect.

STÉTTI (*stéi*),	I stood.	**STÉMMO,**	we stood.
STÉSTI,	thou stoodst.	**STÉSTE,**	you stood.
STÉTTE (*sté*),	he stood.	**STÉTTERO** (*stéro*),	they stood

Future.
STARÒ, I shall *or* will stand.

SUBJUNCTIVE MOOD.
Present.

io **STÍA,**	that I stand.	*stiámo,*	that we stand
tu **STÍA** or **STÍI,**	that thou stand.	*stiáte,*	that you stand
égli **STÍA,**	that he stand.	**STÍANO** or **STÍENO,**	that they stand

Imperfect.
io **STÉSSI,** if I stood *or* should stand.

CONDITIONAL MOOD.
Present.
STARÉI(*staría*), I should, would, *or* could stand, *or* might stand.

IMPERATIVE MOOD.

sta (*stá'*) *tu,*	stand thou.	*stiámo,*	let us stand.
STÍA *égli,*	let him stand.	*státe,*	stand ye.
		STÍANO or **STÍENO** *églino,*	let them stand.

IRREGULAR VERBS. 219

Stáre is sometimes varied with the conjunctive pronouns, *mi, ti, si,* etc., and the particle *ne:* thus, ME NE *sto,* I remain here; TE NE *stái,* thou remainest here; etc. *Me, te,* etc., are then mere expletives.

Contrastáre, signifying to deny, to dispute; *soprastáre* or *sovrastáre,* signifying to stand over, to threaten; *ostáre,* to oppose; *restáre,* to remain, — are *regular,* and are varied like *amáre.*

The foregoing verbs, *andáre, dáre, fáre,* and *stáre,* in all those forms in which, when they are simple, they make but one syllable, have, in their compounds, the grave accent on the last syllable; as, *rò, dà, fè', stà:* Rivò, I go again; ridà, he gives back again; *disfè',* he destroyed; *instà,* entreat thou; etc.

VARIATION OF THE IRREGULAR VERBS OF THE SECOND CONJUGATION.

Variation of the Irregular Verbs in ēre *(long).*

The simple irregular verbs in ēre (long) are the following viz.: —

cadére,	to fall.	rimanére,	to remain.
dissuadére,	to dissuade.	sapére,	to know.
dolére,	to grieve.	sedére,	to sit down.
dovére,	to owe.	tacére,	to be or keep silent
giacére,	to lie down.	tenére,	to hold.
parére,	to seem.	valére,	to be worth.
persuadére,	to persuade.	vedére,	to see.
piacére,	to please.	volére,	to wish, to will, or to be willing.
potére,	to be able.		

Cadére (*varied with* Éssere).

INFINITIVE MOOD.
cadére, to fall.

PARTICIPLE.
cadúto, fallen.

INDICATIVE MOOD.
Present.

cádo (cággio),	I fall.	*cadiámo (caggiámo)*,	we fall.
cádi,	thou fallest.	*cadéte*,	you fall
cáde,	he falls.	*cádono (cággiono)*,	they fall.

Perfect.

CÁDDI(*cadéi,cadétti*),	I fell.	*cadémmo*,	we fell.
cadésti,	thou fellest.	*cadéste*,	you fell.
CÁDDE (*cadéo*),	he fell.	CÁDDERO (*cadéro, cadéro*),	they fell.

Future.
caderó (cadró), I shall *or* will fall.

SUBJUNCTIVE MOOD.
Present.

io cáda,	that I fall *or* may fall.	*cadiámo (caggiámo)*,	that we fall.
tu cáda,	that thou fall.	*cadiáte (caggiáte)*,	that you fall.
égli cáda,	that he fall.	*cádano (cággiano)*,	that they fall.

CONDITIONAL MOOD.
Present.
caderéi (cadréi, caderia, cadria), I should, would, *or* could fall, *or* might fall.

IMPERATIVE MOOD.
cádi tu, fall thou.

Dissuadére (*varied with either* Avére *or* Éssere).

INFINITIVE MOOD.
dissuadére, to dissuade

PARTICIPLE.
DISSUÁSO, dissuaded.

INDICATIVE MOOD.
Perfect.

DISSUÁSI,	I dissuaded.	*dissuadémmo*,	we dissuaded.
dissuadésti,	thou dissuadest.	*dissuadéste*,	you dissuaded.
DISSUÁSE,	he dissuaded.	DISSUÁSERO,	they dissuaded.

Dissuadére, properly speaking, is a compound of the Latin verb *suadére*, as well as *persuadére*, to persuade, which has the same irregularities.

Dolére (*varied with* Éssere, *and the Conjunctive Pronouns*, mi, ti, si, *etc.*).

INFINITIVE MOOD.
dolér-si, to grieve.

PARTICIPLE.
dolúto-si, grieved.

INDICATIVE MOOD.
Present.

mi DÓLGO (*dóglio*),	I grieve.	ci DOGLIAMO (*dolémo*),	we grieve.
ti DUOLI,	thou grievest.	vi doléte,	you grieve.
si DUÓLE (*dóle*),	he grieves.	si DÓLGONO (*dógliono*),	they grieve.

Perfect.

mi DÓLSI,	I grieved.	ci dolémmo,	we grieved.
ti dolésti,	thou grievedst.	vi doléste,	you grieved.
si DÓLSE,	he grieved.	si DÓLSERO,	they grieved.

Future.

dorrò (by contraction for *dolerò* *), I shall *or* will grieve.

SUBJUNCTIVE MOOD.
Present.

mi DÓLGA (*dóglia*),	that I grieve.	ci DOGLIÁMO,	that we grieve.
ti DÓLGA (*dóglia*),	that thou grieve.	vi DOGLIÁTE,	that you grieve
si DÓLGA (*dóglia*),	that he grieve.	si DÓLGANO (*dógliano*),	that they grieve

CONDITIONAL MOOD.
Present.

dorréi (*dorria*), by contraction for *doleréi* (*doleria*),† I should, would, *or* could grieve.

IMPERATIVE MOOD.

		DOGLIÁMO-ci,	let us grieve.
DUÓLI-ti,	grieve thou.	doléte-vi,	grieve ye.
si DÓLGA (*dóglia*),	let him grieve.	si DÓLGANO (*dógliano*),	let them grieve

The compounds of *dolére*,— as, *condolére*, to condole, etc.— have the same irregularities.

---

* To distinguish it from *dolerò*, future of the verb *doláre*, to defraud.
† To distinguish them from *doleréi* (*doleria*), forms of the conditional of the verb *doláre*, to defraud.

Dovére (varied with Avére).

INFINITIVE MOOD.

dovére (devére *), to owe.

PARTICIPLE

dovúto, owed.

INDICATIVE MOOD.

Present.

devo or débbo (déggio),	I owe.	DOBBIÁMO (debbiámo),	we owe.
dévi (déi),	thou owest.	dovete,	you owe.
déve or DÉBBE (dée dé'),	he owes.	dévono or DÉBBONO,	they owe.

Perfect.

dovéi or dovétti, I owed.

Future.

doveró or dovró, I shall or will owe.

SUBJUNCTIVE MOOD.

Present.

io DÉBBA (déggia),	that I owe.	DOBBIÁMO (deggiámo),	that we owe.
tu DÉBBA (déggia),	that thou owe.	DOBBIATE (deggiáte),	that you owe.
égli DÉBBA (déggia),	that he owe.	DÉBBANO (déggiano),	that they owe.

CONDITIONAL MOOD.

Present.

doveréi or dovréi (doveria or dovria), I should, would, or could owe, or might owe.

IMPERATIVE MOOD (wanting).

---

* The Latin debére, from which dovére derives some of its forms.

Giacére (*varied with either* Avére *or* Éssere).

INFINITIVE MOOD.

giacére, to lie down.

PARTICIPLE.

giaciúto, lain down.

INDICATIVE MOOD.

Present.

GIÁCCIO,	I lie down.	GIACCIÁMO,	we lie down.
giáci,	thou liest down.	giacéte,	you lie down.
giáce,	he lies down.	GIÁCCIONO,	they lie down.

Perfect.

GIÁCQUI,	I lay down.	giacémmo,	we lay down.
giacésti,	thou layest down.	giacéste,	you lay down.
GIÁCQUE,	he lay down.	GIÁCQUERO,	they lay down

SUBJUNCTIVE MOOD.

Present.

io GIÁCCIA,	that I lie down.	GIACCIÁMO,	that we lie down.
tu GIÁCCIA,	that thou lie down.	giacciáte,	that you lie down.
égli GIÁCCIA,	that he lie down.	GIÁCCIANO,	that they lie down

IMPERATIVE MOOD.

		GIACCIÁMO *nói*,	let us lie down.
giáci *tu*,	lie thou down.	giacéte *vói*,	lie ye down.
GIÁCCIA *égli*,	let him lie down.	GIÁCCIANO *églino*,	let them lie down.

The compounds of *giacére* (as, *soggiacére*, to be subject, etc.) as well as *piacére* and its compounds (*compiacére*, to please *dispiacére*, to displease; etc.), have the same irregularities.

Piacére, and its compounds *compiacére*, etc., in the second person plural of the present of the subjunctive, and in the second person plural of the imperative mood, make PIACCIÁTE, etc.

Parére (varied with Éssere).

INFINITIVE MOOD.
parére, to seem.

PARTICIPLE.
parúto (*pá so*), seemed.

INDICATIVE MOOD.
Present.

PÁIO,	I seem.	*pariámo*,	we seem.
pári,	thou seemest.	*paréte*,	you seem.
páre (*pár*),	he seems.	*paróno*, or PÁIONO,	they seem.

Perfect.

PÁRVI (*pársi*),	I seemed.	*parémmo*,	we seemed.
parésti,	thou seemedst.	*paréste*,	you seemed.
PÁRVE (*párse*),	he seemed.	PÁRVERO (*pársero*),	they seemed.

Future.
parrò (by contraction for *parerò* *), I shall or will seem.

SUBJUNCTIVE MOOD.
Present.

io PÁIA,	that I seem.	*pariámo*,	that we seem.
tu PÁIA,	that thou seem	*pariáte*,	that you seem.
égli PÁIA.	that he seem.	PÁIANO,	that they seem.

CONDITIONAL MOOD.
Present.
parréi (*parria*), by contraction for *paréréi* (*pare-iat*), I should, would, or could seem.

IMPERATIVE MOOD.

pari tu,	seem thou.	*pariámo nói*,	let us seem.
PÁIA *égli*.	let him seem.	*paréte vói*,	seem ye.
		PÁIANO *églino*,	let them seem.

Persuadére.
(*See* "Dissuadére," p 220.)

Piacére.
(See "Giacére," p. 223.)

---

* To distinguish it from *parerò*, future of the verb *paráre*, to parry, to adorn.
† To distinguish them from *paréréi* (*pareria*), corresponding forms of the verb *paríre*, to parry, etc.

Potére (*varied with either* Avére *or* Éssere).

INFINITIVE MOOD.
Potére, to be able.

PARTICIPLE.
potúto, been able.

INDICATIVE MOOD.
Present.

pósso,	I am able.	possiámo,	we are able.
puói (*può*),	thou art able.	potéte,	you are able.
può (*puóte, póte*),	he is able.	póssono (*pónno*),	they are able.

Future.
potrò (by contraction for *poterò*),* I shall *or* will be able.

SUBJUNCTIVE MOOD.
Present.
póssa, that I be able, *or* may be able.

CONDITIONAL MOOD.
Present.

potréi (*potria*), by contraction for *poteréi* (*potería,† poria*),	I should, would, *or* could be able, *or* might be able.

IMPERATIVE MOOD (wanting).

---

* To distinguish it from *potrò,* future of the verb *potáre,* to prune.
† To distinguish them from *poteréi* (*potería*), corresponding forms of the verb *potáre* to prune.

Rimanére (*varied with* Éssere).

INFINITIVE MOOD.

rimanére, to remain.

PARTICIPLE.

RIMÁSTO (*rimáso*), remained.

INDICATIVE MOOD.

Present.

RIMÁNGO (*rimágno*),	I remain.	*rimaniámo*,	we remain.
rimáni,	thou remainest.	*rimanéte*,	you remain.
rimáne,	he remains.	RIMÁNGONO,	they remain.

Perfect.

RIMÁSI,	I remained.	*rimanémmo*,	we remained.
rimanésti,	thou remainedst.	*rimanéste*,	you remained.
RIMÁSE.	he remained.	RIMÁSERO.	they remained

Future.

rimarrò (by contraction for *rimanerò*), I shall *or* will remain.

SUBJUNCTIVE MOOD

Present.

io RIMÁNGA (*rimagna*),	that I remain.	*rimaniámo*,	that we remain.
tu RIMÁNGA (*rimágna*),	that thou remain.	*rimaniáte*,	that you remain.
égli RIMÁNGA,	that he remain.	RIMÁNGANO,	that they remain.

CONDITIONAL MOOD.

Present.

rimarréi (*rimarria*), by contraction for *rimanerèi* (*rimaneria*),	I should, would, *or* could remain, *or* might remain.

IMPERATIVE MOOD.

rimáni tu,	remain thou.	*rimaniámo nói*,	let us remain
RIMÁNGA égli,	let him remain.	*rimanéte vói*,	remain ye.
		RIMÁNGANO églino,	let them remain

Sapére (varied with Avére).

INFINITIVE MOOD.
sapére, to know.

PARTICIPLE.
sapúto, known.

INDICATIVE MOOD.
Present.

so,	I know.	SAPPIÁMO,	we know.
SAI,	thou knowest.	*sapete*,	you know.
SA (*sape*)	he knows.	SÁNNO,	they know.

Perfect.

SÉPPI,	I knew.	sapémmo,	we knew.
sapésti,	thou knewest	sapéste,	you knew.
SÉPPE,	he knew.	SÉPPERO,	they knew.

Future.
saprò (by contraction for *saperò*), I shall or will know.

SUBJUNCTIVE MOOD.
Present.
io SÁPPIA, that I know, *or* may know.

CONDITIONAL MOOD.
Present.

saprèi (*sapria*), by contraction for *saperèi* (*saperia*),	I should, would, *or* could know, *or* might know.

IMPERATIVE MOOD.

SAPPI *tu*,	know thou	SAPPIÁMO *nói*,	let us know.
SÁPPIA *egli*,	let him know.	SAPPIÁTE *vói*,	know ye.
		SÁPPIANO *églino*,	let them know

The compounds of *sapére* — as *risapére*, to learn, *or* to come to know — follow the same irregularities.

Sedére (*varied with* Avére).

INFINITIVE MOOD.
sedére (séggere*), to sit down.

GERUND.
sedéndo (seggéndo), sitting.

PARTICIPLE.
sedúto, seated.

INDICATIVE MOOD.
Present.

SIÉDO or SÉGGO,	I sit.	sediámo,	we sit.
SIÉDI,	thou sittest.	sedéte,	you sit.
SIÉDE (séde),	he sits.	SIÉDONO,	they sit.

Perfect.
sedéi or sedétti, I sat.

Future.
sederó (sedró), I shall *or* will sit.

SUBJUNCTIVE MOOD.
Present.

Io SIÉDA or SÉGGA,	that I sit, *or* may sit.	sediámo or SEGGIAMO,	that we sit.
tu SIÉDA or SÉGGA,	that thou sit.	sediáte (seggiáte),	that you sit.
egli SIÉDA or SÉGGA,	that he sit.	SIÉDANO or SÉGGANO,	that they sit

CONDITIONAL MOOD.
Present.
sederéi (sedréi, sederia), I should, would, *or* could sit, *or* might sit.

IMPERATIVE MOOD.

SIÉDI *tu*,	sit thou.	sediámo or (seggiámo) noi,	let us sit.
SIÉDA or SÉGGA *égli*,	let him sit.	sedéte vói,	sit ye.
		SIÉDANO églino,	let them sit.

Sedére is sometimes varied with the pronouns *mi, ti, si,* etc., and then it requires the auxiliary *éssere;* as, *mi siédo,* I sit (myself); *ti séi sedúto,* thou hast sat (thyself); etc.

The compounds of *sedére* — as, *possedére,* to possess; *risedére,* to reside; *soprassedére,* to supersede — have the same irregularities.

---

* This verb, now become obsolete, is still used in many of the forms of the modern verb *sedére*.

Tacére (varied with Avére).

INFINITIVE MOOD.
tacére, to be or keep silent.

PARTICIPLE.
taciúto, been silent.

INDICATIVE MOOD.

Present.
tácio (táccio), I am silent.

Perfect.

I was silent.	tacémmo,	we were silent.
thou wast silent.	tacéste,	you were silent.
he was silent.	TÁCQUERO,	they were silent.

TÁCQUI,
tacésti,
TÁCQUE,

SUBJUNCTIVE MOOD.

Present.
to tácia (táccia), that I be silent *or* may be silent.

CONDITIONAL MOOD.
taceréi, I should, would, *or* could be silent.

IMPERATIVE MOOD.
táci tu, be thou silent.

Tacére is sometimes varied with the pronouns, *mi, ti, si*, etc., and then it requires the auxiliary *éssere: mi tácio*, I keep silent; *si è taciúto*, he has kept silent; &c.

The compound of *tacére — ritacére*, to become once more silent — follows the same irregularities.

20

Tenére (varied with Avére).

INFINITIVE MOOD.
tenére, to hold.

PARTICIPLE.
tenúto, holden.

INDICATIVE MOOD.
Present.

TÉNGO (*tégno*),	I hold.	*teniámo* (*tegnámo*),	we hold.
TIÉNI (*tégni*),	thou holdest.	*tenéte*,	you hold.
TIÉNE,	he holds.	TÉNGONO,	they hold.

Perfect.

TÉNNI,	I held.	*tenémmo*,	we held.
tenésti,	thou heldest.	*tenéste*,	you held.
TÉNNE,	he held.	TÉNNERO,	they held.

Future.
terrò (by contraction for *tenerò*), I shall *or* will hold.

SUBJUNCTIVE MOOD.
Present.

io TÉNGA (*tégna*),	that I hold.	*teniámo* (*tegnámo*),	that we hold.
tu TÉNGA,	that thou hold.	*teniáte* (*tegnáte*),	that you hold.
égli TÉNGA (*tégna*),	that he hold.	TÉNGANO (*tégnano*),	that they hold.

CONDITIONAL MOOD.
Present.

terréi (*terrìa*), by contraction for *teneréi* (*teneria*),	I should, would, *or* could hold, *or* might hold.

IMPERATIVE MOOD.

TIÉNI (*te'*) *tu*,	hold thou.	*teniámo* (*tegnámo*) *nói*,	let us hold.
TÉNGA (*tégna*) *égli*,	let him hold.	*tenéte vói*, TÉNGANO *églino*,	hold ye. let them hold.

Tenére is sometimes varied with the pronouns *mi, ti, si*, etc., and then it requires the auxiliary *éssere*; as, *mi sóno tenúto*, I have holden *or* restrained myself; etc.

Valére (*varied with either* Avére *or* Éssere).

INFINITIVE MOOD.
valére, to be worth *or* to avail.

PARTICIPLE.
valúto (*válso*), been worth.

INDICATIVE MOOD.
Present.

VÁLGO (*váglio*),	I am worth.	*valiámo*,	we are worth.
vali,	thou art worth.	*valéte*,	you are worth.
vale (*val*),	he is worth	VÁLGONO,	they are worth

Perfect.

VÁLSI,	I was worth.	*valémmo*,	we were worth.
valésti,	thou wast worth.	*valéste*,	you were worth.
VÁLSE,	he was worth.	VÁLSERO,	they were worth

Future.
varrò (by contraction for *valeró*), I shall *or* will be worth.

SUBJUNCTIVE MOOD.
Present.

io VÁLGA *or* VÁGLIA,	that I be worth.	*valiámo*,	that we be worth.
tu VÁLGA *or* VÁGLIA,	that thou be worth.	*valiáte*,	that you be worth.
égli VÁLGA *or* VÁGLIA,	that he be worth.	VÁLGANO,	that they be worth.

CONDITIONAL MOOD.
Present.

varréi (*varría*), by contraction for *valeréi* (*valería*).	I should, would, *or* could be worth, *or* might be worth.

IMPERATIVE MOOD.

vali tu,	be thou worth.	*valiámo nói*,	let us be worth
VÁLGA (*váglia*) *égli*,	let him be worth.	*valéte vói*,	be ye worth.
		VÁLGANO *églino*,	let them be worth

Vedére (*varied with* Avére).

INFINITIVE MOOD.
vedére, to see.

GERUND.
vedéndo *or* veggéndo, seeing.

PARTICIPLE.
vedúto (visto), seen.

INDICATIVE MOOD.

Present.

védo, véggo,	I see.	vediámo *or* veggiámo,	we see.
védi (vè'),	thou seest.	vedéte,	you see.
véde,	he sees.	védono *or* véggono,	they see.

Perfect.

vídi,	I saw.	vedemmo,	we saw.
vedésti,	thou sawest.	vedéste,	you saw.
víde,	he saw.	vídero, (víder),	they saw.

Future.

vedrò (by contraction for vederò), I shall *or* will see.

SUBJUNCTIVE MOOD.

Present.

io véda *or* végga,	that I see *or* may see.	vediámo *or* veggiámo,	that we see.
tu véda *or* végga,	that thou see.	vediáte *or* veggiáte,	that you see.
égli véda *or* végga,	that he see.	védano *or* véggano,	that they see.

CONDITIONAL MOOD.

Present.

vedréi (vedría), by contraction for vederéi (vederia),	I should, would, *or* could see, *or* might see.

IMPERATIVE MOOD.

védi (vé') tu,	see thou.	vediámo nói,	let us see.
véda *or* végga égli,	let him see	vedéte vói,	see ye.
		védano églino,	let them see.

Volére (*varied with* Avére).

INFINITIVE MOOD.
volére, to wish, to will, *or* to be willing

PARTICIPLE.
volúto, been willing.

INDICATIVE MOOD.
Present.

vóglio *or* vò',	I am willing.	VOGLIAMO (*volémo*),	we are willing.
VUOI (*vuóli, vuó'*),	thou art willing.	*volete*,	you are willing.
VUOLE (*vóle*),	he is willing.	VOGLIONO (*vónno*),	they are willing.

Perfect.

VOLLI,	I was willing.	*volémmo*,	we were willing.
volésti,	thou wast willing.	*voléste*,	you were willing.
VÓLLE,	he was willing.	VÓLLERO,	they were willing

Future.

vorrò (by contraction for *volerò* *), I shall *or* will be willing

SUBJUNCTIVE MOOD.
Present.

io VÓGLIA, that I be willing *or* may be willing.

CONDITIONAL MOOD.
Present.

vorréi (*vorria*), by contraction for *voleréi* (*voleria* †), | I should, would, *or* could be willing, *or* might be willing.

IMPERATIVE MOOD (wanting).

The compounds of *volére* — as, *disvolére*, to desire the contrary of what one has wished; *rivolére*, to wish again, or to be once more willing — have the same irregularities.

---

* To distinguish it from the *future* of the verb *voláre*, to fly.
† To distinguish them from the corresponding forms of *voláre*, to fly

VARIATION OF THE IRREGULAR VERBS OF THE THIRD CONJUGATION.

The following are the simple irregular verbs of the third conjugation; viz.,—

dire,	to say or to tell.	udíre,	to hear.
moríre,	to die.	uscíre,	to go out.
salíre,	to ascend.	veníre,	to come.
seguíre,	to follow.		

Díre (*varied with* Avére).

INFINITIVE MOOD.
DÍRE, to say.

GERUND.
dicéndo, saying.

PARTICIPLE.
DÉTTO (*ditto*), said.

INDICATIVE MOOD.
Present.

díco,	I say.	diciámo,	we say.
díci or dì'	thou sayest.	DÍTE,	you say.
díce,	he says.	dícono,	they say.

Imperfect.
Io dicéva or dicéa, I said.

Perfect.

díssi,	I said.	dicémmo,	we said.
dicésti,	thou saidst.	dicéste,	you said.
DÍSSE,	he said.	DÍSSERO,	they said.

Future.
DIRÒ (by contraction for *dicerò*), I shall or will say.

SUBJUNCTIVE MOOD.

Present.
to *dica*, that I say *or* may say.

Imperfect.
to *dicéssi*, if I said *or* should say.

CONDITIONAL MOOD.

Present.

DIREI (*diria*), by contraction for *dicerèi* (*diceria*),	I should, would, *or* could say; *or* might say,

IMPERATIVE MOOD.

di' tu,	say thou.	diciámo nói,	let us say.
dica egli,	let him say.	DITE vói, dicano églino,	say ye. let them say.

The compounds of *dire* — as, *ridíre*, to say again; *contradíre* or *contraddíre*, to contradict; *interdíre*, to forbid; *bendíre*, to speak well of; *maldíre*, to speak ill of — have the same irregularities.

Benedíre, to bless, and *maledíre*, to curse, in the perfect are both regular and irregular, and make *benedii* or *benedissi,* I blessed; *maledii* or *maledissi,* I cursed.

Moríre (*varied with* Éssere).*

INFINITIVE MOOD.
moríre, to die.

PARTICIPLE.
MÓRTO, dead.

INDICATIVE MOOD.
Present.

MUÓRO (*mòio*),	I die.	*moriámo*,	we die.
MUÓRI,	thou diest.	*moríte*,	you die.
MUÓRE (*muór*),	he dies.	MUÓRONO (*muóiono*),	they die.

Future.
moriró or *morró*, I shall *or* will die

SUBJUNCTIVE MOOD.
Present.

io MUÓRA (*mòia*),	that I die *or* may die.	*moriámo*,	that we die.
tu MUÓRA (*mòra*),	that thou die.	*moriáte*,	that you die.
égli MUÓRA (*móra*),	that he die.	MUÓRANO (*mórano*),	that they die.

CONDITIONAL MOOD.
Present.
moriréi or *morréi* (*moriría* or *morría*), I should, would, *or* could die, *or* might die.

IMPERATIVE MOOD.

MUÓRI *tu*,	die thou.	*moriámo nói*,	let us die.
MUÓRA (*móra*) *égli*,	let him die.	*moríte vói*,	die ye.
		MUÓRANO *églino*,	let them die.

The compounds of *moríre* — as, *premoríre*, to die before, etc. — have the same irregularities.

---

* *Moríre* may be varied also with *avére*; but it then takes the nature of an active verb, and signifies " to kill," and not " to die."

IRREGULAR VERBS. 237

Salire (*varied with either* Avére *or* Éssere).

INFINITIVE MOOD.
salire (*saglire* *), to ascend.

PARTICIPLE.
salito, ascended.

INDICATIVE MOOD.

Present.

SÁLGO (*ságlio*),	I ascend.	saliámo or SAGLIÁMO,	we ascend.
sáli or salisci (*ságli*),	thou ascendest.	salíte,	you ascend.
sále or salisce (*ságlie*),	he ascends.	SÁLGONO (*ságliono*),	they ascend.

Perfect.

salii (*sálsi*),	I ascended.	salimmo,	we ascended.
salisti,	thou ascendedst.	saliste,	you ascended.
salì (*sálse, salío*),	he ascended.	salírono (*salíro, salír*),	they ascended.

SUBJUNCTIVE MOOD.

Present.

io SÁLGA (*ságlia*),	that I ascend.	saliámo or SAGLIÁMO,	that we ascend
tu SÁLGA (*sághi*),	that thou ascend.	saliáte or SAGLIÁTE,	that you ascend
égli SÁLGA or salisca,	that he ascend.	SÁLGANO (*ságliano*),	that they ascend

IMPERATIVE MOOD.

		saliámo nói,	let us ascend
sáli or salisci tu,	ascend thou.	salíte vói,	ascend ye.
SÁLGA or salisca égli,	let him ascend.	SÁLGANO églino,	let them ascend.

The compounds of *salire* — as, *risalire,* to re-ascend; *assalíre,* to assail; etc. — have the same irregularities.

---

* From this verb, now become obsolete, are derived many of the forms of the modern verb *salire*.

Seguíre (*varied with either* Avére *or* Éssere)

INFINITIVE MOOD.
seguíre, to follow.

PARTICIPLE.
seguíto, followed.

INDICATIVE MOOD.
Present.

séguo or siéguo,	I follow.	seguiámo,	we follow.
séguí or siégui,	thou followest.	seguíte,	you follow.
ségue or siégue,	he follows.	séguono or siéguono,	they follow.

SUBJUNCTIVE MOOD.
Present.

io ségua or siégua,	that I follow.	seguiámo,	that we follow.
tu ségua or siégua,	that thou followest.	seguiáte,	that you follow.
égli ségua or siégua,	that he follow.	séguano or siéguano,	that they follow.

IMPERATIVE MOOD.

séguí or siégui tu,	follow thou.	seguiámo nói,	let us follow.
ségua or siégua égli,	let him follow.	seguíte vói,	follow ye.
		séguano églino	let them follow.

¶ The compounds of *seguíre* have the same irregularities.

Udire (*varied with* Avére).

INFINITIVE MOOD.
udire (odire), to hear.

PARTICIPLE.
udito, heard.

INDICATIVE MOOD.
Present.

ÓDO — I hear. — *udiámo,* — we hear.
ÓDI, — thou hearest. — *udíte,* — you hear.
ÓDE — he hears. — ÓDONO, — they hear.

Future.
udirò or *udrò,* I shall *or* will hear.

SUBJUNCTIVE MOOD.
Present.

ch'io ÓDA, — that I hear *or* may hear. — *udiámo,* — that we hear.
tu ÓDA (*òdi*), — that thou hear. — *udiate,* — that you hear.
egli ÓDA, — that he hear. — ÓDANO, — that they hear.

CONDITIONAL MOOD.
Present.
udirèi or *udréi* (*udiria* or *udria*), I should, would, *or* could hear, *or* might hear

IMPERATIVE MOOD.

ÓDI *tu,* — hear thou. — *udiámo nói,* — let us hear
ÓDA *egli,* — let him hear. — *udíte vói,* — hear ye.
 — — ÓDANO *églino,* — let them hear.

The compounds of *udire* — as, *riudire*, to hear again, etc. — have the same irregularities.
Esaudíre, to grant, is regular, and varied like *esibire.*

Uscíre (*varied with* Éssere).

INFINITIVE MOOD.
uscire (escire), to go out.

PARTICIPLE.
uscito, gone out.

INDICATIVE MOOD
Present.

ÉSCO,	I go out.	usciámo,	we go out.
ÉSCI,	thou goest out.	uscíte,	you go out.
ÉSCE,	he goes out.	ÉSCONO,	they go out.

SUBJUNCTIVE MOOD.
Present.

io ÉSCA,	that I go out *or* may go out.	usciámo,	that we go out.
tu ÉSCA,	that thou go out.	usciáte,	that you go out.
égli ÉSCA	that he go out.	ÉSCANO,	that they go out.

IMPERATIVE MOOD.

ÉSCI *tu*,	go thou out.	usciámo nói,	let us go out.
ÉSCA *égli*,	let him go out.	uscíte vói,	go ye out.
		ÉSCANO églino,	let them go out.

The compound of *uscire* — *riuscíre*, to succeed — has the same irregularities.

IRREGULAR VERBS.

Veníre (*varied with* Éssere).

INFINITIVE MOOD.
venire, to come.

PARTICIPLE.
VENÚTO, come.

INDICATIVE MOOD.
Present.

VÉNGO (végno),	I come.	veniámo (vegnámo),	we come.
VIÉNI,	thou comest.	veníte,	you come.
VIÉNE,	he comes.	VÉNGONO (végnono),	they come.

Perfect.

VÉNNI,	I came.	venimmo,	we came.
venisti,	thou camest,	veniste,	you came.
VÉNNE,	he came.	VÉNNERO (véniro),	they came.

Future.

verrò (by contraction for *venirò*), I shall *or* will come.

SUBJUNCTIVE MOOD.
Present.

Io VÉNGA,	that I come *or* may come.	veniámo (vegnámo),	that we come.
tu VÉNGA,	that thou come.	veniáte (vegnáte),	that you come.
égli VÉNGA,	that he come.	VÉNGANO (végnano),	that they come.

CONDITIONAL MOOD.
Present.

verréi (verría), by contraction for *veniréi* (venirìa),	I should, would, *or* could come, *or* might come.

IMPERATIVE MOOD.

VIÉNI tu,	come thou.	veniámo nói,	let us come.
VÉNGA égli,	let him come.	veníte vói,	come ye.
		VÉNGANO églino,	let them come.

Venire is sometimes varied with the conjunctive pronouns *mi, ti, si,* etc., and the particle *ne:* thus, ME NE *véngo,* I am coming thence; TE NE *viéni,* thou art coming thence, etc. *Me, te,* etc., are then mere expletives.

The compounds of *venire* — as, *convenire,* to agree; *divenire,* to become; etc — have the same irregularities.

TABLE OF IRREGULAR VERBS.

INFINITIVE.	PRESENT.	PERFECT.	FUTURE.	PARTICIPLE
Accéndere, *to light*	accéndo	accési	accenderò	accéso
Accórgersi, *to perceive*	m' accórgo	m' accórsi	m' accorgerò	accórto
Addúrre, *to allege* (Addúcere), *to allege*	addúco	addússi	addurrò (ad lucerò)	addotto (addátto)
Affliggere, *to afflict*	affliggo	afflíssi	affliggerò	afflitto
Ancídere, *to kill*	ancído	ancísi	ancidrò	ancíso
Andáre, *to go*	vádo (vo)	andái	andrò	and.to
Apparire, *to appear* (Appárere), *to appear*	apparisco (appáro) (appájo)	appárii appárvi (appársi)	apparirò apparerò	apparito apparso (apparúto)
Appartenére, *to belong*	appartèngo	appartenni (appartenétti)	apparterrò apparteneró	appartenúto
Applaudire, *to applaud* (Applaúdere), *to applaud*	applaudisco applaúdo	applaudii (applaúsi)	applaudirò applauderò	applaudito (applaúso)
Aprire, *to open*	ápro	aprii, apérsi	aprirò	aperto
Árdere, *to burn*	árdo	ársi	arderò	árso
Ascéndere, *to ascend*	ascéndo	ascési ascendéi ascendétti	ascenderò	ascéso
Ascóndere, *to conceal*	ascóndo	ascósi	asconderò	ascóso, ascósta
Aspérgere, *to sprinkle*	aspérgo	aspérsi	aspergerò	aspérso
Assídere, (Assédere), } *to sit down*	assído	assísi	assiderò	assíso
Assístere, *to assist*	assísto	assistéi	assisterò	assistito
Assólvere, *to absolve*	assólvo	assolvéi, assolvii	assolverò	assolúto
Assórbire, *to absorb* (Assórbere), *to absorb*	assorbisco (assórbo)	assorbii (assórsi ?)	assorberò	assorbíto
Assúmere, *to assume*	assúmo	assúnsi	assumerò	assúnto
Astringere, *to compel* (Astrignere), *to compel*	astringo (astrigno)	astrínsi	astringerò (astrignerò)	astrétto
Atténdere, *to wait*	atténdo	attési	attenderò	atténto
Avére, *to have*	ho	ébbi	avrò	uv .to
Avvéllere, *to root up*	avvéllo	avvélsi	avvellerò	avvelto
Bévere, *to drink* (Bére), *to drink*	bévo (bibo), béo	bévvi, bevéi (bébbi)	beverò, bevrò (berò)	bevúto, beúto
Bollíre, *to boil*	bóllo	bolli	bolirò	bolíto
Cadére, *to fall*	cádo (cággio)	cáddi, cadéi	caderò, cadrò	cadúto
Calére, *to care for*	cále	cálse	calerà (carrà)	calúto
Capére, *to comprehend* (Capíre), *to comprehend*	cápo (capísco)	capéi (capétti)	caperò, capirò	capúto, capíte
Cédere, *to submit*	cédo	cedéi, céssi	cederò	ced ito. césso
Chiédere, *to ask*	chiédo	chiési	chiederò	chiésto
Chiúdere, *to shut*	chiúdo	chiúsi	chiuderò	chi úso
Cignere, *to gird* (Cíngere), *to gird*	cingo (cigno)	cinsi	cingerò	cinto
Cógliere, (Corre), } *to gather*	cóglio, cólgo	cólsi	coglierò, corrò	cólto
Cómpiere, *to accomplish* (Cómpire), *to accomplish*	cómpio	compiéi comp i	compierò	compíte
Concepíre, *to conceive* (Concépere), *to conceive*	concepísco (concípio)	concepii (concepétti)	conceperò (conceperò)	concepito concepúto
Connéttere, *to connect*	connétto	connettéi (connéssi) con bbi (connerétti)	connetterò	conn.sso (connettúto)
Conóscere, *to know*	conósco		conoscerò	conosciúto
Consumáre,* (Consúmere), } *to consume*	consúmo	consúnsi	consumerò	consúnto
Coprire, *to cover*	cópro	copr.i, copérsi	coprirò	copérto

* This verb is regular.

TABLE OF IRREGULAR VERBS. 243

INFINITIVE.	PRESENT.	PERFECT.	FUTURE.	PARTICIPLE
Córrere, *to run*	córro	córsi	correrò	córso
Costringere, *to constrain*	costringo	costrinsi	costringerò	costretto
(Costrìgnere), *to constrain*	costrigno		(costrignerò)	
Créscere, *to grow*	crésco	ucbbi (crescétti)	crescerò	cresciuto
Cuòcere, *to cook*	cuòco	còssi (cocci)	cocerò	còtto
Dàre, *to give*	do	diédi, diéi	darò	dato
Decìdere, *to decide*	decido	decisi (?)	deciderò	deciso
Delùdere, *to delude*	deludo	delusi	deluderò	deluso
Deprimere, *to depress*	deprimo	depréssi	deprimerò	depresso
Difèndere, *to defend*	difendo	difesi	difenderò	difeso
Dire, *to say*	dico	dissi	dirò	detto
Dirigere, *to direct*	dirigo	diréssi	dirigerò	diretto
Discèndere, *to descend*	discendo	discesi	discenderò	disceso
Dispergere, *to disperse*	dispèrgo	dispérsi	dispergerò	dispèrso
Distìnguere, *to distinguish*	distinguo	distinsi (distinguétti)	distinguerò	distinto
Divedére, *to*	divédo	dividi (dividéi)	divedrò	divedúto (diviso)
Divéllere, *to root out*	divéllo	divélsi	divellerò (diverrò)	divélto
Dolére, *to grieve*	dólgo, dòglio	dólsi	dorrò	doluto (dólto)
Dovére, *to owe*	debbo, devo	dovei, dovétti	dovrò	dovuto
(Devére), *to owe*	(déo)	(devei)	(doverò)	
Emèrgere, *to emerge*	emergo	emersi	emergerò	emérso
Erìgere, ergere, *to erect*	érigo, érgo	eréssi, érsi	erigerò, ergerò	erétto (érto)
Esigere, *to exact*	esigo	esigéi	esigerò	esatto
Espèllere, *to expel*	espèllo	espulsi	espellerò	espúlso
Espónere, *to expose*	espóngo	esposi	esporrò	esposto
(Espórre), *to expose*	(espóno)	(esposi)	(esponerò)	(esposito)
Esprìmere, *to express*	esprimo	espréssi	esprimerò	espresso
Essere, *to be*	sóno	fui	sarò	stato
Estèndere, *to extend*	esténdo	estési (estendétti)	estenderò	estéso
Estìnguere, *to extinguish*	estinguo	estinsi	estinguerò	estinto
Facére or fare, *to do*	fo (faccio)	feci (féi)	farò	fatto
Féndere, *to cleave*	féndo	féndei (féssi)	fenderò	fésso
Figere or figgere, *to fix*	figo, figgo	fissi (fisi)	figerò, figgerò	fitto, fisso, fisso
Fingere or fignere, *to feign*	fingo (figno)	finsi	fingerò	finto (fitto)
Fóndere, *to melt*	fóndo	fusi (fondéi)	fonderò	fuso, fondúto
Frangere, (Fragnére), } *to break*	frango	fransi	frangerò	franto
Frìggere, *to fry*	friggo	frissi	friggerò	fritto
Genuflèttere, *to kneel*	genuflétto	genufléssi	genufletterò	genuflèsso
Giacére, *to lie down*	giàccio	giàcqui (giacétti)	giacerò	giaciúto
Gìre, *to go*		gii	girò	(gito)
Giùngere, *to arrive*	giúngo	giúnsi	giungerò	giunto
Giùgnere, *to arrive*		godétti, godéi		
Godére (gaudére), *to enjoy*	gódo		goderò	goduto
Illùdere, *to delude*	illúso	illúsi	illuderò	illúso
Immèrgere, *to immerge*	immèrgo	immérsi	immergerò	immèrso
Impéllere, *to impel*	impéllo	impúlsi	impellerò	impúlso
Imprìmere, *to print*	imprimo	impréssi	imprimerò	impresso
Incìdere, *to grave*	incido	incisi	inciderò	inciso
Incórrere, *to incur*	incórro	incórsi	incorrerò	incórso
Incréscere, *to be sorry*	incrésco	incrébbi (increscétti)	increscerò	incresciúto
Intèndere, *to understand*	inténdo	intési	intenderò	intéso, intenso
Intèssere, *to weave*	intèsso	intesséi	intesserò	intessuto
Intrìdere, *to temper*	intrìdo	intrisi	intriderò	intriso
Intrùdere, *to intrude*	intrúdo	intrúsi	intruderò	intrúso
Invàdere, *to invade*	invàdo	invàsi	invaderò	invàso
Invòlgere, *to wrap up*	invòlgo	invòlsi	involgerò	involúto
Invòlvere, *to wrap up*	invòlvo		involverò	
Ire, *to go*			irò	ito
Irrìdere, *to deride*	irrìdo	irrisi	irriderò	irriso

244 ITALIAN GRAMMAR.

INFINITIVE.	PRESENT.	PERFECT.	FUTURE.	PARTICIPLE
Iscrìvere, *to inscribe*	iscrivo	iscrissi	iscriverò	iscritto
Istruìre, *to instruct*	istruisco	istruii	istruirò	istrutto
Lèdere, *to offend*	ledo	(lési) (ledéi)	lederò	léso
— Lèggere, *to read*	lèggo	léssi (leggéi)	leggerò	létto
(Lécere), (Lécere), } *to be lawful*	lice, léce			(lìcito) lecìto
Maledícere, Maledìre, } *to curse* (Maladìre),	maledìco	maledéssi	maledirò	maledétto
Mérgere, *to dive*	mérgo	mérsi	mergerò	mérso
Méscere, *to mix*	mésco	mescéi	mescerò	(mesciùto)
♦ Méttere, *to put*	métto	misi, (méssi)	metterò	mésso (misso)
Mólcere, *to assuage* {	2d pers. mólci 3d pers. mólce	(mulse)		
— Mórdere, *to bite*	mórdo	mórsi	morderò	mórso
— Morìre, *to die*	{ muóro, móro { muójo, mójo	morii	morirò, morrò	mórto
Múgnere, Múngere, } *to milk*	múngo	múnsi	mugnerò	múnto
- Muòvere, *to move*	muòvo	móssi (movéi)	moverò	mósso
- Nàscere, *to be born*	násco	nácqui	nascerò	náto
⸗ Nascóndere, *to conceal*	nascóndo	nascósi	nasconderò	nascóso
Negligere, *to neglect*	negligo	negligéi	negligerò	neglètto
Nuócere, (Nócere), } *to hurt*	nuóce, noccio	nocqui	nocerò	nosciúto
Offèndere, *to offend*	offèndo	offéssi	offenderò	offéso
— Offerìre, *to offer*	offerìsco	offerii	offerirò, offrirò	
Offrìre, *to offer*	òffro	offérsi	(offerrò)	offérto
(Offerere), *to offer*	òffre			
Opprìmere, *to oppress*	opprìmo	oppréssi	opprimerò	oppresso
- Parére, *to appear*	pájo (páro)	párvi (pársi)	parrò (parerò)	parúto (párso)
- Páscere, *to feed*	pásco	pascéi	pascerò	pasciúto
Percuótere, *to strike*	percuóto	percórsi	percuoterò	percósso
-- Pèrdere, *to lose*	pèrdo	perdéi	perderò	perdúto
Persuadére, *to persuade*	persuádo	persuási (persuadéi)	persuaderò	persuáso (persuadúto)
— Piacére, *to please*	piáccio, piácio	piácqui	piacerò	piaciúto
Piàngere, Piàgnere, } *to weep*	piángo, piágno	piansi	piangerò	piánto
- Pingere, pignere, *to paint*	pingo	pinsi	pingerò	pinto (pitto)
Piòvere, *to rain*	piòvo	piòvvi, piovéi	pioverò	piovúto
⸗ (Pónere) or pórre, *to put*	póngo (póno)	pósi (puósi)	porrò	pósto
— Pòrgere, *to offer*	pòrgo	pòrsi	porgerò	pòrto
— Potére, *to be able*	pòsso	potéi, potétti (possétti)	potrò (poterò)	potúto
Precìdere, *to shorten*	precìdo	precìsi	preciderò	preciso
Prèmere, *to press*	prèmo	preméi	premerò	premúto
⸗ Prèndere, *to take*	prèndo-	prési	prenderò	préso
Presúmere, *to presume*	presúmo	presúnsi	presumerò	presúnto
Protèggere, *to protect*	protèggo	protéssi (?)	proteggerò	protètto
Púngere, púgnere, *to prick*	púngo	púnsi	pungerò	púnto
Rádere, *to shave*	rádo	rási (radéi)	raderò	ráso
Recìdere, *to retrench*	recìdo	recìsi	reciderò	reciso
Redìmere, *to redeem*	redìmo	redìméi	redimerò	redénto
Règgere, *to govern*	règgio	réssi	reggerò	rètto
Rèndere, *to render*	rèndo	rendéi	renderò	rendúto (réso)
Repèllere, *to repel*	repèllo	repúlsi	repellerò	repúlso
Reprìmere, *to repress*	reprìmo	représsi	reprimerò	représso
— Rìdere, *to laugh*	rìdo	rìsi (ridéi)	riderò	riso
Rilúcere, *to shine*	rilúco	rilússi	rilucerò	
⸗ Rimanére, *to remain*	rimángo	rimási	rimarrò	rimáso
— Risólvere, *to resolve*	risólvo	risólsi, risolvéi	risolverò	risólto
— Rispóndere, *to answer*	rispóndo	rispósi	risponderò	rispósto
Ristáre, *to desist*	risto	ristétti	ristarò	ristáto
Ristrìngere, Ristrìgnere, } *to restrain*	ristringo	ristrinsi	ristringerò	ristrétto
Ròdere, *to gnaw*	ródo	rósi	roderò	róso

TABLE OF IRREGULAR VERBS.

INFINITIVE.	PRESENT.	PERFECT.	FUTURE.	PARTICIPLE
Rómpere, *to break*	rómpo	rúppi (róppi)	romperò	rótto
Salíre, *to ascend*	sálgo, salísco	salíi (sálsi)	salirò (sarrò)	salíto ✓
Sapere, *to know*	so (sáppo)	séppi (sapéi)	saprò (saperò)	sapúto
Scegliere (scérre), *to choose*	scelgo, scéglio	scelsi	sceglierò	scelto
Scendere, *to descend*	scendo	scési (scendéi)	scenderò	sceso
Scindere, *to cleave*	seindo	scinsi	scinderò	scisso
Seignere, (Scingere), } *to ungird*	scigno, scingo	scinsi	scignerò	scinto
Sciogliere, Sciorre, } *to untie*	sciòglio	sciòlsi	scioglierò	sciòlto
Scorgere, *to perceive*	scòrgo	scòrsi	scorgerò	scòrto
Scorrere, *to lay waste*	scórro	scórsi	scorrerò	scórto
Scrivere, *to write*	scrivo (scribo)	scrissi	scriverò	scritto
Scuòtere, *to shake*	scuòto (scúto)	scòssi (scotéi)	scoterò	scòsso
Sedere, *to sit down*	siédo, séggo	sedéi, sedètti	sederò (sedrò)	sedúto
Seguire, *to follow*	séguo, siéguo	seguii	seguirò	seguíto
Serpere, *to creep*	serpo	serpéva		serpénte
Soffrire, (Sofferire), } *to suffer*	sòffro	soffrii	soffrirò	sofferto
Solére, *to be wont*	sòglio	sóno, solito		solito
Sòlvere, *to solve*	sòlvo	solvéi	solverò	solúto
Sòrgere (súrgere), *to arise*	sòrgo (súrgo)	sòrsi (súrsi)	sorgerò	sòrto (súrto)
Sospèndere, *to suspend*	sospèndo	sospési	sospenderò	sospéso
Spándere, *to pour out*	spándo	spandéi	spanderò	spandúto
Spárgere, *to spread*	spárgo	spársi	spargerò	spárso
Spégnere, Spengere, } *to extinguish*	spéngo	spénsi	spegnerò	spénto
Spéndere, *to spend*	spéndo	spési	spenderò	spéso ✓
Spèrgere, *to disperse*	spérgo	spérsi	spergerò	spérso
Spingere, (Spignere), } *to push*	spingo	spinsi	spingerò	spinto
Stare, *to stand*	sto	stétti (stéi)	starò (sterò)	státo
Sténdere, *to extend*	sténdo	stési (stendéi)	stenderò	stéso
Strídere, *to cry out*	strído	stridéi	striderò	
Stignere, Stingere, } *to stain*	stingo (stigno)	stinsi	(stignerò)	stinto
Stringere, Strignere, } *to bind fast*	stringo	strinsi	stringerò	strútto ✓
Strúggere, *to dissolve*	strúggo,	strússi	struggerò	strútto
Svèllere, Svégliere, } *to root up*	svèllo, svélgo	svèlsi	svellerò	svèlto
Súggere, *to suck*	súggo	suggéi (sússi)	suggerò	taciúto
Tacére, *to be silent*	tácio (táccio)	tacqui (tacéi)	tacerò	taciúto
Téndere, *to tend*	téndo	tési (tendéi)	tenderò	téso
Tenére, *to hold*	téngo (tégno)	ténni (tenei)	terrò (tenerò)	tenúto
Téssere, *to weave*	tèsso	tessèi	tesserò	tessúto
Tignere, tíngere, *to dye*	tingo (tigno)	tinsi	tignerò	tinto
Tògliere, Tòrre, } *to take away*	tòglio, tòlgo	tòlsi	torrè	tòlto
Tóndere, *to shear*	tóndo	tondéi	tonderò	tonduto
Tòrcére, *to twist*	tòrco	tòrsi	torcerò	tòrto
Tórpere, *to be benumbed*	tórpo			torpénto
Trarre, (Tráere), } *to draw* (Trággere),	trággo (tráo)	trássi	trarrò	trátto
Uccídere, *to kill*	uccído	uccísi	ucciderò	ucciso
Udire, *to hear*	òdo	udíi	udirò (udrò)	udíto
Úgnere, úngere, *to anoint*	úngo (úgno)	únsi	ungerò	únto
Uscíre, *to go out*	ésco	uscii (escíi)	uscirò	uscito (escito)
Valére, *to be worth*	válgo (váglio)	válsi (valéi)	varrò (valerò)	valúto (válso)
Vedére, *to see*	védo, véggo	vidi (véddi)	vedrò	vedúto (visto)
Veníre, *to come*	véngo	vénni (venii)	verrò (venirò)	ven ito (vénuto)
Víncere, *to conquer*	vinco	vinsi	vincerò	vinto (vítto)
Vívere, *to live*	vivo	vissi (vivéi)	viverò	vivúto ✓
Volére, *to will*	vòglio, vò'	vòlli (vòlsi)	vorrò	volúto
Vólvere, *to turn*	vólgo	vòlsi	volgerò	vòlto
Vólgere, *to turn*	vólvo		volverò	

Defective Verbs.

Defective Verbs ending in ēre (long), accented.

calére,	to care for.	parére,	to fear.
colére or cólere,	to adore.	silére,	to be or keep silent
licére and licére, }	to be lawful.	solére,	to be wont.
lícere and lícere, }		stupére,	to be astonished.

Defective Verbs ending in ĕre (short).

álgere,	to be chill.	riédere,	to return.
ángere,	to afflict.	sérpere,	to creep.
arrógere,	to add.	soffólcere, }	to support.
cápere,	to contain.	soffólgere, }	
chérere,	to ask.	tángere,	to touch.
convéllere,	to convulse.	tóllere,	to take away.
fiédere,	to wound.	tórpere,	to be benumbed.
lícere,	to shine.	úrgere,	to urge.
málcere,	to assuage.	vígere,	to be vigorous.

Defective Verbs ending in íre.

íre,	to go.
gíre,	to go.
olíre,	to smell.

VARIATION OF DEFECTIVE VERBS.

(These verbs are used only in the tenses and persons which are here given.)

Calére.

INFINITIVE MOOD.

Present.		*Past.*
calére, to care for.	éssere calúto,	to have cared for.

GERUND.
caléndo, caring for.

PARTICIPLE.
calúto, cared for.

INDICATIVE MOOD.

Present.		*Imperfect.*
cále or cál, he cares for.	caléva or caléa,	he cared for.

Perfect.
CÁLSE, he cared for.

SUBJUNCTIVE MOOD.

Present.		*Imperfect.*
CÁGLIA, that he care for.	calésse,	if he cared for.

IMPERATIVE MOOD.
CÁGLIA égli, let him care for.

Calére is generally used with the conjunctive pronouns *mi, ti, ci, vi, gli*. thus, *mi cále*, I care for; *ci caléva*, we cared for etc.

Colére or Cólere.

INFINITIVE MOOD.
colére or *cólere*, to adore.

INDICATIVE MOOD.
Present.

(*cólo*),   I adore.
(*cóle*),   he adores.

Lecére and Licére, or Lécere and Lícere.

INFINITIVE MOOD.
lecére and *licére*, to be lawful. | *éssere lécito* or *lícito*,* to be lawful.

INDICATIVE MOOD
Present.
léce or *líce*, it is lawful.

Pavére.

INFINITIVE MOOD.
pavére, to fear.

INDICATIVE MOOD
Present.
páve, he fears.

Silére.

INFINITIVE MOOD.
silére, to be or keep silent.

INDICATIVE MOOD
Present.

síli,   thou art or keepest silent.
síle,   he is or keeps silent.

---

* From this form are derived *è lécito*, it is lawful; *éra* or *fu lécito*, it was lawful; *sarà lécito* it will be lawful; etc., which are used to supply the tenses in which *lecére* is defective.

Solére.

INFINITIVE MOOD.

to be wont. | *éssere sólito,* | to be wont.

GERUND.
soléndo, being wont.

INDICATIVE MOOD.
Present.

solére,

sóglio, | I am wont. | sogliámo (*solémo*), | we are wont.
suóli, | thou art wont. | soléte, | you are wont.
suóle (*sóle*), | he is wont. | sógliono, | they are wont.

Imperfect.
io soléva or *soléa,* I was wont.

SUBJUNCTIVE MOOD.
Present.
io sóglia, that I am wont *or* may be wont.
Imperfect.
io soléssi, if I were wont *or* should be wont.

Stupére.

INFINITIVE MOOD.
stupére, to be astonished.

INDICATIVE MOOD.
Present.
stúpe, he is astonished.

Álgere.

INFINITIVE MOOD.
álgere, to be chill.

INDICATIVE MOOD
Perfect.

álsi, | I was chill. | algémmo, | we were chill.
algésti, | thou wast chill. | algéste, | you were chill.
álse, | he was chill. | álsero, | they were chill

Ángere.

INFINITIVE MOOD.
ángere, to afflict.

INDICATIVE MOOD.

Present.	*Imperfect.*
ánge, it afflicts.	angéva, it afflicted.

Arrógere.

INFINITIVE MOOD.
arrógere, to add.

GERUND.
arrogéndo, adding.

PARTICIPLE.
ARRÓTO or ARRÓSO, added.

INDICATIVE MOOD.
Present.

arróge,	he adds.	arrogiámo, arrógono,	we add. they add.

Imperfect.
io arrogéva or arrogéa, I added

Perfect.

ARRÓSI,	I added.	arrogémmo,	we added.
arrogésti,	thou addedst.	arrogéste,	you added.
ARRÓSE,	he added.	ARRÓSERO,	they added.

Cápere.

INFINITIVE MOOD.
cápere, to contain.

INDICATIVE MOOD.

Present.	*Imperfect.*
cápe, it contains	capéva, it contained

Chérere.

INFINITIVE MOOD.
chérere, to ask.

INDICATIVE MOOD.
Present.

| *chéro,* | I ask. | | | |
| *chére,* | he asks. | | | |

Convéllere.

INFINITIVE MOOD.
convéllere, to convulse.

GERUND.
convelléndo, convulsing.

PARTICIPLE.
CONVÚLSO, convulsed.

INDICATIVE MOOD.
Present.

convélle,	he convulses.	*convéllono,*	they convulse.
		Imperfect.	
convelléva or *-léa,*	he convulsed.	*convellévano* or *-léano,* they convulsed	
		Future.	
convellerà,	he shall convulse.	*convelleránno,*	they shall convulse

SUBJUNCTIVE MOOD.
Imperfect.

| *convellésse,* | If he convulsed. | *convelléssero,* | If they convulsed. |

CONDITIONAL MOOD.
Present.

| *convellerébbe,* | he should convulse. | *convellerébbero,* | they should convulse. |

Fiédere.

INFINITIVE MOOD.
fiédere, to wound.

GERUND.
fiedéndo, wounding.

INDICATIVE MOOD.

Present.

fiédo,	I wound.	
fiédi,	thou woundest.	
fiéde,	he wounds.	*fiédono,*

Imperfect.
io *fiedéva* or *fiedéa*, I wounded.

Perfect.
fiedéi, I wounded.

SUBJUNCTIVE MOOD.

Present.

io *fiéda* (*fiéggia*),	that I wound.	
egli *fiédia* (*fiéggia*),	that he wound.	*fiédano,*

Imperfect.
io *fiedéssi*, if I wounded.

Lúcere.

INFINITIVE MOOD
lúcere, to shine.

GERUND.
lucéndo, shining.

INDICATIVE MOOD.

Present.

lúci	. . . .	*luciámo,*	we shine.
lúce	thou shinest.	*lucéte,*	you shine.
	he shines.	. . .	. . . .

Imperfect.
io lucéva, I shone.

Perfect.

. . . .	. . . .	*lucémmo,*	we shone.
lucésti,	thou shinest.	*lucéste,*	you shone.

Future.
luceró, I shall *or* will shine.

SUBJUNCTIVE MOOD.

Present.

. . . .	. . . .	*luciámo,*	that we shine.
		luciáte,	that you shine.
égli (lúca),	that he shine.	*(lúcano),*	that they shine.

Imperfect.
io lucéssi, if I shone *or* should shine.

CONDITIONAL MOOD.

Present.
luceréi (luceria), if I should, would, *or* could shine, *or* might shine.

Mólcere.

INFINITIVE MOOD.
mólcere, to assuage.

INDICATIVE MOOD.

Present.			*Imperfect.*
		io molcéva,	I assunged.
mólci.	thou assungest.	*molcévi,*	thou assungedst.
molce.	he assuages.	*égli molcéva,*	he assuaged.

Riédere.

INFINITIVE MOOD.
riédere, to return.

INDICATIVE MOOD.
Present.

riédo,	I return.	. . .	. . . . .
riédi,	thou returnest.	. . .	. . . . .
riéde,	he returns.	*riédono,*	they return

Imperfect.

io riédeva or riedéa,	I returned.	. . . .	. . . .
riedévi,	thou returnedst.	. . . .	. . . .
egli riedéva,	he returned.	*riedévano,*	they returned.

SUBJUNCTIVE MOOD.
Present.

io riéda,	that I return.	. . .	. . . . .
tu riéda,	that thou return.	. . .	. . . . .
gli riéda,	that he return.	*riédano,*	that they return.

Sérpere.

INFINITIVE MOOD.
sérpere, to creep.

GERUND.
sérpendo, creeping.

INDICATIVE MOOD.
Present.

sérpo,	I creep.	. . .	. . . .
sérpi,	thou creepest.	. . .	. . . .
sérpe,	he creeps.	*sérpono,*	they creep.

Imperfect.

io serpéva,	I crept.	. . . .	. . . .
serpévi,	thou creptest.	. . . .	. . . .
égli serpéva,	he crept.	*serpévano,*	they crept.

SUBJUNCTIVE MOOD.
Present.

io sérpa,	that I creep.	. . .	. . . . .
tu sérpa,	that thou creep.	. . .	. . . . .
égli sérpa,	that he creep.	*sérpano,*	that they creep

DEFECTIVE VERBS. 255

Soffólcere *or* Soffólgere.

INFINITIVE MOOD.
soffólcere or *soffólgere*, to support.

PARTICIPLE.
soffólto, supported.

INDICATIVE MOOD.

Present.
soffólce or *soffólge*, he supports.

Perfect.
soffólse, he supported.

Tángere.

INFINITIVE MOOD.
tángere, to touch.

INDICATIVE MOOD.
Present.
tánge, he touches.

Tóllere.

INFINITIVE MOOD.
tóllere, to take away.

INDICATIVE MOOD.
Present.

tólli, thou takest away.
tólle, he takes away.

SUBJUNCTIVE MOOD.
Present.

tu tólla, that thou take away.
égli tólla, that he take away.

IMPERATIVE MOOD.
tólla égli, let him take away.

Estóllere (to lift), compound of *tóllere*, is defective only in the participle, and in all the persons of the perfect of the indicative.

Tórpere.

INFINITIVE MOOD.
tórpere, to become numb.

INDICATIVE MOOD.
Present.

tórpo,   I become numb.
tórpe,   he becomes numb.

SUBJUNCTIVE MOOD.
Present.

o tórpa,   that I become numb.
u tórpa,   that thou become numb.
gh tórpa,   that he become numb.

Úrgere.

INFINITIVE MOOD.
úrgere, to urge.

INDICATIVE MOOD.
Present.
úrge, he urges.
Imperfect.

égli urgéva or *urgea*, he urged. | *urgévano*,   they urged.

Vígere.

INFINITIVE MOOD.
vígere, to be vigorous.

INDICATIVE MOOD.
Present.
vige, he is vigorous.
Future.
vigerà, it will be vigorous.

Gíre.

INFINITIVE MOOD.
gíre, to go.

PARTICIPLE.
gíto, gone.

INDICATIVE MOOD.
Present.

g'iámo, we go.
g'íte, you go.

Imperfect.
g'íva *or* g'ía, I went.
Perfect.
ιo g'íi, I went.
Future.
giró, I shall *or* will go.

SUBJUNCTIVE MOOD.
Present.

g'iámo, that we go *or* may go
g'iáte, that you go.

Imperfect.
ιo gíssi, if I went *or* should go.

CONDITIONAL MOOD.
giréi, g'iría, I should, would, *or* could go, *or* might go.

IMPERATIVE MOOD.

g'iámo, let us go.
g'íte, go ye.

Íre.

INFINITIVE MOOD.
íre, to go.

PARTICIPLE.
íto, gone.

INDICATIVE MOOD.

Present.
íte, you go.

Imperfect.

ío íva,	I went	ívano,	we went.
égli íva	he went.	. . .	. .

Perfect.

ísti,	thou wentest.	(íro, ir),	they went.

Future.

. . . . .	. . . . .	irémo,	we shall or will go
. . . . .	. . . . .	iréte,	you will go.
. . .	. . . . .	iráno,	they will go.

CONDITIONAL MOOD.
(iriano), they should, would, or could go, or might go.

IMPERATIVE MOOD.
íte, go ye.

Olíre.

INFINITIVE MOOD.
olíre, to smell.

INDICATIVE MOOD.

Imperfect.

ío olíva,	I smelled.	. . .	. . . . .
vívi,	thou smelledst.	. . .	. . . . .
égli olíva,	he smelled.	olívano,	they smelled

PROVERBS.

A word to the wise is enough,	A buón intenditór póche paróle.
All that is fair must fade,	Bélla cósa tósto è rapíta.
A ragged coat finds little credit,	A véste logoráta póca féde vien prestáta.
Any thing for a quiet life,	Álla páce si può sacrificár tútto.
A great liar has need of a good memory,	A un gran bugiárdo ci vuól buóna memória.
An old horse for a young soldier,	A gióvane soldáto vécchio cavállo.
A buttered mouth cannot say no,	Bócca únta non può dir di no.
A good appetite needs no sauce,	Buón appetíto non vuól sálsa.
A good beginning makes a good ending,	Buón princípio fa buón fíne.
A barking dog does not bite,	Can che abbaía non mórde.
A voluntary burden is no burden,	Cárica volontária non cárica.
A gold key opens every door,	Chiáve d'óro ápre ógni pórta.
A fat kitchen, a lean testament,	Grássa cucína, mágro testaménto.
A new broom sweeps clean,	Granáta nuóva spázza ben la cása.
Aught is better than naught,	Méglio è póco che niénte.
All is not gold that glitters,	Óro non è tútto quel che risplénde.
A sin confessed is half forgiven,	Peccáto confessáto è mézzo perdonáto.
A little spark kindles a great fire,	Piccóla favílla accénde gran fuóco.
A rolling stone gathers no moss,	Piétra móssa non fa múschio.
A little gall makes a great deal of honey bitter,	Póco fiéle fa amáro mólto miéle.
As you would have a daughter, choose a wife,	Qual fíglia vúoi, tal móglie píglia.
Anger increases love,	Sdégno auménta amóre.
All's well that ends well,	Tútto è béne che riésce béne.
A married man is a caged bird,	Uómo ammogliáto, uccéllo in gábbia.
An ounce of discretion is worth more than a pound of knowledge,	Val più un' óncia di discreziúne che úna líbbra di sapére,
A fasting stomach has no ears,	Véntre digiúno non óde nessúno.
After the horse is stolen, shut the barn-door,	Dópo che i caválli sóno prési, serrár la stálla.
A bird in the hand is worth two in the bush,	È méglio un uccéllo in gábbia che cénto fuóri.
Bend the tree while it is young,	Piéga l'álbero quándo è gióvane.
Better late than never,	Méglio tárdi che mái.
Better a happy heart than a full purse,	È méglio il cuór felíce che la bórsa piéna.
Better bend than break,	È méglio piegáre che rómpere.
Better give the wool than the sheep,	È méglio dar la lána che la pécora.
Big head and little wit,	Cápo grásso, cervéllo mágro.

Bad news travels fast,	Le cattíve nuóve vólano.
Counsel is nothing against love,	Cóntro amóre non è consíglio.
Comparisons are odious,	I paragóni son tútti odiósi.
Christmas comes but once in a year,	Natále non viéne che úna vólta l'ánno.
Do what you ought, come what may,	Fa quel che dévi, n' arrívi ciò che potrà.
Do not count your chickens before they are hatched,	Non far cónto dell' uóvo non ancór náto.
Delays are dangerous,	L' indugiáre è pericolóso.
Different times, different manners,	Áltri témpi, áltri costúmi.
Drop by drop wears away a stone,	A góccia a góccia si trafóra la piétra.
Do not look a gift horse in the mouth,	A cavál donáto, non guardár in bócca.
Every thing is good in its season,	Da stagióne tútto è buóno.
Every dog is a lion at home,	Ógni cáne è leóne a cása súa.
Every truth is not good to be told,	Ogni véro non è buóno a díre.
Every body knows where his shoe pinches,	Ognúno sa dóve la scárpa lo strínge
Every one for himself, and God for us all,	Ognún per sè, e Dío per tútti.
Every body praises his own saint,	Ognúno lóda il próprio sánto.
Every body's friend, nobody's friend,	Amíco d' ognúno, amíco di nessúno.
Every one thinks his own cross the heaviest,	Ad ognúno par più gráve la cróce súa.
Extreme ills, extreme remedies,	Ai máli estrémi, estrémi rimédi.
Friends in need are friends indeed,	A bisógni si conóscon gli amíci.
For a web begun, God sends thread,	A téla ordíta Dío mánda il fílo.
Fair words, but look to your purse,	Bélle paróle, ma guárda la bórsa.
Four eyes see more than two,	Vedón più quattr' ócchi che dúe.
Fortune comes to him who seeks her,	Vién la fortúna a chi la procúra.
Forbidden fruit is sweet,	I frútti proíbiti sóno dólci.
Father Modest never was a prior,	Fra modésto non fu mái prióre.
From those I trust, God guard me; from those I mistrust, I will guard myself,	Da chi mi fído, mi guárdi Iddío; da chi non mi fído mi guarderò io.
God helps him who helps himself,	Chi s'aiúta, Dío l'aiúta.
Give to him that has,	Dà del túo a chi ha del súo.
Give time, time,	Dà témpo al témpo.
God sends meat, and the devil sends cooks,	Dío ci mánda la cárne, ma il diávole i cuóchi.
Great griefs are mute,	I gran dolóri sóno múti.
Great smoke, little fire,	Gran fúmo, póco arrósto.
Gold does not buy every thing,	L'óro non cómpra tútto.
Good wine makes good blood,	Buón víno fa buón sángue.
He who succeeds is reputed wise,	A chi la riésce béne, è tenúto per sávio.
He who knows nothing, knows enough if he knows how to be silent,	Assái sa, chi non sa, se tácer sa.
He is blind who cannot see the sun,	Ben è ciéco chi non véde il sóle
He who sings drives away sorrow,	Chi cánta, i suói máli spavénta

PROVERBS.

He who buys in time, buys cheap,	Chi cómpra a témpo, cómpra a buón mercáto.
He laughs well who laughs last,	Ríde béne chi ríde l'último.
Hear, see, and say nothing, if you would live in peace,	Ódi, védi e táci se vuói vivér in páce.
He is master of another man's life who is indifferent to his own,	È padróne délla víta altrúi chi la súa sprézza.
He gives twice who gives in a trice,	Chi dà présto, dà il dóppio.
He who stands may fall,	Chi è rítto può cadére.
He that reckons without his host must reckon again,	Chi fa il cónto sénza l'óste, gli convién fárlo dúe vólte.
Hell is full of good intentions,	Di buóna volontà è piéno l'inférno.
Habit is a second nature,	L' ábito è úna secónda natúra.
In at one ear, and out at the other,	Déntro da un orécchio e fuóri dall' áltro.
Ill weeds grow apace,	La mal érba crésce présto.
Look before you leap,	Guárda innánzi che tu sálti.
Like master, like man,	Tal padróne, tal servitóre.
Live, and let live,	Vívi, e láscia vívere.
Love me, love my dog,	Chi áma me, áma il mío cáne.
Love rules without law,	Amór régge sénza légge.
Love me little, and love me long,	Amami póco, ma contínua.
Love knows not labor,	Amór non conósce travàglio.
Let him who is well off stay where he is,	Chi sta béne non si muóva.
Long tongue, short hand,	Lúnga língua, córta máno.
Marry in haste, repent at leisure,	Chi si maríta in frétta, sténta adágio.
Many a true word spoken in jest,	Quel che páre búrla, ben sovénte è véro.
Much smoke and little fire,	Mólto fúmo e póco fuóco.
Make me a prophet, and I will make you rich,	Fámmi indovíno, e ti farò rícco.
Nothing venture, nothing have,	Chi non s'arríschi non guadágna.
Nothing is difficult to a willing mind,	A chi vuóle, non è cósa difícile.
Near the church, far from God.	Vicíno álla chiésa lontán di Dío.
Old reckonings, new disputes,	A cónti vécchi, contése nuóve.
One enemy is too many, and a hundred friends are too few,	È tróppo un nemíco, e cénto amíci non bástano.
One hand washes the other, and both hands wash the face,	Úna máno láva l'áltra e tútt' e dúe lávano il víso.
One word brings another,	Úna paróla tíra l'áltra.
One swallow does not make a summer,	Un fióre non fa Primavéra.
One man warned is as good as two,	Un avvertíto ne val dúe.
Out of sight, out of mind,	Lontáno dágli ócchi, lontáno del cuóre.
Poor as a church mouse,	Povéro cóme un tópo in chiésa.
Poverty has no kin,	Povertà non ha parénti.
Physician, heal thyself,	Médico, cúra te stésso.
Pluck the rose and leave the thorns,	Cógli la rósa, e láscia le spíne.
Rather hat in hand than hand in purse,	Piuttósto cappéllo in máno, che máno álla bórsa.
Roses grow among thorns,	Ánco trà le spíne náscono le róse.

Saying is one thing, and doing is another,	Áltra còsa è il díre, áltra il fáre.
Silence gives consent,	Chi táce, acconsénte.
Strike while the iron is hot,	Bátti il férro quánd' è cáldo.
See Naples, and then die,	Védi Nápoli e pói muóri.
Savings are the first gain,	Lo sparágno è il prímo guadágno.
Seeing is believing,	Chi con l'ócchio véde, di cuór créde.
Second thoughts are best,	Il secóndo pensiéro è il miglióre.
The full belly does not believe in hunger,	Córpo satóllo non créde al digiúno.
To pay one in his own coin,	Pagár úno délla súa própria monéta.
Think much, speak little, and write less,	Pénsa mólto, párla póco, scrívi méno.
Translators, traitors,	Traduttóri, traditóri.
The weakest goes to the wall,	Sémpre ha tórto il più débole.
They say, is a liar,	Si díce, è mentitóre.
The people's voice, God's voice,	Vóce di pópolo, vóce di Dío.
To fall out of the frying-pan into the fire,	Cadér délla padélla nélle brágie.
The biter is sometimes bit,	Chi búrla, víen burláto.
The world is governed with little brains,	Con póco cervéllo si govérna il móndo.
True love never grows old,	Amór véro non divénta canúto.
The liar is not believed when he speaks the truth,	Al bugiárdo non si créde la verità.
The workman is known by his work,	All ópera si conósce il maéstro.
There is always a calm before a storm,	La bonáccia burrásca mináccia.
The beard does not make the philosopher,	La bárba non fa il filósofo.
There is no love without jealousy,	Non c'è amór sénza gelosía.
There is no smoke without fire,	Non c'è fúmo sénza fuóco.
The steed is starving whilst the grass is growing,	Méntre l'érba crésce il cavállo muóre di fáme.
The devil is not so ugly as he is painted,	Il diávolo non è cósi brútto cóme si dipínge.
The best is the cheapest,	Il miglióre è men cáro.
Teaching we learn,	Insegnándo s'impára.
To cast pearls before swine,	Gettár le marghérite ai pórci.
The earth covers the errors of the physician,	Gli erróri del médico gli cópre la térra.
There is no disputing about tastes,	Dei gústi non se ne dispúta.
The doctor seldom takes medicine,	Di rádo il médico píglia medicína.
The world was not made in one day,	In un giórno non si fe' Róma.
Tell me the company you keep, and I will tell you what you are,	Dímmi con chi trátti, e ti dirò chi séi
Whoever brings, finds the door open for him,	Apérta ha la pórta chiúnque appórta
Where there is a will, there's a way,	A chi vuóle, non máncano módi.
Well begun is half done,	Buón princípio è la metà dell' ópra

Who does too much often does little,	Spésso chi tróppo fa, póco fa.
Who knows most believes least,	Chi più sa, méno créde.
Who comes seldom is welcome,	Chi ráro viéne, vién béne.
While there is life, there is hope,	Finchè v'è fiáto, v'è speránza.
Who knows nothing never doubts,	Chi niénte sa, di niénte dúbita.
What's done can't be undone,	Quel che è fátto non si puo disfáre.
What costs little is little valued,	Quéllo che cósta póco, si stíma póco
Who judges others condemns himself,	Chi áltri giúdica se condánna.

IDIOMS.

Non vále un ácca,	It is not worth a pin.
A bèll' ágio,	Leisurely.
Mangiár cárne d' allódola,	To take pleasure in being praised.
Fáre álto e básso,	To do as one pleases.
Amíco da bonáccia,	A table friend.
È all' artícolo di mórte,	He is at the point of death.
Dar la báia,	To laugh at.
Da básto é sélla,	Fit for any thing.
In un bátter d' ócchio,	In an instant.
Dirizzáre il bécco ágli sparviéri,	To attempt impossibilities.
Andáre di béne in méglio,	To grow better and better.
Un uómo da béne,	A good honest man.
Dir del béne,	To speak well of a person.
Mi convién bérla,	I must bear it.
Tenér l'ánima co' dénti,	To be almost dead.
Dal détto al fátto v'è un grán trátto,	To say and to do are two different things.
Chi dórme non píglia pésci,	Idleness begets poverty.
Quésta cósa non m'éntra,	I do not comprehend this.
Non è érba del vóstro órto,	This is not of your own making.
Mangiársi l'érba sótto,	To spend what one has.
Ascónder l'ámo nell' ésca,	To deceive one under the color of friendship.
Le cóse sóno in buón éssere,	Things are in a good way.
Éssere all' estrémo délla víta,	To be at the point of death.
Státe all' érta,	To be upon one's guard.
Ésser di buóna bócca,	To be a great eater.
Favelláre con le máni,	To strike.
Non avér fiéle,	To be good-natured.
Far filáre úno,	To make one do what you please.
Pagár il fío,	To pay dear for.
Dáre ad úno cárta biánca,	To give one full power.
Fra tre giórni,	In three days.

Dolérsi di *gámba* sána,	To complain without reason.
Dárla a *gámbe,*	To run away.
Vincere la *gára,*	To carry the prize.
Con bel *gárbo,*	In a civil manner.
Fáre la *gátta* mórta,	To dissemble.
Cóme méglio vi aggráda,	As you think fit.
Imbarcársi sénza biscótto,	To undertake a thing without means.
È *impastáto* di vizj,	He is very vicious.
Véndere all' *incánto,*	To sell by auction.
Dár l' *incénso* a' mórti,	To make almanacs for the last year.
Il túo *inchióstro* nón tígne,	Your credit is not good.
Mostráre altrúi *lúcciole* per lantérne,	To make one believe that the moon is made of green cheese.
In cása súa v' è il *látte* di gallína,	In his house they always eat of the best.
Uno máno *láva* l' áltra,	To help one another.
Legársela al díto,	To owe one a spite.
Tenére in *líbra,*	To keep in suspense.
Dáre in *lúce,*	To publish.
Veníre *mánco,*	To faint.
Uscír del *mánico,*	To be extravagant.
Far un *marróne,*	To make a mistake.
Méttere álla véla,	To set sail.
Miráre con la códa dell' ócchio,	To cast sheeps' eyes.
Ti farò *mórdere* le únghie,	I'll make you repent it.
Mutár vérso,	To alter the course of one's life.
Dar l' última máno,	To finish.
Fuór di máno,	Out of the way.
Éssere álla máno,	To be ready.
Avére la máno,	To have the advantage.
Métter máno ad úna cósa,	To begin a thing.
Imbottár *nébbia,*	To lose time.
Tésta di pollástra,	Giddy brained.
Fáre il bécco all' óca,	To finish any work.
Ócchio mío,	My darling.
In un bátter d' ócchio,	In an instant.
A quáttr' ócchi,	Face to face.
Va in buón *óra,*	God speed you.
Far *orécchie* di mercánte,	To give no ear.
Tútto' l móndo e *paése,*	One may live everywhere.
Col témpo e cólla *páglia* matúrano le néspole,	Time brings every thing to maturity.
Stársi ne' própii *pánni,*	To be contented with what one has.
Cavár le pénne maéstre,	To take away the best one has.
La vóstra opinióne non mi *quádra,*	I am not of your opinion.
Quésto è il *quánto,*	This is the point.
Di *quándo* in quándo,	Now and then.
Dár nélla ragnátela,	To fall into a snare.
Menár tútti a *rastréllo,*	To use all alike.
Rénder l'ánima,	To give up the ghost.
Rídere ágli ángeli,	To laugh at nothing.
Ha póco *sále* in zúcca.	He has not a great deal of judgment

I a gallína che cánta è quélla che ha fátto l'uóvo,	The man who is too earnest in justifying himself is guilty.
Venír la schiúma álla bócca,	To be in a great passion.
Levársi all' álba de' tafáni,	To rise late.
Chi tárdi arríva míle allóggia,	Those who come too late must kiss the cook.
Tenére il piède in due stáffe,	To have two strings to one's bow.
Pigliár gli uccéllini,	To play the fool.
Uccèl da válle,	A sly man.
Ugnér le máni,	To bribe one with money.
Far veníre l'ácqua all' úgola,	To make the mouth water.
Vedére il pel nell' uóvo,	To be clear-sighted.
Dár le véle a' vénti,	To set sail.
A véla e rémo,	With all speed.
Vendémmia méntra hái témpo,	Get money while you can.
La candéla è al vérde,	The candle is almost out.
La veritá sta sémpre a gála,	Truth always prevails at last.
I miéi affári hánno préso buóna piéga,	My affairs are going on successfully.
Náscer vestíto,	To be born lucky.
Fára a chi tócca,	Let every one care for himself.
Far d'úna láncia un zípolo,	To make a little out of a great deal
Cantáre ad úno la zólfa,	To chide.

ITALIAN AND ENGLISH VOCABULARY.

Abbáglio, mistake.
accánto, aside.
ácqua, water.
addósso, on, upon.
affánno, grief.
affátto, entirely.
affétto, good-will, kindness.
ágo, needle.
álba, dawn.
álbero, tree.
allóra, then.
allóro, laurel.
álma, soul.
alméno, at least.
al par, equal, alike.
altéro, proud.
áltro, other.
amarézza, bitterness.
ámbo, both.
amicízia, friendship.
amíco, friend.
amistáde, friendship.
ámo, fish-hook.
amóre, love.
ancélla, waiting-maid.
anélito, panting.
anéllo, a ring.
ánima, soul.
ánimo, courage, mind.
ansánti, panting.
antíco, ancient.
apértura, hole, gap.
áquila, eagle.
arátro, plough.
arcáno, secret.
ardénte, hot, burning.
aréna, sand, gravel.
argénto, silver.
ascóso, hidden.
aspétto, aspect.
assennáto, sensible.
astánte, by-stander.
ástro, star.
augellétto, small bird.

áura, gale, breeze.
avéllo, grave, tomb.
avvenénza, comeliness.
avveníre, future.
avverténza, precaution.
avvíso, advice.

Bácio, a kiss.
baléna, whale.
bállo, bull.
bambíno, child, infant.
bandíto, an outlaw.
bellézza, beauty.
beltà, beauty.
benchè, although.
bicchiére, drinking-glass.
bíle, anger, passion.
bióndo, fair, light.
birbánte, vagabond.
bisógno, need, want.
bizzárro, whimsical.
bórgo, suburb.
bórsa, a purse, bag.
bósco, a wood.
bottéga, shop.
bráccio, an arm.
brándo, sword.
brézza, cold, breeze.
brína, frost.
brúno, brown, dark.
brútto, ugly.
bugía, a lie.
buói, oxen.
burrásca, tempest.
búrro, butter.

Cáccia, hunting.
cágna, dog.
cálca, confusion.
calvézza, baldness.
cálvo, bald.
cálza, stocking.
cambiavalúte, broker.
cammíno, way, road.
cámpo, field.

cánto, song.
canzóne, song.
capánna, cottage.
capélli, pan.
cáro, dear.
cárne, meat.
carabína, carbine.
carézza, caress.
carnéfice, executioner.
cárta, paper.
cascáta, cascade.
cáso, case.
caténa, chain.
cattedrále, cathedral.
cattívo, bad.
cáuto, wary, cautious.
cávo, hollow.
céna, supper.
cénere, ashes, cinders.
céppo, stump, log.
céra, wax.
cérto, certain, sure.
cétra, cithern.
cervéllo, brain.
chéto, quiet, still.
chiáro, clear, fair.
chiáve, key.
chiaróre, brightness, clearness.
chína, declivity.
chiódo, nail.
chitárra, guitar.
ciabbattíno, cobbler.
cíbo, food.
siéco, blind.
ciélo, sky, heaven.
címa, top, summit.
cinghiále, a wild boar.
cittadíno, citizen.
códa, tail.
cognizióne, knowledge.
cognáto, brother in-law.
colazióne, breakfast.
cólle, hill.
cóllera, anger.

ITALIAN AND ENGLISH VOCABULARY.

coltivatóre, farmer.
concorrénza, competition.
contadíno, peasant.
cónto, account.
contráda, country.
convíto, banquet, feast.
cóppa, cup.
cortína, curtain.
costúme, custom, manner.
crúccio, anguish.
cucína, kitchen.
cúlla, cradle.
cuóre, heart.
cupidígia, covetousness.
cúpo, deep.

Dabbéne, good, honest.
danáro, money.
delítto, crime.
débole, weak.
détto, word.
dì, day.
difétto, fault.
disgrázia, misfortune.
dóglia, grief, pain.
dólce, sweet.
dolcézza, sweetness.
dóno, gift.
donzélla, damsel.
dótto, skilful, learned.
droghiére, druggist.
drítto, right, straight.
duólo, grief, pain.

Ebbrézza, drunkenness.
élmo, helmet.
élsa, the hilt of a sword.
entrámbi, both.
erário, the treasury.
érba, grass.
erbóso, grassy.
eréde, the heir.
eróe, hero.
erránte, wandering.
érto, steep, ascent.
estáte, summer season.
età, age.
etáde, age.
eteree, ethereal.

Fáccia, face.

fálce, scythe.
fállo, fault.
fáme, hunger.
farfálla, butterfly.
fáta, fairy.
fatíca, fatigue.
fáto, fate, destiny.
favélla, discourse, speech.
féde, faith.
férro, iron.
fiámma, flame.
fiánco, side.
fiáto, breath.
fíco, fig.
fidánza, trust, hope.
figúra, figure, shape.
figliuólo, son.
fiéro, cruel, savage.
fiévole, feeble, weak.
fióre, flower.
fiócco, tassel, flake of snow.
fischiáta, whistling.
fiórido, flowery.
fólla, crowd.
fórte, strong.
frettolóso, hasty.
fúlgido, bright.
fúmo, smoke.
fúne, a rope.
fuóco, fire.
furibóndo, like a madman.

Gállo, a cock.
gélo, ice.
gélido, frozen.
gémito, groan.
gemebóndo, groaning.
génere, gender, kind.
genitóre, father.
génte, people.
ginócchio, a knee.
giója, joy, a jewel.
giórno, day.
gióvane, young.
gioventù, youth.
giúbilo, rejoicing.
giubilánte, merry-making.
giudízio, judgment.
giuraménto, oath.

giustízia, justice.
góbbo, hunch-backed.
góla, the throat.
góta, cheek.
gradásso, a boaster.
gragnuóla, hail.
grásso, fat.
gráta, grate, an iron grate.
grído, cry.
grifágno, rapacious.
guái, woe.
guáncia, check.
guárdo, look, sight.
guásto, spoiled, havoc.
guerriéro, warrior.
guiderdóne, reward.

Ignóto, unknown.
imbandigióne, setting of dishes on the table at a feast.
ingánno, deceit, fraud.
indovína, fortune-teller.
ingégno, wit, art, skill.
intórno, about.
invérno, winter.
invídia, envy.

Là, there.
lábbro, lip.
lácrima, a tear.
ládro, thief.
laggiù, below.
lárva, ghost.
láto, side.
lavóro, work.
légge, law.
legúme, pulse.
lénto, slow.
lettóre, reader.
léve, light.
líbbra, pound.
líto, bank, shore.
liéto, merry, cheerful.
liéve, lightly.
língua, tongue, language.
líte, strife.
lógoro, worn out.
lórdo, dirty.
lucénte, shining.
lúme, light.

lúngo, long.
luógo, place.
lusinghiéro, flattering.
lústro, lustre.

Maciléute, thin.
magía, magic.
máglia, mail, armor, a net.
máyro, lean.
mále, ill.
malattía, sickness.
malóri, ills.
malóra, ruin.
mánto, cloak.
máre, sea.
maríto, husband.
mariuólo, a cheat.
mascélla, jaw-bone.
masnáda, a crowd of soldiers.
méno, less.
ménte, mind.
ménsa, table.
méntre, whilst.
mercanzía, goods.
merlétti, lace.
meschinéllo, poor.
mestízia, melancholy.
mésto, sad.
metà, moiety.
mézzo, middle, midst.
migliáia, thousands.
minéstra, soup.
miséria, misery.
módo, manner.
móglie, wife.
mólle, tender.
monéta, money.
móndo, world.
mórso, bit.
montágna, mountain.
mórte, death.
móto, motion.
motteggiatóre, a jester.
mulíno, mill.

Náno, a dwarf.
náso, nose.
natále, nativity.
náto, son, child.
náve, ship.
ne, of it, of them.

nébbia, mist, fog.
nemíco, enemy.
nequízia, wickedness.
néve, snow.
niénte, nothing.
nója, weariness.
nóce, walnut-tree.
nótte, night.
nózze, marriage.
núbe, cloud.
núvola, cloud.

Occúlto, hidden.
olézzo, odor.
óltre, besides.
ómbra, shadow.
ónda, wave.
óra, an hour, now, at present.
orgóglio, haughtiness.
órdine, order.
oriénte, east.
órma, track, trace.
oriuólo, watch.
óro, gold.
órso, bear.
oscúro, obscure, dark.
ósso, bone.
ostéllo, tavern.

Páce, peace.
paése, country.
palágio, palace.
pálma, palm.
palúde, marsh.
pánca, bench.
paragóne, comparison.
paréve, opinion.
pári, equal.
paróla, word.
párroco, pastor.
pásco, pasture.
pásqua, easter, passover.
passéggio, a walk.
pásto, food.
pátto, bargain.
pazzía, folly.
pázzo, mad.
péggio, worse.
péna, punishment.
penóso, painful.
pensiéro, thought.

péntola, pot.
perchè, why, because.
perícolo, danger.
perénne, perennial.
pésce, fish.
péssimo, worst.
pétto, breast.
pézzo, piece.
pío, pious.
piáno, plain.
piánto, tears.
piázza, square.
piccíno, little one.
piétra, stone.
pigióne, house-rent.
pióggia, rain.
pittóre, painter.
piúma, down, feathers.
póco, little.
podágra, the gout.
podére, farm, power.
podestà, power, dominion.
póggio, hill.
pói, then.
poichè, since.
pólvere, dust.
pomeridiáne, post-meridian.
pórco, hog.
pórpora, purple.
portaménto, carriage.
poténza, power.
potére, power.
poltróne, poltroon.
pózzo, a well.
práto, meadow.
prédica, sermon.
prémio, recompense.
premúra, importance.
presciútto, ham.
présso, near.
prénce, prince.
primavéra, spring.
progétto, project.
prodézza, prowess, valor.
próprio, proper.
pugnále, poniard.
púre, yet.

Quà, here.
quaggiù, down here.
quálche, some.

ITALIAN AND ENGLISH VOCABULARY.

qualúnque, whoever.
quarésima, lent.
quási, almost.
quassù, here above.

Rádo, rare, scarce.
rággio, beam, ray.
ragióne, reason, faculty.
rámo, branch.
ráme, copper.
rè, king.
reáme, kingdom.
rédina, rein of a bridle.
regálo, present, gift.
regína, queen.
régola, rule, regimen.
ricchézza, riches.
ridénte, smiling.
rimembránza, remembrance.
río, crook, wicked.
ripiéno, full.
ríso, laughter.
ritrátto, portrait.
ríva, shore.
rózzo, rough.
romíta, hermitess.
rugiáda, dew.
rúggine, rust.

Sággio, sage, wise.
sála, a hall.
salsíne, sausage.
sálice, willow-tree.
sángue, blood.
sapiénte, learned.
sásso, stone.
scále, stairs.
scápolo, not married.
scárpa, a shoe.
scárso, rare.
scémpio, simple.
schérno, raillery.
schiáffo, a box or cuff on the ear.
schiéra, a troop.
sconfítta, defeat.
scopérta, discovery.
scúdo, a shield.
scúro, dark.
sdégno, anger.
sè, himself, herself.
sécolo, a century.

sécco, dry.
séga, saw.
ségno, sign.
segréto, secret.
sélva, wood.
sembiánza, face, look.
sémpre, always.
sénno, judgment.
sénso, sense.
sentiéro, path.
séta, silk.
símile, equal.
síto, situation, seat.
soáve, sweet, agreeable.
sógno, a dream.
sólito, accustomed.
sómmo, top, height.
sónno, sleep.
sórcio, a mouse.
sorríso, smile.
sórte, destiny.
sospíro, a sigh.
sótto, under.
spáda, a sword.
spásso, amusement.
spécie, sort.
spéme, hope.
speránza, hope.
spésso, often.
spína, a thorn.
spóglia, clothes.
spónda, shore.
spórco, dirty.
squallóre, paleness.
stanchézza, weariness.
stélla, star.
stivále, boot.
strépito, noise.
stréga, witch.
súbito, quick.
súcco, juice, sap.
suólo, earth, ground.
suóno, sound, noise.

Tále, such, like.
tárdi, late.
tázza, a cup.
tedésco, a German.
téma, fear.
ténebre, darkness.
térra, earth.
tésta, the head.
tóro, bull.

tórtora, a turtle-dove.
tósto, quick.
trà, between.
trécce, tress of hair.
tríbolo, sorrow, a thistle.
tróno, throne.
tútto, all.

Uccéllo, bird.
uffízio, office.
uómini, men.
úscio, passage.

Vácca, cow.
vágo, fine, handsome.
vámpo, a flame, flush.
váno, vain, empty.
váso, vessel, pot.
vécchio, an old man.
véce, (in), instead.
vélo, veil.
véltro, a grayhound.
vénto, wind.
ventúra, fortune, luck.
vergógna, shame.
vérno, winter.
véro, truth.
veróne, gallery, balcony.
vestíto, clothes.
vézzo, pastime, pleasure.
vía, way, road.
vicíno, near.
villággio, village.
viltà, cowardice.
vínte, vanquished, per suaded.
vísta, sight.
víso, face.
víta, life.
vittória, victory.
vivánda, victuals.
vóglia, mind, desire.
vólo, flight.
vólpe, fox.
volpíno, cunning.
vólta, turn, revolution.
vólto, face.

Zíngara, gypsy.
zimbéllo, allurement.
zítto, hush, silence.
zólla, clod, lump.
zóppo, lame.

23*

ENGLISH AND ITALIAN VOCABULARY.

Accident, accidénte.
acquaintance, conoscénza.
act (action), átto.
admirable, ammirábile.
advantage, vantággio.
adversity, avversità.
advocate, avvocáto.
age, età, sécolo.
ago, a while ago, long ago, qualche témpo fa, mólto témpo fa.
agreeable, piacévole.
almighty, onnipoténte.
aloud, fórte.
although, benchè.
always, sémpre.
ambition, ambizióne.
ancient, anziáno.
anger, sdégno.
answer, rispósta.
appearance, apparénza, fáccia.
apple, pómo or méla.
architect, architétto.
army, esército.
art, árte.
assiduous, assíduo.
astonishment, stupóre.
auditors, ascoltatóri.
author, autóre.
away, via.

Back, dósso.
baker, fornáio.
baldness, calvézza.
balloon, pallóne.
banker, banchiére.
bargain, contrátto.
base, vile.
battle, battáglia.
beard, bárba.
beautiful, béllo.
beauty, beltà.
because, perchè.

bed, létto.
beggar, mendicánte.
behind, per di diétro.
behold, écco.
bell, campána.
benefit, benefício.
better, miglióre.
birth, natività.
bishop, véscovo.
black, néro.
body, córpo.
bold, ardíto.
bouquet, mázzo di fióri.
breakfast, colazióne.
broth, bródo.
burst (of laughter), scoppiáre délle rísa.
business, affáre.

Cabbage, cávolo.
cabinet-maker, ebanísta.
calm, cálma.
candle, candéla.
caricature, caricatúra.
carriage, carrózza.
cause, cáusa.
certainly, cérto.
chance, ventúra.
change, mutazióne.
charming, affascinánte.
chimney, cammíno.
chair, sédia.
character, caráttere.
charitable, caritatévole.
child, fanciúllo.
chin, ménto.
circle, círcolo.
civil, civíle.
clear, chiáro.
clever, ábile.
climate, clíma.
cloak, mantéllo.
coast, cósta.
coat, vestíto.
conducive, profittévole.

confessor, confessóre.
consequence, consequénza.
contrary, contrário.
conquest, conquísta.
copper, ráme.
correct, corrétto.
country, paése or pátrio.
coward, poltróne.
crazy, pázzo.
crime, delítto.
crowd, túrba.
cruel, crudéle.
cup, cóppa, tázza.
cupidity, cupidígia.
custom, costúme.

Dangerous, pericolósa.
day, giórno.
debt, débito.
decay, declinazióne.
decent, decénte.
defeat, sconfítta.
defiance, disfída.
desire, desidério.
despite, dispétto.
despotic, dispótico.
difference, differénza.
difficult, diffícile.
discovery, scopérta.
disease, malattía.
distance, distánza.
doctor, dottóre.
dress, gónna.
dry, sécco.

Early, mattutíno.
eclipse, eclíssi.
effect, effétto.
eloquence, eloquénza.
employment, impiégo.
empire, impéro.
end, fíne.
endurance, sofferénza.
enemy, nemíco.

ensuing, seguénte.
enterprise, intraprésa.
entirely, interaménte.
envy, invídia.
eternal, etérno.
evidently, palpabilménte.
ever, sémpre, tuttávia.
executioner, carnéfice.
eye, ócchio.
eyebrows, cíglia.
eyelids, palpébre.

Face, fáccia.
false, fálso.
falsehood, menzógna.
fancy, fantasía.
farmer, fattóre.
fat, grásso.
fault, fállo.
favor, favóre.
fear, timóre.
feather, piúma.
feature, fattézza.
fellow, uguále, compágno.
fellow-citizen, concittadíno.
few, póco.
fine, fíno.
finger, díto.
fire, fuóco.
firebrand, tizzóne.
fleet, flótta.
flock, grégge.
flower, fióre.
fog, nebbia.
fool, mátto.
forehead, frónte.
foreigner, forestiéro.
fork, fórca.
fox, vólpe.
fruit, frútto.
fury, fúria.

General, generále.
genius, génio.
gentle, gentíle.
gentleman, gentiluómo.
girl, fanciúlla.
glass, vetro.
'glory, glória.
gloves, guánti.
goodness, bontà.
grandchild, nipotíno.

grandfather, ávo or nónno.
grandmother, áva or nónna.
grain, gráno.
grateful, gráto.
grief, dolóre.
grocer, droghiére, bottegájo.
gross, grósso.
guide, guída.
guilty, colpévole.
guinea, ghinéa.

Hail, gragnuóla.
hair, capéllo.
happiness, felicità.
hare, lépre.
haste, premúra.
head, tésta, cápo.
heaven, ciélo.
health, salúte.
heart, cuóre or córe.
heavy, pesánte.
heel, calcágno.
here, quà, quì.
hero, eróe.
high, álto.
hip, ánca.
historian, istórico or storico.
hither, quì o quà.
home, dimóra.
homely, rózzo.
hope, speránza.
how, cóme.
human, umáno.
humble, úmile.
hunger, fáme.

Idea, idéa.
idle, pígro.
ill, mále.
immediate, immediáto.
indolence, indolénza.
infinite, infinità.
influence, influénza.
ingenious, ingegnóso.
inhabitant, abitánte.
inheritor, eréde.
injury, tórto.
inn, albérgo.
inquisitive, curióso.

instrument, istruménto.
Joke, búrla.
journey, viággio.
joy, gióia.
judge, giúdice.
judgment, giudízio.
just, giústo.

Key, chiáve.
kingdom, régno.
kitchen, cucína.
knife, coltéllo.
knowledge, cognizióne.

Labor, lavóro.
lace, merlétto.
lame, zóppo.
language, língua.
large, gránde.
laughter, ríso.
law, légge.
lawyer, legísta.
leaf, fóglia.
least, mínimo.
leg, gámba.
lie, menzógna.
life, víta.
light, lúme.
lightning, lámpo.
lion, leóne.
lip, lábbro.
lock-maker, chiavajuólo
loss, pérdita.
loud, álto.
love, amóre.

Maid, fanciúlla.
majesty, maestà.
manner, maniéra.
marriage, sposalízio.
marvelous, maravíglioso.
mask, máschera.
master, maéstro.
meal, farína.
meat, cárne.
medicine, medicína.
merriment, allegría.
midst, mézzo.
mind, spírito, ménte.
mindful, diligénte.
minister, minístro.

miserable, *miserábile.*
miser, *aváro.*
misery, *miséria.*
misfortune, *sventúra.*
mistake, *erróre.*
money, *denáro.*
motion, *móto.*
mouthful, *una boccáta.*
moon, *lúna.*
much, *mólto.*

Nail, *chiódo.*
name, *nóme.*
napkin, *salviétta.*
natural, *naturále.*
naughty, *cattivéllo.*
navigator, *navigatóre.*
near, *vicíno.*
necessary, *necessário.*
neck, *cóllo.*
need, *bisógno.*
neighbor, *vicíno.*
neither, *nè.*
new, *nuóvo.*
next, *seguénte.*
night, *nótte.*
no, *nò, non.*
noble, *nóbile.*
north, *settentrióne.*
nose, *náso.*
notice, *notízia.*

Oats, *aréna.*
object, *oggétto.*
obstinate, *ostináto.*
occupation, *occupazióne.*
odd, *impári.*
often, *spésso.*
opinion, *opinióne.*
order, *órdine.*
ostrich, *strúzzo.*

overseer, *sopraintendénte.*

Page, *pággio.*
panegyric, *panegírico.*
painter, *pittóre.*
patriarch, *patriárca.*
paper, *cárta.*
paradox, *paradósso.*
parrot, *pappagállo.*
peace, *páce.*
perfidious, *pérfido.*
perhaps, *fórse.*
person, *persóna.*
picture, *pittúra.*
piece, *pézzo.*
pike, *pícca.*
pity, *pietà.*
plate, *piátto.*
pleasure, *piacére.*
plenty, *abbondánte.*
portrait, *ritrátto.*
poverty, *povertà.*
power, *poténza.*
precipitately, *precipitaménte.*
pretty, *leggiádro.*
price, *valóre.*
pride, *orgóglio.*
prisoner, *prigioniéro.*
prompt, *prónto.*
promise, *proméssa.*
purple, *pórpora.*
purse, *bórsa.*

Quarrel, *queréla.*
queer, *stráno.*
quick, *vívo.*
quite, *tutt' affátto.*

Remembrance, *memória.*

rich, *rícco.*

Secret, *segréto.*
signal, *ségno.*
sink, *sentína.*
sleeve, *mánica.*
sleepiness, *sónno.*
smile, *ríso.*
soil, *suólo.*
soldier, *soldáto.*
solidity, *solidézza.*
spectacles, *occhiáli.*
step, *pásso.*
strife, *líte.*
superstitious, *superstizióso.*
surprise, *maravíglia.*

Tear, *lágrima.*
thief, *ládro.*
thirst, *séte.*
title, *título.*
treasury, *erário.*
truth, *verità.*
tyrant, *tiránno.*

Umbrella, *ombréllo.*

Vase, *váso.*
vice, *vízio.*
victory, *vittória.*

Walk, *passéggio.*
weariness, *stanchézza.*
wit, *ingégno.*
witness, *testimónio, monuménto.*
work, *ópera.*
word, *paróla, détto.*
wound, *cicatríce.*

INDEX.

INDEX.

THE NUMBERS REFER TO THE PAGES.

A.

A, 22, 40, 44, 91, 123, 163.
Accent, grave, 3, 29, 219.
Active verbs, 188; variation of, 188; agreement of participles of, 188; change in tenses of, 188; become passive, 205; become pronominal, 209. (See "Verbs.")
Adjectives, 61; remarks on, 64; agreement of, 32, 64, 69, 84; termination of, 61; plural of, 32, 61; number, gender, etc., of, 32, 61; used as nouns, 19, 62; nouns used as, 62; invariable, 62, 70; signification of, altered, 64; suppression of syllables in, 63; elision of, 64; place of, 64; comparatives of, 67; superlatives of, 73; formation of superlatives, 73; of quantity, 62; numeral, 82; possessive pronouns, 97; demonstrative pronouns, 103; indefinite pronouns, 109, 115; past participles and, 73; adverbs and (see "Adverbs") interjections and, 183.
Adverbs, 171; formation of, 123, 172; the comparisons of, 172; termination in *mente*, 73; of time, 172; place, 173; order, quantity, quality, affirmation, negation, doubt, 174; comparison, interrogation, choice, demonstration, 175; adjectives and, 172, 175; adjectives used as, 175; article and, 20; elision of, 172.
Adverbial phrases, 125, 124, 176.
"All," 111, 112; used as adverb, 112.
Alphabet, Italian, 1.
Alquánto, 63.
Altro, 110, 111; *altrúi*, 116; *áltri*, as a noun, 116.
Amáre, conjugation of, 188; its passive form, 204. (See "Verbs.")
Andáre, 160, 166; its compounds, 166; Italianisms with, 167; conjugation of, 215; conjunctive pronouns and, 215. (See "Verbs.")
Apostrophe, 3.
Article, 16; agreement of, 18; indefinite, 16, 43, 83; definite, 17; variations of definite, 17; use of, 18, 19, 20; omission of, 18, 19; elision of, 17, 18; exercise upon, 20; union with prepositions, 21, 41, 122; suppression of, 74; partitive, 41–43; numerals and, 83 86; possessive pronouns and, 20, 98, 99; transposition of, 106; preposition *in* and, 131; verbs and, 20; adverbs and, 20.
As ... as, 69, 175.
Augmentatives, 76, 81; formation of. 76; double, 79; irregular 79; frequent use of, 81.
Auxiliary verbs, 141, 186. (See "Verbs.")
Avére, 98, 141, 161, 209, 213; conjugation of, 186; used idiomatically, 143. (See "Verbs.")

B.

"Be," auxiliary verb. (See "*Éssere*.")
Béllo, 63.
"Better," as adjective and adverb, 67.
Bisognáre. 148.
"Both," 85, 86.
Buóno, 63.

C.

Cardinal numbers, 82.
Cases, 15, 16; of nouns, 40; governed by prepositions, 121.
Che, 68, 90–93. 110, 162; interrogative, 91, 92; the subjunctive and, 93, 155; connection with other words, 93; the present participle and, 162.
Chi, 90–93, 110, 116.
Ci, *vi*, etc., 48, 51, 56, 100. 118, 142, 148, 149, 162, 211, 213, 215, 247.
Ció, 104.
Cóme, 69, 70.
Comparison of adjectives, 67; of adverbs, 172.
Compound sounds, 3.
Con (with article, 22, 24). 125, 130, 164.
Conjugation of verbs. (See "Verbs.")
Conjunctions, 179; in common use, 180; phrases, 181; the subjunctive mood and, 156.
Conjunctive pronouns, 48, 55, 57, 97, 209 with *andáre*, 215; *stáre*, 219; *dolére* 221; *sedére*, 228; *tacére*, 229; *temére* 230; *calére*, 247.

[275]

INDEX.

Consonants, sounds of, 2; double, 4; when doubled, 53.
Contraction of *lo, gli,* etc., 22 (see "Union of Articles and Prepositions," 22); of participles, 161.
Conversazióne, 21, 26, 31, 39, 46, 54, 60, 66, 71, 76, 81, 88, 95, 103, 108, 114, 120, 123, 134, 140, 145, 151, 158, 165, 170, 178, 185.
Costúi, colúi, 106.
Cosi, 69, 70.
Cotále. (See "*Tále.*")
Cotánto. (See "*Tánto.*")
Cotésto, 104.
Cùi, 90, 91, 162; the article and, 92

D.

Da, 22, 40-44, 121-126, 136, 147.
Dire, 166; conjugation of, 216; its compounds, 166, 216. (See "Verbs.")
Days of the week, 39.
Declension, 15; of articles, 22-24; of nouns, 22-24, 41; of possessive pronouns, 98.
Defective verbs, 246; list of, 246; variation of, 247. (See "Verbs.")
Definite article. (See "Article.")
Demonstrative adjective pronouns, 103; added to possessive, 105.
Di, 22, 40-44, 121-126, 163; when used for "than," 68. *Di.* 23.
Diminutives, 76; formation of, 77; irregular, 79; added to verbs, 79; frequent use of, 81.
Diphthongs, 2.
Disjunctive possessive pronouns, 97.
Donáre, 148, 149, 222.

E.

E, sounds of, 2.
Elision, 3; of articles, 17, 18, 22, 23, 85; of pronouns, 52, 56; of adjectives, 64; of adverbs, 172; of verbs, 189, 195.
Élla, use of, 56; its inflections, 11, 56.
Elliptical phrases, 42.
Epochs, 86.
Equality, comparative of, 69.
Éssere, 141, 142, 161; conjugation of. 187; its own auxiliary, 142; its formation of the passive, 142, 204; past participle, 187; used impersonally, 142, 147, 212; infinitive and, 161; neuter verbs and, 206; pronominal verbs and, 208. (See "Verbs.")
Etymology, 1, 15.
Euphony, 17, 26, 33 43, 49, 52, 55, 57, 64, 118, 125.
Exercises, mnemonic, 16, 21, 26, 32, 40, 46, 47, 48, 55, 61, 67, 72, 79, 82, 89, 96, 103, 109, 115, 121, 129, 135, 141, 146, 153, 159, 166, 171, 179
Exercise in pronunciation, 4, 5-15.

Exercises for translation, 20, 25. 31, 38, 45, 53, 59, 65, 71, 75, 87, 94, 102, 107, 113, 119, 127, 133, 139, 144, 151, 157, 164, 169, 178, 184.
Expletives, 149.

F.

Fáre, 166; conjugation of, 217; its compounds, 217; Italianisms with, 168. (See "Verbs.")
Fio, 34.
First conjugation, 147, 166, 188; irregular verbs, 166, 214. (See "Verbs.")
Future tense, 155, 188; contraction of, 211.

G.

Gender, 15, 18; of nouns, 27, of adjectives, 32, 61; of augmentatives, etc., 76; of possessive pronouns, 97; of demonstrative pronouns, 104; participles, 161.
Gerund, 159, 162. (See "Verbs").
Gli, as article, 17; elision of, 18; contraction of, 22; as pronoun, 48, 51, 55, 100, 162, 247; joined to *lo,* etc., 56.
Gli, adverb, 173.
Gliélo, etc., 56.
Grammar, Italian, 1.

H.

H used with *c* before *e* and *i,* 2, 73, 150; in the formation of plurals, 33, 34.
"Have," auxiliary verb. (See "*Avére.*")

I.

I (the sign of plural), 28, 32; exceptions, 33; elision of, 18, 189, 195; addition of, 200. (See "*Il.*")
Idioms, Italian, 263.
Il, i, 17; contraction of, 23; as pronouns, 55, 98, 162; suppression of, 74; used for prepositions, 42.
Imperative mood, 160, 214; pronouns after, 51; irregular verbs and, 214.
Imperfect tense, 150, 156.
Impersonal verbs, 147, 155, 210, 212; how varied, 210; list of, 147. 211; *éssere* and, 147, 212; pronouns and, 49, 148. (See "Verbs.")
In, 129, 136, 163; where placed, 130; union with article, 22, 131; becomes *ne,* 22.
Indefinite adjective pronouns, 109, 115. (See "Pronouns.")
Indefinite article. (See "Article.")
Indicative mood, 154, 155, 162, 196, 198, 201; irregular verbs and, 214.
Inferiority, comparative of, 68.
Infinitive mood, 159; article and, 20, 147; pronouns and, 57; terminations of, 147; used as a noun, 147, 100; as third person, 160; present participle and, 163; *éssere* and, 161; *lúi, lèi,* and, 160; imperative and, 160; contraction of, 214.

Interjections, 182; in common use, 182; derivation of some, 183; agreement of, 183.
Interrogative pronouns, 50, 91; phrases, 50, 91.
Irregular plurals, 36.
Irregular verbs, 166, 214; how varied, 214; *first* conjugation, 214; *second*, 219-233; *third*, 234-241; table of, 242. (See "Verbs.")
Issimo, 73, 74.
Italian alphabet, 1; grammar, 1; idioms, 263; proverbs, 259.
Italianisms, with possessive pronouns, 100; with *tutto*, etc., 112; with *andàre*, *dàre*, 167; *stàre fàre* 168.

L.

La, 17; its plural, 17; contraction of, 23; as pronoun, 55, 162; as inflection of *élla*, 11, 56; before verbs, 56; its place, 57; before numerals, 83; elision of, 18, 56. *Là*, adverb, 173.
Le, 17, 18; contraction of, 23; as pronoun, 48, 51, 55, 162; before verbs, 56; its place, 57; before numerals, 83; elision of, 18.
Letters, 1; sounds of, 1.
Li, article, 17; as pronoun, 55; before verbs, 56; its place, 57. *Lì*, adverb, 173.
Lo, 17; its plural, 17; contraction of, 22; as pronoun, 55, 162; before verbs, 56; its place, 57; used for preposition, 42; elision of, 17, 22, 56.
Lòro, 48, 52, 97.

M.

Màno, 125.
Mèco, *téco*, *séco*, etc., 51.
Méno or *màneo*, 17, 68, 70, 74, 172, 174.
Mèzzo, 63.
Monosyllables, union of, 55, 57.
Months of the year, 39.

N.

Names, proper, 19, 35, 41, 65.
Ne, 51, 55, 118, 142, 149, 162, 213, 215, 219. (See "*In*.")
Neuter verbs, 206; how varied, 206; become pronominal, 209. (See "Verbs.")
Non, 56, 58, 117, 149, 160, 171.
"Nothing," 93, 110, 116, 117, 174.
Nouns, 26; general remarks on, 29; gender of, 27; plural of, 32; double plurals, 37; irregular plurals, 36; cases of, 40; terminations of, 27-36; proper 19, 35, 41, 65; abstract, 19; invariable, 33; relation expressed by *di*, *a*, *da*, 40; variation of nouns, 41; words used as, 19; possessive pronouns used as, 98; infinitive used as, 20, 147, 160; numeral adjectives and, 83; nouns used as adjectives, 62; suppression of the noun after *uno*, 85; exercise upon the noun, 38.
Number, 15; of articles, 17; of nouns, 32 of adjectives, 32, 61; pronouns, 36, 97.
Numeral adjectives, 82; how divided, 82; cardinal numbers, 82; ordinal, 84; fractional and collective, 84.

O.

O, sounds of, 2.
Objective, repetition of, 66.
"Of," rendered by *il* or *lo*, 42.
Ogni, 109-111; *ognidì*, 109.
Onde, 93; *dónde*, 173, 175.
Ora, 83, 172; *ognóra*, 109, 172.
Ordinal numbers, 84.
Orthoëpy, 1.
Orthography, 1.
Òsso, 34.

P.

Paradigms of verbs. (See "Verbs.")
Pàri, 62.
Participles, 161; agreement of, 161; place of, 64. Present, 162; how expressed, 162; of active verbs, 188; prepositions and, 163; infinitive and, 163; *che* and, 162. Past, 161; of active verbs, 188; of passive, 204; of neuter, 206; *avére*, 161; *éssere*, 142, 161, 187. Pronouns and, 58, 162; irregular verbs and, 214; as qualificative adjectives, 73; contraction of, 161.
Particles, 41, 43, 211; expletive, 149.
Parts of speech, 15.
Passive verbs, 147, 204; much used, 147; formation of, 142, 204; how active verbs become passive, 147, 205; past participle of, 204.
Per, with the article, 24; contraction of, 24; as preposition, 122, 129, 131.
Perché, 175, 181.
Perfect definite, 150, 192, 194, 214.
Personal pronouns. (See "Pronouns.")
Phrases, adverbial, 123, 124, 176; conjunctive, 181; idiomatical, 143, 263; interrogative, 50, 91.
Più, 17, 67, 70, 74, 172, 174.
Plural of articles, 17; nouns and adjectives, 32, 61; pronouns, 36, 97; irregular, 36.
Poetical pieces, 176, 183.
Possessive pronouns. (See "Pronouns.")
Prepositions, 121, 129, 135; in common use, 122; union of articles and, 22, 41, 125; use of various, 137; after personal pronouns, 137; present participles and, 163; repetition of prepositions, 85.
Pronominal verbs, 208; variation of, 209 (see "Verbs"); pronouns and, 51.
Pronouns, 46; place of, 49, 57; suppression of, 49; transposition of, 58; apposition of, 49; elision of, 52, 56; Impersonal verbs and, 49; pronominal verbs and, 51; infinitive and, 57; past parti

ciples and, 58; euphonic rules, 57; doubling of consonants, 58. Personal pronouns in the nominative, 46, 49; in the objective, 47, 50, 55; verbs and, 148, past participles and, 162; prepositions and, 137. Possessive adjective, 20, 97; plural of, 36, 97; division of, 97; variation of, 98; agreement of, 98; personal pronouns and, 99; as nouns, 98; as Italianisms, 100; as expletives, 149; use of, with article, 20, 98, 99; demonstratives added to, 105. Indefinite, 109, 115; used in singular, 109, in plural, 110. Relative, 89, 97. Demonstrative, 103; added to possessive, 105. Interrogative. 50, 91. Conjunctive, 48, 55. 97, 209, 215, 219. Disjunctive, 97. Reflective, 51.
Pronunciation, 1; exercise in, 4; reading-exercise in, 5-15.
Próprio, 98.
Prosody, 1.
Proverbs, Italian, 259.
Pure, 181.

Q.

Quále, 36, 90, 116, 155, 162; use of, 91.
Quánto, 62, 69, 70.
Quéllo, 104.
Quésto, 104-106.

R.

Reading-lessons, 5, 20, 25, 30, 37, 44, 52, 59, 65, 70, 74, 86, 94, 100, 106, 113, 118, 126, 132, 138, 143, 150, 156, 164, 169, 176, 183.
Reflective verbs, 208. (See "Pronominal Verbs.")
Regular verbs, 188; synoptical table of the variations of, 202. (See "Verbs.")
Relative pronouns, 89, 97.

S.

Se,* 47, 50, 51, 118.
Second conjugation, 192; division of, 192; first class, 192; second class, 194; irregular verbs, 219-233. (See "Verbs.")
"Self," 40.
Si, 51, 57, 100, 117. 147, 149, 162, 205, 209, 219, 221, 228, 229, 230, 247.
Signóre, *Signóra*, etc., 19, 56, 99; elision of. 19.
"Some," 43, 110, 112.
Sómno, 73.
Sópra, used for *su*, 24.
Sounds of vowels, 2; of consonants, 2; of *e*, 2; of *o*, 2; compound, 3.
Speech, parts of, 15.
Sta, abbreviation of *quésta*, 105

Stáre, 169, 166; conjugation of, 218; its compounds, 166, 219; Italianisms with, 167; conjunctive pronouns and, 219.
Stra, as particle, 73.
Su, with article, 22, 24; contraction of, 24; preposition, 122; *sópra* used for, 24.
Subjunctive mood, 153; when used, 154; tenses of. 156; irregular verbs and, 214; conjunctions and, 156.
Substantives. (See "Nouns.")
"Such," 62. 106, 110, 112.
Superiority, comparative of. 67
Superlatives of adjectives, 73; of adverbs, 172; of interjections, 183.
Syllables. 4; termination of, 4, exceptions, 4; union of, 55, 57; suppression of, 63.
Synoptical table of regular verbs, 202.
Syntax, 1; of verbs, 146.

T.

Table, synoptical, of regular verbs, 202; of irregular verbs, 242. (See "Verbs")
Tále, 36, 62, 106, 110, 112.
Tinto, 69, 110.
Tenses of dependent verbs in a compound sentence, 155.
"Than," rendered by *di* and *che*, etc., 68; by *cóme* and *cosi*, 69.
Third conjugation, 196; division into three classes, 196; first class, 196; second, 198; third, 201; irregular verbs, 234-241; list of, 234.
Titles, 19, 56, 99.
"To be hungry," "thirsty," etc., 143.
Tútto, 110, 149; its agreement with the noun, 111; as an Italianism, 112.

U.

Uómini, 36.
Unipersonal verbs, 210. (See "Impersonal Verbs.")
Úno, *un*, *úna*, 16, 43. 85, 110; when suppressed, 85; elision of, 85.
Uscíre, 42, 125; conjugation of, 240

V.

Variations of regular verbs, 202.
Veníre, 125, 142, 148, 160; conjugation of, 241.
Verbs, 141; syntax of, 146; general rules, 147; irregularities of. 214; moods of (see "Infinitive," "Indicative," "Imperative," and "Subjunctive Moods"); tenses of (see "Imperfect," "Perfect Definite," and "Future Tenses"); participles of (see "Participles"). Place of the verb, 149, 160; terminations of, 147 Article and verbs, 20, 147. Nouns

---

* *Se* (himself) was formerly written with an accent, — *sé*.

and verbs, 20, 147, 159, 160. Pronouns and verbs, 49, 51, 57, 91, 148. Union with diminutives, 79. Auxiliary verbs, 141, 186; conjugation of *avére*, 186 (see "*Avére*"); of *éssere*, 187 (see *Éssere*"). Regular verbs, 188. Active verbs, 188 (see "Active Verbs"). First conjugation, 188; conjugation of *amáre*, 188; of *cercáre*, 190; of *pregáre*, 191. Second conjugation, 192; conjugation of *temére*, 192; of *téssere*, 194. Third conjugation, 196; conjugation of *sentíre*, 196; of *esibíre*, 198; of *cucíre*, 200; of *abborríre*, 201. Synopsis of the variations of regular verbs, 202. Passive verbs, 204 (see "Passive Verbs"); conjugation of *éssere amáto*, 204. Neuter verbs, 206 (see "Neuter Verbs"); conjugation of *partíre*, 206. Pronominal or reflective verbs, 208 (see "Pronominal Verbs); conjugation of *pentírsi*, 208. Unipersonal verbs, 210 (see "Impersonal Verbs); conjugation of *piòvere*, 210; of *éssere* (unipersonally used), 212. Irregular verbs, 214 (see "Irregular Verbs"). First conjugation, 214; conjugation of *andáre*, 215; of *dáre*, 216; of *fáre*, 217; of *stáre*, 218 (see "*Andáre*," "*Dáre*," "*Fáre*," "*Stáre*"). Second conjugation, 219; conjugation of *cadére*, 220; of *dissuadére*, 220; of *dolére*, 221; of *dovére*, 222 (see "*Dovére*"); of *giacére*, 223; of *parére*, *persuadére*, *piacére*, 224; of *potére*, 225; of *rimanére*, 226; of *sapére*, 227; of *sedére*, 228; of *tacére*, 229; of *tenére*, 230; of *valére*, 231; of *vedére*, 232; of *volére* (see "*Volére*") 233. Third conjugation, 234; conjugation of *díre*, 234; of *moríre*, 236; of *salíre*, 237; of *seguíre*, 238; of *udíre*, 239; of *uscíre* (see "*Uscíre*"), 240; of *veníre* (see "*Veníre*"), 241. Table of Irregular verbs, 242. Defective verbs, 246; conjugation of *calére*, 247; of *colére* or *cólere*, *lecére* and *licére* or *lécere* and *lícere*, *pavére*, *silére*, 248; of *solére*, *stupére*, *álgere*, 249; of *ángere*, *arrógere*, *capére*, 250; of *chérere*, *convellère*, 251; of *fiédere*, 252; of *lúcere*, *mólcere*, 253; of *riédere*, *sérpere*, 254; of *suffólcere* or *saffólgere*, *tángere*, *tóllere*, 255; of *tórpere*, *úrgere*, *vígere*, 256; of *gíre*, 257; of *ire* and *ohre*, 258.

"Very," before participles, 73.
Vi, *ci*. (See "*Vi*.")
Via, 85, 147, 149.
Vocabulary, Italian-English, 266; English-Italian, 270; of exercises, 45, 54, 60, 66, 71, 75. 88, 95, 102, 108, 114, 120, 128, 131, 139, 144, 151, 157, 165, 170, 178, 185.
Volére, 148; with *ci* and *vi*, 148; conjugation of, 233.
Vosignória, 56.
Vowels, 1, 4; sounds of, 2.

W.

"Who." "which," "what," etc, 90, 91
Words, union of, 21, 55, 57.

EXERCISES

ADAPTED TO

CUORE'S ITALIAN COURSE.

EXERCISES FOR TRANSLATION.

Exercise I.

The Article.

The father and mother. The uncle and his son. The brother has the pens. I have the books. Who has the house? What has he? He has the wine. She has not the book. The servant has the apples. What has the shoemaker? The shoemaker has the shoes. Hast thou the penknife? Which seal has she? Who has the peach? I have not the peach. I have the bread and the meat. He has the herbs. The man has a fig. The scholar has a book. Thou hast a pear. Have I a mirror? Who has a house? Has he a record? She has a guide. The tailor has money. What has the domestic? The domestic has the linen. Who has a friend? My uncle has a friend. The mistress has no time.

1. There are seven primitive colors, — red, orange, yellow, green, blue, indigo, and violet. 2. See the churches, the palaces, the amphitheatres, and the arches, which have outlived so many generations of men! 3. Annina looked at her weeping sister, at her dear old father, and then expired. 4. Vasco di Gama presented to the King of Malabar the gifts, and the letters written, one in Arabic, and the other in Portuguese. 5. The ant is the emblem of industry. 6. Exercise and temperance strengthen the constitution. 7. Iron and steel are more useful than gold and silver. 8. Secrecy is the key of prudence. 9. Avarice is despicable. 10. The end crowns the work. 11. Walking

increases the appetite. 12. The gentle answer appeases anger. 13. Errors and wickednesses draw ridicule upon us. 14. Nations ought to love peace, and avoid war. 15. Employ your time well; cultivate your mind; love order. 16. Reading forms the heart, and enlightens the mind. 17. Health is the first condition of a happy life. 18. Gratitude produces all the other virtues. 19. At the age of eighteen, Romulus laid the foundation of a city which gave laws to the world.

Exercise II.

Union of the Articles and Prepositions.

The gardens of the brother. We are in the room. The knife is upon the table. The friends are in the garden. I have the handkerchiefs in my pocket. You are his friend. The voice of the man. The shoes are in the room. The wine is upon the table. I am not in the house. They are not in the city. The girl has no spectacles. She has no gold. Who is in the street? Has he the neighbor's book (the book of the neighbor)? Who has the father's stick? Is she in the house? No; she is in the garden, under a tree. Has the tailor my brother's horse? Who has your mother's pocket-handkerchief? I have it in the pocket of my coat. Is the key in the door, or under the table? The man has bread and wine for his dinner. In the streets of the city. He has the roses from his friend. He writes with a pen.

1. Give me some bread, wine, butter, cheese, boiled meat, mutton, veal, pie, mustard, and salt. 2. The power of speech is a faculty peculiar to man. 3. The bird is known by his song. 4. Flowers are the ornament of gardens. 5. Riches are often the tariff of esteem. 6. They say that our honor is in the opinion of others. 7. The eyes are the mirror of the soul. 8. The value of things is founded upon wants. 9. Climate influences the character of men. 10. We prove gold and silver with the touchstone, and the heart of men with gold and silver. 11. The

law of necessity is always the first law. 12. The miser allows himself to die of hunger in the lap of plenty. 13. Poverty and misfortune bring about equality. 14. Best is the enemy of good. 15. Fortune has the first place in the things of the world. 16. Abundance of words is not always an (the) indication of the perfection of language. 17. History is the picture of times and of men. 18. The lamb and the dove are the emblems of meekness and humility. 19. True merit is always accompanied by modesty. 20. Clouds and fogs are formed by the vapors which come out of the earth. 21. He who opens his heart to ambition shuts it to repose. 22. The wise man prefers the useful to the agreeable, and the necessary to the useful. 23. Poverty and ignorance are the followers of negligence and sloth. 24. The road from virtue to vice is much shorter than from vice to virtue. 25. Health is the daughter of exercise and temperance. 26. A salutation, a word of love to the unhappy, is a great kindness.

Exercise III.

The Noun.

My brother is a dentist. Your father is my neighbor. My mother is your neighbor. We have a horse and a mare. They have a peach-tree and an apple-tree in their garden. This woman has flowers in her garden. Have you seen the king? Is the soup cold? This is a hare. Is study a pleasure? They have seen the Pope of Rome I have an apple in my hand. Have you a fig and an orange? Give some fruit to my brother. The man has a cow and an ox. Iron is a metal. Silver is also a metal. We are in the path. My uncle has a crane. Is this your daughter? Am I your friend (f)? Who is a philosopher? Is your neighbor poor or rich? Who has gold? This man has gold; but he has no heart. The cathedral of this city is rich; but the people are poor. I am a neighbor to a poor woman. The frog is in the hedge. In the morning The basket of fruit is on the table. Eggs are good for breakfast.

Give me some bread and butter with my good eggs. My brother has a basket of good fruit. The cat is in the yard. Is the meat in the kitchen? The child has a dove. This woman has some currants.

1. Paper, pencils, inkstand, ink, slate, chalk, sand, &c., are used in school. 2. The bench, chair, desk, stool, cupboard, and sofa, are articles of furniture. 3. Among instruments, we have the hammer, the awl, the axe, the mallet, the saw, the needle, the file, and the gimlet. 4. For table-ware, there are the table-cloth, the napkin, the carving-knife, the plate, the salt-cellar, the porringer, the knife, the fork, the fruit-dish, &c. 5. The mason, the smith, the tailor, the shoemaker, the weaver, the baker, the carpenter, the farrier, the knife-grinder, the barber, the butcher, the hatter, are all artisans. 6. Affected behavior is the mask of ignorance. 7. We should never judge of the good or bad character of persons by the expression of their face. 8. The rose without thorns only grows on the highest Alps. 9. Tobacco is an American plant. 10. A good conscience is a good pillow. 11. The moth which flies about the lamp finally burns his wings. 12. We obtain love and friendship by modesty and humility. 13. The eye delights in the verdure of the earth and the beauty of the sky. 14. In that valley, I saw a little village, an old castle in ruins, and a convent.

Exercise. IV.

The Plural of Nouns and Adjectives.

The good sisters. Celebrated men. Gray coats. The men are good, and the women are good. The girl has handsome hands. My shoes are narrow. The kings are in the city. You are not unhappy. The tailor has a pair of boots. Her sleeves are narrow. This baker has good bread. Give me some of his bread and cheese. Is the king in his palace. I have a cow and two oxen. The physicians are in a hotel. We have asparagus upon the table. I have seen mice upon the table.

She has rings on her fingers. Give me two bushels of oranges. Who has two wives? The Romans have good oxen. We have good horses and cows. Children are not fools. Your sisters have no sweetmeats for supper. I have seen the bones and the claws of the crane. Has your sister seen the beautiful houses of the rich ladies? No; but she has seen their beautiful lakes and woods.

1. The merchants sell tea and chocolate. 2. The shoemaker makes boots and shoes. 3. There are many ancient temples in Italy. 4. The scholars have neither ink, writing-paper, nor pens. 5. The stone urns in the garden came from Naples. 6. I have sent a dozen handkerchiefs to the washerwoman. 7. The tailor makes cloaks and overcoats. 8. Oxen and horses are useful animals. 9. There are birds upon the flowers and upon the trees. 10. The strangers have bought coats. 11. There are diamonds, pearls, emeralds, and other precious stones. 12. The streets of B. are narrow. 13. The country bakers are not friends of the city bakers. 14. All workmen and workwomen are employed at this season. 15. God is the father of man, and the preserver of all creatures. 16. The inhabitants of Gadara honored poverty with a peculiar worship; they considered it as the mother of industry and the arts. 17. The man who does not see good in others is not good himself. 18. Misers resemble the horses who carry wine and drink water, and the asses who carry gold and eat thistles. 19. The rivers of Nigrizia and Guinea do not flow through plains and valleys, but rush from cataract to cataract. 20. It has been said, that a fine city without monuments is like a beautiful woman without a soul. 21. Ribbons, flowers, and lights make incredible metamorphosis. 22. The variety of trees and precious shrubs of landscape gardening were things unknown to the ancients. 23. The verdant, rich, and luxurious plains which are found in Piedmont are the best-cultivated lands of all Europe. 24. The order and beauty of the world are manifest proofs of the existence of a Supreme Being. 25. We know good fountains in dry

weather, and friends in adversity. 26. The grass grows to the height of twelve feet in the vast plains of Africa; and, under this gigantic grass, wander panthers, lions, and the enormous reptile boa. 27. When Orpheus was playing on the lyre, tigers, bears, and lions came to fawn upon him and lick his feet. 28. The muses were goddesses of science and art. 29. Men kill oxen, sheep, deer, and even birds and fish, to feed upon them.

Exercise. V.
Cases of Nouns.

I have no good letter-paper. I wish to write letters to Paris. Have you a pocket-dictionary? Is it not time to dine? Give me the silver spoons. My brother has a cask of good wine. The children are in the yard. Have you not seen the flowers on the walls? Here are your father's books. We see with our eyes, and hear with our ears. The cows are in the water. The eggs are in the nests of the birds. My father has a saddle-horse and two hunting-dogs. Have you my brother's pens? Who gave me this book? Have you seen the gunpowder? Have you dined to-day? Yes; I have dined with some relations. What have you for breakfast? I have bread alone for breakfast. What does he sell? He sells tobacco and gunpowder. Let us go to buy some ink. Send Luigi to the post. Whose hat is this? It is not my friend's hat. To whom do you write? Write to your sister. I write to my friends. Whom do you see? I see some girls in the street. Have you money? No; but I have good friends. Is this a hunting-dog?

1. In the city, there are tailors for men and women, and shoemakers for men and women. 2. The sun shines by day, and the moon by night. 3. No one is sheltered from calumny. 4. The language of a modest man gives lustre to truth. 5. A babbler is troublesome to society. 6. A foolish man doubts nothing. 7. Abundance of riches do not make us happy. 8. Adonis was a youth of extreme beauty. 9. Hope leads us by an agreeable

road to the end of life. 10. The goods which the merchant consigned to his sons have arrived. 11. The soldiers have come from Georgia. 12. The rules of this Grammar are easy. 13. Patriarchs are monarchs of the Church. 14. Mr. A. has received the catalogues from the bookseller. 15. Success is for him who seizes upon it. 16. Fanaticism is, to superstition, what excitement is to fever; what rage is to anger. 17. Woe to the man whose only ambition is to please mean men! 18. The religious fanaticism of the Puritans was the promoter and the support of the revolution in England.

Exercise VI and VII.

Pronouns.

Who are you? I am your friend. What do you wish of me? Have you money? I have need of money. He has written a letter. What have you said to me? A daughter is born to him. Does it rain? No; it snows. They are with her in my father's house. Tell him and her that I love them. I wrote a letter to her. They are writing to you. I shall go to the post myself. Do you think of me? I think of you. Give me a good stick. Think no more of them. What has he said to you of them? Let him do it. I do not wish to do as you do. Who is there? It is I. It is he. He speaks of us. I give you this ring because I love you. Will you send this letter to him? He loves his friend. I love you, and you love me. I will go with you. She speaks of you. Think no more of him. Go with them. I wish to see you. She can speak to him of it. Do not ask it of her. Behold him. Behold her. Behold us. He gives it to us. We lend them to you. He will give the flowers to her. I will give them to him. She does not deny it. Give it to her. She gives it to her neighbor. I do not wish to see them. Tell them so (it).

1. Silvio Pellico says, "We read, or meditate in silence, a great part of the day." 2. "I wrote the tragedy of 'Leoniero da

Dertona,' and many other things." 3. "From my heart, I pardon my enemies." 4. "Although Mr. M. was in a deplorable state, he sang, he conversed, and did every thing to conceal a part of his sufferings from me." 5. If you do not embrace fortune when she presents herself, you may hope for her in vain when she has turned her shoulders upon you. 6. Do not disturb opinions which render a man happy, unless you can give him better ones. 7. If we wish to know what any one says of us when we are absent, let us only observe what they say of others in our presence. 8. Some one asked Diogenes what was the best method of revenging himself on his enemy. "You will succeed," said Diogenes, "by showing yourself an honest man." 9. A vagabond dog went into a forest, and, finding a lion, he said to him, "You go wandering through the woods; you suffer from hunger and the inclemencies of the season. See me: I live, and enjoy much, without any trouble. Does my life please you? Will you come with me? You know it will be for your good." The proud and generous lion answered, "You eat; you are sheltered; you take pleasure, and have no trouble, it is true: but you are a servant, and I am free, and will never serve upon any terms." 10. It is not the abundance of riches we possess which can make us happy, but the use we make of them. 11. Behold! it is Rome which presents herself to your view; it is Rome, the eternal city, the city of wonders. 12. Misfortunes shake hands; they seldom come alone. 13. The joys of friendship make us almost forget our misfortunes. 14. The prisoner said to the chief keeper, "What is your name?" To which he answered "Fortune, sir, made fun of me, giving me the name of a great man. My name is Schiller." 15. All the most amiable gifts of mind and heart are united in Raphael to render him dear to me 16. Every one complains of his memory, and no one of his judgment. 17. The soul of Bice was worthy of the heaven which now possesses it; and her example sustains me in the fear which often oppresses me since her death. 18. I heard Ellen praying; and, kneeling down without interrupting her, I followed her words, with my eyes filled with tears. 19. A bad poet had a satire printed against Benedict XIV. The pontiff examined, corrected, and returned it to the author; assuring him, that it would sell better thus corrected. 20. Great men recognize, fraternize, and embrace each other, through the lapse of ages. 21. A crow dressed himself with the fallen feathers of a peacock, and, despising his companions, went among the peacocks, who, recognizing him, stripped him of his false plumes, and drove him away. Then he returned in confusion to his companions, seeking to unite with them again; but they made fun of and refused to receive him. Let the misfortune of the crow be a lesson to us.

Exercise VIII.

Adjectives.

The honest man. The diligent scholar. A sweet apple. Good books. Are you idle? She is generous. They are obedient. We are merry. Who are weak? He is not strong. I am tired. Life is short. Who is ready? That boy is a good scholar. The little girl has a new dress. We are poor. Mrs. S. is modest and amiable. Your friend (f) is generous. I am not strong. Give him half a bottle of good wine. Have you seen the beautiful flowers in the king's garden? Those strangers are not innocent of the great crime. We are in a small house. There are beautiful trees in this garden. That lady has fine eyes. I have many apples and few pears. Have you many friends? Is he deaf, or is he dumb? My dog is faithful. The poor woman was lame. Your coat is not blue; it is black. Her hat is white, and mine is yellow. That girl is not ill; she is obstinate and ungrateful. Who is that proud young man? The lady is very polite. The streets of Boston are not large. What useless work! Is she inquisitive? This writing-paper is not good. They are imprudent. The men who are in that large white house are honest and wise.

1. Milton's "Paradise Lost" is a fine poem. 2. The Queen of England is a kind lady; she loves the good and industrious. 3. The German lady is very generous; she always thinks of the poor, and takes care of many orphans. 4. There are large forests in France and Germany. 5. A constant, sincere, and disinterested friend is rare. 6. The short dress, the close black-velvet waist, and the coarse red handkerchief which partly covered her face, clearly showed her to be an Alpine girl (to have come from the Alps). 7. Doctor S. had great love for justice, great tolerance, great faith in human virtue and in the help of Providence, and a vivid sentiment of the beautiful in art. 8. All social posts can be occupied by honest men. 9. The moral and political vicissitudes of nations transform a people of heroes into a horde of slaves. 10. Why are there upon the earth so much beauty and so many imperfections? why, in man, so much grandeur and so much misery? 11. Aosta, a Roman city, is full of beautiful ruins of the time of Augustus. 12. Columbus said, "My thoughts are such as please few (persons): they are, as I think, wise, certain, reasonable, meditative; but yet, to most men, they would appear vain, foolish, adventurous, and frivolous." 13. I love Torino: I love its beautiful squares, its large and clean streets; and I love, more than all, its slow, but industrious, silent, and progressive life. 14. Crescenzio, of illustrious birth and fine person, was rich, and brave in arms. 15. The Dutch are generally a patient, laborious, neat, sober, frugal, and industrious people. 16. Death spares neither rich nor poor. 17. The diligent hand conquers want; and prosperity and success accompany the industrious. 18. The tongue is a little member; but it says great things. 19. A mild, polite, and affable person is esteemed by everybody.

Exercise IX.
Adjectives in the Comparative.

Charles is more inquisitive than his sister. Maria is handsomer than her mother. These pears are sweet; but the plums are sweeter. The dog is more faithful than the cat. We are more tired than unhappy. He is happier than his brothers. You are more wicked than I. He is as dexterous as generous. You are happy; but we are happier. Mr. L. is richer than his neighbor. In summer the days are longer than in winter. Gold is more valuable than silver. The girls are more discreet than the boys. Rafaello is handsomer than his brothers. Her cheeks are red as roses. White as milk.

1. The richer man is, the more avaricious he is. 2. The more Napoleon conquered, the more he wished to conquer. 3. The term of life is short; that of beauty is still shorter. 4. The stork has a longer neck than the goose. 5. In summer the days are longer than they are in winter. 6. Brass is more useful than lead. 7. The General was less successful than skilful. 8. Charles fell into an indifference, which was worse than doubt. 9. There is more true glory in forgiveness than in revenge. 10. Antonio was perhaps as great a man as Augustus; but he was less fortunate. 11. The Savoyards have more active blood than we have: they have more of the impetuous temper of the French; we, more of the blessed " far niente " of the Italians. 12. Nothing is so contagious as example. 13. Generally, the more populous a country, the richer it is. 14. Few people have a more celebrated, and, at the same time, a more miserable country. 15. It is in thy own power, O man! to be less unhappy. Arm thyself with firmness against present ills, and forget the happier days which are passed. 16. Women produce much stronger sentiments in the heart of man by their wit than by their beauty. 17. A philosopher said, that it was better to consult women than learned men in doubts concerning language;

because the latter do not speak so well or so easily as the former, who study less. 18. There are as many kinds of hypocrisy as there are virtues. 19. Alphonso, King of Spain, said, "I am more afraid of the tears of my people, than the strength of my enemies."

Exercise X.

Adjectives: their Superlatives.

How do you feel to-day? I feel very well; I have no pain in my head; I am very strong. They have little bread, and less meat. Your house is convenient, ours is more so; but that of Mrs. S. is the most convenient of all. That is the finest tree in the country. We have the best water in town. Your well is the deepest I ever saw. Her hat is more fashionable than handsome, and very large. It is better to have too much than too little. Maria is more industrious than Sarah; she is the most industrious person in the house.

1. The Campidoglio was the most celebrated edifice of Rome 2. Nestor was the oldest and the wisest of all the Greeks who were at the siege of Troy. 3. It is a most bitter thing to be forever separated from our friends. 4. There are very valiant men upon the American battle-field. 5. Princes are often more unhappy than the greatest part of their subjects. 6. Self-love is the most cunning of all flatterers. 7. The most pernicious of all sins is calumny: it very often ruins the reputation of the most honest people, makes discord among the most intimate friends, in fact, it is the most abominable sin in the world. 8. The most agreeable quality that a man can have, is to be civil and courteous. 9. He who is difficult in selecting, often chooses the worst. 10. A philosopher says, that the grandest object in the world is a good man struggling against adversity. 11. Intemperance and idleness are our most dangerous enemies. 12. It is said that there was a very happy and a very rare exuberance of loyalty in C. Balbo, which commanded love and respect. 13. "The Life of Dante" is a work about which history and literature

dispute, as to which shall enumerate it among the best in their respective categories. 14. Naples and Florence are among the most ancient and most beautiful cities. 15. We call that medium distance, which holds the middle place between the longest and the shortest. 16. The most noted States are not those which possess the most fertile country, but those which give themselves up with the greatest activity to arts and trade. 17. The discovery by Columbus was the fruit of a most vivid intellect, exalted by a very warm imagination, and sustained by an iron and indomitable nature. 18. Fidelity, which comprehends in itself almost all virtues, has no merit, is almost no virtue, when it can be inculcated by fear; but it is one of the sublimest virtues when it is inspired by love.

Exercise XI.

Numerals.

My sister has five books, and I have but two. Your brother has a new cane. The farmer has 54 apple and 10 pear-trees in his little orchard. I have two horses, three cows, one dog, and 50 hens. There are four weeks in a month. February has 28 days. A year has 12 months, 52 weeks, or 365 days. He is 25 years old; he was born in the year 1840. Is your father 60 years old? No, he was born in 1810. I have bought three bottles of wine, and six bottles of cider. Give me 22 rolls for 20 cents. In Boston there are 104 churches, 19,500 houses, and nearly 185,000 inhabitants. How much is 5 times 25? 9 times 72? 40 and 50 make 90. 65 and 70 make 135. We sailed for Europe on 1st of June, 1820, and returned Oct. 17, 1827. The first day of the week. The third month of the year. We have had sixteen bottles of wine, and this is the seventeenth. My son is three years and a half old. Lula is the third in her class. Give me five different kinds of fruit. We are in the nineteenth century. This is the sixth bird I have seen to-day. He has spent three dollars and three-quarters for trifles. Tell us what o'clock it is. It is a quarter past five, and almost time for supper. Fifteen gentlemen and ten ladies. Twenty boys and three girls. Twenty-one dollars and seventy-five cents. The poor old woman said she was eighty-one years old.

1. In our times, it is not rare to see decrepit people of twenty-five years. 2. Cæsar conquered more than eight hundred cities in less than ten years. 3. Sophocles and Euripides, two famous tragedians, were both Athenians. 4. The exhibition which Titus gave to the Roman people, at one time, cost him eighty millions. 5. Lewis Fourteenth was said to be one of the greatest kings in the world. 6. Where do we see men of the stamp of those depicted by Dante in the fifteenth and sixteenth canto of his Paradise? 7. Herodotus relates of the ancient Persians, that, from the age of five years to twenty, they taught their children only three things, — to manage a horse, to use the bow, and to tell the truth. 8. About the year one thousand, St. Bernard, a Savoyard, founded the useful and famous monastery on one of the highest summits of the Alps, which still flourishes. 9. A foolish young man asked an old lady how old she was. "I do not know exactly," she replied; "but I have always heard, that an ass is older at twenty years than a woman at seventy." 10. Masinissa, King of Numidia, died at the age of ninety-seven years, leaving forty-four children; he had been an ally of Rome nearly seventy years. 11. Hospitality is one of the first duties of man. 12. The Venetians imposed a singular tribute upon the Patriarch of Aquila, in the year one thousand one hundred and seventy-three: every year, on Shrove-Tuesday, he was obliged to send a bull and a dozen pigs to Venice; they represented the Patriarch and his twelve canons. They were led through the city in pomp, and then killed. 13. Henry Dandolo, whose eyes had been put out by order of the Emperor Manuel Comnene, was, however, elected Doge of Venice, in the year one thousand one hundred ninety-two, at the age of eighty-four years. Soon after, he took command of the Venetian fleet of five hundred vessels, and succeeded in taking possession of Constantinople in

the year one thousand two hundred and four. After this conquest, he added to his other titles that of Lord of the Fourth and Eighth of the Roman Empire. 14. The activity of the Savoyards is shown on both sides of the Alps: it not only sends street-sweeps and servants into France, but soldiers also, fifteen or eighteen Savoyard generals having been in the French army 15. Count Cæsar Balbo expired on the evening of the third of June, one thousand eight hundred and fifty-three, after a few days of acute suffering.

Exercise XII.

Relative Pronouns.

Who are you? What is that? Which is it? What have you for me? To whom did you give the chocolate? Whose coat is that? What does he say? Whose children are they? Which of these oranges is the sweetest? A man eats what he likes. He will give this book to her whom he likes best. The shoes which you bought are not good. Which flowers are the handsomest? Of whom have you bought this linen? What have you given for it? To whom does she write? For what do you study? What is good for you? What have you seen? That is the lady of whom I spoke. He who is rich is not always happy. Upon what does he live? What a beautiful tree! What beautiful flowers! He who is speaking is the teacher. The lady for whom she works has much business. Which of these two pears do you wish? What is the (f) domestic doing? Who is going with you? The boy whom you have seen with me. Whose horse is that? It is mine; I bought it of your father's friend. What is the use of appetite without food? That of which you think the least is to amuse yourself.

1. Cleopatra wore two pearls in her ears, each of which cost more than a million. 2. Tell me whose company you keep, and I will tell you who you are. 3. There are faces in which the character of goodness is well expressed. 4. He who acts conscientiously may err; but he is pure in the sight of God. 5. What

is learned in youth is easily impressed upon the mind. 6. Happy are those who can content themselves with the necessaries of life. 7. He who does not love his brother does not deserve to live. 8. Modesty is to merit what a gauze veil is to beauty: it diminishes its splendor, but augments its value. 9. That which is most delicate in a work is lost by translating it into another language. 10. There is a certain art in conversation which gives grace to the simplest thing. 11. Contact with other men is necessary for him who has to write history. 12. The cocoanut-tree is of medium size; the leaves of which fall and shoot forth alternately, so that it is always covered with foliage. 13. Venice is a city unique in the world by its situation; it is precisely like an immense ship, which tranquilly reposes upon the water, and which no one can reach, but by means of boats 14. There is nothing, however mean it may be, that is not useful for something. 15. Charles Bonnet, who was almost perfect in heart and mind, tells us that after death all the species mount one round of the ladder which leads to perfection. 16. At the commencement of a feast, the Romans used to present a list of the viands which were to appear upon the table to the guests, in order that each one might reserve his appetite for that which most pleased him. 17. A preacher had annoyed all his audience preaching upon the beatitudes. After the sermon, a lady told him that he had forgotten one. "Which?" asked the preacher. "That," answered the lady, "blessed is he who did not hear your sermon." 18. Listlessness is a disease, the only remedy for which is labor. 19. That which is called Eldorado is only a sandy desert, which will not offer you a drop of water if you are thirsty, nor the shade of a tree if you are weary.

Exercise XIII.

Possessive Adjective Pronouns.

Is this your brother's pen? No, it is mine. All that I have is hers. His book is very good. Our relations are not poor.

The daughter loves her father and mother. The son loves his mother and sister. I love you and your children. Do not speak against my relations. It is one of my sisters. She is in the kitchen with her aunt. To-day she will put on her best white hat, and her new shoes. Go in her stead. He spoke continually of his father, mother, and sister. Their female friends are not in the city. Is that your glove? No, it is not mine; it is yours. Their good dog is not in our yard. Look at your watch. Give me my property. Go to his store. These are your apples, his pears, and my cherries. Who has her nice ribbons? Where is my lace? Give my aunt her money. My dear friend, I have nothing to give him. They were her people. Her neighbor was left to guard her house and her cows. She and her mother. My dear children. Put it in your pocket. She put it upon her head. He did it with his hands.

1. England owes her wealth to the protection which she accords to her commerce. 2. Oh, what a longing a prisoner has to see his fellow-creatures! 3. There is no doubt, that every human condition has its peculiar duties. 4. Nothing serves better to confound our enemies, than not to notice their offence. 5. Every condition has its pleasures and its pains. 6. The great wisdom of man consists in knowing his folly. 7. Our friends forsake us when fortune ceases to favor us. 8. A wise man often doubts: a foolish man never; he knows every thing but his own ignorance. 9. Euripides complained to one of his friends, that he had been three days making a few verses. 10. Conscience is a just judge of our actions. 11. A sick man almost always says to his physician, My head and all my body pains me. 12. Hannibal distinguished himself from his equals not by the magnificence of his dress, but by the beauty of his horse and his arms. 13. Self-love is our prime mover. 14. "And he also, when he saw me, arose, and, throwing his arms about my neck, embraced me." 15. A simpleton joked a man of wit about his large ears. "I acknowledge having them too large for a man," he answered; "but you must at the same

time agree, that yours are too small for an ass." 16. If you attempt to enter into conversation with an Englishman who does not know you, he will certainly take you for a knave. He will button up his vest, put his handkerchief well into his pocket, see that his watch is safe, and look crabbedly at you. Notice his face: it says to you, "Leave me alone." Yet this same person is perhaps the most friendly of mortals; he only wishes to protect his own independence. 17. A fox seeing a crow, which had a piece of cheese in her beak, upon a tree, began to praise her very much. "What fine feathers!" he said; "what a beautiful body! If you knew how to sing, upon my word there could be no finer bird." The foolish bird, to allow her voice to be heard, opened her beak, and let the cheese fall; and the fox, seizing it, carried it away. But the fox soon paid for his fraud; for the shepherd came, and killed him for his skin.

Exercise XIV.

Demonstrative Adjective Pronouns.

This is my penknife; that is yours. These are her pens. Is that ink good? Who is he? Who is she? Who are they? This house no longer belongs to me. What have you in that trunk? Who are those men? What did your father buy to day? Who has given me this beautiful bouquet? What is in that closet? She will do what the master tells her. We shall go and take a little walk this evening. In the meantime you can go to our neighbors. Take this inkstand, and give me that. That is the lady of whom I was speaking. This rich man is sick. Those poor women are well. That poor child is handsome and good. Give those gloves to that man. To this or to that? This man was learned, that was ignorant. That axe was lost. I have found this gold axe. Is this your axe, sir? This morning I worked in the garden. He planted those seeds which you gave him. This book is incorrect. That grammar is much used. He loves those dear children. Where have I seen those faces? To whom have you given those plums? Have you written to that lady? What did she say to that news? I prefer this table to that. This hat is very becoming to your daughter. She likes these red ribbons, not those yellow ones. Give me that small piece of cheese.

1. Happy are those who love to read. 2. We love those who admire us; but we do not always love those whom we admire. 3. Those who believe that happiness consists in riches deceive themselves. 4. We often forgive those who annoy us, but rarely those whom we annoy. 5. Ariosto is the poet of the imagination, Tasso that of the intellect. 6. James I. was one of those men who are discontented with their condition, and envious of others' glory. 7. Plato banished music from his republic. 8. All the works of nature merit our admiration. 9. The words of a sincere man are the thoughts of his heart. 10. " His eyes were closed by his physician, his friend from infancy, and a man all religion and charity." 11. " I have never known a more noble spirit than his, and few similar to his." 12. True grief weeps little; the tear of the soul is much more bitter than that shed from the eye. 13. Those who flatter the great, ruin them. 14. We must do what God sets us to do, and take what he sends us. 15. There are human beings to whom nature shows herself a real step-mother; poor Joanne was one of these unhappy creatures. 16. The hour of twilight exercises a mysterious influence upon gentle spirits; that light and those shadows which seem to meet only to take leave of each other (to give an adieu) awaken a thousand delicate and affectionate thoughts. 17. From time to time, conscience wars against pride, and attempts to conquer its bad reasonings (the bad reasonings of this) by bearing witness to the truth. 18. That sky, that country, that distant motion of creatures in the valley, those voices of the country girls, those laughs, those songs, exhilarated us very much. 19. The wounds of the body are nothing in comparison to those of the mind.

Exercise XV.
Indefinite Adjective Pronouns.

They have spoken of nobody. She gave it to somebody. I had nothing for dinner. The children love each other. One goes, and another comes. Both are in the city. Give him all you have. Tell me all you know. The woman knows everybody. The good man loves everybody. Has any one been here? It is said that Celia will go to France. No one is without faults. Some are good, others are bad. I hear somebody's voice. They are not going into Washington Street. They say it was a long procession. Is there any thing new to-day?

1. Every man is exposed to criticism. 2. All men are subject to death. 3. Every one has his faults. 4. Take those books, and put them each in its place. 5. Justice includes all other virtues. 6. Scipio displayed grandeur in all his actions. 7. All nations appear to desire to obtain merit from the splendor of their origin. 8. We must have patience, and every thing will come right in time. 9. People judge others' things in a different manner from that in which they would judge their own. 10. People drink good wine in France, and eat good meat in England. 11. Every period of life has pleasures proper and natural to it. 12. Whatever reasons one may have for being absent from his country, there can be none sufficiently strong to make him forget it. 13. Vice disunites men, keeping them on guard, one against the other. 14. That which thou desirest others to keep silent, keep thou silent. 15. Other times, other customs. 16. It is foolish not to wish to know any thing. 17. No language is perfect in itself. 18. It is easier to be wise for others than for ourselves. 19. Every body seeks happiness, few find it. 20. A preacher, who had not been invited to dine with any one through Lent, said, in his last sermon, that he had preached against all sins except that of gluttony, because it had not appeared to him that such a vice

ruled in the country. 21. Some one asked an American, why there had not been a monument erected to Christopher Columbus. 22. Every beginning is difficult.

Exercise XVI.
Indefinite Adjective Pronouns Continued.

What is the best news? What is the talk about town? There is no news. I have read no paper to-day. Do they still speak of war? No, they speak only of peace. Every flower has its beauty. Every man has his virtues. Our friends will remain in France some weeks. She spends her time in some useful occupation. They have some good books. One sees that he is only a child. No servant was ever more faithful. We shall remain in the city all summer. He goes somewhere every season. Every one is her friend, because she is good. One can do much. Every little helps. It is not well to do nothing. Some make money, others lose it. The girls were jealous of one another. One has a fine face, the other a handsome hand. Both mother and child were here.

1. Any loss is more honorable than to lie. 5. All the laws and the prophets, all the collection of sacred books, is reduced to the precept of loving God and man. 3. The pleasure derived from things, in appearance almost nothing, when we wish well to some one, is indescribable. 4. Speaking with one and another is a pleasant recreation for every one. 5. No friendship, however intimate it may be, can authorize the violation of a secret. 6. God knows how much more pleasant the name of Naples, the city of my fathers, is to me than that of any other name of Italian country. 7. Nothing is durable here below. 8. Every thing has its time; and the usages of war, perhaps, more than any other thing. 9. In plains we wish for hills, and on hills we naturally wish to walk on plains. 10. There is almost no great capital in Europe where they do not

seek servants from some remote, hidden province, and for the most part from the mountains.

Exercise XVII.

Prepositions di, a, da.

Have you come to find me? Do not go near the bed. That boy has fallen from the tree. Give the boy milk to drink, and some bread to eat. Have you good writing-paper? My sister has a good saddlehorse to sell. They say that our enemy is out of danger. Whilst the child is starving at home, the mother goes to church to pray. Give that man something to do. Do not say it in jest. That domestic is not fit for many things. The little boy plays the teacher, and the little girl the mistress of the house. He lives out of the town, and keeps arms for defence in his house. Why have you not something to do? I have been sick since last year. Those girls depend upon their aunt. Have you learned your lesson by heart?

1. We must be careful not to expose ourselves to danger. 2. Cæsar said to some one who was reading in his presence, "Are you reading, or are you singing? If you are singing, you sing very badly." 3. When the gods love princes, says an ancient philosopher, they pour a mixture of good and evil into their cup of fate, so that they may never forget that they are men. 4. There is no true friendship without virtue. 5. Riches and poverty have great influence upon men. 6. The city of Florence enjoyed tranquillity and abundance under the government of the Medici. 7. Have three things open to your friend,— your face, your purse, and your heart. 8. Charlemagne sealed treaties with the hilt of his sword. 9. " Dying, we find an asylum against the misfortunes of life," said Seneca. 10. We ought to learn more from observation than from books. 11. " The eternal God has poured out happiness; and I, I alone, am without help, without friends, without company." 12. God save you from living alone, by force (being forced to live alone)! 13. It was ordered

by Providence, that, when man is struck with calamity, woman shall be his support and consolation. 14. The last of the Vallesa was one of the best and most noble — noble in actions — among the ministers of our good and popular king. 15. It is not possible not to find some enchantment in the presence, in the looks, and in the conversation, of a good, vivacious, and affectionate old lady. 16. It is said that the suffering of man upon earth is for the good of mankind.

Exercise XVIII.

Prepositions in, con, per.

From this time forward. From that time forward. My house is in one of the principal streets of the city. Are you angry? Where is the bunch of grapes which your uncle had for me? Go to the tailor's for your father's coat. With whom do you study music? We study with the schoolmaster. Are you going to Mrs. G.'s to-day? How did the boys go into the church? They went four-by-four. The lady saw a little girl pass over (through) the meadow with a faggot of wood upon her head. I only wish to speak with you. We earn our bread by labor. Money is to pay the house-rent. What do you do to earn your food? Will you come with me? The hostess led us into a clean room. The father returned with the clothes which he had bought in the village. A dog was sleeping at his ease in a manger full of hay. An ox came to the manger to eat. The envious dog barked, and would not allow the ox to approach the hay. The poor hungry animal was angry at such an overbearing act, and said to the ribald dog, "May God reward you according to your deserts, uncharitable villain! You do not eat the hay yourself, nor permit others to enjoy it. Make use of the good things given you by Heaven, and permit others to enjoy theirs."

Exercise XIX.

Prepositions.

She will be here in ten days. It is said there is nothing new under the sun. We will go together after dinner. They praise her to the skies. Until now I have been your friend. He is beloved even by his enemies. Do not hesitate. I shall have finished this book shortly. He has been in France nearly three years. There are nearly one thousand souls in this town. I can do nothing without you. Poor women! They appear to be friendless. The good man cannot see my husband without speaking to him. There is no entrance for any one. Mary set out for the city with her mamma. She had a little bed at the side of the lady's bed.

1. Before publishing his poem, Tasso wished to submit it to the criticisms of the bravest men of his times. 2. The poet was presented to the king by the generous duke. 3. To that unfortunate woman, Rome alone appeared to be a secure asylum. 4. The soldier has every proof of esteem from the most celebrated men who live here. 5. Mrs. U. presents her compliments to Mr. M. She cannot have the pleasure of seeing him to-day, and begs him to excuse her. 6. Mrs. U. presents her compliments to Mrs. M., and requests the favor of her company on Tuesday evening next. 7. If you do not call upon me in the morning, I shall certainly wait on you in the evening. 8. The country is submerged from time to time, and once Charles was up to his head in water. 9. Who lives according to the laws of nature, in this city? 10. Caroline has found some strawberries between the two stones at the side of the wall. 11. Mr. L. was silent; and sadly he fixed his eyes upon Peter, who cast his down to the earth. 12. Captain S. yields to civil orders, is a sincere lover of peace, and aspires to no other dignity than that of being able to be useful to his beloved country. 13. The captain was named Schiller; he was a Swiss, of a peasant family;

he had served against the Turks under General Laudon in the times of Joseph II.; then in all the wars of Austria against France, until the fall of Napoleon. 14. The hospitality of the French is the most complete in the actual state of society. 15. Among the Sybarites, women invited to feasts and public dinners were notified a year previous, that they might have time to appear with all the pomp of beauty and dress.

Exercise XX.
The Verbs essere and avere.

We are poor and sick. Are you not rich enough? Were they all here? Have you had time to go to Rome? I shall be at home next week. There is no time to lose. Why are you in such a hurry? Be quiet, and you shall have some figs. Be so kind as to to give that old man a glass of wine. There are many people who do not love to work. We have no meat for dinner. I am ill, and have no appetite. The physician is charmed with the progress of his patient. They have a cold. The parents of those children have been too indulgent. He has been to the tailor's; but the coat was not finished. I shall be happy to see her in my new house. They have been very polite to us. She is about to marry. I will come to your house to-morrow. It may be that I shall not be at home. Her things are all in a good way now. I look upon thee as a good friend. There is no hope left. Mr. R. is a rich man, or a man of great wealth. The rich are not always happy. Good health is better than wealth. What is the matter with you? I am no longer hungry. That would be useless. Is his bird tame? Have they green worsted? Give her needle, thread, and cotton.

1. The city of Brünn is the capital of Moravia. 2. To be a slave to the judgment of others, when you are persuaded that it is false is the height of baseness. 3. Happy are those who hate violent pleasures, and know how to be contented with an innocent life. 4. Whoever is capable of lying, is unworthy of being enu-

merated among men. 5. It was a sweet pleasure to hear those songs and the organ which accompanied them. 6. It is easy to give advice, but very difficult to follow it. 7. Albert R. had changed his hope of being one of the great of Europe, into that of being one of the first of his own little province. 8. Arduino, Marquis of Ivrea, was the last Italian king of Italy. 9. It is curious that Piedmont, one of the most picturesque countries perhaps in the world, was nevertheless one of the last to admit picturesque gardening. 10. The city of Tyre is refreshed by the north wind which comes from the sea. 11. The greater the number of men there are in a country, provided they are industrious, the more abundance they enjoy. 12. The ambition and avarice of men are the sole origin of all their misfortunes. 13. The most unhappy of all men is he who believes himself to be so. 14. The most free of all men, is he who can be free even in slavery. 15. Misfortune is the school of great intellects. 16. Friendship and religion are two inestimable advantages (goods). 17. Not to remember happy days is a great diminution of misery, particularly when we are young. 18. General B. said, "I have always believed that the education of war is the best education that a man can have."

Exercise XXI.

The Verbs and their Syntax.

Have you seen the violets? There are beautiful tulips in your cousin's garden. How fresh every thing looks! Every thing looks alive. The rain has done a great deal of good. This is the warmest summer I can remember. I think we shall have more rain. I have a little business to do. I have had a very pleasant journey. You never will do like others. You wait for nobody. I will not stay a moment longer. I wish for a steel pen and a sheet of paper. Tell me to whom you write. I write to the dear friend whom you have seen at my house. What noise do I hear? You said it. I thought you were mistaken. Come home before it grows dark. Take away those things. Never speak without thinking. They say that he has never enjoyed a moment's happiness. Do not go out; it rains. She was about writing a letter when you entered. It is Henry's turn to go to the city. To-morrow I shall play the cook: will you come to dine with me? We shall have maccaroni with cheese for dinner. Now they ring the bell for supper, and we are not all ready to go. Let us wait a little. See, my suit of clothes is finished. How well he plays the violin! it is a pleasure to hear him.

1. The music of Bellini says sadly, as he who hopes for nothing here below, "Weep and pray." 2. Let us remember that suffering is the common heritage of the sons of man; that earth without heaven would be too hard an exile; and that life without God is an insoluble enigma! 3. "Heaven be thanked, that I can remember my good mother without the least remorse!" said R. 4. The will of God be done. 5. It is a shame to the human race, that war is inevitable at certain times, or on certain occasions. 6. Labor and cares do not frighten the wise man; they are the exercise of his mind, which they keep in vigor and health. 7. Those disasters which cast down, discourage, and mortify the spirits of a man, seem to rouse up the energies of the softer sex. 8. We should foresee danger, and fear it; but, when it comes upon us, we have only to despise it. 9. In war, fortune is capricious and inconstant. 10. Men wish to have every thing, and make themselves miserable with the desire for superfluity. 11. Great conquerors, like those rivers which overflow their banks, appear majestic, but lay waste all those fertile countries which they should only water. 12. Everybody says what comes into his mind. 13. When the heart of a man is exercised and strengthened in virtue, he ought easily to console himself for the wrinkles which come upon his face. 14. Justice, moderation, and good faith are the securest defence of a State. 15. Misfortune fraternizes souls, stifles bad passions, and binds around us ties of love. 16. St. Cecilia is a popular institution which

appears to be transmitted from the middle ages. 17. Letters! are they not the children of heaven, descended to earth to console us in grief? 18. Ah! there is much comfort in the alternations of care and hope for a person who is all that is left to us. 19. Who, in the noise of our streets, with railways, the smoke of the engines, and the monotonous rolling of the omnibuses, would not sometimes sigh for the quiet of a country life?

Exercise XXII.
Subjunctive Mood.

The mistress of the house ordered her to go. I fear that you will be late to school. Tell her that she cannot do as she likes. He does not know if he ought to buy it of him. If he knew it, he would not tell it to me. We are assured that your friend (f) has come. If you had studied, you would be more learned. It seems that she will not give the cake to her son. It is possible that she may give it to him to-morrow. I want to be home in good time. I am afraid the roads are very dusty. I think we shall have some rain. Do you not think that it is very warm for the season? I want something good to eat. Here is a piece of toast, which I think will please you. Make yourself at home. What fruit do you like best? It does not appear to me that there is much difference. You say so, that you may not blame me. She seems to be growing homelier. The master asked me who I was, and where I went to school. What does he think that I know? I wish to give her the flowers which please her. She appeared to me more beautiful than ever. More beautiful than any other lady in Boston. If I had such a house. He wishes to know who she is. I wish that you would write to my mother. Let me feel your pulse. Is there any thing I can do for you? It seems to me to be very late. Now I must see your flower-garden and your kitchen-garden. Although it is difficult, I will do it. If he knew how much he was beloved! I must go. I am afraid that I shall not be able to go there.]

cannot believe any such thing. What is it to you if he comes or not?

1. The preacher said to his hearers, "If I offered you only promises, you would be excused for not believing me; but I offer you certain and present things." 2 "Let us see if you now have the courage to do better, and to allow yourself to be humiliated by the truth which condemns your weakness." 3. Do not say things which are not true. 4. Do not go in search of perils, when necessity does not require it. 5. We must found public schools, where we can teach our youth to prefer honor to pleasure. 6. Very soon James and Charles had the same confidence as if they had passed their lives together, although they had never seen each other before. 7. People generally pray that God would reward them for every good action. 8. If we do not flatter ourselves, the flattery of others will never hurt us. 9. "Alas!" cried Mrs. P., "I fear that my son is dead; and I know not what I shall do." 10. Whatever may have been Louisa's intentions, she has not done as well as she might. 11. The larger a kingdom is, the more officers are required to do what the chief magistrate could not accomplish by himself. 12. What a shame it is, that the most elevated men make their grandeur consist in their money-bags. 13. Who has not need of a friend who loves the truth only, and who will tell you the truth in spite of yourself? 14. The statue of Zenobia was in so life like a posture, that one could almost believe that she would walk. 15. How many exiles have exclaimed, "Would to God that I had never left my country!" 16. When a good general is killed, all the camp is like a disconsolate family which has lost the father, who was the cherished hope of his tender little ones. 17. It was only with the good parent, that the discreet child did not use circumspection in manifesting all the secrets of his heart.

Exercise XXIII.

Infinitive and Participles.

We are beloved by all our friends. I have been out of town all winter. They have arrived in England. When he arrived at the church door, he found it shut. She is very acute at raillery. They have not found the dog which was lost. I have seen a green worm on the rose-bush. It is not all in commencing. The fire is spread throughout the city. Do not fear that I go away; your manners please me too much. She has had time to repent of it. Who can say much in few words? Seeing her going away. It seemed to him that he saw his lady. When I had said thus. Who can have done that? She must go very soon. I have always loved good old people. He has been very kind to us. She has given two dresses to her servant. Having rested his weary body, he got up. On his departure, he gave each child a dollar. I believe that you are all asleep. Who has told all these things to our father? Where has he bought that fine horse? I have paid more for my feathers than they are worth. If I could have some pretty ribbon to trim my dress. That man has gained much money. Your son has spent more than you can ever earn. He has not rendered an exact account of every thing. Never speak at random. When the night was spent. He is oppressed by cares. To be master of a thing. He has been the Lord Mayor of London. They have spent about twenty crowns. I walked about ten miles. To condemn one without hearing. My friend is about to marry a rich woman. Have you fed that little white dog of yours? Mr. S. has brought you a gold ring from the city. I have eaten so much that I cannot go. Who would have believed it? How can that be? It looks so very nice. Will you have the goodness to ring the bell? My brother has taken three cups of tea, and asks for more.

1. The providence of God keeps us from perishing; the power

of God prevents us doing those things which displease him; and the goodness of God preserves us from suffering. 2. There are but few people who are satisfied with their lot. 3. It is easy to give advice, but difficult to follow it. 4. Signor Domenico, believing himself a learned and wise man, but not knowing what to with his knowledge, made a physician of himself, without ever having studied medicine. 5. Even in prison, there are persons afflicted to console, sick to cure, weak to comfort, and strong to confirm. 6. We are obliged to confess that our soul, mind, heart, and all our affections, have too restricted limits. 7. Many cities have desired to become the capital of a great empire. 8. The lack of maritime power is a great injury to a nation. 9. We are machines moved by habit. 10. Let us write from the dictation of our heart, provided it is free and uncorrupt. 11. We see ruined churches, castles, and convents of the middle ages throughout all Europe; the surface of Italy is covered with them. 12. "I stood at that window palpitating, shuddering, and staring about until morning, when I descended oppressed with a mortal sadness, and imagining myself much more injured than I really was." 13. It is always sad to be obliged to leave one's country through misfortune; but to leave it in chains, and be carried into horrible climates, is so afflicting that no terms can express it! 14. Saint Nilo, moved to pity by the cruel treatment inflicted on his countryman Filigato, went to the young emperor Otto, and, supplicating and weeping, demanded mercy for the prisoner. 15. The twins Romulus and Remus, being exposed by order of the king, were found and secretly educated by a shepherd named Faustolo.

Exercise XXIV.

The Verbs andare, fare, stare, and dare.

The sun sets. I have much to do. Three months ago. I have never harmed any one. He will go at daybreak. He did his best. He will set sail at three o'clock. We live a regular life. He did not know how to wish a happy new year. He h*a* just published my new work. That parrot has disturbed me very much. She pretended not to hear what the beggar said. I beg you to come to live with us. We are accustomed to take breakfast at seven o'clock. Can you not keep still? Tell her, that I say she may do as she likes. How she stands like a marble statue! How is it that this man is your husband? Go for the doctor. Mr. Lewis has given me a beautiful white hen. I am on the point of leaving for Europe. Where do you live? How do you do? How is your mother? Are your sisters well? When I was standing at the window, I saw the soldiers pass by. Be quiet, child! This is the question. Stay as long as you please. Where does she live? This city stands in a plain. He is obliged to live on bread and water. These clothes cost me twenty crowns. Why are you so thoughtful? I am reading. I love to live friendly with everybody. When the worst comes to the worst, he will sell the house. You must welcome him. Give me good fruit, bread, and wine, and I shall be satisfied.

1. True dignity is not in pride. 2. So goes the world. 3. Minerva gave the olive, fruit of a tree planted by her, to the inhabitants of proud Athens. 4. Wild beasts are not so cruel as men: lions do not wage war upon lions, nor tigers upon tigers: yet man alone, despite his reason, does that which animals without reason never do. 5. Is there not land enough to give to all men more than they can cultivate? 6. If we eat more food than is necessary, it poisons instead of nourishing us. 7. Hasten, O young man! to go where destiny calls: go unhesitatingly to the field of battle. 8. As represented, the frightful Pluto was seated upon a throne of ebony. 9. Virtue is the greatest gift which the good God can give us. 10. We must not take the life of one man into account, when the safety of the nation is at stake. 11. "Go, good mother, go to heaven, and find your child." 12. When misfortunes commence in a house, it often happens that even indifferent people fear for themselves. 13. "Then I

saw how things came, how they went, and how they would go." 14. "This silence is not to my taste," said the captain; "it presages no good." 15. The country of Phœnecia is at the foot of the Lebanon Mountains, whose tops pierce the clouds, and go to touch the stars. 16. The unhappy father does not know where he is, what he is doing, or what he ought to do, and goes calling his lost son. 17. True praise is that which is given in the absence of the person praised. 18. Whilst we are in the midst of delights, we do not wish to see or hear any thing which can interrupt their enjoyment.

Exercise XXV.

Adverbs.

Where are you going? Where is your stick? They are often unhappy. My aunt is seldom satisfied. Henceforth I shall do nothing for that family. They have treated me most ungenerously. Bravo my friend! you have spoken very well. I am afraid it will be too late to do good. We will go directly. Have you finished already? You read newspapers continually. I shall finish in the twinkling of an eye. The young man came unexpectedly. We seldom go out. I am always in a hurry. How quickly he moves! They must go very soon. I heard of it a short time ago. They were seen near the house. The men whom you wish to see are not here. The good general is welcome everywhere. I am better to-day than I was yesterday. Now-a-days she is seldom at home. They are constantly coming here. I am almost asleep. I have waited a long time, and she does not come. In general, he is very proud to his inferiors. When he leaves, I shall leave also. You are advised to go immediately. At what o'clock does the packet start? Let us walk faster. Write to me immediately. Without fail. They can sleep here. Your rooms are ready. How much are we indebted to you? It is very disagreeable to travel alone. I have travelled this way several times. With best wishes, yours truly. Do not wait longer.

1. Sextus V., when he was cardinal, pretended to be extenuated by years and infirmities, and went very stooping. 2. It often happens that men reap more advantage from their mistakes, than from the good deeds they have done. 3. Happy are those who have never wandered from the straight road of virtue! 4. People are continually talking of virtue and of merit, without knowing what they are. 5. The wise man loves truth, and never tells a lie. 6. We seldom repent of speaking too little, but often of speaking too much. 7. Cato the censor never ceased to represent to the Senate the sad consequences of luxury. 8. Perhaps there is no greater absurdity than that so often repeated, of the peace of mind of the just. 9. At any rate, Napoleon was certainly, in a military point of view, greater than Charlemagne, or any other; and particularly so in the conception of the wonderful campaign of 1800. 10. Good-luck, like ill-luck, never comes alone. 11. Behold me, then, in a sort of society, when I was prepared for a greater solitude than before. 12. The secretary was very humane, and spoke of religion with affection and dignity. 13. In Germany, priests are accustomed to dress like laymen. 14. True dignity consists in being ashamed only of mean actions.

Exercise XXVI.

Promiscuous Exercises.

Go! what nonsense (childishness)! And so! What is it? Speak, then. The man is never satisfied. Will you never have done? The sky is as fine now as it ever was. He was near his end. Oh, how happy I am! He is so-so. Such like. Whilst you read, I write. Come with me, and show me where I may go. He goes so well. I am very well. It would go ill with me if I had nothing else to live upon.

1. Alas, how full of contradictions is man! 2. Oh, how pleasant is the sympathy of our fellow-creatures! 3. Oh, how

unjust are men, judging by appearances, and according to their own superb prejudices! 4. O Italy, Italy! when shall I have the pleasure of seeing you again? 5. Oh! if I could do it, I would do it willingly. 6. He loves me because I merit it. 7 Oh, so! let us speak of something else. 8. There is no honorable retreat for a good and wise man, except in company of the Muses. 9. We should never be prejudiced against a man because he has a fierce aspect. 10. The rich, who have never experienced want nor the necessity of considering or paying for the comforts of life, know nothing of the pleasure of economy.

11. Have you made all your preparations for departure? 12. Every thing is ready. 13. Send for a porter to carry my luggage. 14. I shall take the railway omnibus, and start in five minutes. 15. It seems to me to be very late. 16. How soon shall we be at the terminus? 17. I am afraid of being too late for the nine o'clock train. 18. Here we are at the terminus: we are never too late. 19. The train will start in five minutes. 20. Make haste and take your ticket. 21. What luggage have you? 22. I have two trunks, three carpet-bags, and one hat-box. 23. Here is the locomotive engine that is to draw us. 24. Have we two engines? 25. It requires a very great force to draw a train of twenty-five carriages. 26. What is the power of those engines? 27. They are each of twenty-horse power. 28. Are you going by the express train? 29. No, this is the accommodation train. 30. At what o'clock does the baggage train start? 31. There are two a day: one starts at ten o'clock in the morning, and the other at three in the afternoon. 32. Does your father come with us? 33. No: he goes in the express train. 34. Make haste: the train is just going to start. 35. That is the signal for starting. We are off. 36. We are already far from the terminus. 37. We have already gone four or five leagues. 38. We have gone just six miles. 39. We went the last mile in two minutes. 40. We go a mile and a half in a minute. 41. This is quick travelling. 42. But for your assistance, I should have lost all. 43. Should you have undertaken it, if you

had thought it so difficult? 44. Persevere, and you will succeed. 45. I heard them firing all the morning. 46. I felt her hand trembling in mine. 47. He saw his dog torn in pieces at his feet. 48. It would be necessary for him to see her. 49. I want some sealing-wax. 50. Do you want any thing else? 51. We often lose more time in idly regretting an evil than would be necessary to remedy it. 52. I would certainly do it, if it were necessary. 53. You might have broken your neck. 54. You might have forwarded your letter by his servant. 55. He would answer though he had been advised not to speak. 56. It must not be told to any one. 57. I would not have acted thus. 58. They would have neither roast beef nor pie. 59. His sister is ill: he must go and see her. 60. The fact must have taken place an hour after nightfall. 61. He owes me now a thousand pounds; last year he owed me twelve hundred. 62. Always carry an umbrella when it is fine. 63. Is not friendship the greatest of earthly blessings? 64. Have you not been to see the crater of Mount Vesuvius? 65. Did you not go as far as Turin by the railroad? 66. Is your uncle's agent yet arrived? 67. Should you be displeased, if I gave you any more examples? 68. Do you write to her sister to-day? 69. He is so silly and so tiresome that I cannot bear him. 70. He has so much wealth that he does not know what to do with it. 71. I like neither his person, his family, nor his fortune. 72. In the sweat of thy brow shalt thou eat bread till thou return to the ground from whence thou wast taken; for dust thou art, and to dust thou shalt return. 73. You shall not speak English: you shall speak Italian, nothing but Italian, with your teacher. 74. Do not go into the current: you will be drowned, as you cannot swim. 75. I shall die in a land of strangers, and not a tear will be shed upon my grave. 76. Yes; and your death will be just as much felt in the world as that of a worm or a fly. 77. True; but it will not be the less a matter of infinite moment to me. 78. Speak well of your friend; of your enemy, neither well nor ill. 79. The truly virtuous may fears neither poverty, afflictions, nor death. 80. The poor man has neither relatives, acquaintances, nor friends. 81. Either say nothing of the absent, or speak like a friend. 82. The good man possesses a happiness which the world can neither give nor take away. 83. On the fifteenth of next month, when I have won the capital prize. 84. Chaucer, the father of English poetry, was born in thirteen hundred and twenty-eight, and died in fourteen hundred, in the seventy-second year of his age. He had thus lived in the reigns of Edward the Third, Richard the Second, and Henry the Fourth. 85. Swans are an ornament to lakes and rivers. The swans of Australia are black. 86. Knowledge is the eye of youth, and the staff of age. 87. I flatter myself you will be satisfied with your daughter's pronunciation. 88. One should avail one's self of every opportunity to acquire knowledge. 89. Mr. B. thinks himself a great man; but he deceives himself. 90. The horseman and horse that fell down the precipice are both dead. 91. Is this the lady from whom you received the letter which you mentioned? 92. That is the goldsmith by whom this ring was made. 93. The fruit of that forbidden tree, whose mortal taste brought death into the world. 94. The lightning has blasted that beautiful tree, the fruit of which was so delicious. 95. Never defer till to-morrow what you can do to-day. 96. Shun poverty: whatever be your income, spend less. 97. This is bad; that is worse: these are so-so; those are the worst of all. 98. There is but one lasting affliction,— that which is caused by the loss of self-esteem. 99. Share this melon with your play-fellows; give each of them a slice. 100. My brothers are both returned from college; each has obtained a prize. 101. All fools are not knaves; but all knaves are fools. 102. Mr. A. has failed: shall you lose the money he owes you? 103. I shall have published the second edition of my Dictionary before the end of the year. 104. When you have studied Italian two years, you will understand what you read. 105. He will have spent half his fortune before inheriting it. 106. He who listens through a hole may hear what will not please him. 107. "Doctor, may ma eat oysters for supper?" "Yes: she may eat shells and all, if she likes." 108. My brother might have made a fortune by his trade. 109. Before you say or do any thing, reflect what the consequences may be. 110. If I went by the steamer, I should be sea-sick. 111. You would arrive sooner if you went by the mail. 112. While you are passing through the Tunnel under the Thames, hundreds of large ships are sailing over your head. 113. Since habit is a second nature, let us early form good ones. 114. The universe is composed of two things only, — mind and matter. 115. In educating the mind, we should not forget to educate the heart. 116. In Italy the eye sees much, but the memory more. 117. Victoria the First, Queen of the United Kingdom of Great Britain and Ireland, is the grand-daughter of George the Third, and the neice of King William the Fourth. 118. The Arabs call the camel the ship of the desert. 119. Egypt was the cradle of arts and sciences. 120. There are, in your exercise, as many errors as words. 121. The prospect brightens as you ascend. 122. Beauty is potent, but money is omnipotent. 123. Though I had written the letter, I had not forwarded it. 124. He is still rich, notwithstanding his losses. 125. He has acted an unworthy part: nevertheless I will assist him. 126. I forgive him, on condition that I never see him more. 127. Tell the truth: otherwise you will be despised by every one. 128. She was both young and lovely, and rich also. 129. The earth is divided into five parts; namely, Europe, Asia, etc. 130. You might learn a great many things: as, for instance, music, painting, etc. 131. It has happened just as I expected. 132. Whence comes it that you are so melancholy? 133. You are young and inexperienced: therefore you ought to be guided by the advice of your elders. 134. You have promised: then you must perform 135. Since she has written to you, you must reply.

The pagan gods chose various trees. The oak pleased Jupiter; the ash, Mars; the pine, Cybele; the poplar-tree, Hercules; and the laurel, Apollo. Minerva and Pallas asked why they took unfruitful trees. Jupiter replied, "On account of the honor." "Say what you will," added Pallas, "I like the olive on account of its fruit." "You are right, dear daughter," replied Jupiter, and immediately they all called her the Goddess of Wisdom, because, if what we do is useless, the honor is vain.

The celebrated Venetian painter, Titian, let his pencil fall whilst painting the Emperor Charles V. The emperor picked it up immediately, saying, "A Titian merits to be served by an emperor." There are few fine galleries where pictures of Titian and Correggio are not to be found.

Aspasia of Miletus was celebrated in Athens for her wit and her beauty. She was so skilful in eloquence and politics, that Socrates himself took lessons of her. She was the teacher and wife of Pericles, and lived 428 years before the Christian era.

Count Mansfield, one of the greatest captains of the age, had certain proofs that an apothecary had received a considerable sum to poison him. He sent for him; and, when he appeared before him, he said, "My friend, I cannot believe that a person whom I have never injured should wish to take my life. If necessity induces you to commit such a crime, here is money: be honest."

Whilst a countryman was sowing his field, a young man passed by, who, trying to be witty, said with rather an insolent air, "Good man, *you* have to sow, and *we* reap the fruits of your labors." To which the countryman replied, "It is very probable, sir; for I am sowing hemp."

A young man of distinction, having just returned from making the tour of Europe, and using the privilege of travellers to embellish things with the flowers of invention, was telling an officer, one day, of the magnificent presents which he had received from different reigning princes; among others, he mentioned a very superb bridle, which had been given to him by the King of France. "It is so elegantly ornamented with gold and precious stones," said he, "that I cannot persuade myself to put it into my horse's mouth; what can I do with it?" — "Put it into your own" (mouth), replied the officer with whom the traveller was speaking.

www.ingramcontent.com/pod-product-compliance
Lightning Source LLC
Chambersburg PA
CBHW030009240426
43672CB00007B/887